# DRIVER

# DRIVER

## SIX WEEKS IN AN EIGHTEEN-WHEELER

PHILLIP WILSON

The Lyons Press
Guilford, Connecticut
An imprint of The Globe Pequot Press

The Lyons Press is an imprint of The Globe Pequot Press.

10 9 8 7 6 5 4 3 2 1

Printed in the United States of America.

Designed by Kirsten Livingston

Library of Congress Cataloging-in-Publication Data

Wilson, Phillip.
   Driver : six weeks in an eighteen-wheeler / Phillip Wilson.
      p. cm.
   ISBN 1-59228-679-8 (trade cloth)
   1. Wilson, Phillip. 2. Truck drivers—United States—Biography. 3. Working class—United States—Biography. 4. United States—Description and travel. I. Title.
HD8039.M7952U575 2005
388.3'24'092—dc22

2005002248

# CONTENTS

WEEK One

ONE OF THE REASONS I EVEN MESS WITH GETTING UP IN THE morning is to have about a pot of coffee. Real coffee. Not that French stuff or some foamed hot chocolate or blueberry-flavored brew . . . pure Arabica bean coffee. Right from the mountains of Central America if I'm in control of the type and quality, and as near that as possible if I'm not. I do that pot of coffee every day, and have for years. Many years, to the point it is a habit, some would say. Nothing more than a morning ritual, others might say. A pleasure, I'd say, and the time spent in the drinking of it allows me to reconnect. I can't jump from sleep and get right to anything, and I bitterly resent the expectations of someone who can. I sit and sip and do nothing taxing. I learned long ago not to make critical decisions the first 45 minutes of my day. I sip and wait. Wait until I am aware and I can think deliberately. The coffee doesn't necessarily wake me so much as gives me something to focus on until I do wake, and that sort of camouflages me from those who may suffer the misfortune of having my company for the first hour of the day. And, I like the taste of it. Two good things in one effort, and that suits my "economy of motion" philosophy.

To be on my parents' deck just past the farm–country dawn is more pleasure to mix with the coffee. Cool and calm, the stillness and dampness of the air. Morning sounds all around. Late rooster in the far away. No city noises. Hummingbirds up before the heat. First faint breeze rustling the dewy leaves just enough to cause those little bitty droplets that form on the tips to fall. They patter onto the earth. Quiet conversations. Cups and saucers clinking. Comfortable silences. The damp boards of the deck, cool against the soles of my feet. Acceptance. The kind only your parents can give you.

I hate to leave all these good things, but my new career starts today and I need to be in Texas later this morning to meet my trainer in that new career, so i collect my stuff, express my thanks to my parents, and drive off, arm waving out the window like I always do, until we can no longer see over hill and dale . . . and then wave a little more just in case one can still see the other. My dad on the corner and me looking in the mirror. He is the only really good man I've known, and I wish I could have known him as a friend as well as a relative.

His arm waving high, and mine out the window as high as I can reach, driving away, until his hand in the distance is all I see above the hill. I turn onto the highway and we lose sight, him maybe seeing the top of my pickup and me seeing only his hand, but I wave another few hundred yards down the road, like I know he is waving a few more seconds. We are never sure what the other can see, and I don't want him to think I'd turn my back on him. Not even for a instant. Not even driving away.

As a boy, I was never afraid of making my parents angry or getting a beating. That wasn't why I was a comparatively good kid. I didn't do a lot of things simply because I didn't want to disappoint them. I still don't.

Along the Oklahoma countryside I've traveled at least a thousand times, I still see new things and think about the old ones. How things really haven't changed all that much in my lifetime of being and coming here. And that brings on a whole thought process involving just what all has changed in my life since I quit spending my summers here so many years ago. I remember childhood friends and long, hot days spent fishing, working in the hayfields, and playing in the lake. Water moccasins and watermelons, blue jays and blue skies. Sitting next to my grandmother right by the open window in church and listening to the newest student circuit preacher, since no real preacher wanted our little out-of-the-way town, drone about Jesus, Joseph, and Mary while mud daubers droned in and out the unscreened window. Sometimes a car would go by, and I'd watch the dust hang in the air above the bone-dry gravel road. I would sit on the rock-hard oak pew waiting to see which way it drifted. It seemed like the dusty cloud took hours to drift away or dissipate in the breezeless heat of the early day. But, it seems like everything takes a long time when you're a kid.

The womenfolk in their Sunday dresses had fans made of tongue depressors and pasteboard pictures of Jesus in Gethsemane. They would sit idly moving the fans back and forth during the sermon, but the little butterfly-shaped fans were no help at all in the August Sunday morning and stagnant heat of the old church house. Parenthetically, I find it strange how those things buried so deep come back so vividly, my having not thought about those things for years, and I wonder if I try to recall those things or if they merely pop up of their own accord. I'll have to think more on that subject some other time, I guess.

I remember, too, walking home from church along the sidewalk built by the WPA, grass growing in the cracks, and purposefully stepping on fallen plums to hear them pop beneath the soles of my Sunday shoes. I had to hang back from my grandparents a little to do that. My grandmother would get onto me for messing up my good shoes if she'd see me, but she was usually busy talking to one of her friends on the way back home. My grandfather didn't care. If he saw it at all, he'd just shake his head and keep walking. It wasn't far; we just lived a block from the church.

At the midday meal, not just Sunday, but every day, the table was heaped with fried food and garden-grown veggies. Tomatoes the size of softballs with a serious acid whang. Old folks sitting in the shade of a Sunday afternoon drinking iced tea in goblets that came in soap powder; the condensate dripping from the glass would leave wet spots on their shirts. The old folks must have been in their late forties. I hated Sundays, because on Sundays I had to hang around the house and stay clean in case I was brought out to the adults to see how much I had grown. Like a lot happened since last week when they saw me. No fishing or swimming permitted on Sundays, but I'd sneak off to the creek in the canyon, to meet my sneaky buddies, or get caught trying. If that happened, I'd have to go sit with the adult males in the shade of the front yard and listen to conversations about the business end of farming. Price of beef. Whether or not God would send the rain. Sometimes they would talk about fishing or hunting, but not often enough to keep me from fidgeting. If I fidgeted enough, I'd be told to sit still or go find something to do. Always tried for the latter, but sometimes overfidgeted and got the former. Timing, duration, and intensity are everything when it comes to being obnoxious.

There are few things that speak to me of my days gone by like the smell of a fresh-cut Johnson grass meadow drying in the sun, or the slow boil of a distant black-bottomed thunderstorm and the low roll of thunder across the Oklahoma miles, but those things can be had here still. Life was good, surrounded by intelligent and caring people in this pastoral country, and the memories of it flood back as I drive past the scenes of events imprinted long ago. Fishing with my grandfather in that pond at the top of the hill. The scent of recently plowed earth as I drive through it now instantly takes me back to his tractor and sowing seed in a hayfield on a textbook June morning 45 years ago.

Scents, of all the stimuli, seem to stimulate memories most quickly for me, and the desire to remember, through these scents, may be as much why I have the window down as is the desire to feel the summer wind on my arm as I go carefree and alone along the hilly lane to the highway many miles away.

Most of us have two families, the one we were born into and the one we create, and I'm a lucky guy. My born-into family is intact and the one I created is all grown and gone. That means my life is mine and it's time to change some things. I read somewhere the average person has seven different careers in a lifetime, and I don't know if I buy into that, but it is comfortable to know there may be others out there no more able to decide what they want to be than myself, and as possibly out of whack as I am.

Those fortunate souls born knowing what they want to do, and go do that, are happy, I'm sure. Most folks just fall into something that pays their way, get into a little debt and realize there are bills to pay, then have no financial room to do what they want careerwise. They simply fall into something and get trapped there. I did that, for a very short time; however, my days of being financially responsible to others are behind me. I can do what I want. Robert Louis Stevenson said, "Happy is the man who has found his work," and I absolutely agree. A job takes up about a third of a life, so bad decisions in that arena usually lead to long-term unhappiness. I never did a job I didn't like overall, and have no intentions of starting at this stage of the game, and like every little boy, I've always wanted to drive one of those big trucks. Recently, and luckily, I've been offered a chance.

So today, I'm driving out of this sleepy little county and into what may be a new career. One of those seven, I think. Not long ago, my position at the distribution center for one of the department store chains evaporated when the company evaporated, and I sat around for five months before I decided to see the country, if nothing else, and figure how to get someone else to pay for it. That exercise led me to trucking. So, here I am . . . off to be a truckdriver.

I went to a school funded by a major trucking company to learn how to get a truck to do what it needs to do, and went from never having sat in one to driving in downtown traffic in 10 days, but that's a whole 'nother story. The company spent a great deal of money in preparing me to get my commercial license, but I took some time off right after training and getting that license to get some other things done. A universal truth says there are things that cannot happen when you are home; that you must be gone for them to take place, and I ran afoul of that truth. Some things happened in my absence.

I eliminated those problems in my time at home, and then another one popped up. The company that trained me didn't appear interested at all in having me back after I took that time away. In fact, the person who would have been my boss was plainly not interested in my return to the company. I still occasionally wonder why. Anyway, after a few phone calls, another company was interested, so I hired into that company as an OTR, or, over-the-road, driver.

Changing gears here, so to speak, and moving from the preamble to the main story, and, just so you'll know: Before a company trusts a new-hire driver with $150,000 worth of equipment and a load ranging from worthless to millions of dollars in goods, they want to make certain the hiree can operate the equipment properly, complete the paperwork properly, and treat the customer properly. They put a new driver into a thing called Orientation, which is essentially specific policies, procedures, and performance specifications peculiar to that company, and it comes in two phases: classroom and over the road. I just completed the classroom phase about a week ago, and it is time now for the roadwork. Those companies pay people to train newbies in the classroom, and they also pay people to train those newbies on the road. We'll call those people "trainers."

The plan is to meet my over-the-road trainer in the company compound, where we'll undertake an entry-level approach to driving a big truck across the country and doing all the things a good driver does. I don't know the man very well, but I'm certain he is fully accredited, his being a trainer. Gotta know what you're doing to train, right? Or is it a case of when you teach, you learn twice? Those things aside, I'm about to spend several weeks within five feet of the guy. I've never been that close to anyone for that long in all my days, so this project could probably double as some category psych study. Human saturation, maybe.

I go past the gate guard and into the area known as the "yard," and park my pickup in the employee parking lot. I was told earlier to meet the man in the smoking area outside the training building, so I go that direction, and meet him there. I recognize him, having met him in the past during the classroom phase of orientation. He is a huge man. Not so much fat, just big. Smiles regularly and broadly. Laughs with all his body and one eye closed. A genuine laugh. This is good. We are about to spend a long time very close to one another.

After the pleasantries, he begins with the basics, like getting a truck. After some wandering around looking for the right people in the right offices, and some paperwork, we are assigned a power unit—that's what the company calls tractors, drivers call them "mules"—and we set out to find that unit in the yard. It is here somewhere since someone just turned it in. If a person drives constantly, they get to keep the same tractor, assuming they take only a few days off every now and again. If a person takes more than about five days off, that person loses that tractor. No one really wants to lose a tractor they like, since they are accustomed to the idiosyncrasies that machine has, plus the hassle of getting all their gear out and having to move it all back into another one. But, the tractor has to move freight to make money for the company, so the company can't let one sit for long. It makes sense to most people, but some drivers get frizzed when their mule disappears while they're away for two weeks.

We get the keys to one that belonged to someone going on an extended vacation, and actually found it on our first tour of the acreage. It has been cleaned out, washed, and has no red tags stuck on the driver's window, meaning it is mechanically safe to operate. Roadworthy, in the vernacular. That's another good thing, because now we don't have to wait for some adjustment or repair to be made. We can roll once we get a load assigned to us.

Trainer does a walkaround with me where any obvious defects or problems would be noted. Kinda like pilots do. Anything bent, broken, loose, or leaking. All is well, as we suspected it would be. We know these things have been resolved by the maintenance department when it came into the yard, but it is a point of professionalism for the driver to inspect the unit himself, and it is a point of legality out on the road. I want to learn to do this stuff by the book, so I can develop my own bad habits, not modify someone else's bad habits, so I make mental notes of what needs doing by referencing the company procedure manual, hauling it around during the process. That kinda irks Trainer. Like it impugns his accuracy, and position as trainer, but he says nothing.

Trainer satisfied, I am given the keys, so I climb in and begin the start-up procedure. The 425-horsepower Cummins diesel engine chugs to life. This is the point a professional driver realizes his hometime is over and he is back on the road. I see that in Trainer's face. It's a solemn look. He knows what lies ahead of us jobwise. *Not* knowing what's ahead of us jobwise, I'm up on adrenaline, it is all new and a kind of game to me. I am looking forward to this much like a paid vacation. It is possible, however, neither of us know about five weeks of close quarters with a person who may or may not meet the other's general standards, but we are about to find out.

I ease the tractor into second gear and guide it across the yard to an area designated for loading personal gear into the tractors, where we do that. I've been instructed to bring no more than five small bags or one duffel, so my stuff goes quickly onto the upper bunk I've been assigned. Trainer gets the big bunk on the bottom; it's about a twin-size bed. Space is at a premium. Trainer loads lots of stuff. More and more. I wonder, but say nothing. It's his truck. I'm just a renter.

It is early afternoon in north-central Texas, and the July sun is scorching the black asphalt of the yard. Several acres of it. The truck is loaded now with stuff to wear, eat, read, and use since that truck will be home, office, vehicle, and cafeteria for the foreseeable future. Gotta plan ahead, and we have taken full advantage of the mobility of a car to collect what Trainer knows we'll need and I think we'll need. These trucks hooked up and loaded out are 70 feet long and weigh 80,000 pounds. You can't just whip into the burger joint, or stop by a supermarket; we need to have the stuff on board, and we have taken care of that at a local deep-discounter. Trainer and I sit in the cool of the Kenworth's air-conditioned cab looking onto the poor souls staggering around in the heat as we get acquainted while we wait for a load to take us somewhere.

Where doesn't matter, I think. What difference does it make when we will be traveling nonstop for five weeks?

Trainer administered my company driving test and arranged for me to be under his wing during this phase of my career, but we have spoken little apart from that, so now is a good time to learn some things about one another. We want to come through these next weeks at least on speaking terms.

Trainer smokes. I don't. He lives to eat. I don't. He has no cash. I do. He does not bathe every day. I do. He is deaf in one ear. I'm not. He speaks loudly. I don't. These differences will present themselves again in the coming days. Others will surface. There are similarities as well: We share a coffee thing. He is faithful to his woman. I believe in that, and it is easy to be unfaithful in a driver's world; the opportunities abound. He likes "truckin'." I think I will. He likes eighties rock. So do I. He likes to laugh. I do, too. He is easygoing, and doesn't ruffle easily. I think I am that way. We both like to read, and we have some books to exchange. He has a copy of Crichton's *Timeline*; I stake an immediate claim and stash it on the shelf above my chair. Conversation dies.

Trainer looks out the windshield into the heat waves emanating from the pavement and says we should get over to dispatch to see what the holdup is. It has been more than three hours. Says we "need ta roll." I agree. I came to drive, not sit around, but little do I know at this point just how much sitting around is involved in trucking. Climbing down from the cool of the tractor cab, we set out for a mirage in the distance I hope is a building.

The rush of cool air as the door opens to the office is like stepping into a waterfall and almost made the trip from truck to building worthwhile, and the dispatcher offers up two choices for us. Had 'em all along, he just forgot about us. A load of film to Laredo, or a load of chicken to Pueblo, both dropped here by guys going on hometime. Trainer says we'll take the load to Laredo. He says Laredo is a busy port of entry into the U.S. and we won't have to lay over long, if at all, after dropping the trailer we take there. Makes sense to me. Says we might get stuck in Pueblo waiting for a load out, and he gets paid by the mile. No miles, no money. Don't want to lay over. If we gotta be away from home, let's be loaded and rolling and getting paid. That makes even more sense to me.

Since all crafts have trade secrets and easy ways to avoid common complications, I felt Trainer had done a great deal of training in letting me know that particular problem existed. No telling what misery Trainer had just saved me. I watch carefully as basic information about the load is exchanged. There is considerable paperwork involved in moving merchandise around the country, and even more if that load is going out of the country. This load is going out of the country. The driver doesn't have to deal with all of it, but what the driver does deal with has to be right, or someone may not be paid, and worse, the load may get stuck in bureaucratic limbo at the border. I notice I am a bystander here. I am not involved, and I should be. Seems like I should be doing this paperwork thing hands on, and Trainer is not allowing me this opportunity. I write it off as an oversight on his part, his not being used to having a trainee. I glance up and see a weather screen on the monitor just over the dispatch window. Irregular green patches moving across the outlined image of the North American continent as the images cycle. I think that is rain. It occurs to me the weather is a big factor in a driver's workday. I'll learn later just how big it really is. And why Trainer does the paper shuffle. He isn't sure how it works either, and doesn't want me to know that. At least not at this point.

The taxonomy of transportation has it that a mover of freight is a carrier. A shipper of freight is a consignor, and a receiver of freight is a consignee. All those terms are interchangeable, depending upon whom is talking. There are dozens of carriers. Some move heavy loads and oversized loads. Some move pressure-sensitive loads. Some move dry goods. Some move cold stuff. Some move hot stuff. Some move liquid loads. Some move hazardous loads. Some move all those things. There are common carriers, private carriers, and specialized carriers. There are small, midsized, and large carriers. There are intrastate, regional, interstate, intercontinental, and forty-eight-state carriers. There are LTL, or less-than-truckload, and TL, or truckload carriers. The company I have chosen is a midsize intercontinental temperature-controlled truckload carrier. We move loads that must be kept in a particular temperature range, and we move them all over the North American continent. The trailers have a refrigeration unit on the front that heats or cools as the load requires. In the case of the load we are about to take to Laredo, it is to be kept cold. It is camera film destined for the department stores and malls and small shops of Mexico. It will record moments of people's lives there and be important to those people. Some of those moments will be saved in dresser drawers for generations and referenced many times by many loving fingers. Some of it will record happy days. Some will not. We just became responsible for getting all those things to the border on time and in good condition with the proper paperwork.

Off we go to find the trailer now in the rows of trailers. Trailer number something or another. It is a 53-footer. Some refrigerated trailers are 48-footers, and a very few are 57-footers. It isn't legal to pull a 57-footer in all states, so our company doesn't use them. The 48-footers don't hold as much stuff, so the company only uses those for local trips that don't cost too much to run the tractor. There are shorter trailers, usually 28-footers, called "pups" that can be pulled in tandem, triples, or individually, but this company doesn't use those at all.

Refrigerated loads are almost always at or near the weight limit just by virtue of the goods. Usually, a refrigerated load is dense merchandise like meat, juice, or produce, and the shipper wants to ship as much as possible to keep costs down for the customer. To get the contract, some carriers agree to overweight loads from major shippers and deal with the overweight problem as it arises at the weigh stations along the route to the consignee. That's not a problem with this load. Film is not dense, and a trailer crammed full of it isn't really that heavy. It is well within the state weight limits according to the bill of lading, which is the paperwork that goes with the driver. The bill, as it is known, is a vital document for anyone associated with the movement of the merchandise, right up to and including the state officials who want to know what is on that truck, and has the pertinents like the weight, number of pieces, number of pallets, type of merchandise, temperature range, the shipper and receiver, and other less impressive information. It is a kind of receipt for the load, saying we have it and all is well legally and practically. We more or less accept ownership and responsibility for the load after we sign for it. This load is legal and ready to go according to the bill.

We find our trailer waiting for us among the other trailers awaiting a ride. The reefer units are diesel powered and have their own fuel tank slung below the trailer frame near the landing gear so they can operate independently of the tractor. It looks kinda neat when one cycles on, the engine cranks up and coughs a small exhaust puff into the sky. Looks really neat when that many are lined up doing it, like a gigantic diesel calliope. Dozens of cooling units cycling off and on in the Texas summer sky, all in a row.

I set up to back the tractor under the trailer, angling the tractor just so and straightening to back beneath the trailer apron. I am careful. I have only done this in a training setting, and want to do as well as I can now that I am "out here." That's what drivers call being on the road: "out here."

This is the first part of a critical operation. Failing to properly connect to a trailer is unpardonable. Not properly connecting is called a highhook, or bad hook, and is so preventable that failing to do so is a termination offense in any company I know about. Trailers have been known to ride hundreds of miles not properly secured to the tractor, only to disconnect at a pothole or sharp curve—sometimes with catastrophic results, and always with career-ending results for the driver. There is a rock-simple procedure to prevent that event: get out and look into the back of the fifth wheel when the connection is made, and see whether or not the kingpin is seated properly into the notch of the fifth wheel. No magic here. Get out and look. It is an industry-wide acronym: G.O.A.L. Don't assume everything back there is okay. Get out and look any time we do something we can't see from the windshield.

Little stickers on the very bottom, or very top, of lots of outside mirrors have that advice on them as a constant reminder. Trainer watches me carefully to satisfy himself I know to do that. Once the kingpin is seated properly, very little will cause the tractor and trailer to separate. Trucks fall off mountain roads, and the units stay coupled. Trucks flip over, turn on their sides, and jackknife. They stay coupled. That kingpin–fifth wheel connection is unbelievably strong when done properly. Despite physics' best efforts, the connection stays intact. I will see many crash sites in my days behind the wheel, but never will I see a trailer disconnected from a tractor at one of those sites.

We want this load to stay connected, so we both get under the trailer apron. Me to look, and Trainer to make certain I know to look. Satisfied, we move on to less critical maneuvers involved in hooking up. Then, before we actually get out on the road with a trailer, we do what is called a tug test. The trailer brakes are applied and the tractor pulls forward. If there is a bad hook, it will show up now in the form of the trailer falling off the fifth wheel and onto the tractor frame. The tractor torques sideways, and the trailer doesn't budge. If it is hooked properly, an empty trailer will skid on its tires, called tandems. Loaded trailers go nowhere, because there is a lot of weight on those locked tandem wheels.

Trainer says we need to get rolling here. It is into the afternoon now, the load is due at the international broker's lot at noon tomorrow, and the Mexican border is a long way from the Red River Valley.

All the paperwork done, the trailer located and hooked, and we are ready to ride to Laredo. I wend a way out the lanes of trailers toward the gate, past the drivers' lounge, where some drivers live, literally, and pull up to the guardhouse. The guard notes whatever guards note on outbound loads and waves us through. A safety sign on the driveway to the road admonishes us to mind our following distance. I pay attention. Trainer underlines the sign with a nod. I understand. This thing won't stop like a Ferrari.

I feel like an astronaut must feel when he leaves the safety of the capsule and shoves out into space untethered. A mix of dread and excitement. Trainer sits uneasy in the second seat. Looking. Watching.

I don't blame the poor guy. I wouldn't do what he does. Truck driving is one of the ten most deadly things a person can do employment-wise for many reasons, most of them obvious. That a person would add an exponent to that danger, by allowing a newbie at the controls into the mix, is not rational to me. But he has. And he knows that.

Uncomfortable at first as I go up the gears—the tractor's controls are new to me, it isn't like the training tractors, this is a real road tractor—but I relax a little out on the freeway, or the big road. It is properly said all one word, though: bigroad. Traffic thins out as we go south away from the city, and my comfort levels out just below anxiety. My brain has to learn what input is important and what can be disregarded. So many things to do. Mirrors, little cars, road conditions, warning signs, following distance, staying in the lane, panel lights and gauges . . . I'm all sensory organ right now. Trainer offered nothing but directions since we left the yard. Maybe he knows I can't deal with more input. I wonder if this is what it is like to be autistic. Information overload. I've got it.

On the interstate for a while, and out of the blue, he looks pained and says we have to scale the load. He's right. We don't know how much we weigh. We both forgot to do that. I should have known from schooling and he should have known from experience. All states have weight limits to, among other things, prevent their roads from being crushed into gravel. The loaded truck must be put onto a truck-sized scale and the weight must be below that state's limit, or the driver will be cited at the next weigh station, called a chicken coop, he has to go into because they have a scale the truck must cross to get out of the place. Many are closed on the interstates, due to budget cuts and manpower constraints, so some overweight trucks get away with it. Others are open all the time, and not getting off the bigroad to go into an open coop is a DOT offense, and a memorable one. The chase car officer will be irritable when he catches the offender. Had to fly the coop, so to speak.

DOT is an acronym for the Department of Transportation, and they regulate lots of things. Interstate transportation is one. Though the DOT has its own people, almost all state police are also DOT-qualified persons. They operate the weigh stations and can issue DOT citations even when they are not at the coop. Drivers call them "diesel cops" or "diesel bears," and they don't mess around. Don't have the time, I guess. Lots to do, and one of the things they do is make trucking companies and truckdrivers play by the rules. Like not going down the road overweight.

There are two different kinds of weights. One is called "axle" weight and the other is "gross" weight, or how much the whole truck weighs; tractor, trailer, driver, fuel, soft drinks, socks, everything. All states are concerned with gross weight. Most are concerned with axle weight, or how much weight is on each set of axles, as well. The front axle is called a "steer," the set of eight wheels on the tractor is called the "drives," and the set of eight wheels on the trailer is called the "tandems." The tandems are attached to a carriage and can be slid backward or forward along the trailer frame to shift weight onto them, or onto the drives. The fifth wheel can be slid forward or backward on the truck frame to shift trailer weight onto the steers or onto the drives. The trailer must be scaled with all aboard and full of fuel, or we get skewed numbers. We don't want to scale with fifty gallons of fuel, then go down the road and take on another one hundred fifty gallons, and its weight, then go into a coop. Or scale with one of us out of the truck. Might be okay, and might not. Depends on how heavy the trailer is to start with.

Most big truck stops have scales, and we locate one a couple of exits down the road. Good thing. We need to see if we are axled out properly, meaning we are below the maximum weight per axle, and we need to do it now. We may get little warning for the next coop, because Texas is famous for portable weigh stations. Lots of states have them, but Texas is famous for them. The Texas Department of Public Safety has portable scales and they will set up in locations they know they'll catch overweight trucks trying to avoid the coops on the bigroad. That's a good thing, too.

Most drivers know that, and not many try to get far with an overweight load in Texas. Helps keep the roads among the best in the nation.

I slow down for the exit, and we pull off the feeder into a truck stop and ease through the lot, get onto the scale, and I make sure all our wheels are on. Won't do a lot of good to weigh a trailer with a couple of tires off the scale. These scales axle it out, so we know which way to move the tandem carriage to shift the weight from one set of axles to the other. We are already full of fuel from the pumps in the yard, so we don't need to fuel. The voice from the box near the window wants to know if it is our first weigh. I say it is. Voice says "Gotcher weight, come on in."

First weigh paperwork, called a scale ticket, tells a driver how much weight is on which wheels, and that information along with some fig-gerin' will tell us what corrections need to be made to get the load legal. A simple set of factors in a simple equation determine which direction and how far the tandems or fifth wheel, or both, need to move to get the proper weight onto each set of axles. That not only gets it legal, it also helps the trailer pull smoothly and safely. We don't want a tail-heavy trailer trying to pick up the back end of the tractor, or a nose-loaded trailer squashing the drives and lifting the steer tires every time we hit a bump in the road. Then, mechanical adjustments made, the driver takes the truck back onto the scales for the second, and hopefully, the final weigh, to see if he got it right. Sometimes it takes a few trips for rookies.

I pull off the scale and park while trainer goes into the truck part of the truck stop. There are few old-time truck stops anymore, most have been overshadowed by gleaming corporate operations. Most now are known as travel stops or travel centers, and they are for cars, motor homes, and trucks of all types. Brightly colored, well lit, clean, usually with a couple of fast-food outlets inside, as well as a convenience store, and many have a top-drawer restaurant. Big trucks have their own fueling area simply because of the nature of big trucks. Big trucks need lots of room to get in and out. Like bigroad, the term "big truck" is properly said as one word and emphasizing the word "big." Like BIGtruck. That's how drivers say it. Bigtruck. Anyway, huge amounts of fuel require huge nozzles. Occasional spills—a lot bigger spill than an unleaded nozzle for a car would generate. Keep the big mess in one area, and have that area set up for a potential big mess. It is a good practice, and one that pays off on occasion. I have seen a couple of pretty nasty events at fuel islands.

The place bigtruck drivers go to do the paperwork for fueling is called a fuel desk. In some truck stops it has restrooms, a small convenience store, and a coffee/soda bar. In others, it is part of the convenience store. Drivers also get their scale tickets at the fuel desk. From the fuel island entry there is usually a ritzy entry marker beckoning the "PROFESSIONAL DRIVER." Kinda keeps us segregated and makes us feel special. In reality, the plan is to keep the grubby truckers, the regular customers, away from the upscale public, the moneyed customers. Good business plan really, and customer friendly for both groups.

Trainer is coming across the lot. He hops into the cab. Says we are good to go. All the axles are under the limits. Says the plan is to get to San Antonio and stop for the night, so let's get goin'. Okay.

He's made this trip before, so I'm thinking it is a repetitive thing, and he knows what's up with this route. I am okay with that, too. San Antonio is not that far down the road from here and I'll be about ready for a shower, meal, and a bunk by then. I've been up since about 5:30 A.M. and we left the yard about 5:30 P.M. Trainer has about the same waking period. San Antonio will be about right.

My being a trainee changes the complexion of things, and we will not do some things considered commonplace to a veteran team of drivers. Like let me drive at night for the first week or so. Don't want to risk unnecessary corporate exposure. Most midsize trucking companies are at something near three miles per second exposurewise, meaning every second company trucks cover three miles of highway, and no company wants to compound that exposure by letting a greenhorn blow down the road in compromised visibility. And darkness seriously compromises visibility, whether anyone believes that or not. Tired drivers are just as dangerous as drunk ones, whether anyone believes *that* or not, and we are about to be tired drivers.

Twilight comes on us, and I am directed to stop at the first safe place. Rest stop, truck stop, picnic area, whatever comes along first. I exit the interstate and slow into a picnic area. No restrooms. Just tables and shelters. No matter. We go to the backside of the trailer, away from the road, and pee on the tandems. No one here but us, and it's near dark, but I look around to see if anyone is looking anyway. We trade chairs while we stop.

The driver's seat is known as the first chair. That chair is assigned to a driver based on several things, experience being one of them. The actual chair is always known as the first chair, but the responsibility of the first chair remains attached to one person in the team. That person is responsible for everything about the operation of the truck. Money, repairs, communications, timeliness, everything. Second chair driver just drives and rides. I take the second chair literally and figuratively.

Trainer has said little except directions. We exchange seats in silence, and I watch his technique in all he does as he gets the truck moving and back onto the interstate. Like most people by whom we are taught, I will learn as much what not to do from this man. I see that coming at this early stage of the game. There is an uncertainty in his motion, and an inconsistency in his execution that tells me he is not completely confident. Maybe he's just not used to someone watching every little thing he does.

It is noisy in the cab. Engine sounds, road noise, wind noise, radios. It's hard to carry on a conversation in normal tones. Communication is an effort. Trainer is also deaf in his right ear. I'm on his right. Could be why he doesn't say much. He may not hear what I am saying.

San Antonio exits are coming up and I figure he knows which one to take for our stop, him having done this trip before. We roll right through the city. All the exits go past and he drives on. No San Antonio stop. It is the first in what will be a string of unilaterally changed and uncommunicated plans. That ain't how this is supposed to go according to the trip planning and teamwork exercises we did in class. I am wondering if this could be that "real world" I've heard so much about. I am a little put off, but not enough to create an issue this early in the trip, so I ride along and try to take in the sights to rise above my aggravation. I hate changed plans. Especially if I am involved in those changed plans.

Near midnight we do stop. As we are exiting the bigroad to pull into the truck stop, Trainer says he wanted to get closer to Laredo tonight so we wouldn't have to drive so many hours to get there. I say nothing. I realize at that point he wouldn't understand if I put that plan to any test of logic regarding a noon delivery time. Maybe he's just tired. I hope he isn't stupid. Turns out later he isn't. He is really pretty sharp. He just does and says stupid stuff sometimes, like all of us do.

We drive into the huge lot behind a restaurant and a long, covered row of diesel pumps, and begin the search for a parking place. Most drivers have shut down earlier and have taken most of the parking places. Trainer drives slowly around the lot, and we locate one at the ab- solute back of the lot and he sets up to back in. Trainer has some diffi- culty but I regard it a result of late and tired, since backing is easily as much art as science, and therefore not perfect when the chemistry isn't right. We get into the slot and Trainer sets the brakes. Big hiss of air from beneath the truck, as though it is exhaling a weary sigh of relief. Trainer looks over at me and says, "Honey, we're home." Hoots of laughter from two tired guys in the middle of the night.

But really, we kinda are home.

Setting the brakes in an overnight stop is equivalent to pulling into a driveway after work and traffic. Mechanically, pulling the brake knob on the dash drains the air from the tractor brake lines, then the brake pads are pulled out by springs to contact the drum and keep a set of drive wheels from turning. Like an emergency brake. Intangibly, on the other hand, the workday is done, responsibility behind us, and every- thing done from now until bunktime is discretionary. We can be as irre- sponsible as we want till bedtime, which for us, is right now.

I was assigned the top bunk at the rear of the cab both for sleeping and storage, and that is a good thing. Trainer is six foot six, 275 pounds, or near it, and I don't want that floating over me all night, nor stepping on me on its way out in the morning. Problem is, I'm not sure what to do next, but it certainly involves getting to the stuff on my bunk, and now that I'm about to get out of the seat I've had the past several hours, the cab is incredibly small. Two of us trying to do whatever is next and staying out of the other's way in the process. We need a plan.

At this hour, there is only one possible goal, and that is to get into the bunk. But, I'm not going to do that until I get a shower. I refuse to get into bed, any bed anywhere, without a shower. I tell Trainer, who has jumped from behind the wheel and landed on the bottom bunk, as much. He says do what I want, that he's going to sleep.

Dig out the shower gear, hike to the shower, and endure the return trip. It all takes about an hour. Now, after a hot shower, I am really ready for the bunk.

I climb back into the tractor and step over the refrigerator and Trainer's stuff on the floor. I move my gear bags from my upper bunk onto the second seat, put them in a neat stack and climb onto the bunk. The idling engine noise, cool air from the air conditioner vents and exhaustion take their toll quickly.

After a better sleep than I would have expected, strange bed and place and all, I wake at dawn. It takes a few seconds for me to establish my whereabouts, then the fog thins a little and I realize I don't know quite what to do. I don't have a morning routine. Another case of no plan. I am too much a creature of habit. I have to pee. Trainer snores away beneath me. Should I wake him? When? I decide first pee, then dress, then find coffee. Will plan from coffee. Locate the relief bottle. Two liters. All sane drivers have one of some kind. Biological emergencies first. I am surprised by the volume and how warm the bottle feels. Good thing it's a big bottle. Done. Where's the lid? What to do with the bottle? How substantial are these apple juice bottles anyway? Do I get out and empty it, or just set it down and hope no one knocks it over? This is Trainer's house. Is it bad form to leave a bottle of pee in your host's house? I decide to put it on the top of my locker wedged in by a rolled-up rain suit.

Hope it stays. Wonder how tight those lids seal? Am I going to remember it is there? Will I remember it isn't apple juice? What if Trainer thinks it is?

I realize I am way overanalyzing this. Enough thinking about a pee bottle. Locate last night's clothes and step into shorts and polo shirt. I get the shirt on backward and inside out. Start over. Dammit. Even getting dressed is confusing without a plan.

It is warm even at dawn in the Texas scrub desert, and the air feels good as I climb down from the chilly bedroom, called a sleeper, in the tractor cab and climb out and down the side of the tractor. I hike past the rows of idling tractors. So many kinds and colors. Each has its own distinctive idle. Collectively, they are a localized low rumble. I pass one brand-new Kenworth. It is spotless and has a million-mile safe driver wreath and star on each side of the upper part of the sleeper, called a condo. A million miles. Ten years of driving. The cab curtains are drawn indicating the driver is asleep. I picture the driver. I almost have enough of a database now to do that. He is 50-plus, race unimportant, neatly dressed and maintained, classic shades, smokes and drinks coffee. He is a professional, regards himself a professional and drives like one. He is confident and proud of his craft and enjoys the results any journeyman would enjoy. I'll bet I'm not far off the mark. They are the only drivers that get those million safe mile awards, and companies stand in line to hire them.

Finally get to the building housing the coffee bar. Get my coffee. Pay my dollar and eight cents and start the hike back to the truck. My reflection in the glass outside tells me I haven't combed my hair. Didn't think about it really. I don't have a bathroom mirror to tell me those things in the truck. I already relieved myself, so no compelling reason to go into the restroom near the coffee shop and pass a mirror and shock myself. My gray hair is three inches long, thick and wiry. Serious pillow hair this morning. Worse than usual. The close-cropped beard doesn't help any. I look like a cross between a Rhodesian Ridgeback, a Rasta, and an Afghan hound.

I hope I get back to the truck before anyone notices. I hurry back toward the truck, head down. I hear tires rolling behind me. I try not to look as the tires come up beside me. Cow horns come into my peripheral vision. Attached to a long hood. Hood moves past me. More hood. A window powers down on passenger side of an ancient Cadillac limo. Would I like a ride back? It's free. Wanting to put my head in a bag, I say no, thanks. No telling who is in there or how many. All well dressed and ready for the day. Maybe not. Maybe they all have bed hair and I'd fit right in. Maybe not even be noticed. Maybe I'd be the only one in it and I could save myself the walk. Window powers up, five or six doors go by, and the thing idles past, chuffing light blue exhaust. I console myself. Limo driver's probably not shocked. Sees bad hair every day.

Trainer must be coming around. The tractor is jostling about as I get to it. I open the passenger door and climb up and into the second seat. He's fumbling for cigarettes. Fumbles for lighter. Finally gets both together and takes a deep draw, has a coughing episode, and sits back in the first seat in some satisfied state smokers go into behind that first hit. The air conditioner is blasting. Smoke swirls around the cab. I look at him, disgusted, holding my coffee.

After three or four puffs he courteously rolls down his window. The light breeze is against it, and nothing leaves the cab. He thumps the ash at the window, and it blows back in and all over him. Doesn't register. I roll my window down and try not to breathe until the smoke is out with the draft.

Trainer wordlessly grabs a huge plastic mug, opens the door, climbs down, and strikes off toward the coffee bar. I wordlessly watch him disappear beside the cab and reappear in front of the fender, walking away in the soft morning light. I feel like a forced guest in someone's house, not really comfortable since both of us have to be there. Maybe a morning routine will develop and make us both more comfortable soon. It's just a matter of timing and coordination of behavior patterns. And a little consideration.

Trainer sleeps like a brick, but hooks up quickly once conscious. I sleep well, but lightly, and it takes about 45 minutes from the time my eyes open until I am connected well enough to function. Another hour, and I am as fine-tuned as I will be all day, and I think we have covered that already.

In the coming days, it will happen, in this routine development, that I am the first to awaken, and I will wake Trainer by opening the light-proof curtain dividing the cab from the bunks, and stay in my bunk snoozing while Trainer gets up, dresses, hacks, grubs around for, finds, and lights a cigarette, sits back in first seat, fills the cab with smoke from one puff, rolls down the window, focuses a minute or two, grabs his un-washed mug, and sets out for the coffee bar. Then, I'll start a behavior pattern that will stay with me until my training period is finished.

I wake automatically around 6 A.M. daily and have for years, unless I'm home in my own bed. I will become the alarm clock. After Trainer gets out of the truck, I get down from the bunk, pee, dress, comb my hair, sit in the second seat, stare out the windshield, find my mug, and follow Trainer some minutes later.

Sometimes we pass one another. Rejoining back at the truck we sit and sip our coffee, look out the windows, listen to the radios, both the CB and the FM, and comment on what we see or hear. Both of us are touchy in the mornings. We learn we can ruin the morning by pissing one another off, so we try not to do that, and maintain the small talk or short comment approach to any subject. I usually go back for a second mug full, and when I return that will become the signal to begin our business day. Logs, trip plan reviews, fuel, food, and rest stops, who drives when and how far, and the day-to-day operation of the truck; who checks the oil, coolant, tires, hoses, fuels the tanks, cleans the wind-shield, and so on.

Eventually I will drive the morning shift and Trainer will drive the midafternoon and evenings. He likes a late-morning nap and will come soon to trust my driving to the point he will do that. I like a midafter-noon nap and I will do that as well. Trainer is good at making the truck go forward and down the road, and I will come to trust his ability to keep us upright. Backing is another subject.

We start today with the logs, and I am immediately taught to falsify one. Not in the sense that safety is disregarded, but that we retain hours enough to drive. There are regulations for the number of hours that a driver can drive the truck, work aside from driving the truck, sleep in the truck, and take time away from the truck. Logs are the daily record of those hours. I have to learn which one of those categories each hour of my day falls into. We fudge a little. Nothing dangerous, or I wouldn't do it, but enough so we don't have to sit out a day every so often, which happens if the hours are logged real time. That sitting out a day is a result of government, aka DOT, intervention and totally unnecessary if you are rested enough to drive safely. The spirit of the regulations are maintained, but the letter of them is not. The sole purpose of a log is to keep tired drivers off the road, and few will argue that.

Logs done, and I stand amazed at how much misinformation is out there, particularly among drivers, regarding hours and how to log them, when to sign what and how long to keep that log. For as many people as have to log hours, there aren't many that really know about the logging process, and how to do it properly. Most knowledgeable folks wouldn't believe the stories I've heard. Then again, being knowledgeable folks, maybe they would.

I am elected to drive first this morning, and the truck handles well as we work our way through the lot and get onto the bigroad south for Laredo. Like any other job, some days it feels good to be at work.

One of many things about driving over the road is that I'm never late for work. I wake up there. Another is the constantly changing wallpaper. Every office I ever had in any capacity, had no windows. I bitched for years. I wanted an office with windows just so I had some connection with the outside world. Never happened, so I settled for cool pictures on the wall. Ansel Adams. Annie Liebowitz. Van Gogh repros.

Well, another real benefit of my new office is the pictures on the wall. It's a nonstop natural history video. I am taken by the South Texas desert in the early morning, and after all his miles, Trainer is rapt as well. The beauty in the emptiness of it. Shadows, scrub brush, and sand. I wonder what interesting and adapted manner of life must be out there. I recklessly think on walking across here one day to see for myself.

The bigtruck rumbles toward Mexico in the slanted early light, gritty sand and khaki dust billowing up from the shoulder of the road behind us. Our wake, I guess, as we sail atop the dusty road between the waves of mesquited dunes.

Our mission, now that we have accepted it, is to get this load of film to the international broker and drop it in his yard, so he can arrange to get it into Mexico. In that effort, and after a long enjoyable trip across the Texas scrub desert, we come to the edge of the fabled Rio Grande river and exit the bigroad onto a street that is just like what one would see in a Mexican neighborhood. Narrow, tree lined, dusty, and small, well-kept houses with no lawns. Doors open right onto the street. The bigtruck is about five feet from a house on either side. I drive slowly listening to the branches scrape the top and sides of the tractor and trailer as I watch for pedestrians. Don't want to squash someone coming out a door. I feel like a whale must feel, snooping through a coral reef or kelp beds. The tree branches are trimmed away on the bottom by countless other bigtrucks, a kind of sculpted arboreal tunnel, so I know we are on the right track, but I'm still uncomfortable with my skill level and the current conditions. That brings on heightened awareness, but not stress.

At the end of this quaint and picturesque lane is our broker . . . and no place to park. How does that happen? How can a guy run a business that requires something this big and not have a place to put them? First off, this little lane was never intended to accommodate vehicles 70 feet long and 9 feet wide. The street is only 12 feet wide. Turning at one of the intersections should be out of the question, but I manage without taking out a house. I pull alongside the desert sand–blasted building while Trainer goes in to find out what to do with the trailer. I sit back, try to relax a second, and look around at the culture I'm amid.

I'm privileged to see from this vantage point. Vibrant colors on clothes and in windows. Lived in, but small and neat houses. Cooking facilities outdoors. Antique lawn chairs askew and a couple of beer bottles tattling on the last social event. Kids playing with used-up toys in the dusty shade of the sparse-leafed trees. Happy though, or seem to play that way.

Jammed-together small businesses, decades old. Family owned. Handed down, maybe, or carefully sold. Proprietor sweeping the sidewalk with worn broom. Busy. Small people comfortably dressed. No corporate soldiers here. Carrying the day's groceries home in bags that have made the trip many times. No hurry. This is a slice of daily life in an old neighborhood of a legendary Texas border town. Laredo was Laredo before Texas was Texas. The Rangers shot it out with desperadoes on these very streets. I'll bet Gus and Call rode right through here, Gus wanting to kick a pig. Maybe like that one, right over there.

Trainer wanders back from the broker's and says the drop yard is one block over. Dang. I am not set up for a left turn in these tiny streets. While it is true that two wrongs don't make a right, it is also true that three rights do make a left, so go three right turns instead. That's not easy either, but I get it done, coming within inches of corners of houses, and idle to the drop yard. No speeding through the 'hood hereabouts.

Guard directs me in and we slip right in between two trailers. Slick as glass. Trainer says nothing, but I know he is put off by the smoothness of it since a pro would have had some difficulty getting into that slot. He thinks it is a lucky event, but I think I have the knack. We exchange glances, and hop out into the dusty heat to unhook, or drop, the trailer. We hop a lot. Crank down the landing gear, unhook the air hoses and electrical cable, and pull the release handle that opens the fifth wheel notch and frees the kingpin. Hop back into the air-conditioned cab and move the tractor forward so it is disengaged, but not from beneath the trailer completely, so that if the ground is not stable enough to support the trailer, it will sink onto the tractor frame and not into the ground. Sometimes trailers do sink into a soft surface, and it is a major operation to raise a 60,000-pound loaded trailer high enough to be re-hooked. Expensive, too.

The trailer stays put. Another feather in my hat. I grin and continue from beneath the trailer apron and turn sharply to avoid other trailers, steer the tractor onto the street, and park just outside the broker's building, following Trainer's directions, behind a row of cars nosed against another building, preventing their backing out. Illegally parked. Trainer goes back in to clear the paperwork. I stay in case the tractor must be moved, which happens twice in five minutes. Trainees are not to move the truck without the trainer aboard, but I have no choice and no one from headquarters is here anyway. I feel important, backing out of the way to let the other cars out, then returning to the original spot.

The passenger door flies open and Trainer reappears. Surprisingly agile for such a big man, he lands in the second seat, the air shock hisses in angry agony, and he motions me to go. Shift into second gear, idle down the street and back the way we came minus the trailer. It is called bobtailing and it is dangerous. These tractors were designed to be under a 30-ton load, and they do not handle properly without it. It is much easier to maneuver with no trailer, and that's fine in close quarters, but at speed on the interstate, the rear wheels tend to hop on rough spots and during braking. Both those are unsafe events and I don't like getting involved. Just have to be extra careful with following distances since we, in effect, have no brakes.

Trainer called headquarters, HQ henceforth, while in the broker's office to ask what was next and was told to bobtail over to the company yard on the other side of town to wait and a message would be sent via the satellite system. It is a neat little keyboard e-mail device wired to a CPU under the bottom bunk with an antenna on the roof that allows direct communication with the shirts at HQ. Saves a lot of phone calling. The device also pings the server in San Diego once an hour and gives the truck's location in GPS coordinates, or latitude and longitude. Don't even bother lying about where the truck is. They know. Some drivers cover the little white antenna dome with aluminum foil when they are making an unauthorized stop or trip so the truck can't send that info. It works, too. HQ thinks the truck is parked inside a dock or under a loading awning, so they don't get too excited. Then the driver forgets to uncover the dome for a few hours. With a hundred-thousand-dollar tractor off the screen for any length of time, the company smells a rat and assumes it's a missing truck, then they start looking for it with all available resources. The results of those searches are pretty comical. Like where the truck is and what is going on inside when the gendarmes find it.

We bobtail back up the interstate to the loop around town, down a maze of industrial-type streets, past some produce warehouses and into a dusty gravel lot with two shabby portable buildings. The company yard. No expense spared here. Trainer says that building is the lounge with a shower in it and he doesn't know what is in the other. I can't imagine what it might be. Storage shed of some kind, I guess.

I back the tractor into a space between two other tractors. There is plenty of available space and I don't know why I chose the spot between the others. Showing off, I guess. We grab our shower gear, unclimb the tractor, and head into the building we know about. Trainer pushes open the door at the top of the three steps and cigarette smoke literally pours out, along with gunshots from a western on TV. We step in to mumbled greetings and more gunplay. The smoke burns my eyes. I'm not comfortable at all. Ten or more drivers, some male, some female, fat, thin, old, young, all smoking. The smoke has accumulated in the upper third of the atmosphere in the confines of the portable building. The straining air conditioner has created a thermocline about 5 feet from the floor. I stoop a little to stay in cleaner air and knock on the bathroom door. A one-holer with a shower. Clean, too. That's a pleasant surprise. I close and lock the door, set my gear on the homemade bench against the flimsy panel wall. I can hear the goings-on right through the paneling. Oh well.

I am showered and out of the bathroom so Trainer can get in. I collect my gear and move into a smaller partitioned area with its own a/c next to the bathroom and stand directly in front of the vent since I am the only one in there. Try to keep from sweating and invalidating my shower. Summer afternoon in Laredo. Metal building. I figure it will be cooler in the tractor, so I collect my gear and hold my breath as I make my way toward the door through the smoke and gunshots. No one looks away from the movie. I take a breath outside. My first full breath in some time. No smoke out here, just dust. I move quickly to the tractor and get the a/c going and sit real still, vent blowing on me, trying not to move.

The satellite communication device is made by a company called Qualcomm. Many drivers have trouble pronouncing that registered trademark because they are not from a world that uses three-letter acronyms, or abbreviations, or dotcom names. Just not used to saying those things, and their mouth doesn't work to the proper end. Those results are hilarious. First time I heard it was when a driver said "quail-comm." I wasn't sure I heard correctly. I heard it again in another conversation, and realized it was easier to say than "qualcomm" and that's why it appeared in conversation. Quail is a word we are semi-accustomed to saying. Qual is not. Farther into my training, I heard it morph into "quailcall" by one of the more cerebral drivers and liked it at once, so I added it to my company-specific vocabulary, as well as to these pages.

The quailcall beeps a message alert, and I punch that message up on the little screen. The message gives us instructions to pick up a load of asparagus, when, where, and how. More messages follow telling us where to fuel, how much to buy, and which route to take. Even the trucking industry is computer controlled. Still more messages. Where the load is going, who to call there, arrival appointment date and time, and how many miles it pays. This kind of dispatch is called "forced." We have no choice in whether or not we want to take the load. The mainframe computer looks at where the truck is, what loads are available in that area, and whether or not the driver has the time to deliver by the appointment date in its assignment of those loads. It also looks at current road conditions, weather, and other factors affecting the driver's performance. It hands that information to a human, a Dispatcher, and he or she makes the final call as to whether or not we should be assigned the load. Apparently the computer thinks we can get the asparagus to California on time. Apparently Dispatcher does, too. We think we can as well, so we acknowledge the load via the quailcall. We tell the computer and Dispatch we'll take it. Like we have a choice. I crank up and we drive out of the baking, dusty parking lot of the luxurious company yard.

As it happens, the place we'll pick up the load is just around the corner. Better still, the trailer is already loaded. We don't have to wait for it to get that way. The refrigeration unit is chilling the asparagus at 35 degrees Fahrenheit. Don't want it to freeze, but do want it cold enough to keep further degradation to a minimum and stun any bugs that may be hiding out in the greenery. We go through the same hookup procedure as before, taking the same special care with the kingpin–fifth-wheel attachment. Trainer watches me carefully.

Hot. Wow, it's hot here. Getting into the chilled trailer to arrange the loadlocks is a pleasure. A loadlock consists of two pieces of pipe, one inside the other, that expand outward with a ratcheting mechanism such that the two ends contact the inside trailer walls and wedge themselves in that position to keep a load from shifting, or falling backward. Refrigerated loads almost always have them in place since the load doesn't go all the way back to the trailer door for the door to hold the load steady. Can't put anything in the last four feet of a reefer trailer or the air cannot circulate properly around the goods. The reefer unit blows conditioned air across the ceiling to the rear of the trailer where it falls across the face of the door and returns under the merchandise through grooves in the floor to the return-air vent in the bottom of the front wall to be cycled back again. There are sensors throughout to notify the driver when something's not right. An alarm light in a panel outside the nose of the trailer that the driver can see in his left mirror signals a problem if one develops. Seeing that light, a driver knows to pull over and investigate. Not much he can do usually, but there are many facilities around the country that are equipped to deal with whatever may happen. If it is load threatening, the driver will take it to one of those places. More waiting. More downtime. Fortunately, it is not a regular occurrence. These reefer units are very dependable and can even diagnose themselves when they are not well. Some of the newer ones can adjust themselves electronically to compensate for a partial systems failure. Technology is good.

I like putting the loadlocks in place. It's 35 degrees in the trailer and near 100 outside. Never thought I'd want to be in 35-degree weather. I don't want to get out, but we have to move. The shipper needs the dock to load another truck. I climb in the truck and tug the trailer to test the connection, pull out into the street and wait for Trainer to close the doors, so the cold air and asparagus won't fall out on the way to California.

We idle out the lot and up to the guardshack so the guard can clear us to leave. Pleasantries all around. The guard checks the papers for whatever it is guards look for on papers. Smiles and waves, and we head to California via the local supermarket. I've had a TexMex attack. Trainer says he feels one coming on himself. We'll take this opportunity to stock up on local cuisine since it is a favorite for the both of us, and this is the last chance we'll have to get it from an authentic source for a while. Plus the parking lot of the supermarket is big enough for us to get in and get out safely, and that is an infrequent occurrence.

I've been in every state of the Union over the years, contiguous and otherwise. I have eaten in every state of the Union. There is no better food than is found along the Gulf Coast of these United States. We enjoy a blend of cultures possibly like no other place on Earth, and they all have their culinary arts. The Spanish came here 600 years ago and brought a style of cooking. The Aztecs and Maya were already here cooking. The French sailed over about the same time and left a recipe or two with the coastal aborigines that were pretty good at seafood prep already. The Africans came along and showed everyone how to do leftovers. The Asians showed up in the mid-1800s and added about 5,000 years of cooking experience to the mix. Across the centuries, the food, and the blends of it, get nothing but better along the Gulf Coast. It is one of the reasons I live there.

We are real close to Mexico, and knowing once I leave here the TexMex just gets worse as I go farther from Texas, I wanted to tank up.

I speak just enough Español to get real lost real fast, so we did that looking for a recommended restaurant. We couldn't quite get there. Didn't
want to get off the main roads in the bigtruck. That will be a continuing problem with getting directions from people that drive small vehicles. They don't know to warn drivers about low wires, low clearances,
restricted routes, impossible turns, and no place to park or turn around.
If you are in a bigtruck, get directions from a bigtruck driver.

   We settle for this supermarket out here on the loop. Go in and get
the goods from the deli. Tamales, beans, rice. It'll have to do, and deliMex
here is better than restaurant Mex farther away from South Texas. I
know it'll be a while before I get it again.

   We need sandwich goodies as well. The truck has a small refrigerator aboard, and now is a good time to stock it. Recognize opportunity
and capitalize on it. Trainer says that's a good idea, whatever that means,
so let's do it.

   Eating on the road is its own problem. Restaurants are out for two
reasons. First, they are hard to access. Bigtruck won't fit. Secondly, eating out three meals a day is expensive. Breakfast, seven dollars. Lunch,
seven dollars. Dinner, seven dollars. Every day. With cigarettes and
sodas and snacks, it is possible to get into a cost-equals-income situation
on trainee pay. A wise driver gets a loaf or two, some sandwich-type
meats and cheeses, chips, and soda to minimize that food expense. We
are wise drivers, so we do that. Back to the truck with my deliMex, several bags of homemade fast-food ingredients, chips'n'hotsauce, that's all
one word here, and load it up.

   We set out for California with 40,000 pounds of asparagus, sandwich stuff, and fresh deliMex.


It is late in the afternoon, late in July, and hot as we pull into the line at
the border patrol inspection station. The breeze off the desert only
makes it worse. It is a hot wind, and does more harm than good. It dries
everything and cools nothing. The line of trucks and cars is three quarters of a mile long and serpentines out the station and along the shoulder

of the interstate. This is dangerous as well, having bigtrucks parked along the shoulder. Heat waves rising from cars, road, landscape. Makes me thirsty just looking out the window. We move slowly but steadily, and sooner than I thought, we are almost to the officers doing the inspections beneath a huge shed three or four lanes wide. They stop every vehicle, look into the compartments, and badger the people inside. Anyone else in there? Where have you been? Where are you going? Are you a U.S. citizen? How long? I have the window down and can hear them asking the questions to other cars and trucks. A dog sniffs around each vehicle in the process. Several cars are off to the side undergoing different levels of inspection. Some have the people out, some have everything out.

A rattletrap pickup is motioned out of the queue and into the search area. An older Hispanic couple exits the cab and a troop of kids swarm from the camper. The old man has an uh-oh expression and his mate has a confused look as the agents close in on the old truck.

We are motioned forward and quizzed. I look at the agent in disbelief upon the U.S. citizen question. He must see that expression a thousand times a day. He also notes the refrigeration unit running and the temperature readout on the side of the unit and surmises there are no illegals in the trailer. If there are, he further surmises, they are of no real consequence to the Immigration Department. He steps off the running board and motions us through.

The rattletrap pickup has stuff all out of it now and the dog is really busy. I don't know what happened, but it doesn't look good. We idle past and I hope the old folks don't get into trouble because someone stashed something on their truck to get it across the border. You never know, but I think they are too old to be smugglers. I only hope they didn't get used as transporters, and would have had the goodies taken back from them on the U.S. side at gunpoint, if necessary, by the bad guys. If that is the case, maybe it will go better for them that they were caught here. Smugglers don't have too many rules when it comes to getting their stuff back.

I shift up through the gears and am surprised at how little effort the engine puts forth to get such a load up to roadspeed. These things are very powerful. Each gear must be double-clutched and shifted at the proper combination of engine RPM and road MPH, or the transmission will not allow that shift to be completed. It is a practiced art and not one easily mastered. Much gear clashing and profanity is involved in learning, and the transmission is unforgiving but durable beyond belief. There is no way to cheat. The mechanical process must be correct, or the transmission hangs in neutral. Not only is that an aggravation on level land, it is illegal to have a commercial vehicle in neutral for any period while it is rolling, and in the mountains it is simply dangerous. No one wants 80,000 pounds stuck in neutral going up, or coming down a mountainside.

I am shifting smoothly and have made it a point of my apprenticeship to get this part down. Shifting and backing are the mark of a driver. Some drivers never get one or the other. A few never get either. Watch the tachometer and the speedometer. Proper engine speed and proper roadspeed for each of ten gears. Double-clutch and move the shifter. There are five gears in low range, and five gears in high range. There is a range selector button on the shifter knob. Move the button up for high, down for low. Fail to move the button from high at a stop, and the transmission will still be in high range. Embarrassing. Truck hops a couple of times and dies. More hopping. Fail to move the button to high from fifth gear, and it will not go into sixth gear. Great grinding noises. More embarrassment. Castigating looks from Trainer. I make all those mistakes the first few days. That's how I know the things are very nearly indestructible.

The tenth gear is called the money hole, or the big hole. It is only used on the highway and the truck must be at speed to get it into tenth gear, so the truck will be rolling for a while and racking up the miles if it is in that gear. I have it in the money hole, in the hammer lane, on the bigroad. The hammer lane is the fast lane. Granny lane, or travel lane, is the other one. The faster you go, the more miles you cover and the more money you make. It's a simple business.

Got the hammer down, headed for our overnight stop in Fort Stockton. The computer told us to fill up at a particular truck stop there, and since we want to incorporate as many things as we can into one stop, we may as well stay the night. I figure we'll get there between midnight and 1 A.M. I like the availability of morning coffee at a truck stop, as opposed to other places we may have to stay the night, so I am okay with riding till that hour to get there. I have a coffee thing, you know.

The route chosen by the computer is as direct a means as is possible. It is usually wise to go that route for many reasons, but mainly because it is usually the best way to go. We still have to check local road conditions and look in the atlas for low clearances and restricted routes, but ordinarily that's the way to go. Restricted routes are on a table in the front pages of the atlas. Those routes are not roads bigtrucks can travel. There is some reason for a bigtruck to not be there, and the fines for using a restricted route can be staggering. Thousands, even tens of thousands of dollars in some cases, for a transgression. We do not want to get caught on a restricted route in a bigtruck.

The company will not be responsible for the fine in the case of that offense. The company will sometimes pay a huge fine for various DOT offenses and charge the driver for it through a payroll deduction, but only if that driver is an asset to the company. Nonetheless, it is a painful experience. In addition, in some situations, the offender's truck is not allowed to leave under its own power, and the expense of a tow is incurred. Tow trucks that can pull a bigtruck are not cheap. Driver has to pay that, too.

This route is a truck route, but is not heavily traveled, for several reasons: there is no reason to be here unless one is going to Fort Stockton or Laredo, there are few fueling places, and it crosses a desert. It parallels the Rio Grande through mesquite forests, if forest is the word, and is wonderfully smooth. And that is good, because the weight these trailers carry squashes the suspension and therefore stiffens it considerably, and the frame is shaken as a result. And, the engine is attached to the frame. More vibration. The cab is suspended on air bags and that helps a lot, and the chairs are mounted on an air system as well. The chairs have an oscillator on them that helps remove some of the pitching motion of the cab, but the trucks still ride rough. On a rough road, the ride is rougher. On a really rough road, the ride is not comfortable. Drivers wear shoulder belts for more than the possibility of collision.

The drive itself is a good one. The ribbon of asphalt lays over the desert hill and dale like part of the landscape. Doesn't seem added on at all. A constant blur of six- to eight-foot mesquite trees/bushes lines both sides of the road, and we sit about two feet above them in the cab. We rise and fall with the land. It is sparsely populated and therefore starkly beautiful. I see jackrabbits blasting off the road shoulder on occasion. Huge ears. Surprise a deer or two on a crested hill. They blast off as well. This area is where some record rattlers are found, so probably some rattlesnakes blasting around out there, too. Maybe get that way eating the deer.

We are driving into a spectacular sunset. The dust in the air sets the sky aflame above the Mexican desert for two travelers lucky enough to be there, which causes a moron to wonder: If a sunset happens, and no one is there to see it, does it have any color?

Low-latitude sunsets and dawns don't live long, and you might miss them if you look away, but watching the road is a big part of driving. I try to err on the side of safety. The sunset turns to twilight and the sky is a gradient of indigo above to aquamarine at the horizon. Just beautiful. It goes quickly from there to the deep black of a crystal-clear west Texas night. The near full moon, climbing in the eastern sky, is brilliant and bathes the white cliffs and hills in a soft glow. I feel a need to get out and be in it somehow, so I shout at Trainer I need to pee. We have to change chairs anyway, since he has to drive in the dark hours. He huffs an answer I don't understand, but my message was more a statement than request, so I look for a suitable place to pull off the road.

Bigtrucks can't just pull onto the shoulder like a car. Forty tons can crush a weak shoulder and sink in, or worse, fall onto its side. We need hard surface and enough of it to get completely off the road. Anything parked on any part of the roadway or shoulder is called a "sitting duck." We don't want to be one. For the amount of driving the average person does, they are surprisingly bad at it, and as a result they hit something sooner or later, having gotten out of their lane chasing a cigarette or swatting the kids, or just being a bad driver. Being a less-than-excellent, or careless, car driver shouldn't be a death sentence, so we don't leave bigtrucks where less-than-excellent or careless car drivers are likely to hit them.

I find a place. It looks like a place perfectly designed for parking a single bigtruck off the shoulder.

Park the truck, get out and into the just-fallen darkness. I walk across the road to get away from the noise and light of the truck, and look into the black velvet sky peppered with glittering speckles of stars and a couple of really big stars that must be planets. The moonlight diffuses in the dust like the sunset, but still doesn't hide the stars. It gives the sky a closeness. Like I could touch it. City folks don't see this. I revel a moment, and then have to go. I could stay long here, maybe get a permanent bend in my neck.

Trainer doesn't want to drive for some reason. He's still in the second seat. I walk to the passenger side and tell him he needs to drive now. He looks back and down at me from on high. I can't drive past dark, remember? I am a trainee and the safety department says I can't drive after dark for the first week. He sits up at the word "safety." I notice that. The keyword. I will use "safety" in many discussions in the future to get a result and it will never fail to produce. Safety. No one wants to cross that line and be found out. Least of all a trainer. What a tool.

All smug, I climb into the second seat and get comfortable as Trainer goes up the gears and we get back to speed. I look out the window onto the moonlit desertscape. The Spanish have a word for it. *Encanta. Yo soy encanta.* I'm enchanted. And so I am.

Miles and miles, rabbits and deer, moonlight and limestone. And the road is a ribbon of silver. I sit at my window and am *encanta* while the Kenworth rumbles through the darkness, far from anywhere, going somewhere, with me looking out the window thoroughly enjoying the trip through nowhere, across the purple moor.

The cab is lit internally by myriad small lights from myriad instruments indicating the status of myriad functions. Trainer's face is illuminated by a panel of them and he is intent. He is driving. He is focused. I admire that. He works at doing a good job for himself and the company. He takes a pride in his job that is not so common these days. He likes the driver's life and considers himself a driver. A member of the fraternity; a professional. He ordinarily chatters on the CB radio and uses all the dialect. But, in his desire to be accepted, he tries too hard to join in and the other reindeer laugh and call him names. I listen. He is unfazed by it, or appears to be. Just wants to be one of the guys. I know he must feel the rejection and I know it must take its toll. I don't really see what he's doing, or more accurately what he's not doing, that gives him away as a wannabe. Not much chatter out here tonight though, so he's safe enough. We've passed maybe two cars going the other way, and they probably don't have radios.

It's late now, near midnight, and after a long and pleasant ride, the lights of our fuel stop are on the horizon. Looks strange to me, this island of light in the darkness, hazy halo above it. We roll into the glare of Fort Stockton to fuel up and bed down.

As we pull into the fuel stop, other trucks are backed in to the perimeter of the concrete lot and more are parked across the street in a dusty lot, but we are alone at the fuel island. I am not sure what my role is yet in the fuel stops, so I take the entry-level position as service station attendant. Clean the windshield, no mean feat since it is 10 feet off the ground, check the oil, coolant, fluids, belts and hoses on the engine.

We finish fueling quickly. The high-volume pumps on each side of the truck blow about a gallon of diesel per second into a pair of 100-gallon tanks. Good thing, too; I'm tired now, the adrenaline crash is on me. We go in to the fuel desk and square away the bill, get in the truck, and drive across the street to park in the dusty lot. It's easier than backing into a slot on the concrete part, I'm told. Okay.

Set the a/c on blizzard, undress, climb into my bunk, and sleep the desert night away. I don't even remember lying down.

The morning sun is blazing through the windshield and the sapphire blue west Texas sky is blazing through my upper window. I roll out and into my shorts. Where's my shirt? What did I do with it? There it is on the locker top. So's my briefcase. So is that relief bottle from yesterday. Step forward over the refrigerator and between the chairs. All my bags are on the second seat. Musta put 'em there last night. I keep them on my bunk during the day where they are in the road less traveled. Guess I put them there last night in a stupor. It's okay, that's where they should be. I need to sit in that chair though, and that means the bags go back on the bunk. Unfortunately, I need to make the bunk before the bags go back on it. Back over all the stuff to the bunk. Bad hair. I'll bet I have it. Make the bunk. The mattress is half a king sheet wide, so I fold one in half side to side, lay it on top of the mattress, and sleep in it like a taco. A lightweight Mexican blanket tops it off for a bedspread. Very colorful and adds a festive atmosphere to the cab. Back over the stuff on the floor. Pitch the bags onto the bunk, just so. Don't want them transformed from innocent carriers of clothing into cannonballs during panic braking.

Flop into the chair. It hisses. Spray water into my face and hair from a small garden bottle. Dry my face with a paper towel and comb the mist into my hair. I feel a little better. Coffee. Where? Out of the idling tractor and into the warm desert breeze. It is like a caress and I'm the better for it. I set out for where I believe coffee is waiting. I see Trainer heading back with a crusty mug full. I know it's coffee because he has to have it as well. I know the mug is full because of the way he's carrying it. All good signs. We pass wordlessly in the dust, eyeing one another in a mimed affront.

About the middle of the second cup for me, we update our logs. Call it "doing" our logs. Since they have to be "done," and they have to be right, and ours have to match since we are a team, we "do" them together. We can't have both of us driving at the same time. The log can't show us in Dallas at 5 P.M. and San Francisco at 7 P.M. that same day. The log has to make sense. A copy of the logs goes into HQ with a trip package of papers, and there is a special department of each company responsible for logbook compliance. The DOT can show up in any carrier's offices and demand to see the logbooks of any driver. Especially after an accident. The logs had best make sense. The fines can be huge for failure to comply on a corporate level and just as huge proportionately for the guilty driver.

Usually, a driver doesn't have to wait for an accident to get his log inspected. Like we talked about before, any weigh station in any state has a person authorized by the DOT to inspect a logbook. Not just any officer can do that. Most state troopers can demand a logbook. Most city and county officers cannot. Gotta be a DOT person. If one of those authorized to do so finds a discrepancy, like getting from Dallas to San Francisco in two hours, that driver has a problem. An expensive one. And it opens the door to further inspections, for about as far back as that officer wants to look, each located offense ticketed separately. Company doesn't pay those either.

Logbooks are a battleground for the DOT and the driver. Federal management versus common sense. The object of the logbook is to keep tired drivers off the road. Most drivers understand that and don't fudge much on their logs. A very few drivers look at it like a game. Young ones mostly. Catch me if you can. They drive on pills and youth, with two or three logbooks. The more miles, the more money, and a legal logbook shuts a driver down after 10 hours of driving. They have one for inspection by the DOT and one or more for the paycheck. One for the show and two for the money. They are regarded as outlaws by most, which they are, and live life as renegades, so they don't advertise except among their own, but they are still out there. You share the road with them. So does your family. They are the ones that pass you so fast your car is sucked sideways.

Trainer is religious about the logs, and does not like any outright falsification. I am pleased. I had heard much about how a log had to be manipulated to make any real money. I see it isn't so. It could be manipulated to make more, but the risk outweighs the financial gain. Doc-

tored logs are a termination offense in any company, even the companies
that turn blind eye to it. They don't care until the driver is caught or gets
them caught. Then, of a sudden, they care. More miles, more money for
them as well.

Logs done, we pull the bag from the small wastebasket that doubles
as an emergency chamber pot for Trainer, and put the trash out. Amazing how much accumulates in a day between the two of us. Stow the
loose gear, adjust our chairs, buckle up, and we're off in a cloud of dust,
literally.

Most tractors have exhaust pipes that go straight up. Those are
called "stacks." Some have exhaust pipes that go under the cab and exit
in front of the rear wheels. Those are called "weedburners." Our company likes the weedburners because they don't blow hot exhaust onto
the refrigeration unit attached to the trailer and do all the bad things to
reefer units that hot diesel exhaust from a stack would do. Downside is,
if there is any dust in the propwash area of a weedburner, it goes airborne. This whole lot is talcum-fine dust. As we move out, everyone
dives inside something till the cloud passes. The one person who does
not is lost to vision in that cloud. Poor soul never saw it coming. En-
gulfed by an airborne parking lot.

Ease onto Interstate 10 and head west to California by way of El Paso.
As the miles go by we try to talk over the roadnoise of eighteen wheels, a
65-MPH wind outside and the steady roar of the engine. Calidamfornia,
Trainer says. Traffic, regulations, cops, smog, few truck stops, and 55 MPH
for bigtrucks. Can't make no time, he says. Always bustin' a rule whether
yer tryin' to or not. Don't even want to go there, he says.

Trainer's near deafness is a further impediment to our discussions.
He frequently misunderstands the question and launches a detailed answer, trying to be a good trainer, to an imagined query. I see no point in
stopping him. I enjoy the sound of his shout and his innocent butchery
of the language. I smile to myself and look out the windshield at the
landscape as he yells above his deafness and the ambient noise about
why we check the oil when I'd asked about the stuffed animals on the

dash. Little mementoes of important occasions. Like the ones the kids get in those kiddie meals at the fast-food places. They mean a lot to him, though, or they wouldn't be on the dash of his truck. Lots of drivers do that, placing important things on the dash, much like a cubicle worker would have on his or her desk or monitor.

I look onto the vastness as we drive through it, and think on how so many cross the Rio Grande, risking first drowning, then dehydration in the Texas desert, trying for a better life in these United States. Some don't make it, and it is easy to see why. There is no shade and no water here. Once the illegal immigrant leaves the river, there is no more surface water, and he, or she, is faced with miles upon miles of scrub brush, sunbaked sand, and unfriendly critters. No pleasure trip. Ranchers and outdoorsmen find fifty to eighty dead every year in this part of Texas alone, not counting the other states and their deserts, and not counting the ones that aren't found. But they still come, to do our floors, mow our lawns, roof our houses, and pick our lettuce. Stuff we don't want to do, and I have seen firsthand the poverty that drives them to attempt a crossing. Some of the things that cause them to defy death would have to be seen to be believed. And I am not sure I believed my eyes in some cases. We live a good life here, and they will settle for a scrap or two of that good life, risking this wasteland to get that scrap, and I think on that as we drive through it.

The day wears on and heats up. I stop every hour or so, to get out and walk around at the state rest stops. It rankles Trainer, but I am not accustomed to driving long periods yet. The chairs are multiposition and comfortable, but no frills. Theory has it the chair should be comfortable, but not sleep inducing. That mix is hard to get, given the body types and mind-sets that will occupy them. Trainer doesn't like stopping because the wheels don't turn and he's paid by the mile. He gets the miles he drives and the miles I drive. He says nothing. Just body language and Neanderthal expressions. I'm on a salary while I train. Wheels roll or no, it's the same to me. I wonder, could Trainer be more interested in my miles than my training. He wants to drive. We have to stop so he can get into the first chair. He hollers we are stoppin' all the damtime. Ain't makin' no dammoney.

After driving a little, Trainer shouts he knows a stop I need to know. Now he wants to stop. Again. Shouts it's coming along shortly. Got a tiger in there. I nod my head. I'm going whether I want to or not. He slows to exit.

The potholed lot is huge, the contraption of cobbled buildings is odd-looking, and there is a "see the tiger" sign. Trainer parks away from the other trucks. Says he wants me to see the tiger. I think *he* wants to see the tiger and I'm a handy excuse to do that. I don't want to see a caged animal. Or a chained animal. Those things offend me. The people that do those things offend me. I regard zoos as nothing more than animal prisons, no matter how exotic or sophisticated, or what the conservation rationale behind them. Let's preserve the species so it can live in a cage so we can take our kids to see an imprisoned animal. Not everything was put here for our entertainment.

A sizable chain-link compound is attached to a part of the building made of smaller buildings. Trainer goes straight for it. Coming from behind him, I see the filthy cage is empty. Bare concrete, no shade, a nasty blanket stuffed into a corner, and a couple of bleached bones scattered about the deck. I hope those are the remnants of the responsible party. Trainer is looking all around the cage as if he's missing the tiger somehow. Like it can't not be in there. Disgusted, he goes for the door and steps into the market part of the place, cool and moist, determined to find the tiger. He stopped to see the tiger. Where's the tiger. The tiger's gotta be here somewhere.

Just inside, away from the other merchandise, but in the wide route, is a small cage on the linoleum-tiled floor with a small tiger in it. Attached sign says picture with the tiger, ten dollars. Trainer stares. He's miffed. He stopped to see a real tiger. Sets off to find the big tiger. I kneel by the cage and stroke the cub's fur through the fence; he meows and leans against my hand. We bonded. So, I stick my hand in up to the forearm, as far as it will go into the heavy mesh. He is small, maybe 40 pounds and desperate for attention, and far too late I see the danger stamped all over him as he opens his mouth, gently gnaws my hand with two-inch fangs, and his emerald eyes meet mine. A calm, intelligent confidence looks into me, takes my measure and finds me lacking, my hand held loosely in his mouth. I have never felt more vulnerable than in that instant. Like I am defenseless and he knows it.

Looking into the eyes of a tiger, even a little one, is a primal experience. Heart suddenly pounding, I jerk my hand back through the wire mesh, fall back onto my backside and realize what a foolish thing that was to do. Though he meant no harm, there is no mistaking that the cuddly, attention-starved ball of beautifully striped fur is a future top-of-the-line predator. A clerk walks up and says I can hold him and get a picture of me holding him for ten dollars. I sit on the floor and breathlessly say thanks, I've been close enough.

Trainer whizzes around the corner and says he's ready to go and what'er you doin' sittin' on the floor. I get onto my feet, weak at the knees. We leave by way of the other door. Still shaken by my foolishness, I stop by the men's room on the way out. Have to pee badly for some reason.

Out to the truck and on the bigroad again. He wants me to drive again. I think about what just happened and I know it will stay with me always. I know there were people in other places in other times that had the same experience with a tyger burning bright, but did not live to tell the tale, in the forest of the night. I shiver a little, and wonder whether or not it is the air conditioner, the ice-cold soda in my hand or the fearful symmetry.

We have to stop in El Paso and get the reefer unit checked. Distributors that buy produce want to make as certain as they can the stuff arrives in sellable shape. So we have to stop at a third party to get a temperature check. Keeps everyone honest. Plus the third party can head off any potential problems with the unit. They are maintenance personnel as well, since they are a part of the company that manufactures the reefer units. Quality folks, too. They take good care of the units and make us feel right to home anytime we deal with them anywhere. The stop is coming up pretty shortly here.

I exit the freeway for the reefer place and get my first taste of real instant panic that comes with rolling backward from a dead stop uphill. Stopped for the light, I let go the brake to engage the clutch and the whole rig rolls backward surprisingly quickly. We go back two or three feet before I realize what is happening and get back onto the brake pedal to stop the roll. Very luckily, there is nothing behind us, close enough to hit anyway. That incident puts a permanent fear in me, that's two permanent imprints today, causes a complete redo of uphill stops, and it doesn't happen again. I haven't put my arm in a tiger cage again, either.

We get to the reefer place uneventfully, and they do their certifications. It really doesn't take too long, but we see it as a good opportunity for lunch and take full advantage, strolling down to a recommended steakhouse. Only Omaha has steaks that can compete with Texas, and even those would be on a case-by-case basis. Nothing else is close enough to talk about. We go with the steak-and-baker, wander back to the truck, and democratically decide we should roll rather than nap. I vote for the nap. Trainer has two votes, and rolling wins by a landslide. He takes the nap as a perk of winning. I demand a recount, but it doesn't matter. Trainer is also the election judge, and the results stand. I resolve to appeal the blatant ballot box stuffing. Trainer hops in the bunk as I shift into second gear. Says he's the arbitrator, too.

Another thing happened in the west Texas town of El Paso. I saw how the difference of 50 feet can mean feast or famine. The Rio Grande is the dividing entity between Mexico and the U.S. It is the border. Lots of rivers are borders. That doesn't make it different. What makes it different is the fact it separates the have of El Paso from the want of Juarez. I have seen poverty that approached destitution before, but I have never seen such a dramatic economic difference in the space of 50 feet. Never. The wealth of one city and the poverty of another. So close and yet a financial world apart. I am taken completely aback as I drive through the western edge of El Paso and look across the drainage ditch strewn with tires and trash known hereabouts as the Rio Grande in Texas and the Rio Bravo in Mexico. The freeway parallels the river within a few feet for some distance, miles really. I glance through the chain-link fence on the U.S. side and across the river to lock eyes with a man standing in the dust outside a crumbling cinder-block house amid cannibalized cars, and realize a spin of Fortune's wheel is all that made a difference in where we are, he and I.

His face and his place are with me permanently now. Others are already and more will be as well. I have snapshots and video clips of people in my head. I don't know their names in some cases, and I know more about some and less about others than I want to know. But, mainly, I carry with me this mental photo album of individuals and situations. Times and places and people captured and kept for some reason I thought was important at the time. I get them out sometimes and look at them. Maybe we all do that. I don't know. I never really talked to anyone about it.

I feel guilty somehow, my having just had a steak for lunch, knowing that man may have been hungry and there surely being someone over there hungry. Couldn't help but be. Certainly none of them had a steak for lunch. I try to shake the guilt thing by looking straight out the windshield and yelling a question to Trainer about our next fuel stop. He yells from the sleeper he doesn't like hiphop, but there are some country western tapes in his locker we can listen to if I want.

The miles roll by and there is no end to this desert. We stop for a break and change seats. Trainer takes the wheel, fresh from his nap, and we get back onto the bigroad. In the wilds of New Mexico, Trainer is intent on the interstate. He has no distractions now. He's driving. Got the CB on, waiting for some more abuse. I feel like I'm on a tour or something. I am thinking I should be sightseeing rather than looking out the windshield, like I'll burn myself out if I use the windshield too much, so I'm looking out my window and see two bulls sparring a couple of hundred yards into the low brush. As we get more alongside them, and from this distance, I see this is not sparring. They are serious. One is shiny red on the side of his neck. Massive, powerful animals dueling in the sand, intent on damage. A struggle as old as time. Two males of some species determining who's boss. Dust rising into the still air above them giving the whole thing a dramatic effect. Angled shadows in the early-afternoon heat, the sunlight on rippling muscles beneath iridescent hides. Herb Alpert plays his trumpet somewhere in my mind.

Trainer drives westward, oblivious. I sit back in my chair thinking on what I just saw, and how some things are like they always were, and how the most civilized among us can be pushed to lose his control and become a raging bull under the right, or wrong, circumstances. And I think maybe there is such a thing as temporary insanity. But I don't think it is true insanity. It may be we just get pushed to the point of forgetting our training and anger management and etiquette, and revert just for a time, to the animal we really are. It may be that violence is the only solution in some cases. It may be the only thing we really understand. It may be the only real way to determine who's in charge here.

The Kenworth bellows its highway song, unconcerned and determined.

Back from where I was mentally, and back on the road listening to the citizen's band radio, volume above everything else. They are called that because any citizen can use them. Don't have to have a license, and that's a shame. Without some structure other than the ability to afford one, we get what we have. CB radio must be the source of that old crack about two unarmed people in a battle of wits. Foul-mouthed simpletons trading insults and threatening one another. Even some, a very few, of the women are scary. However, most of them, the women, are welcome additions to any conversation, their voices alone an admonition to mind our manners.

These are the same people I see in truck stops that smile, hold the doors for one another, and say hidydoo over lunch. But something happens to them in the anonymity of the airwaves and the mobility of their trucks. Civility, manners, and morals go right into the toilet. Drivers beat one another soundly on the radio. More get into the fray and it becomes a verbal gangfight. Paragraphs of four-letter words. Fortunately the range is only a couple of miles, and we move from one aggressive conversation into the range of another. Whores advertise their services and a pricelist in the truck stops or rest areas. Truck-stop barkers advertise the daily special and Christians thump the Bible; it is a collage of voices and topics, like a tapestry of sound, fringed with static.

Trainer regards the CB as a vital source of information, though misinformation abounds, some innocent and some purposefully malicious. I regard it strictly as some twisted kind of entertainment.

Back when, everyone had a handle. An alter ego with a name. Now, truckers refer to one another simply as "driver." No one is black, no one is white. No one is skinny or fat. No wealth-based social stratification out here. Everyone is "driver." Rarely, someone will ask how are ye known. Many times a hesitant and sheepish response produces that named alter ego, as though the person is embarrassed to reveal their fantasy side even in the shadows of radio. It doesn't matter, really. They will only know one another for a few seconds if going opposite ways, and a few miles if they are going the same way, but they still are reluctant to make that side of themselves public.

With more than a million and a half OTR trucks out there, the likelihood of crossing the other's radio path again is slim. Oddly, it does happen.

One Mensa candidate comes into range talking about getting off the bigroad to get cigarettes and a soda. Says her truck runs on Marlboros and Cokes. Someone asks is she married and she says yeah, but her husband is mad at her. He likes her hair long and had "pissed her off" over something I didn't catch as the result of static, so she cut her hair to "piss him off." I think it is no wonder we have television programs about divorces, if that is what goes on.

We roll into Arizona and a place with big piles of big rocks called Texas Canyon just as a big thunderstorm is getting bigger and positioning itself over the canyon. The rain literally begins to pour just as we drive from beneath it, and the wind is fierce, rocking the cab at roadspeed. It is a headwind, and from above, luckily not much from the side, and the Kenworth's engine doesn't notice. As we go along, the microburst is more from our side and rear, and the Kenworth does notice that. The whole truck rocks uncomfortably. I hold onto the arms of my chair, not knowing how much of a roll angle the truck will survive.

Even with more than 40,000 pounds of asparagus holding us down, the rig is shoved heavily by the gusting wind. It is an obvious effort for Trainer to steer. I am not concerned at this point about the truck being blown over, but I am concerned about being blown onto the shoulder and Trainer losing control. These things don't stay upright long once they leave the pavement. I shout above the engine and windnoise at Trainer to slow down. He thinks for a second and shouts back he wants to get away from here fast. I won't argue, but I know I am right. He knows it, too. It is the first of several power trips for Trainer, and a dangerous means to establish dominance.

A storm is hiding others, and as we emerge from the canyon I can see them lined up for us in the distance. In the mirror I can see behind us and note how much worse the one storm is for those still in the canyon. The clouds are black and ugly, wind-ruffled on the bottoms. Angry and threatening. Not innocuous and fluffy like fair-weather clouds.

The interstate goes onto a high plain about here and the soaked sand tells a violent story. Rivulets still run their fingers through the sand beneath the juniper and creosote bushes. I picture the desert fauna dealing with that. Dry this moment, flooded the next, then dry again. Hot and dry for weeks, maybe months, then with little warning, tons of wind and water, and an hour later it is hot and dry again. As if nothing had happened. Back to sunbaked, hard country. Sunbaked, hard fauna in it.

Some miles farther, Trainer has a biological emergency and exits the bigroad onto a two-lane road into the desert. He must know where he's going. There's nothing out here but an apparently long-abandoned gasoline station. We roll right up to it. Trainer flies out the door and double-times to the back of the building without a word. A guy that big looks funny when he runs. I look around from the cab. Old wheels and sun-charred tires litter the place. Antique gas pumps. Relics from another age. The kind that have those little balls that whirl around in the half-globe at the top. White paint peeling from the side of the cinder-block building. Oil and grease in lumps that leaked from 10,000 cars long ago on the concrete deck both sides of the gas pump island. Sand-scratched sign creaks as it swings in the breeze on the pole by the road. It is so sun-faded I can't make out the logo.

I climb out, step into the sand, and walk beneath the awning over the pumps. Little tabs of peeling paint dangle like tiny stalactites from the underside of the awning and flutter in the hot breeze. The awning seems low, but I guess I'm used to bigtruck fuel islands. This place is a dump. I snoop around and snoop right into more sunbaked fauna. An old man in a tattered old chair against the building beneath the awning. I say hello. He says hello. We eye one another for a few seconds. I comment on the storm that passed by. He says it 'uz a mean 'un. Quiet, but not uncomfortable, moment. He says not many people stop by here no more, least of all them big fancy trucks. More quiet. He asks how much diesel the truck would hold. I tell him 200 gallons. Says he wisht he solt diesel. Said business died away after they put the interstate in years ago. Said he used to do some welding here, too—mufflers and broken tailpipes mostly. Was an Esso station. But they got bought up by some big company and closed him down. Long time gone, now.

Like any isolated soul he just wants someone to talk to and I guess I seem harmless enough, so he talks uninterrupted for a while. About how it was back in the days and life was good. Moved out here from Phoenix after the war. Started a gas station so he could meet people. Wanted to find the right girl and make enough to treat her proper. Take care of his customers so they'd trade with him. And he did those things along with his wife's help after he found and married her. She ran the office, right in there. He did the work, and pumped the gas. Them trucks wasn't as big then, but they used to run on gas, y'know. Liked to see them come in to fill up.

Then they moved the road and his business died. His wife did, too, so now he's right back where he started. And he looked away, into the mountains in the distance for a moment. Said quietly, she liked those mountains. She'd look at them for hours sometimes. Liked to watch the storms come over them.

He moves on to the storm just passed and suddenly brightens. Says he wants to show me something, and to follow him. I follow the spry little man around the corner and into the surprisingly cool building. The grubby linoleum floor is caked with grease. Old glass-front cabinets stuffed with yellowed and dog-eared papers. Receipts and invoices from another age. I follow him to a dusty display case that apparently held candy bars at one time, judging that from the crinkled wrapper in the far corner. In it now are things that appear to be sandstone tree roots. Some are big, like two feet across. Says he watches the storms for the want of anything to do and tries to remember where the lightning bolts hit the ground and goes there when it is safe, to locate these and dig them up. Done it for years. Keeps 'em right here. The ones that make it back. Sometimes they fall apart. Looks for the burned spot where the lightnin' hits and digs real careful there. Gotta be careful 'cause them little branches'll break right off. He stands back to gauge my reaction. I am duly impressed and say as much. The aged little man smiles a satisfied smile, and I bend to get a closer look. I ask if I might hold one and he says sure and I am surprised at how heavy and gritty the things are.

I marvel at the lightning's sandstone fingerprints and the man that tracks them down. I have not known the likes of either. Still holding the sandstone buckhorn, I see motion in my peripheral vision and look through the dusty glass to see Trainer moving carefully back to the truck. I could spend hours here learning to see this man's desert like he sees it, but asparagus waits for no one. It is wilting as we stand here, so I bid my host a thank you, hand back the lightning-glass, and work my way through the maze of junk and greasy litter back to the door and out to the truck. He closes the case and follows me out. Sits back in his chair, resuming the same position as when I first saw him.

Calidamfornia is out there somewhere, and I sometimes lose sight of the fact that's where we are going. There is a lot to see and do along the way, and I get sidetracked easily. It is a thing I have. Short attention span regarding stuff everyone else thinks is important.

There is a gem from Zen that says be where you are and do what you are doing. The purity of that impresses me. Right now I'm in the desert with a desert dweller looking at desert stuff. I'm not sure I want to go to Calidamfornia. This very second, anyway. I don't really care how badly the folks there want asparagus. Right this very second.

I look down from my window and picture the decrepit gas station and its wizened owner in their glory days. Him in his starched uniform and cap with its fifty-mission crush, the station freshly painted with a shiny new Esso sign swinging in the desert sky. Packed with cars and people waving Esso cards at him. One of the Greek scholars, Aristotle, noted the only constant is change, and this is a glaring example of the difference of then and now. Greek scholars were pretty deep, and Aristotle may well have been to Arizona.

Dust and sand boil from the weedburner blast beneath the Kenworth as Trainer shifts into second gear and lets out the clutch. I look in the mirror and see the old man in his chair. I guess he lives here. I didn't ask. I don't guess it matters.

The engine roars as we get to roadspeed from the access ramp onto the interstate and I settle into my chair to work things out for myself, looking out the windshield, into the blinding sun. How we come and go into and out of other people's lives and how all parties concerned are, or are not, the better for having done so.

Trainer shouts that Phoenix is the next town of any size along our way but we ain't gonna stay there. We'll fuel some distance to the west and stay there. We hafta wash the truck, too. If we go into California with a dirty truck, the dam CHiPs will inspect us at the border and find somethin' wrong with the truck. If it's clean they won't.

Say what?. . . I don't think the California Highway Patrol uses dirt as their criterion for inspecting trucks. While a really grimy truck may signify poor maintenance overall to an inspector, I don't think a little road dust is a real red flag.

What red flag? Where? Never mind. We gotta wash the truck before we get to California . . . or we'll get busted. Busted for what?. . . A dirty truck?

Trainer clams up and looks out the windshield, frustrated with the conversation.

Soon the Phoenix skyline hoves into view, and I am impressed with the size of the city. I had thought it smaller. Didn't take into account exponential population growth, I guess. It happens out here in the desert as well. People boinking away everywhere. Making more consumers and taking up more space and building houses and buying cars and driving around plugging up the freeways and polluting the air.

I read once that 3,000 new cars a week hit the streets in the U.S. That many cars take up 11.3 miles of roadway, and we don't build roads that fast, so I guess we are headed for gridlock sooner than I thought. Phoenix definitely has a head start on the other desert towns insofar as the gridlock situation goes.

Going through town on the freeway, two drivers are at it on the CB. One says he'll kick the other's ass if the other will just pull over. The other says he has a gun. The one says he has two guns. We drive out of hearing and shooting range. Wild, wild west. I wonder how that worked out. I watch the papers for a couple of days, looking to see if anyone was shot in Phoenix. These guys are professional drivers . . . well, maybe not professional, but at least getting paid for driving, and I wonder if this an example of professional roadrage. As in not amateur.

Onward, through the metropolitan oasis of Phoenix and into the desert again. Not far down the road, Trainer says we'll wash the truck here and stay the night. Not necessarily in that order. We pull into a big truck stop, eat, shave, shower, and bed down for the night. Trainer usually gets into his bunk as soon as we get back from the shower, and watches some TV. Maybe a videotape. I sit sideways in the second seat with my legs across the space and my feet in the first seat, get comfortable as if I were in a chaise, and read. Trainer drifts away, begins to snort, and I get up to turn the TV off. I regard television as the greatest lost potential of our age, so I rarely watch it, except for a movie, and refuse to watch anything with a laff track. Any program with a laff track tells me it is such poor quality the audience must be prompted to think it is funny. Which tells me something about the audience . . . I'm not sure what. So I just read. Newspapers, magazines, rarely, and what books I can trade. We have a cassette player, and I have thought about the audio books while we drive, but I don't know that I want someone else reading to me. I have several problems with that, and maybe I'll enumerate them one day. But not today. We'll move on to the subject of sleep.

It is easy to sleep in a bigtruck. Most of the time the engine is running. Most of the time the truck is moving. The drone of the engine, the comfort and the rocking of the cab are analogous to the womb. It is easy to drift off. Drivers regularly battle sleepiness. Even sitting still, the effect is the same what with the engine idling so the a/c works. And a medium breeze will rock most cabs because of the air-ride configuration whether the tractor is rolling or sitting still. The cab has a three-point attachment to the frame and is unstable by design. It is set up to rock rather than jolt. Combine those factors with a little fatigue, and the result is a sound sleep. I sleep well in the truck. So does Trainer. About the only thing that brings on battle stations is a change in the idling engine's grumble.

Steady as a heartbeat, these engines are born to run. Built almost entirely of forged moving parts, they have a life span of about a million miles, properly maintained, and missing a beat is so rare as to be non-existent. Therefore, when one does stumble, the implications are far reaching and everyone associated with that engine gets real concerned real fast. A change in the engine's pitch would have both of us on our feet and scanning controls very nearly instantly, even from a deep sleep. No such problem tonight, though, and the morning is on us soon enough.

Awake at first light, I snooze a few minutes and let the sky brighten, then open the light curtains with my foot, kick them aside, and the

Arizona morning washes into the cab. I don't have to get out of my bunk. Trainer flops around and sits up on the edge of his bunk. Orients himself. Falls through the curtains into the cockpit, fumbles for cigarettes and lighter, chair hisses and squeals, lighter clicks open and scratches, flame poofs, deep inhale, lighter clicks closed, window rolls down, exhales outside into Arizona. I snooze and wait. A pattern is developing as the mornings go on.

Trainer dresses and chases his coffee mug all over the dash. I hear it. Plastic mug making sliding plastic sounds on the top of the dash, the handle clicking into the windshield. Sounds like the mug was winning there for a moment. I've heard one contestant knows he has the upper hand in arm wrestling when the other guy breaks wind. Trainer struggling, straining, stretching to get the runaway mug, leans across the dash from his chair, and gives himself away. Way to go, mug. I hope the window is down. I hope there is a breeze.

The door opens on the driver's side, the cab rocks as Trainer's weight hangs on the steps going down, and the door slams shut. That's my signal to get out of the bunk and begin my routine.

Trainer reappears with a sour look just as I'm done. He gets in, I get out. Head for the coffee fountain. I have, thus far, learned quite a bit from Trainer, and one of those things is how to get coffee if we don't have a fuel desk. Free . . . as if we were at a fuel desk. If I go in and fill a Styrofoam cup from the coffee bar in the convenience store part of the truck stop, it costs X. If I go back in with the same cup, it is considered a refill and I'm charged ½X. Further, if I go into the coffee bar with my own cup initially, it is also considered a refill, and I'm only out ½X. But, if I go to the coffee bar with my own mug, and that mug has the logo of the truck stop chain on it, the attendant usually waves me off when I get to the kiosk. Free coffee. It's a good thing. So, I have several coffee mugs. One for each of the major truck stop chains, and I use whichever is called for.

The fuel desk coffee bar in most any truck stop is not nearly as deluxe as the big one in the convenience store part of the place, but the coffee is just as good and the crowd is much less cosmopolitan. Seldom

is anyone in the fuel desk coffee bar concerned with what condiments
there are, or how many of those little hazelnut doobies to put into the
mix. These are coffee drinkers, not dilettantes. Just get the coffee and
go. Sometimes, if there is no fuel desk, I have to put up with some yup-
pie trying to get just the right blend of foofoo in his cup at the convenience store coffee bar. They take a while, especially if they are trying to
impress a woman with their encyclopedic knowledge of additives, and
all they really do is help her mess up a good cup of coffee. I just keep
my mouth shut while it happens, and hope it doesn't take too long.

Back to the truck. Stare out the windshield. Small talk. Back for
second mug. Back to truck. Logbook. Trade chairs. Directed by Trainer,
I take the first chair. From this point forward, in my time with Trainer,
I will drive in the morning and into the early afternoon. Crank up and
maneuver out the parking lot. It isn't easy, and this is where most accidents happen. Low speed and backing accidents in truck-stop parking
lots. Most anyone can drive one of these trucks down the road. It's a lot
like driving a car. Close-quarters maneuvering and backing is another
story. Drivers' abilities range from excellent to awful, much of that dependent on how long they have been driving backward. Low speed, low
impact, but expensive. Most drivers are pretty considerate about parking, but sometimes the lots fill up late in the night, and tired drivers
park anywhere the truck will fit. Most lots hold about fifty to one hundred and fifty trucks. Some hold four to five hundred. This one is about
average with an above-average number of trucks in it. Some are parked
where they shouldn't be. As I pick my way out, I am thinking we need
more truck stops. This one, like many, is overcrowded. Some drivers
don't bother with a truck stop. They just park on the shoulder of an
entry or exit ramp on the interstate. Sitting duck. It's illegal in some
states and dangerous in all states. I am told those are the drivers that
can't back well enough to get into a truck stop. I will find later, however,
while that is true in some cases, many of the drivers that park on the exit
and access ramps ran out of hours there, or are smart enough to not risk
having their truck hit by someone in a truck stop that can't back well.

Interstate 10 west to California. Trainer says we can use the cruise control today. I feel like we've reached a milestone. Drivers call it ridin' and guidin'. It is risky, and that's why drivers are careful when they use the snooze button. Trainer calls it that. The diesel rumbles, the cab rocks, the wind and road noise conspire. Hypnos casts his spell. Gotta be careful with the snooze button on a long stretch of interstate. It is easy to see how something really bad can happen. In fact, I will see the results of that very thing several times before my training is done. Trainer says sleeping at the wheel is an amateur mistake. That veterans know to shut down when they get sleepy. While, at first take, that appears to make sense, I will see deeper into my driving life that this is not necessarily true. Sometimes a vet will overextend himself, or allow himself to be pressured by a dispatcher or broker. Come on, buddy . . . I know you're tired, just get it a hundred miles closer for me, an' I'll getcha repowered. How about an extra hundred dollars?. . . We gotta keep this customer happy.

Trainer initiating a conversation shakes me out of my concentration. Usually he follows my lead. A longtime solo driver, he's not used to having anyone to hold in conversation. Says he's going on vacation in two weeks and needs his birth certificate. I tell him to call the county where he was born, get with the vital statistics group, and they'll mail a certified copy to him for a few bucks. He says he has to go in person. I never heard of that. Says that's the way it is. His birth certificate is in Los Angeles county and he has to go there to get it so he can get a passport so he can go to Cozumel. I tell him to call and they will mail it to his house and he says no, he will get a cab and go into Los Angeles when we get there and I can stay in a truck stop with the truck until he gets back. Tomorrow he says he's gonna get his birth certificate. Okay, suit yourself . . . I give up.

The desert is beautiful in the early light from behind us. Soft colors and shadows on the rock mountains and saguaros. I see no sign of animal life at all. I know it is out there; I've watched those PBS programs about lizards and snakes and scorpions. They are probably just bedded down for the day. Oddly, there is no trash along the roadway like other parts of the interstates we travel. Just rocks and sand. Right up to the road. It had to be a miserable job building this highway along here. Maybe they did it at night. I wonder how Arizona keeps its highways so clean. I wonder if they do that at night.

The California port of entry is right on a lush green bank of the Colorado River that appears from nowhere in the midst of the desert. A good example of an oasis, and must have been heaven-sent for early travelers in these parts. Pleasure boats tied up at a dock that leads from a river onto a desert. Looks strange. A pier coming from the desert. The contrast is sharp, and I understand there is a ferocious fight going on downstream regarding who gets how much of the water. Looks peaceful here for now.

Onto the bridge and into Calidamfornia. We inch along in the bottle-necked traffic on this rusty old bridge. Stop and go off the bridge and through more road construction to the guardhouse, finally. Officer says, What are you hauling? Asparagus. Open up for inspection. Okay. I get out and go to the rear of the trailer and open the inset door, and the officer looks in with a flashlight. Says okay. I close the door and ask what she was looking for. Frozen bugs. What if you see any? We shut you down until we identify the bugs. Did you see any? No. So, we can go? Yep.

I climb back into the first chair, release the brakes, and idle away from the bug house, as the drivers know it. Looking in the mirror, I see the truck behind us diverted into the serious inspection area. Must have had bugs.

Back onto the bigroad and on to Los Angeles to make the first drop of asparagus and so Trainer can get a cab into the city and get his birth certificate. Bless his ignorant heart. He thinks he is going to zip into the Los Angeles county building, they're going to hand it to him, and he'll zip right out. Be back at the truck in no time. Does not understand bureaucracy. Or has a lot of faith.

The southern California desert has nothing to hold my attention except the call boxes. There is only desert and call boxes regularly spaced. They must be spaced using reasonable walking distance, looks like about a mile. They are pretty regular, but still, a bad place to be walk-ing. Very thoughtful of someone, these call boxes. I'll bet those ugly lit-tle gray boxes on those galvanized poles that funky up this desert have looked really good to some unfortunate son in the days before cellular technology. They may look pretty good now to someone without cellu-lar technology.

The early-morning cool and shadows lend the desert a deceptive beauty, but as the day progresses and the sun gets more overhead, that beauty goes away. Midday in a desert isn't the place to be. Glaring, re-lentless, brilliant heat. All those cute little sunbeams gang up and bru-talize this country. Even the distant mountains appear to have wilted. Those poor souls in covered wagons back when. I'm blowing along a paved interstate, sipping an ice-cold soda with the a/c roaring. What a difference a couple of hundred years makes here as well.

I'm riding along thinking about the pioneers, and Trainer says he wants to drive. There is a handy rest area, no facilities, and we make the trade. The asphalt surface is like a griddle. Too hot nearly to breathe, but I like the opportunity to get out and walk just a little, even if it is only around the tractor, so I take the long way around and inspect the tires on the trailer. Things can happen back here I might not see from the front. Better to find a potential problem sitting still than at 65 MPH. All is well. The tires are hot, but just from the road surface. Nothing scary on the truck, but my right ankle has swollen a little. I must have stressed it somehow.

Back into the truck in the second seat. The a/c feels good. Trainer rolls out onto the bigroad and we are off to Los Angeles and a birth cer-tificate. Again.

Rolling along sightseeing, and Trainer says there is a weigh station coming up and I need to get into the back. Why? 'Cause you ain't sup-posed to be up here in that chair. Okay. I hop into the sleeper and close the light curtain. Sort of hiding from the authorities. There are only four categories of time on a log and "riding in the second chair" isn't one of them, so we log that as sleeper time and as such, I need to be in the sleeper. The California DOT guys might want to see our logs. And there I'd be, not in the sleeper.

It's cool and dark in the sleeper, so I close my eyes just for a second, while we inch along in a line of trucks to get to the scale. I know we are on the scale when the truck rocks just a little as we stop. On the scale and I hear an electronically enhanced voice tell Trainer to move into the inspection area. Not good. If things were good, the traffic light over the scale would have turned from red to green and we would have pulled off the scale and onto the access lane for the bigroad. Any voice from the coop is not good.

Operating under the "clean trucks don't get inspected" theory, we had the truck washed last night to the tune of $45 while I watched a huge thunderstorm billow across southern Arizona. Being under that thunderstorm probably wasn't pretty, but from a distance, as the setting sun painted a smashing watercolor on the irregularities of its western side, it was pretty. I sat by a saguaro that had several bullet holes, or what looked like bullet holes, in it and watched the colors on the clouds go from yellow to red to gold and finally to violet and gray in the gathering darkness while we waited our turn. Took about an hour for all that to happen, but it seemed like no time. I came back to see about the truck just as the washer dudes dried it off while Trainer pulled it out of the wash bay, and I sat down on a bench outside by a huge guy having his done as well. His truck was a gorgeous chrome and red conventional Peterbilt. Said he lived in it. Wife died, sold the house, bought the truck, and lives on the road. Seems happy enough. Lot of dead wives out here. If I had one, I think I wouldn't bring her out West. If I wanted to keep her.

Meanwhile, back at the coop, the ol' clean truck trick didn't work for us apparently. We idle on over to the inspection area, and I hear the DOT guy, outside the cab, ask Trainer if he is a team driver. Yep. The DOT guy tells Trainer to hand the logs down to him. Trainer says okay, but the co-driver is asleep. DOT guy says he doesn't want the co-driver, he wants the co-driver's log. Trainer says he doesn't know where the co-driver's logbook is. DOT guy is not fooling around. He says find it . . .

Now. Trainer gets up and rifles my briefcase and produces the log. I'm playing possum. Trainer hands over the logs. The DOT group inside will check the logs for compliance with regulations and see which method of cheating we use. If we cheat within acceptable parameters, no problem. They know we do it and we know we do it. The game is you can't prove nothin' if I cheated right. Neatness counts. They may think sloppy penmanship, or smudged entries were purposefully done, and we don't want to give these guys any reason to really scrutinize the logs. They are already scrutinizing the truck, and the one guy already thinks Trainer sassed him. This is probably not good. Several things have happened here that are not good. Even that is not good.

The state of California is particularly particular about the comings and goings of bigtrucks. No driver I've talked to even wants to go there because of the potential hassles, some real and some imagined. Huge fines, hours held up, shut down for 24 hours at a weigh station for log infractions or mechanical things, and no facilities. However, as I see it, California just wants the trucks legal and safe. Nothing more. If we are safe and legal, no real problems. Many trucking companies, and many drivers, push the limit in both these categories. Some go past the limit in different degrees. Trying to save money, or make more. California knows that. Hence the particular, and hence the hassles.

In the inspection that follows, and while I am hiding in the sleeper, or sleeping in the hider, a dry-rotted air hose is found on the trailer tandems and we are put out of service until repairs are made. Trainer calls HQ and they send a local guy out to make the repairs. Four hundred dollars and five hours later, Trainer climbs back into the cab and cranks up the Cummins. We set out for Los Angeles again, this time with one of the most expensive tandem air hoses in captivity.

Trainer is hot. We are now five hours behind. He was planning on using some of the surplus time we had gained in our schedule to get into Los Angeles. We roll out of the inspection station onto the access ramp and onto the bigroad. I open the curtains and flop into the second chair. Naps are good, even very short ones.

Trainer bitches about the extent of the dry rot and the expense of the repairs. I listen. He says the local guy is in cahoots with the DOT guys. Probably his brother-in-law. I say it isn't likely. A brake problem, no matter how minor, is a major problem in a state with mountains. He gets huffy. Though he has been driving for more than 20 years, Trainer has been with this company about a year. They just made him an over-the-road trainer. I am his first student, I think. I may be his last. We both know I'm right. I'm really not into pressing an advantage, at least in this case, so I don't. We rumble toward Los Angeles and Trainer's birth certificate in silence, except the ambient noise, the new brake hoses doing a fine job.

The Los Angeles basin smog takes me completely aback. I had no idea the haze was that bad. While the air quality in this area gets into any conversation about smog, I am still astounded at what I see, or don't see in this case, as we drop down from the high desert. I can't see more than a mile in any direction. I can barely make out the mountains. I tell Trainer I don't want to go into that muck and I don't care about his birth certificate. He laughs and says wait till we get closer to the city. I tell him I don't think that's funny. He agrees and says it really isn't. That it wasn't this bad when he was a kid here. I can't believe people live here. I can't imagine any responsible adult living here, much less allowing a child to grow up breathing this toxic gas. But, they do. Millions of them.

The quailcall beeps. Eighty thousand pounds of machine and produce moving at 55 MPH. Trainer looks down at the keyboard display and scrolls through the messages. His eyes are on the keyboard for eight, maybe ten seconds. We are on an ten-lane interstate going into southern California traffic. I call his attention to those things. He glances up to the road and then his eyes return to the LED display as if to show me. I remain silent but ready to brace for a collision if Lady Luck gets distracted.

After a moment of alternately looking at the keyboard screen and the road, Trainer informs me I don't have to go into the muck. Our destination has been changed. The customer in Los Angeles has turned down their part of the load and the customer in Marina wants that share as well. Another message from his wife said he did not need to go into Los Angeles for his birth certificate, that they would send it in the mail. He looks at me and says he didn't know they could do that. I look at him expressionless for a moment, then tell him he's gonna love life in the twenty-first century.

A route change loops us around the LA metroplex to the north and east to get to I-5 north into the central valley of California. Even on the loop, the smog is so thick I cannot see any detail of the San Gabriel Mountains, even along their base. I am still astonished it has come to this. I ride along almost shocked. I lived in this area 30 years ago and we accepted the mountains as the beautiful scenery they once were. Many mornings I would look at them as I walked to work in North Hollywood. Now, today at least, they may as well not be there scenerywise. Health-wise, nothing should be here.

I am relieved to be on I-5 north of the city and feel as if I have just escaped something. We climb higher to the edge of the valley and begin a steep descent on a section of the interstate known to drivers as "Grapevine." Named for the little town at the bottom of the hill, this stretch of freeway is what is known as a major hill. It has a grade of be-tween five and six percent for some miles. That means the road drops five or six feet for every hundred feet traveled forward. Purty dang steep in a loaded bigtruck. Brakes get hot. Transmissions blow seals, loads shift. Engines go past the RPM limit and fly apart internally. Ugly stuff. But there is a right way to do this, and nothing bad happens. They told us how to do it in driving school.

Many descents from on high have gained infamy in the trade for being steep, or curvy or lengthy. Difficult to negotiate for one reason or another. This one is famous for all those things. Trainer has spoken at some length in the days past at quiet conversation with other drivers, on the many storied descents around the country. How drivers and rigs came to grief. Of trucks crashed, loads and lives lost from the ages till now. Grapevine, Cabbage, and Soldier. Names spoken with wonder by green drivers, and a pinch of authority by veterans having bested a foe. The mere mention of a major descent brings on "me too" tales from any driver within earshot.

Trainer will now show me how to descend the Grapevine. I say I want to drive down the hill, that I'm the trainee. It is some miles to the beginning of the drop and we have plenty of time to pull over and change chairs. He says he wants me to watch this time, that I don't have enough road miles. Says sit back, relax and watch.

Trainer repeats the classroom gear theory, skill level limits, weight factors, weather and road conditions, ostensibly for my benefit, but really reinforcing his own confidence. He selects ninth gear. Way too tall a gear for this ride down, and I say so. He says to always maintain ten pounds of pressure on the brakes, that way you always have control. I say that won't work in ninth gear and a six-percent grade and 80,000 pounds. They told us in school the brakes will overheat. He says that's company policy. It's company policy to fry the brakes? Silence as we approach the edge. He downshifts to ninth gear. We start down my first major hill with close to 20 tons of asparagus pushing us. I look down the road. This is one steep descent. It would be fun in a car, but this is no car. I am really apprehensive. Trainer is as well. I sense it. Lotta bad chemistry here. You said you'd been driving 20 years, right? Yep, off and on. What do you mean off and on? Well, not all the time. Did you do a lot of mountain driving? Nope, mostly Texas and New Mexico. Sometimes into Oklahoma.

I suddenly don't feel well.

Technique born of misunderstood information, low skill level, between the two of us I don't think we have the skill of one good driver, a heavy load, and we start down Grapevine, a dangerous descent. Why didn't I take that Operations job in Birmingham?

The truck gains momentum. Trainer applies the brakes, the transmission whines, and the engine howls. Cars fly by us. We are doing about 45 MPH. We are going too fast. Trainer is determined to hold 10 pounds air on the brakes. I look over at him and see his face. He is unfocused. Not sure. This isn't good. He is uncomfortable. Doesn't know what to do if plan A fails. Checking gauges. I shout we should downshift to seventh gear. But, I realize we can't. We are going too fast to get the transmission into seventh gear. No response from Trainer. One-third of the way down. Gentle curves but steep road. We pass a CHiP just pulling into a runaway ramp with a truck in it. Must have just happened. Trainer notices and says nothing. I look in the mirror on my side and see wisps of smoke coming from the trailer tandems. I look closer to make certain it is smoke and not dust from the road. It is smoke. Trainer notices I am looking and checks his own mirror. He winces and says to watch the smoke that it doesn't get worse. I look back at him. Like there is something I can do except wring my hands and wish I were in church if the smoke gets worse. I hope there are more runaway ramps down there. I hope they are not all taken.

Runaway ramps are very short exits with steep inclines up a hillside and made of deep gravel or soft sand to provide the drag and rise necessary to stop heavy loads that can't stop themselves. Like we are about to be. Smoke is worse now. I alert Trainer who looks in his mirror and wordlessly confirms that. Beads of sweat on his brow beneath the leather NFL cap pulled on scalp-tight. Wears it constantly. He grips the wheel now. Unsure what to do. Two-thirds of the way down now and the brakes are smoking heavily. Other trucks whiz by us. No load aboard probably. Called deadheading, and they can get away with that since those brakes are not holding back a load that wants to get to the bottom. Other loaded trucks are single file behind us, back some distance. Fearful, I imagine. We are moving faster still. Looks like about 55 MPH from where I sit, parallax considered. Way too fast for this grade and our weight. Trainer looks highly stressed now, so I spare him all that. He has a Tasmanian devil tattoo, a stuffed Tasmanian devil on the dash of the truck, and Tasmanian devil floor mats. As I look at him, I am more reminded of Baby Huey. Strange what comes to us in life-or-death situations. The engine is near the RPM limit and self-destruction, and is screaming in protest. All the brakes are smoking now, even the tractor brakes. I have heard of drivers coming to the inescapable conclusion the truck was out of control and take the chance of jumping out the door rather than being run over by their load in the inevitable stop at the bottom. I wonder if I should begin those preparations. All this is whirling in my head when I look down past the last curve to see the bottom of the hill and a straight run for the couple of miles it will take to get there.

Bad-case scenario: we lose all braking, engine blows, and we coast up to 150 MPH and onto a flat, straight interstate and roll to a smoky stop several miles down the road. Worst-case scenario: all those things and we take out a few cars full of innocent souls that don't see us coming at 150 MPH from behind. Eighty-thousand-pound bowling ball. Possible scenario: Fortune smiles on us and we get down, shaken, but no damage done.

I make the call not to jump. Gonna ride it out. Only a few cars out front and they are far enough ahead of us not to be in danger. We zoom for the bottom trailing a billowing cloud of smoke. The brakes are literally fogging now and may be aflame in that fog for all we know. I look over at Trainer and see a disillusioned man. He knows we will be okay now, and I imagine he imagined that same set of scenarios. Other trucks have let off the brakes, shifted into higher gears, and are taking advantage of a slingshot effect these hills offer when it is safe to do so. They look into our cab as they go past. Trainer avoids their eyes. He has disgraced himself in front of his peers, and his trainee. He knows I was right about the gears. He has done possibly thousands of dollars worth of damage to the truck, and must call HQ for authorization to repair that damage and further dishonor himself. He has endangered a customer's load and exposed his company to untold liability. Risked our lives and the lives of everyone in front of us. And he is still lightly on the brakes. I turned the CB way down at the top of the hill, knowing it would prove a distraction in one way or another, and now turn it back up. A blackness in my soul wanting Trainer to face the music. It is silent. They have all followed us down in mute witness. Not even the most muckraking among them wanting to make Trainer feel worse, and all knowing the potential consequences of such a dangerous ride down the hill. The electronic silence really is deafening.

Serendipity, or good business sense, put a truck stop at the bottom of Grapevine, so unnerved drivers could stop and let their emotions pass while their brakes cool, or fall off in flames, then get the repairs made. We get slowed to the point it is safe to exit the interstate, and heave to a smoking stop at the end of the exit ramp. I can't imagine how the brakes still work. A cloud of acrid, gray smoke envelopes the entire truck as we sit at the stop sign waiting to turn right. Few things smell like burning brakes. Smoke is rolling off the tandems and drives. Like a petrochemical fire, thick and billowy, except gray colored. It is difficult to see through it to turn right onto the access road to the truck stop.

As we idle into the lot by the repair shop, the smoke is still dense, riding the thermals from beneath the trailer and off the drives. Trainer is embarrassed having to drive in under the critical gaze of other drivers in the lot pointing, talking. They know what just happened, they know where we have been, and what could have happened behind it. He is among his own now, holding a smoking gun, so to speak. For someone wanting to be accepted into the club, this is a painful moment. He says nothing, and we idle on to the rear of the lot, far from the looks, shaking heads, pointing fingers and other trucks. In case of fire, we don't want anything else to burn, especially another truck. We may also need room to pull the tractor away from the trailer if the tandem brakes set it aflame, or if the tractor brakes begin to blaze, we don't want the trailer to burn as well. Hopefully we will have neither for a problem.

A grassy knoll and small tree invite me from the cab and to stretch awhile once we have parked the truck. I had it in mind to survey the damage, but the heat and smoke put me off, so I take the knoll and tree up on their kind offer. A vantage point to watch Trainer survey the damage. He circles the truck and trailer three or four times completely. As though he can't believe what has happened. I shout at him to leave everything alone and to let the brakes cool. That we will decide what to do at that point. He walks over, head down, and agrees. We'll lock the truck, get a meal, and decide what to do next. I don't think there is a danger of fire now. He agrees. That means we don't have to hang around to separate the tractor and trailer in the event of a brake fire on either.

We leave the still-smoking truck to itself, and walk some distance to the main part of the truck stop. The part with the convenience store, souvenir shops, fast-food outlets, and whatever else is in there. It is late afternoon, near sundown, and I am hungry. Trainer is always hungry. From the truck parking lot at the rear of the place, we walk past the Dumpster and its attending host of flies, beneath the blinking red neon PROFESSIONAL DRIVERS sign, and go in. We separate to get different meals.

Inside, it is a sort of minimall, with a food court and four or five different fast-food counters and shops all around. Bathrooms on the west wall. I decide on a burger and a soda, and take it to the tables in the middle of the court. Trainer shows up shortly with an armload of burritos. He dumps them all over the table and they roll around. One stops right on the edge of the table. We both look at it, wondering if it will go on over the edge.

I'm not a fan of fast food, but except for the different cooks' skills, it is pretty much the same countrywide. Made to the same top-secret recipes everywhere. At least it's predictable. The same cannot be said for restaurant food. The quality and quantity vary wildly. Some mom'n'pops are a bargain beyond belief. Heaped plates and good. Others, it is a crime to treat food like that, and no wonder the kids left home. So, I have come to be a fast-food dude out here, but it is a distant second choice to the Spanish Asian French Indian Caribbean African blends in the epicurean paradise of the Gulf Coast. Gotta eat, so I just resign myself to be home in a few weeks. Good things come to those that wait.

We eat in silence, though the bustle of commercialism is all around us. Travelers in, travelers out. Dollars in, merchandise out. Young, old, in between with families. Trainer stares into space, grinding a burrito into mush. He has absorbed three or four already. Mentally, he is still coming down the mountain. I look at his hands. They still have the grease stains on them from checking the oil in New Mexico. He lights a cigarette, still chewing the last of the last burrito. I think it is the one that rolled to the edge of the table. Stares and chews some more.

He breaks the silence by announcing he will now call HQ. Sounds resolute. Gonna take his medicine. I tell him we should evaluate further before he does that, such that he can pass on accurate information regarding the current situation. The truck has been stopped nearly an hour and must have cooled to the point we can do a visual inspection of the linings. I see the wheels turning as he exhales another plume of blue-gray carcinogens. Giving himself enough time to appear decisive, he agrees. He is also thinking it will postpone that phone call, and the attending ass-chewing.

Back through the Dumpster flies and out to the truck. No smoke now, only stink, and after a quick look beneath the trailer, no look at all for the tractor brakes, Trainer goes back to call, more confident now that the smoke is gone. I sit on the grassy knoll to watch the peach and rose sky fade in the west. Maybe it's noon in Calcutta or Kashmir or Madagascar. Some far-flung place with an exotic name. Noon, somewhere over the mountains to my west and the ocean beyond them. Some far-off land, or distant shore. The parking lot lights pop on, ruin the sunset and jerk me back to reality. I get up and stretch a little, my back stiff from sitting against the tree for so long.

Trainer comes back and says HQ says to wait another hour and roll. No inspection at the repair shop? Nope. I think he minimized the extent of the problem and we are about to go onward with fried brakes. I say nothing. Trainer says he just can't believe it happened. I look at him intently, to see any sign of aversion, or body language different from his story.

I am put off by the corporate gloss-over, or Trainer's misrepresentation of the situation, or both, and am irritated further by Trainer who says he just doesn't believe it happened. That he did everything right by the book. And tired of hearing that phrase, I ask what book, the stunt driver's manual? You ride the brakes in ninth gear downhill for 10 miles and expect them to still be there at the bottom? Shakes his head. Just can't believe it. I should have gone with him to eavesdrop on that call. Probably talked about hedge trimmers or the weather or something. Anything but crispy brakes.

I walk over to the trailer and around the other side, as much to avoid the temptation of further berating Trainer as the heat from the brakes. Get the trailer between us. Trainer senses this and mopes off to the driver's lounge to call the receiver, the facility to which we will deliver the load. He'll tell them the load will be late.

Most distribution facilities both ship and receive merchandise. Most receiving is done on an appointment basis, or there would be alternate traffic jams and desolation in the receiving lot. It is difficult to staff for highs and lows. Orderly programs staffed properly are the answer. A regulated flow into and from the place. Everyone gets unloaded, or loaded, and no traffic jam. When a driver can't make the appointment, and the driver doesn't tell the receiver, or shipper, it is a problem. Good manners alone dictate a notice, and professionalism demands it. Don't leave the customer guessing the whereabouts of his merchandise. So he calls. We are rescheduled for 3 A.M. tomorrow. I wonder if he told them why we'll be late when they asked, and they do ask: it's their stuff and they want to know what is happening to it. I resign myself to being up all night, or most of it, and imagining the conversation.

I am not comfortable with the decision to roll across the valley and into the mountains without a competent person inspecting the brakes. There is one at this truck stop, and the brakes have been stressed to the point of smoking, for crying out loud. Getting back out among the motoring public with them uninspected is criminal. I say so. Silence. I don't believe it. I voice my concern for about the tenth time. More silence. Gotta get the load delivered. I can hear his brain logicking this misdeed out. No time to inspect 'em. We'll be late enough as it is. But I say nothing.

Trainer knows I am not wanting to play along, and he's not cool with it, his being the trainer, and by some definition of that, being infallible. Aside from that, he knows I'm correctly inside the safety net. His trainer persona is miffed by my insolence and his sense of safety is miffed by my position on this, but he is in too deep to withdraw with any shred of dignity. I sense he has no limit in his effort to prove a point, and back off to prevent any further hardening. I don't want this to be fatal for anyone if Trainer gets an attitude, especially a carload of kids. I reluctantly get into the second seat and look out the window. Trainer climbs in and cranks up. He senses I sense something, and wants to clear it up but doesn't know what to say. I don't either. We set out in silence.

We leave the safety of the truck stop with roasted brakes and head onto the access road to Interstate 5 in the valley, going north, as the dark of night comes onto us.

At least we roll on flat real estate and will for many hours, which will not stress the brakes, and eventually they will cool in the night airstream. We rumble toward the north end of the valley, and the shadowy mountains I know are out there. Going on, I look onto one of the premier agricultural areas on the planet passing my window and glistening in the moonlight. Row upon row of food growing. How can anyone in this country be hungry? How can anyone in the world be hungry? What the hell happens to the food between here and the bellies of the hungry?

The ride along I-5 is a trip through a history of hard work and the trappings of it. Little towns, big towns, agricultural towns all. The smell of what grows in the fields hangs in the still night air as we make our way through the different areas. Onions, garlic, berries, fruit and leaf crops. Like an olfactory salad.

The road lays long before us. Headlights 200 feet into the darkness, backlit by the moonglow. The everpresent background throb of the engine. Baritone hiss of the tires on the pavement, and the rhythmic roll of the air-suspended cab. The hour of my circadian clock and poststress adrenaline vacuum combine to make me doze off in the second seat. Trainer barks, and I snap out of my lapse. He says if I'm sleepy, get into the sleeper, not to sleep in a chair.

Instantly irritated by this abrasive approach, I decide to remain momentarily silent in the face of what I feel is retribution. I gather my consciousness and my thoughts before I defend myself. I think he's proud of himself for having found some imaginary offense to use in his regrouped authority. He senses that and follows up with some quasilogic that says if you sleep in the second chair, you'll sleep in the first chair. I say I doubt that since the responsibility level is different in each chair, and only a murderer would sleep in the first chair. But, it comes to me, as hastily as that premise was generated and by whom, there may be something to it. Insomniacs are cautioned to do nothing but sleep in the bed. Still, I refuse to give him the pleasure. Petty. I'm as petty as he is, and possibly as theoretically dangerous. What's the difference in rolling with toasted brakes and a petty, dozing driver? Both those things have disaster labels all over them.

I am awake now and ruffled. Trainer is vindicated as he sees it, and is satisfied. We move on in noisy silence. The night is beautiful and I am determined to enjoy it, since I'm awake now. But I am still irritated at having been "corrected." I ride in silence, and try to make that silence palpable. So Trainer will know I'm irritated. He knows, I think, but doesn't care. I am trying to decide if that pisses me off.

At the end of the valley is the road up to a lake, or reservoir. The San Luis, I think. The climb up is not bad and the engine seems to run better somehow at night. I don't know that it does, it just seems as though that's the case. Or maybe it is that I am awed by the midnight moonbeams on the lake and the surrounding mountains, maybe it is that the bearable lightness of being here makes everything seem better. Something causes that. It is beautiful. The moonsparkles ricocheting off the wavelets glow softly like pearls, as compared to the brilliant diamondlike sparkles the sun creates on wave tops in the daylight. A kinder, gentler sparkle at night, almost hazy and dreamlike.

I need to be outside, and break out the gotta pee program to force a stop. I want to get the feeling of this place and I need to be outside to do that. The lake, the mountains, the cool, the night. It is like a drug. It is an intoxication I would like to share, but there is no one. Trainer sees none of this as he hoses down the pavement, having just stepped down and turned his bladder loose. A great steaming wet spot on the road, he turns without looking up or around, and gets back into the idling tractor. All this is wasted on him. I walk behind the rig to escape the engine noise as much as possible, and try to absorb some of this before I have to go. Try to get a grip on where I am and what is around me. To be out in it. To feel it if I can. To stand in the California mountains by a lake in the moonlight. To take it with me if I can. I have some memory problems, and it is sometimes difficult for me to recall some things. I don't want this to be one of those things. I want to hang on to this. Put it into my album.

I tarry long enough to cause the air horn to bellow, come back to myself, reluctantly turn and walk along the trailer, look at the sky once, wonder what is out there, then climb into the second chair and am immediately showered in lights.

There are lots of lights in a tractor cab. One particular switch will turn them all on at once and the tractor can be flooded with light. All of them are on. Trainer is a creature of comfort. I am put off by the lights. With the glare of them, I can't even see out the windows. Trainer is shucking a package of peanut-butter crackers, or cheese crackers or some kind of crackers. I watch partly blinded by the glare. Says they don't put many crackers in these little packages. I stare at him, still irked about the lights. I see some weeks of pain coming.

Trainer scarfs the crackers, I watch him in some kind of detached state, and he is not made uncomfortable by it. Glances away and munches on. Blissfully unaware of his existence. He backhands the crumbs from his face and wads the wrapper, tosses it at the trash bucket. Misses. Doesn't notice and doesn't care. He switches off the interior lights, grinds the Eaton transmission into second gear, and we lurch onto the road to Hollister. It is past midnight.

Lots of history here. Some reporter staged a couple of photographs back when, yellow-pressed a story, and, with a little help from Marlon Brando, voílà, the motorcycle culture of the sixties was born. Seems pretty innocent as we roll by, sleeping in the moonlight. John Steinbeck chronicled another culture in several top-shelf docunovels set among these fields and peoples back in the migrant workers' darker days. Tales of ordinary people in extraordinary situations. About that same time, Woody Guthrie warbled his way into the hearts of those peoples and the radios of America singing songs of suffering hereabouts and down in the valley. Of folks come from bad to worse in these fields of broken dreams. He struck the same chord in his music Steinbeck did with his books, and the people loved them for it. Those migrant stories were told in song and print. That pain was made public, and its children grew up to be California. There would be no more mass migrations to a state until the steel factories shut down in the seventies, and those people went to Texas. Bruce Springsteen sang about that one. I wonder what is next, for whom, where they will go, and what artist will chronicle that upheaval in what medium.

Farther into the night, we descend through the foggy forest that lines the coast into Marina, and I can smell the ocean. Damp and salty and fresh in the wee hours of a new day. Still no sleep for either of us. The few cars we pass have no idea they came within two feet of 40 tons and fatigued drivers. A brush with disaster they never knew about.

Looking intently through the fog, we are near our destination and we slow a little. We accidentally blunder into a glowing haze that just happens to be our stop. We pull up to the guardshack centered in a pyramid of light from the overhead sodium vapor lamp. A slight, geriatric woman with bleached blonde hair is busy inside on her two-way radio. The furrowed face looks up as we come to a stop. She looks back down to her work, as though we were not there. Some minutes pass, and Trainer decides to assert himself. He climbs down and walks over to the guardshack to see why she is ignoring us. I can see him standing silent as she speaks without looking up. Trainer comes back. He says she told him we missed our first appointment and now we have to wait till our new appointment time at 3 A.M. Says she told him to park at the edge of the big lot in front of the building. I say that's fine, we need to sleep anyway.

We back in where she said to park. Plenty of space, only a few trucks here, but the dock doors are full of trucks being loaded and unloaded. We climb into our bunks, maybe get a little rest before we are unloaded.

I no more than stretch out, and a banging on the driver's door. Trainer needs to get that. It's his door. More banging. Trainer is snoring. I climb down, kneel on the first chair, and toggle the window down. I look onto the top of a bleached-blonde head. It is either a bad haircut, or not combed for the cut, or both. Nah, no haircut could be that bad. It must be a wig. One of those cheap ones. Probably has a chinstrap. She looks up and says we parked in the wrong place. Not this space, the one just over. I look through her thick glasses into faded blue eyes. The faded blue eyes look back. I say I don't see what difference it makes, there are plenty of spaces all around us. Says we can't stay in this space, that we have to move over one space. She turns away to walk into the cold fog toward the guardshack in the cone of light by the gate.

One of the things that we are taught in orientation is to not upset the customer or the representatives of that customer. Do what they ask within reason. I am thinking this is not reasonable, but to save the hassle, I'll do it anyway. Trainee and all that. Learn the limits before I start being myself.

I climb behind the wheel, crank up the engine, pull out and back into the adjacent space. Shut down and climb back into my bunk. Trainer is snoring and farting. No more burritos for him. I close my eyes and breathe through the sheet.

Banging on the driver door. I hear it as in a dream. Far away and not relevant. More banging. I hear it more clearly and struggle for consciousness. More banging and choking sounds. I am jolted awake by the combination of sounds, thinking something bad is happening. Groggy, I climbstumble out of the bunk, note Trainer in sleep apnea, and more banging on the door. More fumblingstumbling for the window switch, roll the window down, look blurrily down onto the bleached head. She can really hit that door hard for an old woman. Expressionless, she looks up and says put the truck into door three right over there, to be unloaded, and disappears into the fog become light rain. In my boxers, and barefoot, I pull out of the space and idle in front of the assigned door. Spin the trailer on the tandems, pull forward to straighten, back arrow straight between two other trailers with no more than a foot to spare on either side slowly, until I feel the light bump of the rubber pads on the dock door contact the trailer. Done, and it is beautiful. First dock door I ever backed into, and it is perfect. I've not seen anyone do it that well wide awake and in broad daylight, much less half asleep and the middle of the night. I pat myself on the back for a job well done.

Get up from the chair to get back into the bunk. I can sleep while the trailer is being unloaded. Here comes a guy alongside the tractor. He has on the clothes one would see in a cold storage place. I roll down the window. He looks up at me in an almost sympathetic fashion, as though I am too stupid to understand what he is about to say. He says I need to pull the trailer back out and open the doors, and reposition it so he can get in and unload it.

Box trailers have a couple of door designs. One type is called a roll door, because sections of it roll up on a track like some garage doors. The other is called a swingdoor, because it swings to open like the front doors on a house. Roll doors do not need to be opened before docking. The door can be rolled up or down while the trailer is docked. Swingdoors have to be opened before docking. Otherwise, the dock jams the door closed. We have swingdoors on this trailer. I didn't open them. Now, I get to pull forward so I can open the doors. Gotta get dressed, get out, swing the doors, get back in, and redock the trailer. It is cold out, begging to rain harder, and I have to pee. And I'm sleepy. Now, on top of all that other stuff, I'm getting stressed. And embarrassed.

Wide awake now, I have just made a fool of myself in front of people I will hopefully never see again, I have to pee, and it's raining at three o'clock in the morning. I'm irritated like overly tired people get. Maybe I can wait to pee till in the morning. Nope. I don't know where the restroom is, and even if I did, it must be some distance. I can pee between the trailers; it is considered bad form, even among drivers that have to pee, but most have done it. What if I get caught? Making a decision in a pressure situation, I take the moral high road and opt for the facilities. Grim determination and a quick step see me through the gauntlet of weather, time of night, state of mind, and distance. Follow signs to driver's lounge. Restroom's in there. Made it. Push door open and slammed with bright lights and noise. The place is packed with employees not supposed to be there. This place should be deserted except for drivers waiting to load or unload. And quiet. Most drivers would be snoozing, or have the TV down low. This is a party. This is a disco. This is fooling around. These people are hiding from their jobs. Barely noticed, I slip into the restroom and take care of my business.

The place is trashed. Snack machine rifled. Coffee cups, soda bottles, cigarette butts, plastic wrappers litter the floor. The tables needed cleaning days ago. Crusty brown sticky spots on the cheap linoleum tile floor, which is commercial grade yucky-gray speckled tile that is supposed to downplay crusty brown sticky spots. Drivers will get the blame for the mess. They are the only ones supposed to be here. I will hear later that company closed the lounge because the drivers wouldn't take care of it.

Back to the truck. Through the mental and physical rain and fog.

The tractor cab is being jostled back and forth as I climb in. The weight and motion of the forklifts on and off the trailer, moving pallets of asparagus creates an intermittent and violent rocking motion. I can't sleep with that going on, and decide the process shouldn't be long since there are only twenty-two pallets aboard and the rocking is frequent. I sit in the first seat. Waiting. Looking. Foggy rain tapping on the roof. Trainer gagging and wheezing in deep sleep behind me. I doze a little. But I notice any sleep as I am sitting upright causes a round of nausea as soon as I awaken. Most peculiar. It will be a continuing problem, and one I never knew I had till now. Never had to sleep sitting upright before.

The unloading done, I look in the mirror to see a green light has replaced the red one on the wall by the dock door. Red signals the driver not to move the truck, that the DOT bumper has been grabbed by a sturdy hook to secure that trailer to the dock. It prevents a trailer being pulled away during the loading/unloading process. What with forklifts zooming in and out, the results can be imagined. Many facilities require multiple safeguards to prevent premature undocking, or the driver taking off from the dock before the truck is unloaded, possibly with someone aboard the trailer. The driver must be out of the tractor, brakes locked, engine off, tractor disengaged from trailer, wheels chocked, or any combination thereof. Depends on what was learned the hard way at that particular facility.

I see the green light and I know someone in authority inside the building has decided this trailer is ready to pull away from the dock, or some careless employee has leaned on the button. I crank the engine, release the brakes, wait ten seconds for the air pressure to build in the trailer lines so the trailer brakes will release, and shift into second gear. The lurch forward causes the cab to roll and startles Trainer into a phase of consciousness. He sits up on the edge of the bunk behind me and stares out the windshield into the rainy darkness. I coax the truck from the dock and between the other trailers into the lot far enough that I have room to swing the doors closed. I get out and do that.

I get back into the tractor and idle over to the spot we had been assigned earlier to shut down and get some sleep. I have had none now for a full 24 hours.

I turn off the engine and climb into my bunk, clothes and all. Trainer has passed out again in his bunk, gurgling and bubbling and farting. I close my eyes at the same time a banging starts at the driver's door. I know the routine and am instantly highly agitated.

Oddly, Trainer is out of the bunk and at the window in a blur. I hear the crackly old voice outside and Trainer says okay. He gets from behind the wheel to stand in the condo and get better dressed. I stare, irritated, at the ceiling. Trainer fights his way into his clothes, huffing and panting and wheezing and blowing. He flops into the first chair, grabs overhead for his cigarettes, and his lighter clicks open. A huge inhale, lighter clicks closed, productive cough, and the window squeals down. He exhales into the cab and spits whatever was in his lungs out the window. It may have been his lungs. The man is an affront to etiquette. Now I'm angry, sleep deprived, unshowered, *and* disgusted.

Trainer cranks the engine, clashes the transmission into second gear, the torque rocks the cab, and we begin to roll toward the pyramid of light in the foggy rain. I take a deep breath to gain control, knowing all possibility of sleep is gone now, get into my shorts and golf shirt, limp from two days' wear, and plop into the second chair. Trainer aims for the guardshack and hopefully the old woman in it. Without looking up, the corpse waves us through. It must be near dawn.

Trainer says she told him we had to leave the lot since we are done and that a truck stop is just around the corner. He says we will go there for a shower and a nap. We follow the directions in Trainer's photographic memory and wind up in a residential area just as dawn breaks. A lone tree in a field across the way in the soggy first light is my only connection to reality. I somehow identify with that tree. Alone and in a fog.

I can't decide whom to blame. Trainer, the addled old guard, or me for just being here. I should be home wading into the flats with my coffee about now, getting ready for that first sight cast. I get a look at the tree as it goes by my window. Calms me in some indescribable way. I ride in fuming silence and begin to imagine a video of the last four hours and chuckle to myself. Trainer's acute selective hearing picks it up and, feeling the tension may be easing, says welcome to truckdriving. I laugh out loud, and he bongs in with a bass guffaw. I guess I'm tired and sleepy and disconnected like tired and sleepy people get, and shouldn't take whatever emotion I am operating behind out on him.

The rolling hills of northern California take on a dreary beauty as my mood lightens in the misty early morning. I realize I must be so deep in sleep debt I'm losing control, but I promise Trainer the breakfast of his choice any place he wants to stop. He says he thinks we deserve it. I agree and watch Monterey go past my window. I haven't slept for more than 24 hours and feel as alive as I ever have. My senses are fine tuned. This country is beautiful. Huge trees line the edge of the road, as though the road lay at the bottom of a canyon cut from the trees just for it. Huge rocks in the way, such that the road is routed around them. Too big to move, I guess.

We stop at a restaurant in the garlic capital of the universe. The food is excellent, the waitress is funny, the coffee is from God's own tree, and our spirits are much improved for that stop. Mine were anyway. I will come to know in the days ahead, Trainer keys on me for many things; general attitude especially, and because of that, I will try harder to keep the tension to a minimum in our days together. It will not always work.

We have delivered that load of asparagus to the receiver and let HQ know earlier via the quailcall we are ready for another load to take wherever. We just received information via that same device we are to go to a small town just north of here and collect a load of nursery plants and take them to five different places on the East Coast. So, breakfasted and coffeed, we find our way up US 101 through northern California. It is a nice ride, even though we are deadheading. Now, not only have I had no sleep for close to 30 hours, but we have no brakes for two reasons: Trainer smoked them yesterday afternoon, and we are pulling an empty trailer. Good thing Trainer is driving. He got a few hours sleep at least. The weather has cleared and a beautiful day is unfolding for us as we rumble north on this world-famous highway. And I can see why this road is the stuff of travelers' tales. The ruggedness of the place and the vistas are possibly paralleled somewhere, but not surpassed, I'll warrant. Northern California is worth the trip, from wherever one might come.

Riding around northern California, following the directions we were given, we locate the shipper, in this case the nursery wholesaler, and pull in just as another truck belonging to our company rolls in. We wonder whether he is empty or loaded, and whether Trainer knows him or her or them. I take the company interest initiative and walk over to the shipping office to find out what they want us to do and whether or not they are ready to load us, while Trainer sets out to bring this new someone else into his circle of friends.

I get the scoop on our load, walk back, and Trainer is moving into the lives of the poor schnooks in the other company truck, so I decide to get our truck into position to load while Trainer makes himself comfortable with his new buddies, a husband-and-wife combo. Lots of those out here. It is a good way for a married couple to spend some real serious time together, and lots of them do it as a retirement program, or just because the wife wanted to join her driverhusband after the kids fly from the nest. I like it and wish I had that sometimes. Other times, I'm glad it is just me. And Trainer. Jeez.

I get the truck backed in and some resident aliens, the new migrants, are loading the trailer; now seems like the time to rescue the schnooks. The guy has not yet been to the shipping office for details on his load. Trainer has him cornered. I walk up and introduce myself, tell the guy they want him in the shipping office. He knows an exit when he sees one and excuses himself and his wife, and they are off. Trainer is abandoned. I head back to watch the loading process. It is amazing how many potted plants can be put on a trailer when the loaders know what they are doing.

Not much has changed around these parts for migrant workers in the last hundred years or so. Someone has to do the backbreaking part of this agriculture thing, and the cheapest labor to be found these days comes from down south. Way down south. Mexico and south of that. It is hard to enforce the laws for them and against them. Don't ask, don't tell. They won't be here next week anyway, most times. Migrants move with the work mostly, and the work moves with the seasons.

I speak a little TexMex, but their English is better than my Spanish, and I strike up a conversation with a few of them as they load the trailer, more to pass the time than to get involved in their lives. One says he's from Honduras. Left his wife and kids to come here, gonna work two years and make enough to return home and buy some land. Going to grow whatever pays the most back home on his own land. Probably be able to send his kids to college in the Estados Unidos. Another laughs bitterly and said he was going to do the same thing. That was back in 1996. He hasn't been home in two years. He worked the fields and stayed in a room with six other guys from Oaxaca and sent almost every penny home to his wife to pay the coyotes to get her across the river and up here. Kept just enough to eat and share the cost of living. It cost $4,700 U.S. to sneak her across the border and up to Monterey, and the trip took seven weeks. They were staying with some friends close to town, laying low till they could get legal status, but that costs money. He worked in the fields and they planned to get the kids up here with them and get their own place, save the money, educate the kids, and go home wealthy. Maybe buy the land they lived on in Mexico. Things were going well. Until he got home one night and she wasn't there. She was caught by a cop who stopped her for selling flowers on the street without a permit. She had no identification papers. Learned two days later Immigration sent her back to the Mexican border. She was stuck on the Mexican side. Halfway between her husband and her children back in Oaxaca. No *dinero*. Got one letter from her years ago. She was scared and tired and broke and didn't know what to do, which way to go. That she loved him more than life and she was going to try to get back to him. Hasn't heard from her since. He's been home to see the kids because he has a job and he's legal now. But his wife didn't and wasn't. Never made it back and never made it home. She is lost. Says he thinks she is dead. May have killed herself because she couldn't get home to the kids and couldn't get back to him. Married for years, since childhood, and he knows what she'd do. No way she would be a street whore, nor steal, not even to eat. She'd kill herself first. I listen in stunned silence. So does the first man. So do the other three or four guys loading the plants. Man, I hope that is a pack of lies. But I don't think it is.

The story man hasn't slowed his pace, or spoken more. Everyone else stopped at the part where she was caught by the cop. Holding their plants, looking at him. Watching him work and talk.

In a slower, more thoughtful motion, the workers return to loading the trailer. I wonder how this man had held that in for so long that his working partners didn't know. I wonder why he didn't go after her. I wonder how that happened at all. Selling flowers to brighten some recipient's day. Was she really hurting the U.S. economy that badly? Did we have to throw her out? Were we afraid she would pull a leveraged buyout of some major flower firm? Aren't most Americans the children of some kind of immigrants? What are we thinking? What are we doing? We get hysterical about a thing, anything, and common sense goes out the window. And a family is destroyed. A human life lost. Literally. Do we think Emma Lazarus wrote that poem and it was placed where it is because it sounded good? Do we mean what she says? If not, why is it still attached to the Statue? Are we talking out both sides of our mouth? All these things whirl in my brain. I'm going to go and read that poem for myself one day to make certain it says what I was told it says. Then I want someone in some position of authority to explain some things to me because I don't think I understand those things right now.

I wander away to shake that off, leave the loading to itself, and the now quiet crew doing that, to find Trainer and see what he is up to. Sure enough, he has determined that the other company truck is going our way and we need to "run together." The couple looks thrilled. Running together involves a lot of coordinated stopping and starting and yakking on the CB about lawn mowers and the sonsabitches that run the trucking industry while all the parties go the same general direction for an extended period. I think for our part, it will be a good thing. While no individual man is an island, Trainer and myself are gradually becoming one. New conversation partners and topics welcome. I don't care if all I do is listen.

Standing on this snowcapped-mountain-ringed plain, Trainer has decided we will meet, after we've both been loaded, at a truck stop in Sacramento famous up and down the interstates for its steak'n'shrimp dinner. Then we'll all shower and stay the night, rise at first light to avoid the traffic out of town, and head east. We all stand looking at one another, waiting for some sign of acceptance or rejection of all that after he is finished. Uncomfortable silence for some seconds. The light breeze feels good, and the sun is warm on me. I wait and watch to see what and how much of that gets accepted and by whom.

The wife seems to perk up now, having remained wordless all the while. As much to introduce herself as anything, she says she wants that shower soon. I agree. A link is forged in that instant. Some kind of mental connection is made between the two of us. The husband doesn't see that his wife and I have begun a cerebral affair, or doesn't appear to notice anyway. I feel a little wary of such a thing, and I'm not sure why. It seems harmless enough.

Trainer and other driver talk trucks together while his wife and I compare road notes. She says this is her first time out, that the last of the kids just left and she wanted to go along to save the loneliness. She is handsome to the point of being nearly masculine. Says she has taken the unpaid job of navigator/bookkeeper for the truck and is just working into the road routine. We both, being new to the sport, agree the opportunity for a shower is not to be discarded since there may not be another that day, and move on quickly to other aspects of life in a truck for which we were not really prepared. She is easily my match, and as if to underline the limits of the relationship she and I have developed in a few seconds, she brings the subject of her husband into the conversation several times. I smile and listen. I don't play either, and I want her to be at ease. We silently agree to draw the line at unfettered brainsex. The shower subject pops up again to ease the tension. She and I are ready for a shower. Now would be fine. Separately, of course.

At home, I shower ordinarily once in the morning to get my day off right, and once in the evening to remove the day's grime and tension. This spotty shower thing is a major factor in my decision not to pursue trucking as a permanent career. Some things are just not negotiable for me in a given circumstance. Showers are one of those things.

Getting clean, or the urge to, must reside somewhere between always and never in male brains. There is a little boy approach in the male that revels in not having a bath and living like a caveman for a while. Primitive and half wild. But basic washing now and again is a health thing, if not considerate of others, and understanding that, most males, only half disappointed, get a bath when the fun is over. Others of the great unwashed don't grasp that, and see no problem. They are rare, but they are out there. Isolation distorts things. And a solo driver is nothing if not isolated.

Living alone in a truck cab for weeks at a time with infrequent and limited human contact, peculiarities become practice. Cleanliness and social standards can disappear, yet the person can still have a job. Over-the-road truckdriving is at least one of the answers out there for individualism or nonconformity wanting a paycheck. But I'm not there yet. Apparently, she isn't either. We want a shower. Apart.

Our two-truck convoy sets out, both of us loaded with plants now, CB radios popping with static. I'm approaching my 36th hour of sleeplessness. I am driving while Trainer navigates. Turn here, turn there. Watch your speed. Did you see that sign? What did it say? And yaps on the radio with his new friend. Both of these guys are cut from the same cloth. Somehow, I believe I am wide awake and have acute reflexes. Few things are farther from the truth. But, I think I am okay and am therefore okay with driving. I do not know all my warning mechanisms are asleep. I am microsleeping and don't realize it. It will be tomorrow before I understand what is happening today.

My driving role and being new to the trade exclude me from real trucker conversation on the radio. So I just drive and listen and hope the end of my day is not far down the road. And sure enough, it isn't.

I think on what the wife must feel, her just now understanding what her husband had to put up with for so many years to feed the kids. Driving a truck is deceptively simple to a citizen. Change some gears and keep it on the road. Get to see the country. Paid vacation. Dam truckers. Hell, I could drive one o' them big trucks too, honey. Cain't be much to it.

Like a slow-moving freight train, trucks nose-to-tail, idling into the truck stop in the late afternoon as we exit the interstate. I realize my depth perception is shot. It is difficult for me to tell how far ahead the next truck is. The smell of some leaf crop across the fertile fields. Hot. Traffic. CB static. Just let me in so I can get a bath and some sleep, I don't care about the steak'n'shrimp even.

Finally, into the fuel island, diesel up, go past the guardshack, and get our parking ticket. Free parking with 50 gallons of fuel or a truck-wash. Driving around looking for a place to back into. This place is not as big as it should be for the truck traffic it serves. We locate a place near the exit just as another driver is leaving, and I set up to back in.

We are in a line of trucks looking to park, idling slowly through the parking lot, and as such there is no time to waste in grabbing an empty space, since it won't be empty long. There is also no time to waste in getting into that space. The traffic comes to a standstill while a driver sets up to back in. Hopefully, the driver gets in on the first stab, but in a small lot like this one, the trucks are very close together and parked even where they shouldn't be—that is to say, in areas not striped for parking. That takes up maneuvering room. Most drivers are very considerate about where they park, but there is always that percentage of newbies or the generally careless taking up space unnecessarily.

Backing in without taking off someone's mirrors or denting the front end of the tractor, and not having to pull out and retry more than once; they'll give a driver that. Everyone has a bad day at the office occasionally. Anything more than that brings on the CB fire and brimstone. Some are good-natured hoots and taunts. Others are vicious and threatening. Everyone is at the end of their workday, or they wouldn't be looking for a place to park, tired and ready to shut down. Drivers are tempered differently. Some handle the waiting like a part of the job. Some don't.

I am patient, it is new to me, and get my turn. I get set up, turn on the hazard flashers (the universal signal a truck is backing), begin the back, and get in the first time. Trucks everywhere, densely parked, lined up behind me, and I get it in. First try. Blind luck and good training at driving school. A round of applause from the radio, and they don't know I am a trainee. I am validated. Trainer looks out the window and says nothing.

The satisfaction is difficult to measure when a neat piece of work is completed by a skilled craftsman, be he woodworker or surgeon or driver. I may not be a skilled craftsman yet, but I feel like one. I pull the knobs on the dash and the brakes lock with a hiss. My day is done. I'm off duty. Let the others scrap for a parking place, I'm home for the night. A good meal, a warm shower, and I'll see everyone tomorrow.

The four of us reconvene at the door to the restaurant and immediately divide into our respective skill levels. Rookies and veteran drivers. I'm okay with that; she's warm, witty, and intelligent. I'd much rather compare Discovery Channel notes than listen to tales of the time that ol' truck went over the guardrail at a hunnert mile'nour on fire in a blizzard pulling a load of dynamite to China.

The steak'n'shrimp does not disappoint, and we carry on for some time. Until time for a shower. We agree to meet again in the morning for coffee to plan our assault on Donner Pass and have breakfast in Reno. The names roll off veteran tongues in routine conversation. No real namedropping, just places we are going. This job is so dang cool. It's like a ride through a geography and history book. Interstate social studies.

The post-dinner shower is the answer to one of my prayers, and the walk back to the truck is delicious in the cool of the evening, beneath the star-spangled California sky. It feels good to walk along with my shower bag hanging on my shoulder, no cares and knowing I am heading for a long sleep. It is like the walk back is a prelude to that sleep. A light breeze brings that fresh earth scent to me, and I am taken back to a plowed Oklahoma field and my grandfather's lessons on planting forty years ago and a thousand miles away. Strange how neurons and dendrites and synapses get together to run those old videos from the attic like that. So little prompting. Just a scent, and I am there as I wander along, full of the night, thinking on my youthful Oklahoma summers and the faces of loved ones long gone.

I unlock the truck and climb in. Open the vent windows at the head and foot of my bunk before Trainer gets back, to alleviate my suffering at the hands of his steak'n'shrimp dinner, then fold back my genuine Mexican blanket to slip into the sheet for my first real sleep in three days.

The noise is like nothing I've ever heard. An unbelievable screech alternating pitch high and low, like a European siren. An alarm of some kind. I spring from my bed to see what is the matter. Grope for the light switch just as Trainer rips off some ghastly shrimp'n'steak fumes. Simultaneous, like those two events were, I am giggling like an idiot in my frantic sleepsearch for the screaming offender. There is really nothing funny about this. I find a shrieking little purple box in a cloth locker door cover. I start mashing buttons. Nothing, still sounds like a jet-powered siren. Need to find the battery cover and gut the sucker. But where? Gotta be a battery. Cleverly faired into the panel on the side, the manufacturer has thought of everything. This thing will get you up, and there is nothing you can do about it. I get the battery out of the case and it isn't easy. I'm determined, all funny gone now. It shows signs of weakness; it knows I have the upper hand. Battery. Wires. I yank them apart. The battery in one hand and banshee in the other. Silence. Trainer rolls over and grunts and chokes. I stand jockeyshorted and suddenly angry. What the hell is he doing, setting an alarm for this hour? Dazed and successful in the pale light of the overhead panel, I let both items fall from my hands. I climb back into my bunk, victorious. My watch says it's four-thirty.

A faint light glows in my east window as I rouse from a good nap past a good sleep. I take my bearings, and the day's plans pop into my head. I'll stay in my bunk just a minute more in an ode to joy. A new day. Another chance.

I lay still, savoring the cool and calm predawn. Roll over and look out the west window where the sodium glare glints off other trucks and see some have gone. Empty spaces. It comes to me some are idling, and I hear them now. I hear Trainer's gurgling beneath me. These sounds were there, I just didn't hear them. I must be adapting. Time to get Trainer up.

I stick my leg out from beneath the blanket to separate the light curtains. The snoring falters and stops. Rustling bedclothes. Heavy footfalls on the carpet. Works every time. Coughing. Gagging. Lighter clicks. Chair squeaks and hisses. Window hums down. Coffee mug steeplechase. Door opens and cab rocks as 275 pounds of coffeemonster begins the hunt. The door slams shut and I know to begin my routine.

There is a comfort in these few minutes alone at the beginning of my day, I need them and hold them dear. I am developing a kind of mental ease in this life on the road. Taking what I can, when I can, and enjoying it while I can. I am learning to focus on the here and now. Be where I am and do what I am doing.

It will be a walk for Trainer, it would be a walk for anyone, the distance to the coffee bar, so I have more time than usual this morning. Some days the fog is slow to lift, but today the clothes jump on. Spray face and hair with the water bottle, brush teeth and climb out, get into Trainer's tracks and head for the coffee bar in the earliness. It smells agricultural here, the last of the night air heavy with the scent of the plowed earth and that leaf crop, whatever it is.

Past the idling diesels and waking drivers. Lights on in the cabs and the day's business beginning. Waking up at work has its benefits, like not having to go far to the desk from the bed, or having to get dressed to do a little paperwork.

It is going to be a beautiful morning weatherwise. Trainer is hooking up with the other company driver. The other guy probably thought if he got in here early, he could get away clean. I empathize, and say nothing. Trainer probably thought he thought that as well, and that is why the alarm went off at four-thirty this morning.

I think back on yesterday and understand there will be times when any given driver is operating in some degree of sleep deprivation due to the erratic nature of loading/unloading schedules and a host of other influences. Forty tons of machine moving along a crowded freeway piloted by a person microsleeping. Eyes open and brain closed a few seconds at a time. I shudder a little and downplay the seriousness of what

I did by promising myself I won't let that happen again either. I am really racking up a list of things I'm not going to do again. Maybe I should start noting a few on a piece of paper and checking it every so often. Make certain I am keeping all my promises to myself.

This morning I feel good in contrast, rested, and ready to get into the mountains, so I locate the coffee, get back to the truck, and get ready to drive. That involves getting everything I think I'll need for the next six hours within arm's reach of the first chair. Trainer shows up at the window and says he wants to drive. Says he's never driven Donner before and he wants to do that. I say I'm the trainee and shouldn't he be critiquing my mountain driving performance and how will I learn if I don't do it hands on? He says he wants to do it and it's his truck. The old "my marbles" approach. I want to cite day-before-yesterday's mountain adventure, but decide that is overkill in this conversation. I just move my stuff over to the second chair. It isn't worth the hassle. I'll just ride and look. We'll be going up for the next 150 miles anyway. There is not much to the eastbound drop according to the atlas, so that shouldn't be too bad.

He climbs in and says he hates leaving so late, and he is certain he set the alarm for four-thirty to get an early start. I just look over at him and say nothing. Sip my coffee. Sooner or later he will find the gutted banshee.

We set out with Trainer at the wheel. Up the Pacific side of the Sierra Nevada to Donner Pass. It is a beautiful morning, so I just sit sideways in my chair and watch the scenery and reflect on the history of the neighborhood.

In 1846 George Donner and a guy named Reed decided to leave Illinois and head for Californy. That's the place they ought to be. They gathered a group that totaled eighty-seven, headed west, and found a lot more fame than fortune. Things began to unravel across the Great Salt Desert and northern Nevada and they were late in getting to the mountains, but decided to wager they could beat the winter of 1847–48 across the Sierras. Probably the first real bad bet made in Nevada. George and his fellow immigrants rolled craps in the California Sierras. They got stuck in the November snow at what is now Donner Lake, just north-west of Lake Tahoe. The story of what forty-seven of them had to do to live till spring is a grisly account of survivalism versus moralism, of how the Donner party became the dinner party, and worthwhile reading some snowy night by the fire. When you're not hungry.

We cross the Truckee River several times in our ascent. It worms around under the highway in different places, and I am taken by how clear and fast the water is, as we cross the bridges. I am also impressed by how few people seem to be here enjoying it. Then it occurs to me how difficult this must be to access unless you live nearby. It's a long way up here, now that I think on it, and there is no real industry I can see to support a population. That must be why I see so few people. That and the fact it's Tuesday, I believe. Every one with a real job is at work.

We climb a not steep, and not steady, but a mostly-up-and-a-little-bit-down, grade for many miles along the interstate on the way across the Sierras, and the diesel works tirelessly but begins to struggle as the grade increases farther up the mountains. Unloaded or lightly loaded trucks whiz by us going up. We are in the far right lane, called a climbing lane, and slowing considerably, so Trainer downshifts into different gears, we slow gradually in each until we get to seventh gear, and the engine settles into a steady hammering that diesels do under pressure, our momentum lost some distance back. It is just an uphill grind now. The tachometer says the RPM is staying the same, so we are not losing ground. Trainer opts to stay in that gear. The vibration and noise preempt everything. Talking is out of the question. Trainer is intent. Total concentration. I don't know how the engine stays together. The hammering noise it is making must be the result of tremendous internal effort.

Our companions are some distance ahead around the curves, and we occasionally catch sight of them as we talk on the radio when the distance or curves don't cut us off. The other driver has driven this road many times and knows what is coming 'round the bend. It helps in knowing when to speed up and slow down, so he has pulled ahead of us, our not knowing those things. On a road with few curves, it is fairly easy to anticipate those things because they can be seen, and it doesn't matter whether or not a driver has made that trip. In this case, the combination of rises, drops, and curves makes experience a big plus in maintaining the uphill momentum and roadspeed. When to shift, where to brake, and where to take advantage of the slingshot effect. Knowing those things makes the climb much easier on both driver and machine.

I feel the cool, high-altitude forest air up here with just the vent on, blowing the piney scent and river smells into the cab. Rushing water tumbling over the rocks and releasing whatever aromatic agents it holds. Great conifers releasing whatever it is they release to smell so good. Lots of road construction along here as well, barricades making the lanes narrower and moving us closer to the edge such that I can see better down the canyons. The road is old, exposed to severe conditions, and I'm surprised it has lasted as long as it has what with the traffic it carries. Concrete is amazing stuff.

We roll on toward the summit. Trainer is tense. I'm sightseeing. The engine hammers. The morning goes on, and God is in his heaven.

Cresting the pass, and the more than 100-mile climb over, it comes to me only half the job is done. We still have to descend the mountain. The eastbound drop is not the same as the westbound drop. Going east, we will descend only a few thousand feet onto the Nevada high plains. Going west, the drop is from mountaintop to nearer sea level, thus the descent is farther and more demanding. The eastbound drop is relatively short but relatively steep as well. This time we have 20 tons of potted plants shoving us to the bottom.

We both know descents are not Trainer's forté. He is acutely aware I'm watching him with a degree of trepidation. I pretend I'm not. He knows I'm pretending not to watch. It makes him nervous. He decides to get my buy-in and asks what gear would I use as we begin the descent. I tell him. He hesitates and shifts out of the gear he is in and gets the transmission into neutral where it hangs because we coasted past his speed/RPM window as he hesitated. Now we are stuck in neutral beginning a roll downhill. I shout at him to stand on the brake until we slow down and grind it into gear. He does that. Much grinding and clashing and brakes groaning. But he gets it into gear. This is a good sign alongside a bad one. I'm relieved the transmission is in gear, but I fear for the brakes. He just got them hot. Again. Not smoking, but hot, and it is still a distance to the bottom. I loudly suggest the braking method I was taught: to brake down 500 RPMs and let the engine build back up, then do it again. All the way down. Without argument, he tries it and it works. They said it would. I was damsure hoping they were right.

The ride down is without further event, Trainer shines, I am happy for him, and we roll into Boomtown to regroup with our compadres at the breakfast buffet. The blueberry blintzes are too damgood, I win twelve dollars in the slots, get free coffee, and I survived Donner Pass. All's well in my little world, and Reno ranks real high on my list of fun places to be right now. Trainer looks like he's had enough pancakes.

Unfortunately for Trainer, his new buddy is out of hours on his log and therefore has to sit out today. No more running mate. No more stimulating conversation for me with his wife. Oh well. We say our goodbyes and hopetaseeyagins and set out for points east with me at the wheel. Trainer thinks it's safe for me to drive now.

Out of Reno going east, Nevada becomes high chaparral with sweeping vistas. It was mining country in the past and it is beautifully empty country still. Not many people out here. Probably one of the reasons it is still beautiful. I could live easily in Moor, but I don't know anyone who would live there with me. It is about as far from anywhere as any place I have seen.

Across the desolate distances that are northern Nevada and through the Pequop, a serious grade down into Wendover, and the Great Salt Desert comes into view, lit by the late-afternoon sun from behind us, and it is impressive. It is a long way across the desert, Benjamin de Bonneville noted in his travels looking for critters to skin hereabouts in the 1830s, to the mountains on the other side. Shades of blue from new denim to turquoise paint mountain and sky and cloud. A broad band of ivory desert lays long and wide before them, the salt tinted that color by late sunbeams. I decide against a photo for two reasons: A, I'm driving, and B, a photograph would only insult this place.

There is a rest area going onto the desert just past the weigh station into Utah, and we need a break anyway, so I shut down, we get out to stretch. In wandering around the parking lot, there is an observation tower there and I go up onto it just to see what I can see. And actually, more can be seen from that vantage point. It's kind of awe inspiring, the expanse of salt and sky out to the mountains; to me, at least. There is also a plaque at the bottom of the tower detailing the location of the measured mile just out of sight to the north, at the base of the mountains there. Really fast people come here. From all over the world. With really fast machines. Lots of dreams out there. I stand a moment more, looking around, trying to take some of this with me too, I guess, and walk back to the truck. I don't really feel like I've seen the Bonneville racetrack. Something is missing. Maybe it is because I haven't actually seen the raceway, just where it is. There is a difference. To me anyway.

Trainer riding now, I'm driving, on the arrow-straight road that leads to Salt Lake City across the desert. I can see the road go into the vanishing point. Never seen that before. I also never see a living thing on the way across. Not lizard, not snake or scorpion. For what I've seen, there is no life whatsoever. I don't even see a bird flying around. Nothing. For 50 miles. Lots of places claim to be desert, but this is the only real desert I have ever seen, in that it is deserted. Most of what I am told is desert has abundant life. But most of that life comes out at night. Not here. I don't think anything can live in this saltscape. Day *or* night.

Lots of people tracks though. Beer bottles, names spelled out in rocks alongside the roadway, names spelled out in beer bottles alongside the roadway. RUSTY LOVES KAREN. Why do they always use upper case? Peace symbol. Where do they get enough brown rocks in this whiteout to do this vandalism? Must be imported rocks. JOHN LOVE MON. Must have run out of rocks. John saw it coming. Left the "s" off "LOVES."

Bad planning. Loves what? Monica? Money? MON what? Maybe they split up before he finished. Maybe had to make several trips for rocks, and took too long. She may have left him for a faster rock-gatherer.

Vehicle ruts out from the roadway and back to it, old tires and the damdest thing. It looks like a giant saguaro cactus, probably 75 feet tall, with a seed pod broken open on the ground next to it. I ask Trainer what it is. Says he don't know. His curiosity ends there. I ask on the radio. I am told it is a microwave tower, a desert tree, a telephone relay station, something the railroad put there, a headstone for a person that died here years ago, an objet d'art, which it is, and a weather station. I resolve to stop here one day and find out. Too dangerous this trip because we are eastbound and the thing is on the north side of the westbound interstate. I don't want the truck to be a sitting duck for long enough to get across the median, across the westbound side and out to the thing, then make my way back, without disappearing into the salt mire or getting whacked crossing the interstate. I will find later, on a subsequent trip across the Bonneville flats, that thing is a sculpture, and is known as the Utah tree. There is a plaque at the bottom of it that details its existence.

I drive along this monotonous road through the monotonous beauty of the desert and my monotonied brain runs out of things to do. Sometimes that happens on long straight roads. Rolling along, we are alone with our thoughts. The a/c is humming to keep the cab cool, and we ride in silence except the steady rumble of the engine and roadnoise. I'm so acclimated now I rarely hear it, but know to talk above it automatically. It is however, Trainer that speaks. I thought we had talked about everything by now, but we haven't.

There is one more thing.

In the individual solitude of our self-imposed isolation, Trainer has drifted back to an unpleasant childhood after *his* brain ran out of things to do. As is his custom, he roars above the engine when he speaks. He was too little to stop it. The recounting of it takes a while, then he is silent. Looking out the windshield, seeing what is in his mind, and not his eye.

I wish he hadn't told me about it. I don't know what to say. Really, there is nothing to say. Trainer knows that. He just needed to share his burden. I know that. It's an ugly demon I wouldn't want tagging around behind me, and I am heartbroken for him. This gentle giant of a man. Hides his scars behind a squint-eyed laugh and easy manner. He is good to everyone, even people that don't deserve his decency. I want to say something. To make it all go away for him. For his sister. But I opt for silence. Anything I say would trivialize a childhood of suffering.

It is quiet except the continual rumble and roadnoise for a long time. Slumped on the edge of the chair, Trainer is no longer in the truck. Staring through the windshield, but seeing nothing around him, Trainer is banishing Stepfather for today. I see the motionless struggle out the corner of my eye. It is fierce. The memories are powerful, but Trainer is as strong mentally as he is physically, and he gets the door closed. For now.

He sits up straight in the second seat, shortly, and announces his grandson helps him mow the yard. That Trainer pushes the top handlebar and Grandson pushes the bottom one. He begins to glow as he speaks and I listen, happy it is so. Glad for him that his life is good now, that his wife loves him and he loves her. That their marriage is intact since high school, that the kids are grown, gone and he has grandchildren to crown his silver years. I listen to tales of first steps and nasty diapers and cookies lost in the couch. He smiles as he gushes at a roar about the grandkids, and I smile with him. He is putting some distance between himself and that door. I hear the relief in his voice, even through his roaring.

Maybe this desert is a place where some barrier we have is broken down and bad things can get in. Where the miles of baking salt are a warning to stay away, and they have always been. Some just couldn't read the warnings. Pilgrims, prospectors, pioneers, drivers. Maybe it is that we shouldn't be here. That it is a wasteland and all things that come here will be made waste to one degree or another. Maybe a part of the wayfarer stays here and something the desert has goes with that wayfarer, if he makes it across. Even the ones in air-conditioned tractors blowing across the nothingness like a desert wind. Maybe it is a direct proportion thing: the longer stayed, the more damage done. There is nothing here but misery for the unprepared. Seems that dumb animals are smart enough to not come here. No telling the numbers of skeletons, structural and emotional, lying in the salt out there. Those wayfarers who left everything here. The ones that realized too late they were unprepared, or were foolish enough to think there was no hurry or danger, taken by the beauty and solitude. Or wrestled with their demons too long.

Like most beautiful things, the desert is dangerous. Beauty is almost always Nature's warning to stay away.

The salt-crusted miles and the last of the afternoon go by and we roll past the Great Salt Lake where I see sailboats, but no one fishing. Why? No fish. Really? Yup. What is that mosque-looking building at the shore? An old bathhouse from the twenties. No way. Yup.

Trainer guides us off the interstate and into Salt Lake City just as a setting sun watercolors the western sky above the Great Salt Desert I will cross many times, but never again without thinking deeply on Trainer, his ability to prevail, the evil that men do, and how the desert both tempts and takes.

Trainer says to get off at this next exit and we will stop at a truck stop he knows on this side of town to get a shower and a meal. We need fuel as well. In the tone of his voice I sense things are getting back to whatever normal is for us, and adjust the chair for in-town driving. I like the chair high in town so I can see well enough around the truck, and lower on the highway so I can see the mountains and sky. Adjusting the height of the chair also moves the weight from my butt more to my thighs as it goes up and the opposite going down. Helps with the time that can be comfortably spent in the chair, thereby increasing mileage. Thinking like a driver now . . . mo' money.

Salt Lake City is preparing for the winter of 2002 Olympics and the road construction is everywhere. Orange barrels for miles warning of sharp pavement drops and abrupt lane changes. The city is laid against the base of the Wasatch Mountains, and beginning to creep up the sides onto what is called the "Bench." Sort of a residential terrace just downhill from the aspen trees. Known as "quakies" locally for their motion in the wind that frequents the area, these things will be gorgeous in their autumn colors, and add some native flavor for the pre-Olympic crowd. The locals are used to them, and aren't as impressed.

Brigham Young knew real estate if nothing else; a better backdrop for the world sportsfest would be difficult to imagine. I'll try to stop by in 2002. Actually, I'll stop by several times in the coming year, and it will be just as beautiful as I thought it would be.

We ease into Trainer's hideaway for fuel and a shower. Free shower with a fifty-gallon fuel purchase. No problem. We need more than one hundred. Most truck stops do that as an incentive. Everyone needs a bath, and rather than just fueling and allowing a potential customer to roll on, shutting down for a free shower gets that impulse buyer into the store. The showers are in the back and up the stairs so the driver has to tour the emporium to get one. It's good business and helps keep America's drivers clean.

Most franchised truck stops are tidy and color-coordinated for the same reasons. Humans are not much different from crows and raccoons when it comes to bright and shiny. We like it. We pick that place over the dirty and dingy one just about every time. So most places we stop, even for a moment, are well kept. This one, however, is very nice. Spotless, aromatic restaurant and fast-food bar, wide accessible aisles, helpful staff, and palatial, immaculate showers. A warm shower in a beautifully tiled and maintained room, topped off by a warmed plush towel. I luxuriate. Small pleasures at home become privileges on the road, and I look forward to my daily shower. I have given up much of my life to drive. Friends, family, fishing, high-quality food. Sex. My own bed and pillow. Hearth and home. But not my shower. I have not yet sunk deep enough into the trucking lifestyle that I can forgo the shower. While it is true I am no longer a fashionista, shorts and a golf shirt are de rigueur for me, and some of my social graces may be slipping away, I stay clean. I get my shower, and I think we have covered that.

Fresh scrubbed, I wander through the capacious truck stop, among the Salt Lake City consuming public and other drivers. It is enough of a front-running marketplace that civilians shop here as well. It is an island of capitalism and life and light in the early Utah night. I am comforted to be here. Soon enough I will be back in the truck, now affectionately known as Big Blue, and rumbling into the night toward our planned overnight stop in Wyoming. So for the moment, I'll enjoy this unabashed commercialism. Gimme a cheeseburger and fries, please. A little Muenster'd be nice.

Trainer materializes from the crowd as I savor the last of the LDL cholesterol. Says we need ta roll. Says he's got some night mountain driving training for me, but he'll drive to show me how it's done. Roger that. I am too well fed to drive now, and I feel a nap coming on.

The truck parking lot is small for the size of the building, and we sit in a line of bigtrucks waiting to get out onto the street so we can wait in a line of bigtrucks on the street waiting to get onto the freeway. More waiting.

Riding into the city on the interstate I see Salt Lake is just another smoggy, crowded city. What makes it special, if anything does, is the Olympic effort and its proximity to the biggest salt lake in the hemisphere. The freeway is a mess, as in any other city, due in heaping measure to the failure of city planners to envision traffic's exponential growth, and partly due to the Olympic restructuring. Very cool graphics cast into the paneled viaduct walls. They depict Olympic events. Imaginary athletes doing their stuff in an imaginary moment immortalized in cement. What makes Salt Lake City special to drivers is that it is a hub for major truck routes. Interstate 80 goes through it east and west as does Interstate 15 north and south; both are veritable arteries of commerce in the western U.S. Salt Lake City sits right on the junction. There are several major trucking companies based here for that reason. Their drivers can get home easily, and that is attractive to the drivers.

One city right after another in this business. Most of them are similar in that they are a conglomeration of traffic, road repair, litter, strip malls, neon lights, buildings of different sizes, a skyline in most, smog, and people in various states of distress. We will not be there long, so no matter. Another day, another bunch of cities. So they kinda all seem the same. Except two. I am lucky enough to have traveled much, and been in many cities over the years. Two stand alone as standing alone. Las Vegas, Nevada, and New York City. Many cities lay claim to this or that or the other, but Las Vegas, just south of here, is unparalleled anywhere in any country, and New York City, some distance east of here, really is the capital of the world. There are no others like them. Anywhere.

But right now we are trying to get out of Salt Lake City. Up a steep and steady climb on the interstate east into the Wasatch. The engine hammers in seventh gear and Trainer is focused. Says this hill will be dangerous in a couple of months, what with the snow and ice that will grace these canyons. I am sideways in the chair looking back on the lights of the city from on high thinking how pretty it is, how cities take on a different persona after dark. Like they are all business in the day-light, hustle and bustle, then begin to relax and play a little after dark, and settle down for bed after the restaurants and malls close, to sleep for a while with the lights down low, before they go back to work in the light of the morning.

Wyoming is down the road a couple of hours, and the plan is to stay at a truck stop Trainer knows there and shut down for the night. I am somehow under the impression this stop is selected for the quality of the donuts. I have seen him eat an entire box at once, so I know donuts are reason enough to select that particular truck stop. I believe this place sells his brand, if I recall the conversation correctly.

Just into Wyoming is a port of entry where all commercial vehicles must stop and go inside with the pertinent paperwork. It is the way Wyoming does things. A pleasant group of state officials are behind the counter and ask what we have on board and want to see our truck's registration papers. Trainer has stopped here in the past and knew we would be asked for that, so we brought those papers in. We have a loose-leaf notebook with pages of permits and documents sorted by state, kept in the truck. The company provides it and keeps it updated. Occasionally, upon entering a state, we are asked for particular papers and they are in this notebook. In Wyoming, the officials want to see only the registration. We show them that. An entry is made into a database. I ask about it and am told every time the truck comes into Wyoming this will happen. Even though you already have that information in the system? Yes. Okay. Makes government sense to me. Trainer glares. Officer laughs. I ask about the coffee urn I see in the corner of a public area. Help yourself, the coffee's always on here. Thanks. The book is handed back to me with a smile. I think I like Wyoming now.

Trainer stomps behind me to the table with the coffee urn on it. Condiments, too. Real sugar, real cream. We are not supposed to talk to these officials. They are here to make our lives miserable.

No they aren't. They are here to survey us and determine whether or not we are a menace to the state of Wyoming. What is that, a lawyer joke? Do you know how far we would be down the road if we didn't have to stop here? No, but if you will get your coffee and we go, the effect will be minimal. Huffing and glaring. I set out for the truck and leave Trainer struggling to separate the Styrofoam cups locked in a static cling.

He is just tired and stressed. Like trainers get sometimes. Feels good out tonight, cool and dry. The breeze is light and fresh scented. Pine, maybe, or some other conifer.

We set out from the port of entry to Trainer's donut haven some miles into the state, but not far, and exit the interstate into a small, well-lit and neat truck stop. It is near capacity this time of night. We back into an available space, shut down, and finish the coffee with a visit and review of the day's highlights, a couple of chuckles, and climb into our respective bunks. I open my windows at the head and foot of my bunk. I lay back in the coolness flowing through the upper bunk, and wrapped in my Mexican blanket, I close my eyes. Goodnight Ms. Celibate, wherever you are.

I DON'T THINK I MOVED ONCE DURING THE NIGHT. A BREATH OF high-country air rolls in the window and washes over me just after dawn to bring me back from wherever I was. I lie in quiet comfort snuggled in my bunk. Life is good. I opt to sleep for another hour this morning. Trainer will want his donuts as soon as he wakes. He snarkles rhythmically below. I opt to let him sleep another hour as well. Control is good. It's like having the remote all the time.

Shortly I wake again and open the curtain with my foot. The day begins. Trainer is up and hacking and smoking and out the door. Abandon all hope, ye with holes or jelly in your middles.

I languish just a little longer this morning. Climb down, pee, dress, and step into the smashing Wyoming morning. No man lives as well as I do. I pity everyone who isn't me as I look around and smile. No dam wonder those Indians fought so hard for this country. It is spectacular, not to mention their ancestral home. No book of photographs on any coffee table in any waiting room does this place justice. I decide not to waste the film, and I have come to the conclusion landscape photography is an offense to the subject. You have to stand in it. You have to touch it with your eyes. You have to breathe it and feel it on your skin. Anyone that doesn't get out and do that doesn't deserve to know anything sensory about it. Tear up your landscape photographs, show them to no one else, and tell everyone to go and see for themselves. We would have a whole new crop of environmentally aware people. Photographs don't have the magic. It's like showing a man a painting of a beautiful woman. He may admire it and say that is a beautiful woman. He may take in what he sees. But, he will never know anything about her scent, hear her laugh or whisper, or hold her warm, into the night. Never look into her eyes or see her run to him, or listen to her breathe, asleep beside him. Never touch her lips with his. Never embrace her and feel her hair on his cheek, or her softness, alive and tender and holding him close.

That's the difference in the place and the picture.

Free coffee this morning. The clerk waves me on after my turn at the urn. Turn at the urn. Mmmm. Wander back to the truck and climb up to see Trainer already back with a countenance I've not seen before. He usually calls the wife first thing with his coffee and they talk a minute. I like that. Good to see it when it happens, and I'm envious of a happy relationship. She is not well and apparently, I don't know for sure, getting a little worse by the day. Trainer handles it well, but stays uptight. This is the most money he can make for his level of education, so he does the best he can for his family, even if it means his being gone weeks at a time. This morning is different. She's getting worse, I sense, and he doesn't want to talk about it. So I don't ask. He's here and she's there and that's that. Nothing he can do from the road, and no amount of stressing here will fix it.

I stand a little more in this guy's shadow by the day. That he can maintain his attitude as well as he does in the face of his history and the current events is testament to a superior ability or capability. He is a rare person, and I am privileged to have known him. I count myself a lucky man for my small circle of friends and close acquaintances as I set about the start-up procedure and Trainer looks out his window into oblivion. He is at home with his wife, and I don't call him away. He'll return when he's ready.

We roll out of the parking lot and onto Interstate 80 east, a trailer full of plants right behind us. Trainer snaps out of his state and grabbles around in the overhead shelves. He comes up with a Black Sabbath tape from the sixties when Ozzy, in his pre-batbiting days, was with them. He plugs it in and cranks it up. I scream at him it hurts my ears, but I like the music. But it reminds me of a time when I had the chance to take another path, and my life would be different now. If I had lived. Trainer shouts back he is okay and he doesn't have any Hershey bars. I motion to my ears. He nods and says it's okay, he has some brand-new earplugs and I can have them. So he gets up to get them. I reach over and turn the stereo down. He says he can't hear it now. I tell him to find the earplugs and I don't want them if they are all crusted up and orange with earwax. He grubs around in a drawer and hands me a new packet of two. He cranks the stereo back up just as I get them into my ears. He laughs and shakes his head. I smile at the quiet in my head, and the fil-tered music. We head east, the morning sun streaming in the wind-shield, and I feel the heat from 93 million miles away on my shirt, while the Osbourne belts out "Paranoid."

Out of town, I see a peculiar wagon on a hillside with signs of life around. Laundry on a pole, chair away from the wagon, and a washbasin of some kind. The door is open and smoke drifts from a metal pipe out the roof. It looks like a Conestoga Winnebago. Trainer sees my look and shouts it is a shepherd's wagon. Says some folks still watch sheep up in the high country during the summer. When the winter comes, the shep-herds take the sheep to warmer places down in the valleys. Now there's a trade that hasn't changed a whole lot in several thousand years. I won-der what I would have thought had I seen that on some résumé crossing my desk back in another life. Shepherd. I guess someone has seen that on a résumé. I wonder what they wondered. I wonder if the person got the job. I wonder if an interview is necessary for a shepherd's job, and what qualifications a person would need.

I look down a dale farther along the road and see the walls of an old stone house from another age. Windows gone, roof missing sections, walls crumbling, and I wonder who lived there and how long and if they built it. Gone now, this is what is left of their life's work. Makes me wonder if maybe the admonition to Gilgamesh was on the mark. I think on how they saw the same things I'm seeing, but the interstate wasn't here most likely, so they didn't see that. This house was pretty isolated back then. Someone was really proud of it when it was new, and all that went into it. They had to have been. It is a stone house; a lot of time and skill went into building it, not to mention the logistics of getting the building materials on site. Even the rocks had to be brought from somewhere around here. Loaded into a wagon and moved to the jobsite. Timbers cut and seasoned and hewed. Doors made and hung, windows bought and set. No prefab operation here. No power tools. No trips to the home décor store in the family pickup. The place was handmade. Built to last, and I'll bet it is older than I think it is. I wonder what the walls would tell me if the walls could talk. Maybe it was a happy house and the business of housekeeping was a pleasure in it. Maybe it wasn't. Life was harder then, and people had to be a family and work together to make it. Maybe a family lived there, and the kids played among the hills and sagebrush. Maybe not. I wonder if the owners were farmers or ranchers. Whatever the history, now it is little more than a shell waiting for the last wall to collapse and someone someday will remove it for some reason. Maybe by then it will be no more than a pile of rocks bearing little resemblance to a house, and those that bulldoze it away for a developer will have no idea what is being scraped aside by the blade. I would like to have spent a day with the owners in the good days, to know them and to see how they lived. I'll bet they never figured an interstate would pass through the front yard.

Up a hill and downshift to ninth gear to pull it to the top and back up to cruising speed on the straightaway. I settle into the chair and adjust it to suit me. Trainer adjusts it to suit him when he drives, and between the two of us we keep the adjustment buttons busy. Up, down, soft, hard, forward, backward. There is a thing called an oscillator on the bottom of the seat of the chair. It allows the chair to slide freely forward and backward a few inches to compensate for the pitch of the cab when we hit a really rough section of road. It works surprisingly well, too. Sometimes we hit a stretch of road that has a series of gentle sine/cosine waves and the oscillator tries to compensate but gets in synch with the pitch of the cab, and the motion transmitted through the seat to the driver is pretty funny. Like riding a bucking porpoise. I don't have that problem now, but it has happened in the past. When everything is right, or wrong in this case, the motion is so violent I have literally been un-seated, and had it not been for the shoulder belt, may not have been able to stay behind the wheel. Times like that it isn't funny . . . till after it's over and no one is hurt and the truck is still under control.

Anyway, there is much to see along here as we make our way to the plant sellers on the East Coast. This is still wild country and it has what wild country has. Wild people come here to do wild stuff. Ride angry horses and bulls, climb mountains, ride boards and sticks downhill in the snow, dodging trees and big rocks. I ride along this interstate in air-conditioned, well-fed and -rested comfort wondering what a cattle drive must have been like. A couple of places near here were destinations from the cattle ranches in the Southwest, back in the days when the Army bought lots of cattle to feed the soldiers stationed in those forts. There was no interstate here and the railroad went the wrong way, so someone had to take the cows for a long walk.

A thousand miles of wind-whipped dust, cow poo, and sleeping in the dirt. Dollar a week. Maybe. If enough cattle survived the hike. We roll on, sipping coffee at 65 MPH, 32 cents a mile. I guess we are the evolved wagon drivers from back then. Those guys drove the stage-coaches and freight wagons that brought supplies and people out here to "build" the country, maybe down this same path. Put up with hostile locals, bad weather, bad roads, bad directions, and breakdowns, just like us. Maybe there is some continuity to things. They had reins in their hands and we have steering wheels. Moving the freight, just like back then. I resolve to check the trailer for arrows stuck in it at the next rest stop coming up. You just never know.

As I sit and watch the countryside go by my window and think on how things might have been back in the days when this land was a frontier, and knowing my way by the interstate signs, I wonder how those cowpersons found their way around the country. How did a person on horseback find Laredo if he left from Kansas City? How did a person manage to be accurate enough to hit Fort Collins riding from Fort Ticonderoga? I know there must have been trails, but how did they find them, even? What if the trail just kinda played out in the soft sand of the desert. Turn left at the Rockies. I wonder how many got lost and gave up. Could they find their way back? What if their horse got sick? Or worse? How many are still out there, part of the nitrogen cycle now, having set out for the West a couple of hundred years ago with no directions but "go west?"

I like to break every hundred miles or so, and a rest area is advertised just about on time. Let a little of this coffee out and stretch some. Trainer shakes his head, disgusted and derailed, but he is the first one trotting to the facilities when we get stopped. I lock up the idling tractor and trot behind him.

The rest area had some forward-thinking designers. Passive solar heat. Wind breaks. Mini flush. Faucet sensors. There is a conservation effort theme, and a feel that it belongs here, a part of the land. I like it. Take care of my business and mosey outside into the wind. We "mosey" out here in Wyoming. Wait on Trainer to finish whatever it is he's doing in there, I'm not ready to get back into the truck just yet. Look around for a minute. Stretch my 36-inch inseam. Mosey some more.

My wanderings lead to a bas relief monument that details the creatures living on these windscoured hills and how seventeen varieties of sagebrush grow on these rolling plains. Some with a taproot six feet long to get what water is down there, and provide sustenance for the migratory deer types. Antelope and elk and the like. Sagebrush looks pretty nondescript; like it doesn't do a whole lot even though there is a bunch of it out there. I guess how it looks is determined by who is looking at it, a truckdriver or an elk. Dead, the various species of sagebrush break off, become tumbleweeds, and gang up on fences to become a snowbreak in the winter. That's a plus. Further, this whole country would be blown into Kansas if the sagebrush roots didn't hold it down. It's just good stuff to have around, and I come away with a whole new perspective on sagebrush.

Later in the day, we roll into some really pretty country. Badlands. A kind of desert with sedimentary rock formations. Most folks think of a desert as a sandbox, which isn't necessarily so. Deserts are mostly rocks and gravel. Some have lots of sand, but they are mostly rocks if viewed overall. This one isn't just rocks, it is smoothed and rounded formations. The harder rock left after ages of wind and water ply their trades on the softer layers. Impressive. Earth-tone type colors. Real earth tones.

Farther along the interstate, we pass a man-made cliff that has lots of very thin layers of sediment in horizontal strata. More sediment from long ago. This place was probably a lake or sea once, and this is the gunge that settled onto the bottom. I wonder about its composition. Fish bones, river trash that flowed to sea and sank, whale droppings probably. There is a peculiar bump in the strata like something pushed the layers up in that one area alone, and all the strata are concentric in that bump. The surrounding layers are flat. That little aberration would have been hidden in this hill for eternity had we not blown a highway through it. Now, naked to the world, some subterranean cataclysm left its signature for interstate passersby to wonder about.

On to some really prettier country later in the day. The cliffs alongside the interstate are the result of eons of erosion and have multicolored pastel bands of sediment that fairly glow in the late-afternoon sunrays. Flaming Gorge, aptly named, is near here and this must be some of the leftovers, or duplicate parts.

As we roar by, I see the strata are different than what I saw earlier. These are not only different colors, but different thicknesses as well. Some are no more than a fraction of an inch thick and another might be more than a foot thick. No gradient, either. Sharp definition in sizes and colors. The same colors reappear several layers apart. Wonder why. These canyon walls must read like a newspaper to a geologist, but it is confusing for a truckdriver trainee. I can only grasp the beauty and the age of it. But still I wonder about the other things.

Bigtruck rolling. Booming along, in sailboat parlance, with a strong wind on our side. We are loaded heavily, though, and that helps the truck keep all its feet on the ground. Empty or lightly loaded trucks have a rough time in this situation. The trailer can be blown from behind the tractor out to the side, or the wind can rock the trailer onto one side of the tandems, or sometimes all the way over onto its side. Tractor-trailers are the original case of the tail wagging the dog. A fully loaded trailer weighs in around 32 tons and a fueled, loadedtothemax tractor tips the scale at about 8 tons, those numbers depending on several things. It is no contest.

Even empty, the trailer has the advantage. In that case, though the tractor and the trailer weigh about the same, the laws of physics give the trailer a leverage advantage because of its sheer size and windload area. In an ordinary circumstance, the trailer goes where the tractor takes it. In an extraordinary circumstance, the tractor goes where the trailer takes it. We want to live out our driving lives in ordinary circumstances, so we don't put the truck-trailer combination in extraordinary circumstances, or let it get into extraordinary circumstances if we can help it. It is just good business planning.

Currently we are in extraordinary circumstances. But, we have the good fortune to enjoy the weight advantage in this wind, so what would otherwise be foolhardy is more an aggravation than dangerous. Empty, we would shut down until the wind moderated, but I don't think empty trailers should come to Wyoming. Drivers would be shut down all the time with an empty trailer because of the wind. It blows almost incessantly across these plains. I heard a driver this morning say he fell down after leaving Wyoming because he opened his door and got out leaning into a wind that wasn't there.

Big Blue gets a grip on the pavement and rumbles eastward through the early evening and towns founded in the American frontier era. Green River. Laramie. Cheyenne. Names from history. Outposts in the days when wranglers rode into town on horses, not pickups or bigtrucks. Jim Bridger walked these trails when this land belonged to the Cheyenne. Fort Bridger is just down the road. He and a Canadian guy established that fort. Jim Bridger Power Plant is back down the road. The local utility company established that. Jim most likely would not care for the smoke that pours out the stacks and leaves a high-altitude brown haze the length and breadth of the valley that bears his name. I guess whoever named the power plant for him thought that makes everything okay. Like it has his approval or something.

They have a huge rodeo in Cheyenne every year, and I'm told the town swells to three times the population for two weeks. Weekend cowboys everywhere. I hear real rodeos are impromptu. That a bunch of waddies, which is what real cowboys call themselves, just happen to be doing the same things out on the range, and a friendly competition breaks out. Who's the best? Who's the fastest? That's the kind of rodeo I'd like to see. But if that's true, the waddies are the only ones that get to see it. It's over before anyone else gets there. I wonder if drugstore cowboys could cut it for a week on a working cattle ranch. I *would* buy a ticket to see that. Maybe several tickets, since I have friends that would like to see that as well.

Trainer says we need to stop here for the night. He wants some chili, and this place has it just the way he likes it. Reason enough, and I steer off the road for his chili haunt and a night's rest. The chili is great, the shower is warm and soothing, the night's rest is comfortable. Wyoming is a great place to sleep. I never sleep better than when I am there.

It is an early start, and a good one. Trainer is in a pleasant state after we do the logs and have a couple of cups of coffee, and relaxes in the second seat as we take up where we left off last night. No more chili for Trainer, either, or at least not when I will be in the truck with him.

East from Laramie on Interstate 80 is a climb into the Medicine Bow forest. There is a rest area on the top of the hill with a statue of Abraham Lincoln outside. A big statue of Abraham Lincoln. A bust, really, it is his head and shoulders. But a big one.

Some rest areas are pure function. Stop. Get out. Rest. Some are exotic welcome mats to an area with all the amenities and offer a real sample of local color. Some are architectural works of art. Some are not. Some have works of art set about the area, in Nebraska, for instance. Some seem different somehow, and not blended well with the landscape and general theme the state projects, and this is one of those. I can't figure out why a huge bust of Abe Lincoln would be gazing onto a Wyoming interstate in such a thoughtful pose at the edge of a forest named for some aboriginal spiritual artifact. I'll just whip in and find out. Curiosity is a good thing. But I hear many cats are no longer around because of it.

Delighted I am not a cat, I steer off the road and begin the circuitous route from the interstate to the parking lot of the rest area. Trainer is horrified. We ain't got no time for this. Sure we do; what's 20 minutes in the overall scheme of things when we are dealing with thousands of miles and several days? Besides, I'm driving and that is a big factor in the decision-making process. And I gotta pee. It occurs to me I may, however, wind up like those cats, if I'm not careful.

Trainer sits resigned and pouty, staring out the window after I park, set the brakes, and open the door.

I hike inside to see what I can see in the route to the men's room. There is a small theater area and a well-done diorama depicting the local plants and animals. Nice staff, photo gallery, and good coffee. Free, too.

After looking around, I decide to head on back to the truck and, like Abe, bust a move, so to speak. Trainer will be livid by the time I get there. Walking back, I still haven't figured out why Abe is out by the road, even after having read the plaque that explains the evolution of a dirt road from New York City to San Francisco, called the Lincoln Highway, into US 30 and finally into Interstate 80. There is another plaque that further complicates my understanding of the situation by documenting Wyoming's celebration of a sesquicentennial involving Mr. Lincoln. I guess it all ties into the dirt road being named for him, or maybe Wyoming was his favorite state. Plus, it is early and I don't handle complicated input nor abstract reasoning very well until the sun gets a little higher in the sky. I think we have talked about that.

I get into the truck being careful not to spill the coffee, and that isn't easy, climbing in with one hand.

There are a few things we have these days that make my life a lot more pleasant, and one of them is that little snapfit plastic lid on the Styrofoam coffee cups. I have no idea how many total disasters have been averted in my experience alone by those lids. Untold gallons of coffee and fountain sodas saved from the floorboard. To me, they rank right in there with elevators, air conditioners, and outboard motors on the list of waycool things we have these days to make life better. Unfortunately, I don't have one on this particular cup, so I'm careful getting into the cab. It is a one-handed climb. Trainer is huffy. Glares at me as I get in. I pretend not to see him. He hates that.

Back on the road.

At the top of the climb into the Medicine Bow forest, and east a little, is a rest area with a tree growing from a rock. It has a fence around it. Trainer tells me about it and how his daughter loves to stop and look at that tree. We get closer to where it is and I slow down a little. Trainer says why are you slowing down? I say I might want to love that tree as well but I won't know unless I stop to see it. Says we don't have time. Besides you just stopped 15 minutes ago. No matter. I say nothing and slow for the exit. Trainer stares out the windshield as if in some pain. I will turn aside and see this tree growing from a rock. Whatever the cost in time. And nerves. And cats.

Really, I have seen several growing from fissures in rocks along the way, but have not seen one growing from a rock in its own fenced enclosure. It has to be a special tree, and therefore worthy of some interest and us stopping there, so I pull into the small lot and away from some cars already there.

Stopped. Pull the tractor brake knob on the dash. Air brakes hiss. I like to do that. Get out and walk around the fenced area. There is a tree growing from a crack in a rock in there. I think how amazing it is that a tree can separate a rock. Patience is wonderful stuff.

Get back into the truck. Trainer is raging internally. This man has remarkable control. I marvel. The diesel rattles. Trainer fumes. The tree grows. My coffee is still hot. The Rocky Mountain morning is spectacular. I love this job.

Back onto the interstate and up through the gears. I like shifting the gears, too. There is a predictability about it that suits me somehow. Do it right and everything is like silk. Miscalculate RPMs or MPH and it just won't go into gear. I am getting to the stage of my development where I can do other things while I shift. I don't have to focus totally on shifting. I still have to think about what I'm doing, it isn't mechanical yet, but I can do things like watch where I'm going at the same time now.

Western Nebraska. Platte River Valley. Windy and sparse. Lots of tears here as well. Settlers headed for the freebies of the Oregon territory made their way through this valley for its relative flatness, abundant game, and reliable water source. Wagons. Cows. Horses. Breakdowns, sickness, slow going. Shady guides sneaking off into the night. Hostile native landlords. What a trip. Some actually made it to Oregon. I wonder at the soundness of mind of a person that opted to leave the ancestral land and go west. Some probably didn't really want to go, but had done something worthy of leaving the hometown back east. Running from an ex, or the law, or ex-in-laws. Others for the adventure, but I'll bet they were a small percentage. Mess up your life and go west. I really wonder at the mind-set of the spouses that pulled up roots and went along. That's devotion. Or dementia. Or maybe people really married for better or worse back then. And worse came along. So they had to go with the mate. Wasn't like they could go to the mall and find a new wife or husband in one afternoon.

Some didn't go all the way for one reason or another, and I guess the descendants of those folks who just stayed where they broke down mentally or physically, live in Nebraska now.

We change seats at a rest stop well into the state, that has some signs explaining the local geography, and Trainer takes the wheel. There is a sprinkler system in that rest area. It came on while I was reading a lecture panel. Soaked, I ride and look out the window. Trainer thinks that is particularly comical. Saw it all. He has to wait sometimes for the last laugh, but he gets it. Pisses me right off.

I see those icons of technology we know as cell towers on occasion and wonder if 200 years ago a tipi may have been on that same site. Buffalo trails and interstates. The only difference is a couple of hundred years. Onward through the all-day nothingness that is western Nebraska to Ogallala, named for a particular band of Lakotas that frequented the area back when. Trainer says we'll stay the night there. In a truck, not a tipi.

Trainer will now demonstrate entering a crowded truck stop and parking a bigtruck.

We roll in late. Most solo drivers shut down around dark, and the lots fill up quickly around that hour. We get into Ogallala just past dark. Trainer has some difficulty negotiating the entry. There are things that look like tank traps in the lot to keep traffic flowing the proper direction. We nearly hit a couple. Idling around looking for an empty spot, and we see one. Trainer sets up to back in. Bad setup. It isn't really his fault. The trailer needs to be at or near a 45 degree angle to the axis of the parking space at the end of the setup procedure to be pushed backward between two already-parked trucks. He is not set up like that, because he doesn't have the room. This is a small lot, we came in at a bad angle, and there are lots of trucks here. It doesn't look good from where I sit.

Trainer gets frustrated with the pressure of several trucks waiting to get by as he backs and misses several times. Hoots and jeers on the CB, so I turn it off to get that out of the mix. Trainer gives up and pulls away to look for an easier time of it. Decides after some cruising around and nonproductive looking, to go out of the lot and park alongside the exit road behind the service building. That's where they repair the sick tractors in this truck stop. It is dark back here because the place is closed, and a good place to hide. Trainer is frustrated and agitated. Embarrassed.

He thinks he is supposed to be infallible. Thinks he is not setting a good example, and is therefore not doing his job, and exposing himself to ridicule from all quarters. Mine included. Especially my quarter, now that I think about it. We have a new game. It's called "drag the other guy over the coals when he messes up." We both like to play.

I sit quietly pretending not to notice the failed backing attempts. Wounded pride is a bad thing to exacerbate. Trainer turns the engine off. Silence. I let it go on some seconds, and in looking around, I see a burger place down the street. Far from this place of failure. Trainer likes burgers. And it's late, so I know he's hungry. I say there is a burger place down the street and we could walk there to celebrate that backing lesson you just bungled because I know you are hungry and embarrassed. Trainer hops out and slams the door. Big guys can slam doors hard. Kinda reminds me of that old woman in Marino. I grin and take off after him. I don't believe they pay me to do this.

We walk back in the cool of the evening after I redeem myself by paying for both meals, and I listen to Trainer talk about back when in the trucking industry. Back when ya hadda know how ta drive. Didn't have all this automatic damstuff.

Shuffling along the sidewalk, picking the lettuce from our teeth, no hurry, bathing in the Nebraska evening, just fed, a little sleepy and Trainer babbling about weak engines, mountain curves with no guardrail, and sleeping on a board between the seats. Says we got it good these days. I nod my head in silent agreement. I do got it good these days.

Back to the truck, grab my getaway bag, head inside the building for a shower, I get the presidential suite because the others haven't been cleaned yet, back to the truck again and into the bunk. Down for the count; it has been a busy day. And a good one.

Trainer comes in late from his shower, turns on every light in the house, and wakes me. I holler at him for staying out till all hours doing who knows what, then coming in and waking me up, and he says he's sick of coming home to all this bitchin'. I tell him to get his fat ass in the bunk and get the lights off before I have to come down there, and he says be dam glad he's too tired and clean to reach up there and whip my skinny ass all over this condo.

We are learning to live comfortably with one another. It has taken a while, but it's coming along; minor domestic quarrels aside.

Nebraska has, for some atmospheric or refractive reason, the most vivid dawns. The colors are not so much pastel, like the other places, but brilliant colors. I have seen many days begin in many places around the planet, and none are like what I see here. May be all that sunflower and corn pollen in the air. I return from wherever my brain was to my bunk at my usual six in the A.M. and look out my window to watch this day shape up and the clouds scroll through the spectrum while Trainer's apnea grips him below.

I lie here charmed, *encanta*, while the sun rises and blazes the color from the clouds, then open the curtains to wake Trainer.

Muffled snorts. It lives. Beneath me. Like the monster under the bed. I slither to the edge of the bunk to watch. Sorting and huffing through cigarette packs for onesies or twosies. Success. Lighter clicks open. Scratching noises. Flame poofs. Deep rattling inhale. Collapses into hissing first chair. Window hums down. Exhale and wheezing. Productive cough. Trainer's day begins. Grabs at elusive coffee mug. Crusty from yesterday's coffee. Crusty from yesterweek's coffee. Tractor rolls heavily as he gets onto the steps down the side, hacking and gagging. Headed for the coffee bar.

I go through my routine and follow Trainer's trail in to the fuel desk. He is soaking up his second cup when I get there. I load my mug and we head to the counter. He tells the girl at the counter we fueled last night. I look innocent as I can. The girl smiles and waves us away. Leaving with the loot, I say stolen coffee will give you a stomachache. He says he'll risk it to save $45 a month. Now *I'm* going to get a stomachache. Co-conspirator. Since the stomachache is a given, I resolve to enjoy the spoils. Stolen coffee is better than stolen watermelons. Not so messy.

On to Iowa. Fields of opportunities. I become more enamored of Iowa every time I go through it. Iowa is what I picture when someone says the Heartland, or the Midwest. Family farms. Plaid plowed fields. Gentle rolling hills striped with crops. Amber waves of grain. Iowa alone could feed the world. Iowa is where I imagined Dick and Jane lived. Or anyone I read about that lived on a farm. Fields of grainy heads stretching away from the interstate nearly as far as I can see, breezy fingers rustling the goods. Occasionally I see a farmhouse in the middle of an expanse of some grain crop, like an island of humanity in a hilly, rolling sea of agriculture. It does my soul some intangible good to know all this is here. The white limestone rural roads connecting farm to market to neighbor and a pickup zooming along one of those roads leaving a rooster tail of chalky dust drifting over the fields. Given the choice, I think lots of people, in looking back, would opt for an Iowa farm as a childhood development center. These folks live with the seasons and close to the land and the animals that make our lives possible. They have a respect for all those things city dwellers do not have, and may not even know about.

The only problem I see in Iowa is a dearth of nightlife for the GenY'ers. That may be good in the larger scope of things, but if those members of the lost generation live near Walcott, that problem is semi-solved. The metropolis of truck stops is here. It has everything. Barber, dentist, several fast-food outlets, open seating area, second-floor movie theater, laundry, leather store, restaurant, chrome shop, truck repair, and one of the world's great collection of antique toy trucks in a sizable gift shoppe and restaurant. Buffet is good, too.

There are as many locals as drivers inside at any given time, so I have to believe it must rank pretty high on the list of fun things to do after dark around here. Weekend nights the place is really popular with the kids and there is usually a trooper or two walking around to keep a lid on things. Seems pretty tame in the light of day. Mostly drivers here, and they are concerned with getting their business settled and moving on. No trouble from these guys and girls.

The silos, farmsteads, cattle, and cornfields of Iowa stay there and
we settle into the 55 MPH creep across Illinois and into the gradually increasing traffic and more frequent road construction that eventually becomes Chicago. This place hasn't changed a bit in 30 years. I went to a
school here years ago on the north side. Waukegan. Right on the lake. In
your face, cramped, hurried Chicago. We stop on the south side and get
a shower, a meal, and some sleep at a greasy, revamped old truck stop.

This particular truck stop is set right against the freeway and as
such, is busy, crowded, and noisy. Lots of folks trying to get in and get
out, harsh and glaring lights blazing from high above on those stacked
metal poles. Litter blowing everywhere in the constant breeze. Paper,
fountain cups, plastic bottles. Trash, mostly, not rotten garbage.

Dirt dragged in by truck tires and that gritty stuff left from the
snowplows last winter gets blown into little heaps and moves around like
miniature dust storms ankle high, and it mixes with the oil, grease, and
diesel to make a paste that sticks to shoe soles. That paste gets ground
into the cheap tile floor of the building and gives the place a grubby
look. I make my visit inside short; it makes me feel dirty just being in
there. Just the look of it almost negates my shower. We sleep with the
windows closed and the upper a/c on. Don't want that crap in here with
me, or grubbing up my bunk.

Awake in the brown haze of the Chicago dawn. Coffee and logbook.
As we do the logs, I turn on the FM radio, which is something I never
do, preferring the idle of the engine and low fizzing of the CB to the
caffeine-hyped disc jockeys and jockettes that pollute the morning airwaves. It comes on and the scan button lands on a station airing some a
cappella. I stop the graphing on my log and look out the window onto a
trashed cityscape while a choir of angels sings to me. An auditory feast
in a visual famine. Trainer looks up from his work and stares at the
radio. As though he can't believe it would produce such sounds. He
seems pleased somehow, but surprised it doesn't end quickly like a pop
song and cut to a foghorn car commercial. He reminds me of the RCA
dog, Chip, looking at the radio. He says there ain't no music, but that it's

pretty singin' anyway. I smile and agree. It is pretty. I wish I could say the same for the scenery.

It is the morning shift and my wheel watch, so we worm our way out of the trucks, row on row, to the interstate and head for Indiana. Beautiful morning out here, once we roll into the farm country of the upper Midwest and get away from the sprawling Chicagopolis.

Through Indiana and into Ohio. Really nice rest areas built on a rotunda-type architecture that have just about anything a traveler might want or need and spaced at regular intervals along this part of the interstate-become-toll-road. Easy on and easy off. How is it a state can charge a toll on an interstate highway, anyway? How does that happen?

I drive most of the day at Trainer's request, I'm not sure why he requested, but I enjoy driving and am here to learn more about it, so I just drive and enjoy. Trainer seems to be content to ride. All is well.

Into Pennsylvania and onto the turnpike that runs across it side to side. The scenery would be quaint if I had the time or opportunity to look at it. Road construction is here as well. Maybe the turnpike is older than I thought. There is no shoulder on the right and an endless row of orange barrels on the left side of the one lane we have here. Maybe a foot either side to play in. This ride ought to be free, for the inconvenience and danger involved in getting across the state. But it isn't. A bigtruck pays $44 to go across William Penn's namesake land. I was told once he never even came here. That it was just named for him. I don't know if that is true or not, but one thing is certain, I don't feel like I got my money's worth during the trip across it. It is my first experience with outrageous tolls. The piracy begins outside Chicago and continues into the Northeast as far as we are going. By the time we get to New York City and return to about here in Penn's state, we will pay just over $250 in tolls and road use fees. When that number is multiplied by the truck traffic, I don't see road quality on the tollways compared to freeways that would justify the dollars. I wonder where it goes.

Trainer says we'll stay at a place he knows in Breezewood, just off the turnpike. Great cheesesteak, he says. Okay by me; my right leg has begun to bother me at the outside of my thigh, and I want to get out to walk a little anyway. A patch about the two-dimensional size and shape of a football has gone completely numb. The color is okay, and the temperature is no different than the surrounding tissue, so I'm not dreadfully concerned, but it will be seven months before the feeling begins a gradual return, and more than a year and a half before it is completely restored. Never did figure out what caused that.

Exiting the interstate-become-tollway late in the day, there is a more-difficult-than-it-has-to-be means to get across the interstate and into the truck stop. Then once across, there is a curve that becomes a full circle down to the frontage road back to the truck stop, indicated by a warning sign. Another sign warns to do no more than twenty-five miles an hour. That sign also has an icon of a truck tipping over.

Guess what is on its side in the grass alongside the curve.

Nothing is foolproof. Not one single thing is foolproof. Fools are unbelievably ingenious and can easily circumvent almost any safeguard put in place to keep them from doing any damage. One was doing just that right here. Got past several tight turns that should have slowed him down, several warning signs that told him in text to slow down, and a picture representation of what would happen if he didn't.

Kind of amazing when you think about it; every reasonable safeguard in place, and it still happens.

There is no evidence of foul play. No reason I can see for that to have happened. On the bigroad, cars can cut in way too close and the driver may have to go into the bush to prevent a collision. That happens more often than it should. Seventy-mile-an-hour surprises happen out there. Tires blow. Brakes lock. But not here. The driver had to work at this one. The curves alone should have kept his speed down. The orange barrels alone should have kept his speed down. The signs posted regularly were warning enough. General care in a danger zone is called for. This guy missed or disregarded all that.

Troopers in every state have a term for it that has made its way into companyspeak: too fast for conditions. In this case it is a rollover. The truck is on its side and the contents are spilled from a trailer roof ripped away. It is the first of many situations like this I will see, and I will come to resent the foolhardy drivers that do those things. They reflect badly on a craft I want to learn, and the public gauges all drivers by the idiocy of a few.

Rollovers are almost always a termination offense in any trucking company assuming the driver survived. Police reports are reviewed, driver statements are reviewed, and a corporate decision is made. Usually to let the driver go. And it should be that way. Any rollover caused by the agent "too fast for conditions" should be dealt with in that manner. That driver would be dangerous enough in a car, much less hauling a load of hazardous material in a populated area. Some of these trucks are rolling potential environmental catastrophes. Just add a fool.

In some cases it is not only a job-ending, but a career-ending offense, and maybe that is just as well. That kind of person has no business driving a bigtruck. Depending on the circumstances, and whether or not the driver lived, when and if that driver is termed, that information is fed into a database for transportation companies. Those companies search that database regarding potential new hires. If a rollover termination is in there, no front-line trucking company will hire him or her. Too much liability exposure. One megabuck lawsuit and the company goes away. Lots of employees lose their jobs. The risk is too much, even though most companies are screaming for drivers. Few companies will knowingly hire a documented fool.

We get into the parking lot, then the fuel island and head to the restaurant obviously frequented by locals. Trainer was right, the Philly cheesesteak is awesome, even if it is on a hot dog bun. The guy knows his truck stops. Shower and hit the rack. Open the upper windows, the night air feels good, and stretch out to get comfortable in my now familiar bunk.

Excellent night's sleep and in for the morning's coffee. We fill the mugs, and at the kiosk, Trainer goes into his free-coffee spiel about how we fueled last night, which we actually did this time, and the woman behind the counter stares at him expressionless and listens patiently.

Trainer finishes the account and steps back with a smile. The woman says that will be one dollar and eight cents apiece. Trainer looks at her incredulously and I start digging for one dollar and eight cents. I cackle and pay up while Trainer stands shocked and immobile, full mug in hand. I skulk away, smirking as Trainer gouges his pockets.

On the way back to the truck, I sip and enjoy while Trainer grouses about the price of the notfree coffee. I tell him he is ruining his morning coffee. It is a nice walk. He just can't believe it. These Pennsylvania Deutsch don't give away a thing, I tell him. Dam them dutchmans he says, we need to bomb their ass again.

Back onto the turnpike, or what we have left of it, east to Virginia and later into some American history.

It is about time for my morning break and since I drive in the mornings, I get to make those calls. Trainer doesn't like it, but that's the way it is. We stop near a national park and, like most national parks, the countryside is peaceful and quiet. The name of the town nearby is Manassas and we will deliver some plants to a nursery there later this morning. Meanwhile, I get out and stretch a little. Walk around just to get out of the truck. Enjoy the morning. Revel in being alive and take in the surroundings. It is beautiful country now, but the years and flora have hidden what happened in this lovely meadow.

A Civil War battle took place here about 140 years ago called Bull Run by the Union and Manassas by the Confederacy. Looking around, it's hard to believe killing of that magnitude took place in this pastoral setting. But it did. On two separate occasions. Didn't accomplish anything tactical the first time. Had to do it again.

July of 1861, a newly formed and poorly trained Union army of 30,000 men locked horns with a newly formed and poorly trained Confederate army of 22,000 men while a picnicking band of spectators looked on from the hills. No cable network news back then. Five hours later, 2,900 Union soldiers were dead and 2,000 Confederates were killed as well. The Confederate general Thomas Jonathan Jackson earned his nickname "Stonewall" for his stubborn defense of Henry

House Hill, about the only thing between the Union army and the Confederate capital of Richmond, Virginia. That battle changed the face of the conflict between the Union and the Confederacy from a rebellion to an outright war. That war lasted almost five years, cost 600,000 lives, and there are wounds in this part of the country that still have not completely healed. Sons killed fathers and brothers killed one another. That kind of stuff doesn't go away in just a couple of hundred years.

About a year and a month later, a Union army numbering about 35,000, better trained this time, and a Confederate army of 50,000 under Lee and Longstreet with an additional 23,000 serving under Jackson, also better trained, got together again. Same place, and this time they were much better at killing one another. First day nothing was gained, but many were lost. The second day, Longstreet rallied his men and the Confederacy took the field from the retreating Union army. Abraham Lincoln lost 14,500 soldiers and Jefferson Davis lost 9,200 after the body count.

Have a long look at those numbers.

On a late-summer morning, much like this one I am enjoying, maybe, 108,000 men started shooting and stabbing one another not far from where I stand. Two days and 23,700 human lives later, they decided to quit. There was no accurate count of the wounded, only the dead. Simply put, it was a bloodbath. Literally. Carnage is the word that comes to mind, I think, and near biblical proportions. I personally find it difficult to imagine butchery on that level, and as a matter of fact, I can't imagine it. Or, I won't imagine it. Add the 4,900 massacred a year before, and a total of about 29,000 young men lost their lives here, some no more than boys. In this quiet meadow.

I wonder if the picnickers enjoyed the show.

We motor on to Gainesville and into the town of Manassas, where I mail a letter home from the nursery where we drop several hundred plants. We don't actually drop them; "drop" is a term for unloading the truck either partially or totally, or in most cases, leaving the entire trailer itself somewhere. In this case, we have to walk the plants to the end of the trailer, a process known as tailgating, and some nursery workers take them from there. Liability thing. The folks at the nursery are just great and get my letter right out with the morning mail. Finish up the paper-work, which consists of everyone in sight signing the bill, then we close the trailer doors, and head out of town.

Next stop is another nursery in Pennsylvania, about 45 minutes away. I'm not used to the states being so small, so close together, and getting to another one so quickly. The Western states are all big and when the destination is in another state, it usually takes a while to get there. Going to another state around here is like going to another town out west. It's just down the road. Trainer barely has time to make and eat a double-decked sandwich, olives rolling all over the top of the re-frigerator. He doesn't have the touch with condiments, but I think he'll learn. He's used to making a plain old meat-and-bread sandwich, and here he is making huge epicurean strides in the club sandwich depart-ment, having access to all the sandwich garnishes I brought along be-cause I don't care for ordinary sandwiches. A little pizzazz please.

We get to that nursery, and late in the morning it is busy. Crowded lot. Lots of people doing landscaping and gardening projects, I guess. There is no room for the truck, so I park parallel to the building and a few feet away from the roadway. It is a two-laner and not heavily traveled, so I'm okay with that. Trainer doesn't like it for some reason. He says we will move. Where? Over there. Points to a spot about the size of a bath-tub. He will direct me. And he jumps out of the cab, before I have time to register a complaint, motioning me to follow. He wanders the lot ex-pecting me to follow in a tractor-trailer. So, I try to do that, I mean he is a trainer and should know what his own truck can do. Maybe he knows something I don't, and if I follow directions, it will all work out. I shift into second gear and start watching the mirrors and side clearances, overhead wires and shopping baskets full of plants and screaming kids.

There is a utility pole in the middle of the lot and I cannot get where Trainer wants to go because of it. Inching back and forth, within inches of parked luxury cars and high-end carryalls, I inch away and make no real progress.

We are blocking a percentage of the customers trying to come and go. Trainer decides we will cross the road and retry our entry. I see a problem with that in the form of no place to go on the other side of the road. No place to turn around and come back. There is only a ditch and a two-lane road. To do what he wants, we will have to put the truck perpendicular to the road, drive the tractor to the opposite shoulder, double back, and pull the nose of the trailer in an arc across the road and back to the nursery parking lot. There will be a considerable time the trailer will be completely across both lanes as it tries to get back behind the tractor. It will create the scenario necessary for what is called a "rununder."

Trailer sides are much higher than car bumpers, and what would ordinarily be a T-bone-type accident becomes a case of the car going under the side of the trailer rather than hitting it directly. That usually decapitates the car and its occupants. Setting up that rununder scenario is also a termination offense in most any company. There is just no reason to not anticipate the possibility of a rununder. No reason to set one up. No reason to stretch the truck across the roadway. No reason for a U-turn in a bigtruck. None. That's why companies terminate drivers that get caught doing it. It is deadly and unnecessary.

Trainer wants me to set up for a potential rununder. At his command.

I call him over to the window, stick my head out, and remind him of all those things we were taught in driving school. He is adamant. He will stop or direct the traffic on the road and prevent it. Nothing bad will happen, he knows what he is doing. Done it for years. And walks away before I can come up with further objections. Traffic is stacking up in the parking lot behind the truck. People want out. I allow myself to be pressured.

We manage to pull it off, and I still don't know exactly why I went along with it in spite of all we have been taught about right-lane changes, rununders, and rearends. The big three killers; all, generally, caused by the truckdriver.

I drive the truck across the street, into the shallow ditch, break the bottom part of the air dam and the encased fog light in climbing out of the ditch, but get the truck and trailer back across the road before any car comes along. Big relief for me to get that finished, but the relief is short lived once what I have done comes to me.

I jump from the cab, trot to the front of the truck to assess the damage because I heard the crack when the air dam went, walk purposefully to Trainer, just now getting to the front of the truck from his authoritative place in the road, and unload on him. That ranks in the top three stupid things I have done in my life. I semishout at him as I survey the damage, and he says no problem, the maintenance shop can fix the air dam *and* fog light.

I stare at him in disbelief, realize I'm wasting my breath, and go back to the truck, get in, and slam the door to make myself feel better. This door-slamming stuff is better therapy than I would ever have imagined. I see why people do it.

I know now the lengths Trainer will traverse to get a job done. I resolve never to do that again, to never go that far for anyone or anything or any job. I will never knowingly endanger anyone. I'll take the parking ticket, the abuse, the termination. But I will never purposefully endanger an innocent again. I give myself my word, and I can count the promises I've made in 50 years on one hand up to the beginning of this phase of my life. I'll add that one to the growing list of promises I am making to myself regarding truckdriving. This bracket of promises alone may take two hands.

Shaped up, now, to back in and unload this stop's portion of the load, we make our drop, several hundred plants, buckle up, and head for Maryland. Trainer says we will stay just outside Washington, D.C. in a truck stop so big it has a hotel.

Traffic around D.C. is bad but not like LA, Chicago, or Houston. Someone seems to have thought it out and planned ahead a little, and we make our way in that traffic to the truck stop so big it has a hotel.

We get there about the same time every other truckdriver in that part of the world gets there, but going into a lot looking for a parking place has become a regular thing for me. It is just a part of my day. It is a part I could certainly do without, but a part of the day nonetheless. And we find a space some distance from the hotel, about halfway to the end of this side of the lot. Trainer says he doesn't want to walk that far for a shower. It isn't the distance I think, but the effort, and I say no way you are going without a bath; unloading trucks is stinky work.

Trainer has demonstrated another idiosyncrasy lately. He waits until I am finished with whatever I am saying and repeats the last two or three words I said. As if he should comment on the subject, but is too lazy to think of a reply and just echoes the last few words. It annoys me at first, but becomes predictable later, so I have learned to insert selected phrases in the last parts of my sentences for different effects, like "get a shower." So, sure enough, he repeats that phrase, then looks at me scowling. I think he is catching on after his expression changes when he says "stinky work."

After browbeating Trainer into a shower, I announce we may as well eat while we are out, and I saw a sub sandwich shop on the other side of the hotel lobby as we drove in. I lead him around to it, which isn't hard at all, if food is involved.

Before we left Texas, I stocked up on some one-pound bags of different kinds of trail mix and munchy health food like that, and it has been pretty good this far, but a steady diet of nuts and berries doesn't do it for a couple of Southern boys raised on fried food. I need a greasy meat sandwich, and Trainer is having a Pavlovian response to the aromatic cooked meat as we round the corner.

The sandwich shop has really good sandwiches, but no place to sit. Acres of truck parking, a multistory hotel, and no place to sit in the sandwich shop. Must have been designed by an appointed congressional committee, after a factfinding mission.

We get our chips, sandwiches, and soda, go outside, sit on the curb, "kicked onto the curb again" Trainer says, and greet the passersby, sandwiches in hand. We are probably good for business, waving these subs in the faces of hungry drivers trying to decide what to eat at the day's end. It isn't so bad but for the heat, the flies, and the blowing dust.

Billions and billions of truck tires drag tons and tons of road grit into the lot and a couple of tons are in the air around us looking for a sandwich to land on, or an eye to get into. Trainer says he doesn't know what good these flies are, but the cinders are a good fiber source. I just look around and hope I get more of my sandwich than the flies and no really big chunks of grit crack a molar.

Fed, showered and back at the truck, the latecomers are looking to park. I see considerable entertainment value going to waste, so I crank up the CB radio. Those of us already parked have a ringside seat for the abuse being heaped onto unlucky, or unskilled, drivers holding up traffic as they set up the second and third time to back into a tight spot. Tight spots are all that are left this time of evening.

Many of the older metro areas have some structures left from the days gone by when no one foresaw trailers nearly 14 feet high and 53 feet long. Bridges, viaducts, tunnels, and the like. Many of the terminals, docks, and trucklots are expansions of those old facilities that could only expand so far, limited by the available land or existing structural components. But, as the trucks' engine strength grew and the corresponding load-carrying ability grew, the size of the truck grew as well. The facilities and the infrastructure didn't. Over the years, additional layers of asphalt several inches thick have reduced the clearance beneath many of the overpasses and train bridges. All those things combined make for some pretty tight situations sometimes in the older parts of some of these Northeastern cities.

This lot was partitioned for 48-foot trailers, which were thought to be the end of trailer evolution back when, so jockeying a 53-footer in and out with a road tractor, which is 10 to 15 feet longer than a single-drive axle daycab with no sleeper, is no walk in the park. Any given driver in here is positioning a rig 20 to 30 feet longer than the neighborhood was planned to handle.

In the interest of fraternal love, one driver is always trying to help another via the CB. The helper is already parked, or waiting to get there, and is coaching the backing driver on the dos and don'ts. The helper is not responsible for any damages the backer does. The backer is responsible, so it's an iffy situation at best, and the wise backer turns his CB off or way down to minimize the advice. The radio does nothing more than cloud the backing driver's judgment and efforts.

One driver just across from us is having a tough time of it, and I hope his radio is off. The CB hyenas are on him like a straggler. Some of the comments are comical. Some, from tired drivers waiting for their turn to park, are not. Generally, most of it is good for a laugh at someone else's expense, and I tell Trainer as much, drawing the parallel to a boat ramp on any Sunday afternoon. I've seen marriages dissolve and best friends part at boat ramps. I am thinking all we need is a hot dog and a beer to make this entertainment package complete.

The radio settles down after half an hour more parking lot antics, and the whores and hawkers and Christians retake the airwaves. Trainer climbs into his bunk to watch a movie, and I comfy up in the second chair with my kidnapped copy of *Timeline* to see what the professor is doing in the castle of the bad guy.

Trainer begins to snore and choke after a while, which is my signal to turn off the telly, and I relax once again in the air-conditioned idle of the Cummins, feeling the tiredness now that unloading half a trailer of plants brings on. Like the Sandman has a gun at my head, as an old friend of mine said once. I mark my place in the book and trot off to the bunk. We will assault New York City tomorrow, I want to be ready, and it feels good to lie down. I'm a little stiff already. Must have used some muscles that didn't want to work. It can't be that I'm getting older. There may be some aspirin in one of these bags here.

A great rustle of bedclothes beneath me, I startle awake, and Trainer leaps from his bunk. He grabs the trash can, contents and all, and flies out the driver's door. My watch shows 5:45 A.M. A little early, but near enough my waking hour. I roll over to snooze a few minutes. Much jostling as Trainer climbs onto the catwalk between tractor and trailer to relieve himself. I can hear it above the idle of the engine. Sounds bad. Pressurized noises. Groaning.

The driver's door whips open, cab lights come on, and climbing in, Trainer hollers dam them submarine sandwiches. Throws the trash can down on the floor minus the shopping bag liner full of trash. I wonder what became of it. Wrapped in my sheet like a Bedouin, I watch from the safety of my bunk as Trainer begins his cigarette search.

He thrashes around below me, grunting and snorting and rooting. Gets into his shorts, knee-high socks, and tank top, tripping and stumbling. Tractor rocking. Rummaging cigarette packs for a stray, huffing and panting, the creamy aroma of unburned tobacco filling the sleeper as he digs around and stirs up the scent from the opened packages, crushing them in frustration when he finds them empty. It occurs to me there is no toilet paper out there on the catwalk.

Trainer finds a loose cigarette and gets into action. He's out the door and zeroing in on the coffee bar in the hotel. Barely daylight.

I catch up to him in the first floor of the hotel, essentially a cavernous convenience store, with burglar bars all around the glassed exterior walls. The bars look way out of place on a hotel first floor. Get my coffee and a really strange fellow takes my money at the register, more strange than usual. I've heard it said we are all someone else's weirdo, and I guess that's true. This guy is mine. The situation is one that would have to be seen and heard to be believed, but it was an unusual encounter for me, and I've seen some pretty unusual stuff. No reason to go into it here, but if someone told me he was an extraterrestrial, I'd believe it. Anyway, I leave with my coffee and trot down the short stairway to the parking lot and am confronted by a clean-cut fellow who asks do I need any help. It takes me a second to understand what he means, though he has a handful of plastic baggies, it being early for my brain, and answer as much by surprise as intent when I say no. He turns and walks away into the rows of idling trucks. Our nation's capital. The only place I have ever been offered drugs vis-à-vis in my trucking life.

Hurrying back to the truck. Where is Trainer? He shows up shortly saying he had to go to the men's room for something. Probably to get the dingleberries off him. Says he wants me to drive into the City, that

I need the experience. He will drive to the next drop, and I will take it from there. Fine . . . I'll just drink this coffee and ride.

The next drop is in a corner of Pennsylvania that is as close to what I believe colonial America must have been like as anything I have seen in book or fact. I'd have to recommend a ride on US 202 through that area, especially in its autumn colors, and I wouldn't be surprised to see some guy in a three-cornered hat in one of those fields or stepping out the doorway of any one of the houses along that route. If it weren't for the cars parked here and there, a mistake could be made by an unwary time-traveler. Could wind up split as well, I think. I also think I'm reading entirely too much *Timeline*, or it is staying with me too long. Or both.

We made our drop at a wholesaler, and were put a little off our schedule by some really nice folks there. Got the tour, lessons in how to grow plants, coffee, breakfast sweets, and group conversation. Some stops are an above-average pleasure, and this one is. I almost hate to leave. But I'm wanting to see the City, so we bid our la vistas and head out, lighter by several tons of California plants and dirt.

On the Verrazano Bridge from Staten Island, I can see where Henry Hudson sailed into the history books, and the New York City skyline. I don't know what to think about the whole of it. It is more dense than I thought, but not as expansive. The buildings are so tall as to not be believed, even from this distance, but they had to go up since they couldn't go out. The view, I decide, is depreciated by distance. It is a long way across to Manhattan from where we are about to pay $36 and some change for the privilege of crossing this bridge. I wonder if the word "toll" is a contraction of "troll." I wonder if the trolls evolved into tollbooth operators. They both charge for a crossing, I think. There may be some twisted logic there, but it wouldn't take Darwin by surprise, I'll wager.

I am most taken by the World Trade Center towers. They stand head and shoulders above the rest of the beautiful buildings, both in size and appearance. Like twin mirrors, they glint in the late-morning sun. I can't look as long as I'd like, the lanes are narrow on the bridge, matter of fact, it is named the Narrows Bridge, but not for that reason, and the far-right lane we are in has a really low guardrail, plus we sit pretty high up already inside the cab. It's a long way to the water, and Trainer notes that. I tell him not to worry, unless he crosses the Mob or the Tong while we are in town, he won't have to sleep with the fishes. Says it's a damgood thing, that he can't swim very good and he ain't sleepy anyway.

Coming off the bridge, I notice we are the only bigtruck in sight going our way. I comment on that to Trainer, and follow up with a wonder whether or not we are supposed to be here just as I see an orange warning sign telling trucks over 12 feet and some inches high to get off at the next exit. The ceiling is a little low under here, and I decide that is good advice, so I exit the freeway and figure there will be signs to guide us through the detour. I routed this trip yesterday and the atlas did not show low clearances hereabouts, but I am not in the practice of ignoring posted warnings and don't want to find out the hard way why bigtrucks can't go farther. Our trailer, like most trailers, is 13 feet 6 inches tall from pavement to rooftop. Some older, long-established cities have lots of structures built to accommodate trucks and loads common in their day, which is considerably shorter heightwise than what we have, and we just talked a little about that. The atlas notes these structures, and we know not to go that way. Many trucks get what is called "topped" by these bridges, underpasses, and railroad trestles built back in the days. Trucking companies don't like it when the top of a $38,000 refrigerated trailer is sheared away, so we don't want to do that. It would not be nearly as easy to explain as the broken air dam.

No worries, mate. We'll figure it out. Trainer has a catatonic omygod expression and stares out the windshield as we exit the freeway and, like Alice down the rabbit hole, roll through a dark burrow, into the light, and onto Atlantic Avenue into downtown Brooklyn.

Jammed-up vertical housing, open windows with curtains fluttering and fans pumping in cooler air, patchwork neighborhoods, street vendors, little boys selling bottled water from a trash can full of ice for their mom, crowded, narrow, busy streets, shopkeepers sweeping and people visiting among the crates and racks of goods beneath the awnings over the sidewalk on this avenue. This isn't just a city street, people live here. It is self-sufficient. They buy and sell to and from one another, then go home upstairs or around the corner.

A beautiful black girl, hair pulled behind her, in a vivid sundress and high-heeled rope sandals talking to a friend in the shade of an awning over the sidewalk. Brilliant smile and easy manner as she listens. She could have just stepped off the cover of *Cosmo*, or landed at JFK on the last flight from the islands. If this is it, Brooklyn is everything I ever heard it was, and I am absolutely fascinated by it all.

I don't think many bigtrucks get this deep into the 'hood, judging from the looks and thumbs-up we are getting, and the number of tree branches scraping the sides of the tractor and trailer. Usually, if the truck traffic is common, there is a tunnel sculpted into the branches by the thousands of abrasions the trees suffer at the tops and sides of passing trucks. We don't have that here, and the lanes are very narrow. Pedestrians everywhere. Gotta watch for them. Kids especially, bikes and homemade skateboards zipping around and through the slow moving traffic on the pavement.

Trainer is getting more concerned by the minute as we go deeper into uncharted territory. There have been no detour signs. We need to be on the loop around Long Island, he says. I agree. I am *encanta* by this ride through a neighborhood I've heard about all my life, but I know it stops somewhere down the road and I don't want to have to back all the way out. So now *I'm* concerned. Trainer says he doesn't know where we are and decides to hop out and flag down a police car on a corner. And he does that, while I hold up traffic at the intersection, parked in the middle of it, set up to turn right if I have to.

The officers in the police car don't even look at him as he taps on the driver's window. They just look straight ahead and pull away at the first opportunity traffic affords them. Trainer stands in the street looking at me like I can fix it. He runs back and says he will go to the market right over there and find out how to get to the freeway from here and for me to stay with the truck. And he's off.

I have to move the truck, it is blocking a lane of traffic, so I inch around the corner and pull beside the curb, but I can't stay here either, and move around the next corner to the right. Trainer will not be successful and I somehow know that, so I break out the atlas and look up Brooklyn. I see we are currently on 101st Street looking west. It goes straight to the Van Wyck Expressway that goes to the loop. Looking down the street several blocks, I see the expressway a level above the street we are on now. I put the atlas away, relieved the solution is so simple. Get up and rifle the refrigerator for a soda while Trainer is socializing. Frank Sinatra was right about New York, New York. Cool little old guy in a touring cap sitting on a park bench right over there, totally unconcerned with the city going on around him. Must have lived here all his life.

Trainer returns, climbs in, and says we are screwed and we'll never get out alive and he ain't never comin' back to this damtown. The damforeigner in the damstore don't even know how to get the hell out of here. Probly don't even damlive here. I let him vent as I sip a soda and munch some stale tortilla chips. Like a broken man, doomed, he sits slumped on the edge of the second seat, head down. I watch him and sip. He knows I'm watching. I let him soak a minute for effect.

Then, all cheery, I put away the chips, flip the soda can into the trash, and say no sweat, we're outta here. He looks over at me like I just changed color. I outline the plan and he looks nonplussed. I recall the atlas to him, and say it has an inset of the boroughs of New York. He brightens, says yeah, lemme see that, and yeah, . . . hey, let's do it.

I get so sick and tired of being right about every little thing.

We ease onto the expressway we drove beneath half an hour ago, not knowing what it was, and shortly we are on the loop headed for Farmingdale. Trainer is as relieved as anyone I have ever seen for any reason. He beams as we negotiate what has become the afternoon traffic on Long Island. I grin and watch carefully for the road construction and

Mercedes. He high-fives me and says we just did New York City. I'm thinking New York City nearly just did us.

The traffic here has a different tone. It isn't like the traffic in other very heavily congested cities. While none are as bad as Houston where many drivers are just plain rude and reckless, maybe it's the heat there, most cities with a traffic problem just kind of live with it. Traffic mopes along and everyone eventually gets where they intended to go. Not New York. These people seem to love traffic. Radios blasting, smoking cigarettes, hollering at one another, letting cars into tight lines, sipping their bottled water. It is almost a pleasure to be here in this laneswide miles-long trafficinchworm.

Way down, or way up, whichever, the Island we get off the interstate and head south to our drop, and we get there just about the time the place is closing. It is a home repair chain store not far from the Hamptons. Walking in, I am thinking what in the hell is a place like this doing in a place like this? None of the people that live around here would know what to do with a hammer. We find the manager, identify ourselves, and he says his unloader guys have just gone home, or left here anyway, but we are welcome to pull around back and park for the night, and there is a restaurant not far down the street. Pretty good one I way overstep my authority and say we'll take it. Trainer looks down his nose at me for having stolen his thunder, but says nothing. I take over the conversation and say it saves us the trouble of looking for a truck stop. Manager says the crew will be back at daylight and they'll get us unloaded. I say that's okay, we'll be fine right here. This manager doesn't know I'm a trainee, and probably wouldn't care if he did. Trainer stands silent. Stripped of authority. I am proud of myself. He looks better, all that responsibility off him.

Walking back to the truck, Trainer says it is good that we can stay here, but company policy is to be locked into a safe compound or be out of the city before midnight. Fine, then let's go back to New Jersey to a truck stop and get back here by daylight. He just looks at me. I tell him there is a difference in the letter of the law and the spirit of the law. The spirit of the law in this case, is to make as certain as possible the truck and the load are safe. There is no reason to believe the load is in danger butted up to the wall here behind this retail outlet, and we are certainly far enough from the heart of the city to not be concerned about roving bands of truckstealers. He looks around and agrees. Says in this neighborhood ain't nobody needs to steal nothing. Either that, or they already stole a bunch of it and that's how they can afford these houses and cars. Maserati leaving the parking lot with a couple of two-by-fours sticking out the window. Carpentry must pay pretty well around here.

We climb in and I move Big Blue around and behind the place, back as close to the wall as I can so the trailer doors can't be opened, set the brakes, and let the engine idle for the a/c. I forget about the quailcall pinging the server every hour snitching on our whereabouts in GPS coordinates. So does Trainer, but we get away clean. No one ever said anything about it to either of us. They understand the same thing I told Trainer. Those satellite location systems are accurate to within two or three feet, so HQ knew exactly where we were all night, tucked in, safe behind a shopping mall, about a mile from real estate that sells by the square inch. They know no one from these parts will mess with this rig tonight.

We sit on a huge concrete pad at the loading dock looking across the expanse perimetered by a really tall chain-link fence that has that angled arm on the top of the poles that supports the barbed wire. Bobwire in Oklahoma. Bobwar in Texas. The airfield is just the other side of that fence. I say I hope 747s don't land here all night. Trainer says he didn't see no restaurant around here neither.

I look at Trainer. Trainer looks at me. We are not at a truck stop, and neither of us is sure what to do next. Trainer says he's hungry. I say I'm thinking ham and cheese with some dill relish, chips'n'hotsauce with a soda. Maybe a candy bar later. Trainer says candy bar. He stands up and says no deal on the sandwich, we are going to get at least one hot meal a day, and bails out the door. I follow, prepared to walk the distance to whatever fast-food outlet he remembers from miles back, only to see him open the side locker door, and start jerking stuff out the little hole and piling it on the ground. This guy can get more material into a given space than just about anyone I've seen. I don't believe all that junk is coming out that little door on the side of the tractor. Reminds me of all those clowns that pile out of the little car at the circus. Seems to be no end to it.

He whips out a nylon bag and snatches a gas grill out of the bag like a rabbit out of a top hat. Ready to go. Two chairs out of bags, and a table as well. It even has a wooden top. In 30 seconds he has a backyard barbecue set up. All we need is the food. He says what's fer dinner? That has to be my cue to rustle up some grub, so I climb back in and raid the refrigerator and pantry in the tractor to return with a can of refried beans, half a bag of tortillas, a can of tamales, a bag of leftover hot dogs, leftover chili and some salsa, our last bag of tortilla chips, and some peanut butter for dessert.

Trainer is no loser in the culinary arts department, and we soon have a scrapped-together meal, hot off the grill. Kicked back in the lawn chairs chasing the last of the hot refries and salsa around the plastic plate with the last of a hot tortilla, watching a couple of small planes do touch-and-go in the late Long Island afternoon, I feel nothing but sympathy for the Long Island elite, choking down caviar and pâté in their air-conditioned castles, or anyone else that hasn't done this.

We sit and watch the pilots practice and rehash the day's events and giggle like a couple of schoolgirls over our trip through Brooklyn and the things we did and saw there. Trainer recounts the guy in the convenience store who didn't know where he was, and the old man sitting on the bench under a tree. Said the old man looked like he'd never left New York. Like he had lived his whole life here in this town. Must be sad, he says. To have never gone anywhere. And he is quiet for a moment in the quiet of the early evening. He waxes philosophical and says we are drifters. Never home, never knowin' anybody for more'n a few minutes and all the time movin' one place to the next. Grabbin' what we can when we can. Always leavin' the ones we love behind. And he slips away for a while. He misses his mate and his grandkids and his home. I let

him stay till he's ready to come back, knowing he needs the space. He
will be away a while.

Looking into the pale blue twilight, I think how he is right from
where he stands, but everything is attitude and perspective for me, and
I don't see this thing that way. But then, I haven't been an over-the-road
truckdriver for 20 years. I can see how that much time away can make a
man feel the things he feels, now that I am in it.

He shifts in his chair, and I see Trainer has come back to himself,
and doesn't know what to say, fearful he may have left himself vulnerable, again, somehow. It heartens me to know he is comfortable enough
with me to share these insights, even if some of them are only thinking
out loud, and I don't want to shake that fragile trust. Our lives depend
on one another when the truck is rolling. The quality of our relationship
depends on how we accept or reject what the other says and does. We
live and work with one another. We are together almost every minute of
every day. I weigh my words carefully.

I recall more of the day's events for him, the way the New York City
skyline looked from the bridge, the Italian beauty in the white skirt
standing on the esplanade, the relief in getting onto the expressway and
the kids dancing on the sidewalk and the guy juggling the oranges on
the corner of the Brooklyn street. I recall to him the trip across the
country and what we saw and how I pissed him off at the rest stop with
the tree in the rock. I note the terrific meal he just whipped out with
leftovers, and how good it feels to climb into that bunk every night,
clean and fed and tired. How we don't know what will happen tomorrow, or where we will be, and how we don't go to the same office with
the same politics and the same disgruntled people and race the same
route home in the same traffic to flop down in the same chair to watch
the same news every night after night.

We live like kings. We wake up in a different part of the country
every morning. We eat the best food we can find along the way. We roll
down the road in the most expensive vehicle we will see all day. We don't
have to get involved in anyone's troubled life. We don't have to take

sides with any issue. We don't have some jerkboss breathing down our necks making our days long and uncertain. We don't have to look busy. We see more of America in one week than most people see in a lifetime. Spacious skies, amber waves of grain, purple mountains' snowcapped majesty, storms rolling across the fruited plains, cities and places from history. This is no book or tall tale or documentary for us; it is alive. We really have been there. We really have seen that. We don't just live like kings, man, we live like gods. We fly 10 feet off the ground in air-conditioned, air-ride comfort from coast to coast and up and down, eating and drinking sitting in $400 chairs and looking out our office windows watching America go by and feeling sorry for the locals, trapped in their empty lives. And we are paid well enough for the privilege.

I stop to breathe, and what I've said hangs in the air.

He looks at me askance and bursts into a gale of bellowing laughter, squinting that one eye, yelling dammitboy, yer right, an' I never heard it put like that.

They must have heard him at the airport. Success. I smile and wait for the calm behind the bellowing. Trainer is back. I smile and think on how true it is that words are either tools or weapons, depending on how they are used, and by whom.

We sit back in silence past that and take in the last of the daylight, comfortable now, mentally and physically, Trainer adding to the pollution with a cigarette. He sits back in his chair, that oddly is unbowed by his mass, takes deep drags, and blows the smoke far into the sky as he leans back to do so. I watch the little vortices appear and dissipate, tiny smokespirits off to some greater calling, in the bluegray veil rising into the darkening sky.

Trainer announces we'd better clean this stuff up before it gets too dark, totally unaware of the lights popping on around us. More of those orange sodium vapor lights. Bright and glaring. Harsh and unfriendly.

I wash the dishes in a pot of water heated on the grill and Trainer puts the gear away. I am still taken by how it all fits in those little bags. He is just putting the food away and notices the peanut butter. He says we need a break from all this housework and can you put peanut butter on a tortilla? I heat up some water for instant decaf while he smears chunky peanut butter onto a couple of hot tortillas with a little pancake syrup and butter from those tiny plastic containers we stole at a restaurant. Dessert, Long Island style. He looks at me with a mouthful, glances away, and starts to sip his coffee. He knows I'm right. He's just a little homesick. He grins and munches. I know he is worried about his wife, and I would help that if I could. But, my best tack is to let him work it out for himself, and to do no more than listen if I am called upon to do so.

I heat up a couple of gallons of water on the last of the little gas cylinder that fires the grill so we can have a shower later, and hope no one comes along with the bright lights on when I do that on the catwalk between the tractor and trailer. The same catwalk Trainer used earlier. I'd better check it for detritus before dark.

Gear stowed, dishes washed, showered and fed, we make a short evening at home of it and soon we are off to bed. I swear this bunk feels better every night. Or maybe it is that all this adventuring around in New York makes me tired.

The unloader guys show up in the morning just about the time I am ready for coffee and want to start unloading the truck, and I say go with it. We get started and begin to remove the cheap lumber bracing called cheap lumber bracing when it is in place and dunnage when it has dun that job. Most any load that is not shrinkwrapped onto pallets is prevented from shifting too much with bracing that becomes dunnage at some point. Someone has to do something with the dunnage because it gets in the way of the unloading. The contracts and bills of lading usually state whom, and in this case, it is the receiver. That's them.

The supervisor overseeing the unloaders says just pile it up neatly over there and he will have someone take care of it later. So as we tailgate the plants, we do that. As the unloader guys take the plants from us at the tail of the trailer and take them inside, we put the dunnage out and stack it over there. Neat pile just like he said.

Supervisor's supervisor shows up to inspect the progress and says something to supervisor about the dunnage and how she doesn't want the stuff and we need to load that back up and take it with us. I hear it.

Supervisor motions for me to come to him so I bail out the back of the trailer and we meet halfway. He says he can't let us leave the dunnage.

I tell him you said we not only could leave the dunnage, but how and where. Supervisor says he never said that. Yes, you did. I tell him he has no choice, that the bill of lading states the receiver gets the dunnage along with the goods, and I say it loudly enough supervisor's supervisor can hear it, since she is the source of the problem. Be happy to show you a copy of it. Supervisor is recalled by Ms. Supervisor for further consultation. A power struggle. And I was just bragging to Trainer yesterday how we don't have to mess with this stuff. My having had to deal with such crap in a past life tells me they will come up with something piddly to save face, since they know I'm right and a lot of subordinates are watching.

Supervisor comes back, head down, with his supervisor stepping a little closer to hear what happens.

Supervisor says we can leave the dunnage if we break it down to fit into a wheelbarrow. Trainer jumps into the discussion and says we'll do that, no problem. Supervisor backs away from my glare to collect Ms. Supervisor and disappear into the cement block building. Then, I glare at Trainer for a second just to register my irritation. I don't want to glare too long, it is early and he might not be in a good mood. Like I said before, we know not to jack with one another early in the day.

I take the bills into the building for some signatures when we are done and bump into Supervisor and Ms. Supervisor. I figure they'll do, and present the bills. Supervisor says he is sorry about the misunderstanding. I stand silently as the signatures are put onto the bills. Don't want to upset them before I get the bills signed.

Signed bills in hand, I look straight at him and say there was no misunderstanding; you just flat-out lied to save your ass from your autocrat boss, and I'm sorry you have to make your living like that. I'll bet your wife and kids would be really proud of you.

They both look at me in shock, and I turn to walk away. I feel better now, having the last word in.

We close up the trailer and climb into the tractor, the last of the load delivered. Trainer looks at me and asks what happened in there and I say nothing. He looks at me and grins.

I send in some messages on the quailcall telling them we have finished and are empty and waiting for a load. We sit and drink the morning's coffee, speculating on where we will go from here. We have no idea what the dispatcher will come up with since our situation is a little different than either a solo driver or a regular team. The loads are assigned based on several criteria, and ranking among them is delivery date. Trainer says we will probably do coast-to-coast runs because we are a team, and we are into our second week now, so I can do more driving, especially at night. That puts us in a different category than we were in a couple of days ago. My responsibilities are increased by the week in the training process. We will be pushed kinda like a team now, since we can run more miles per day.

A good team of veterans can run the truck 20 hours a day legally. They drive in shifts of five hours on and five hours sleeper time. With good weather and roads, a regular team can move the load 1,000 or 1,200 miles a day. Maine to California in three days. They get a good meal, shower, climb back in, and do it again. Oregon to Florida in three days. Not just once or twice, but day after day.

There is a whole process involved in driving as a team. One sleeps while the other drives. One wakes up and starts driving way down the road from where he or she stopped. There is no continuity to the trip for either driver. Unlike a solo driver who has a regular workday, drive 10 hours and stop for the night, team drivers don't do that. All they do is push the truck. Day and night. Weekends and workdays. Summer and winter. They eat when they can, they shower when they can, and they fuel when they have to. They sleep and drive, and that's about all. But they make a lot of money for a blue-collar worker.

Sure enough, and soon enough, barely finished with the first cup of coffee, we get a note on the keyboard telling us to repower a team load going to California. We are to meet the team in Pennsylvania and take the load they have on to its destination, and we will leave the empty we have with them. Simply trade trailers.

Now, we have to deadhead, pull an empty trailer, to Pennsylvania. Not good and not safe, but no choice. Trainer says he will drive out of town, even though it is the morning shift when I usually drive. I'm cool with that. Gives me time to look at the city and see what I may have missed yesterday.

Back onto the interstate loop and head toward the City. Slow going in the traffic, but again, no one seems to mind. Slow but steady, and soon we ride the elevated freeway above Queens and I look into the open windows and down the streets of another part of New York I've heard about all my life. Everything I ever heard about New York is true. It is a carnival and a wedding and a funeral. There is no other city in the world like it. New York City is alive. Not just the people or the everywhere activity, the city itself has an aura. It is a jillion pieces of humanity and concrete and steel and glass of every color and shape and texture crafted into a magnificent, one-of-a-kind mosaic mural built, and being built, one piece at a time, one second at a time, for the past 500 years. The boroughs have a personality. They are graffitied and lived in. They are homes and neighborhood proprietorships. The spectacular skyscrapers in Manhattan stand with some kind of pride, and project an authority in doing the business of the world. This is no nine-to-five operation, no boom-or-bust oil or mining town. There is a permanence radiating from the City. This place has been here and will be here. There is no city that can realistically compare itself to New York. Matter of fact, no one says New York City. Just say "New York," and everyone on the planet knows the reference is New York City. It is easy to see why people never leave, and don't want to, and I don't even care for city life.

Around the west end of Long Island is the biggest cemetery I have ever seen. We drive past it for miles. There is no telling how many people are buried here. Tombstones, that would qualify as monuments anywhere else, sit in silent memoriam to lives by the tens of thousands. The New

Yorkers that built the place are here. I try to show what mental respect I can as we pass by. John Donne was right. We each really are a part of the main, and the bell really does toll for thee.

We take the bottom level of the expressway to the Verazzano Bridge, and it occurs to me that the other side is the road we were on when I exited in a panic over the low-clearance sign. I have seen bigtrucks going the other way just now past the Atlantic Avenue exit. We seem to be doing okay on this side of the Jersey barriers, although there are regular low-clearance signs just above the hammer lane cautioning bigtrucks about the trestles supporting the upper deck of the expressway. We stay in the granny lane, and the clearance here is fine.

We roll right onto the bridge and pay our thirty-plus-dollar toll to go onto Staten Island, and I savor my last view today of the Manhattan skyline. It is a clarion August morning in the year of our Lord 2001, and the City shines in the early light across the river. I am deeply impressed with all of it as I look backward on it from my window. I will get back to New York, but the skyline will be different, and the cemetery will have more monuments.

Onto Staten Island, and we stop in New Jersey, where I take the wheel, then to Pennsylvania and the turnpike. We are headed for our meeting with the ice cream going to California. We will meet the other team, I'm thinking, at a truck stop designated by HQ and trade trailers, visit a while, like company brothers do, and go our separate ways. Sort of finding a friend you don't know out here. Trainer will get to add to his address book.

Midmorning, we arrive at the appointed place and sure enough, there is the other company truck, already disconnected, the tractor sitting just in front of the trailer. Waiting on us. I find a space in this tiny, cramped lot and back in after a couple of circles around the fuel pumps while I wait for another rig to get out and make a hole for us. Set the brakes and kick back. Trainer hops out ready to assume the role of spokesman, and heads to the other truck, idling and no one visible in the cab. No problem, it isn't uncommon to have to wake them from the sleeper. A wise driver sleeps all he or she can. Especially team drivers. They don't sit still long, and they don't waste a minute of downtime fooling around in a truck stop hitting on the waitresses or playing video games if they are serious moneymakers.

Trainer hikes over and beats on the door. No answer. He turns, looks at me, and shrugs, sets out for the inside of the building. I get out and begin the process of unhooking. It takes a few minutes. It is a process, like many other things, and takes time, so I may as well not waste much by sitting here doing nothing. Besides, I am here to learn, and this is a good opportunity to do something all by myself.

Trainer emerges from the building with a company brother and they talk, heads down as if something is wrong. I wonder where the other driver is. Probably grabbing something to eat. Maybe getting a shower. Unhooked, I climb back in, pull forward a couple of feet to get from beneath the trailer apron, set the tractor brakes, and wait for Trainer to rejoin me.

An early-season cool front is creating a line of thunderstorms in the distance, and the rumble of the thunder through the valleys tells me we need to get this swap done and they need to get back into the shelter of the trucks. They are still talking. If all goes according to plan, the re-power is seamless. We both unhook, trade places, and rehook simultaneously. No wasted space or time. But something is wrong here. Not with the process, but with the people. I can't hear what is going down, but there is no gesturing and laughter and animated posturing going on between the two of them, like there would be ordinarily when company men get together. Backslapping and bonding and what.

A woman walks out to stand by the one man, and I somehow know she is the other driver. She says nothing and stands close. She looks tired. More than tired.

Trainer solemnly acknowledges her presence, says a few more words to the man, ambles back to the truck, and climbs in. Sits silently and looks out the windshield at the pair walking to their truck. The a/c blows, the engine idles, and we got James Taylor on the stereo. Otherwise, it is quiet in the cab. I know I don't want to know. Wordlessly, we wait.

When the other team pulls away from their trailer, Trainer says softly, let's hook up. I shift into second gear and idle in that direction. I've not heard that tone from him before now.

I set up and back under the trailer apron as soon as the other tractor has cleared the space. Back in, bump the kingpin, and go through the hookup procedure by the book. Trainer helps halfheartedly. There must be some parallel between the other team's situation and his own. Maybe not exactly, but there is more than empathy here. Maybe it's a wife thing.

Hooked up and rolling, having bid the other team farewell, we set out on the now-rainy turnpike for another 45 MPH and $44 ride through a one-lane construction zone to the west end of Pennsylvania. This ought to be free.

A long ride in silence and Trainer has squared things away enough to talk about it, out of the blue like he does. He says they are a husband-and-wife team. Young and just starting out. Just kinda getting where they want to be. Few dollars ahead, maybe buy a house. She returned a call to her doctor's office yesterday morning and a clerk blurted out she needs to come in, that she has breast cancer. Real bad breast cancer. And he is silent again, looking out his rain-streaked window. The wet miles go beneath us, the tires hiss and splash. A steady rain pelts the windshield, and the wipers metronome the seconds of the afternoon away. We don't speak. The highway sounds are the only sounds. The weather doesn't help the gloom, the day seems long, and has for a while. There is a heaviness with us difficult to describe.

I feel bad for the woman. I feel bad for her husband. I feel bad for Trainer somehow. I feel bad for all of us associated with this. Donne was right some more. No woman is an island either.

It has been a quiet, slow, wet, depressing, and expensive tour of Pennsylvania as we pay our toll to the trolls and motor into a drier Ohio and settle into the 55 MPH speed limit the buckle of the rust belt has for bigtrucks. Between the construction zones, low speed limits, and weather, we are nowhere near our target 750 miles per day. It is slow going, but we roll steadily, and what miles we do make go by soon enough, I guess. I look forward to stopping tonight, and getting this day behind us. Mentally, it has been a bad one.

The bill we picked up with the load of ice cream from the husband-and-wife team says we have to stop and check the temperature of the trailer's interior twice a day. It is to be maintained at minus 20 degrees. We actually check it several times a day, each time we stop for whatever. I open the inspection door inset in the right swingdoor of the trailer and look at the thermometer hanging in the hole at each stop. I also look at the LED panel on the front of the refrigeration unit. It has several selectable modes that will display the current temperature of the different parts of the trailer's interior. There are sensors on each of the parts, and a look at them all will present an accurate picture of what is happening inside the trailer without actually getting inside, as opening the door will cause a serious loss of cold air. We don't want melted ice cream dripping out the back of the trailer and blowing onto people's windshields, so keeping the doors closed and checking the sensors regularly will help prevent that.

In the first stop where I open the inspection door, there is a plastic shopping bag secured at the door's entry and in pulling it out, I see in it several pints of different flavors of ice cream. I get with Trainer on it and he says this particular shipper does that for the drivers. Gives them a CARE package, so to speak. Another perq of the job. It wasn't given to us particularly, we just sort of fell heirs to it. Trainer says he wants the pint of chocolate crunch. He eats it in the length of time it took me to check the tires on the trailer. I tell him he is going to get sick doing that. Says he does it all the time. He gets sick about 30 minutes later, and we have to stop again.

My feet and ankles have begun to swell a little more for some reason. Lack of activity, I guess. I hope it isn't the ice cream. Maybe it's coach–class syndrome like they get on long flights. Probably a real risk of thrombosis here somewhere. I need to walk more when we stop, and we need to stop more. That will dig into our miles and ruffle Trainer, but I don't want to risk a clot in my leg if that is what the problem is. Maybe I am only getting older, and this is part of that. Things simply don't work like they once did. Lymph system included. I wonder if the numb area in my right thigh is tied into this swollen-feet-and-ankles thing. I wonder if ice cream would help it.

# WEEK Three

WE STOP IN DES MOINES FOR THE NIGHT AND LEAVE EARLY BEHIND three cups of coffee that causes a sooner-than-usual break. I exit the interstate for a roadside rest stop and park. I jump out the door and rather than take the sidewalk to the facilities, being in a hurry, I go across the grassy area. I find myself dodging the piles of dog poo all over the place, and wonder why the dog owners don't put their dogs into the area set aside for that, but learn a lesson in using sidewalks at rest stops. Man, I hate that getting dog exhaust on the sole of my shoe. Then I get in the car, without fail, and smear it on the floor mat. I mean it isn't like I inspect my shoe sole every time I get into my car, but now that I think about it, maybe I should start. Then, worse, it is usually winter and I turn the heater on and it blows hot air across the floor, and that really gets the ol' smearandsniff thing going.

Back in the truck, I look at my shoes and make sure the a/c, not the heater, is on. Just in case.

Back onto the interstate early and westbound in the hammer lane, sun behind us and glaring in my mirrors. I have to keep moving my head to the side in an effort to avoid the brightness. That is not good, in that now not only can I not see in my mirrors, but I'm blinded momentarily

149

when I try. So, I simply don't look, and resolve not to change lanes until I can use them. That is not good for several reasons, but happily, nothing comes of it.

Not far along, and a car eastbound veers from the eastbound granny lane and goes across the hammer lane into the wide and grassy median, crosses that, and miraculously goes across the both westbound lanes without being hit, or hitting anything, and down the steep embankment into the fence at the bottom. Less than 100 feet ahead of us and close enough for me to see the woman's face as she steered across the westbound lanes and down the embankment. She had apparently dozed off and awakened in the median, and was just along for the ride past that. If any of this had happened one second sooner or later, it would have been bad. Timing really is everything. She went between two groups of cars as she crossed our path. It all happened so quickly, I just sat behind the wheel and watched, none of it really registering.

I hold the wheel steady in the event the steer tires blow when we inevitably hit some of the big parts that fell from the car on the woman's trip across the westbound lanes. I hope none of the pieces thrown by the drives fly up beneath the trailer and break an air line to the tandems. We will lose air pressure and the tandems will lock up. That is what has happened in many of the cases where we see four parallel skid marks curve off the road and onto the shoulder. Not that the only reason trailer tandem hoses fail is loose car parts flying around beneath the trailer, but tandem hoses failing is a big reason you see those skid marks veering off the road. The driver was trying to drag a trailer off the road with locked tandems. He lost tandem air pressure for some reason. Once that pressure alarm on the instrument panel goes off, the driver only has seconds to get off the roadway before the tandems lock. In the case of a torn-away or broken air hose, there is little, if any, warning. Most of times they don't make it, the tandems lock, and hence the skid marks. Other times, it was nothing more than the driver using the trailer brakes only in an effort to save his tractor brakes. It is his tractor and someone else's trailer, so use the other guy's stuff.

I manage to avoid all but the smallest pieces, and we go past the scene. I hope she is not hurt badly. Other cars are beginning to panic and swerve behind us. Some fool will lose control, swerving to miss the trash, and cause this to be worse than it has to be.

For all we see as we cross the country, a couple of things have come to amaze me. One, I find it difficult to believe some car drivers drive as much as they do and get no better at it than they are. It seems to me they would get at least fairly good just by virtue of association after a decade or two. But they don't.

Secondly, I find it difficult to believe there are this many cars on the road, the drivers as bad as they are, and no more accidents happen than do. I would think there would be rusted, wrecked car hulks lining the shoulders of every road in every state. That we couldn't haul them away as fast as they would be wrecked. But they aren't, and some law of large numbers says they should be, I think.

Farther along, I see the traffic has thinned out some on the east-bound side, and realize there must be some holdup causing that, and sure enough, there is a bigtruck on its side and most of the trailer roof ripped away. There are some blue barrels smashed open and spilled white powder of some kind all over the roadway. Traffic is bottlenecked to one lane on the median shoulder by the authorities just arrived on that side. Some troopers are just getting out of their cars. It takes them a long time to get on site through the traffic, so most times the emergency vehicles access the crash from the opposite lanes before the lookylews—that's what drivers call rubberneckers—tie those lanes up.

We roll by and know a brother is down. Not a company brother, but one of our own. The initial impulse is to pull over and go see what help we can be, but it is the wrong thing to do. We can do nothing there but get in the way. Neither of us are recently trained paramedics, and neither of us can clean up the mess. If we pull onto the shoulder and just go stand in the way, we have created a sitting-duck situation with our rig on the opposite side of the road, and it will soon be the agent in another collision. People regularly chase dropped cigarettes, drive drunk, doze off and yammer on cell phones, slap at the kids, then go onto the shoulder as they do those things. Another rule of occurrence in the universe we all know as Murphy's Law, plainly states our truck will be parked there when that happens.

It appears to be a one-vehicle accident. I hope there is no car under it, or behind it. At least the trailer didn't run over the tractor. The kingpin did its job. There is no major cab damage, that I can see anyway. I see some people working near the windshield and I hope the guy is okay. I think they are trying to get the windshield out so they can get him out.

The white powder on the road is another story altogether. Trucks hauling hazardous material have placards on the front, back, and sides that display numbers and symbols that tell emergency personnel what is inside, and that gives them a heads-up on how to deal with a spill. They match up the numbers and symbols in a guidebook and determine what the stuff is and what to do with it. Some of it is seriously bad news. Some is nothing more than the chemicals they put in soft drinks. Whatever it is, the guys wading around in it have those white suits and dual-filter masks on. What a mess.

Depending on the material necessary to clean up the site, traffic could be tied up for hours. Some stuff they just sweep off the road and let the wind and rain disperse it, others get a containment structure built and it is hauled away in barrels to be buried. Someone has to pay for that, usually the trucking company that made the mess, as it should be. Taxpayers have enough to support, and some companies should be more circumspect in whom they let pull hazardous loads out among the populace.

I just get over that, and farther down the road another truck is nose-first in the ditch on our side of the interstate. A trooper is just stopping. We are apparently among the first on the scene. Again, the inclination is to stop and do what we can; the trooper senses that and impatiently waves us past, obviously irritated by our slowing presence, and the thought of having to deal with the second accident we may cause. We eye one another as I drive by. I was only slowing to keep the windblast down for him. These things push a lot of air aside, and can blow opened car doors backward and people off their feet under certain conditions. And I don't want to knock a trooper down for all the obvious reasons.

Trainer gets on the CB and alerts the drivers behind us. It is a courtesy among drivers to advise one another about problems ahead, regarding the nature of the problem, the milemarker nearest the problem, and how bad the traffic jam, aka brakecheck, may be at the scene. They are then aware there may be stopped traffic around a bend in the road, or what lane they need to travel to best avoid the bottleneck.

Like any other game of hearsay, the information gets garbled as it goes along from CB to CB. Fortunately, drivers going the other way are able to keep the information semiaccurate, their having just passed by the cause and thereby able to correct the misinformation they hear from the jam. Without that thread of correction in the fabric of news on the CB, the last schmuck in line would hear a message that has no resemblance at all to the real event. Polar bears throwing bananas at cars, or something as goofy, by the time the story gets to the end of the line.

Still farther along, another car drifts off the eastbound interstate and into the median. I see the old man at the wheel as he regains control in the grass when the car slows. At least the car stays upright, and as long as he didn't cardiac, or smack the steering wheel, he'll just have to change shorts. Small pricetag for dozing off at the wheel. It happened so quickly and smoothly, I barely noticed him go off the road, until he was in the grass.

The road is long and straight, the weather is warm and mild, and the traffic is light. Nothing around him to cause him to swerve. He just took a little nap. And under those conditions, it is easy to take a nap.

It is getting worse as we go. Some miles west, heavy black skid marks start in our lane and lead across the shoulder, gouge through the median, scrape the gravel on the opposite shoulder, and streak to a stop at the stripe dividing the eastbound lanes, and a wide scrape on the concrete goes to the trailer end of the bigtruck on its side in the granny lane facing west, looking the wrong way. The roof of the rig is on our side, and one of the steer tires is still slowly spinning. Several cars have stopped and some folks are trying to get the driver out. I hope he is okay and it is a one-vehicle accident. I can't see whether a car is under or behind it. I don't want to look for more than a second because I'm driving. I'll let Trainer look and tell me about it. Which he does, and he says he thinks a four-wheeler caused the driver to lose control westbound and skid into the eastbound lanes. Scary stuff. I don't want to imagine being in a car, driving into the sun eastbound, and seeing an outof-control bigtruck coming into the windshield, and I hope that didn't happen to someone back there just now.

This morning is a personal worst for me. I have seen more bigtrucks and cars leave the roadway and lose control in four hours than I ever will again, aside from snowstorms. Has to be that way. There is no possible way for this to repeat itself. The real miracle, if there is one, is no one apparently was badly injured. At least I didn't see any white sheets or mangled bodies on the pavement. In all the fright, there are only messes to clean up and vehicles to repair. Trainer says one-vehicle accidents are common in this area. Lots of people go to sleep at the wheel. Even professionals. Long, straight roads and no scenery. I have heard, though, from other drivers and Trainer in the past, that sleeping at the wheel is a rookie mistake, and I have found that to be true more often than not. Though it happens to them as well, veteran drivers generally know when to say when, and stop to rest, even if it means a late load.

I drive on, sobered by the morning's events and near catastrophes, and think on my own driving practices and how they may or may not cause or prevent an accident. I cannot imagine a worse thing than to realize something I did or didn't do caused someone to lose their life. I have to believe that realization would have such a profound effect on me that the remainder of my existence would be completely different. That revelation causes me to think back on my initial driving training and how I knew absolutely nothing about driving one of these things, and how I was a clean slate for my driving instructor to work on. I fell in behind him and imprinted like a baby duck. I imitated everything he did and how he did it. I shift gears exactly like he taught me to, and I hold my hands on the wheel just like he showed me. I stop behind the stop signs like he said to do. No Hollywood stops in his truck nor mine. After some of the things I have seen other drivers do out here, I recognize the caliber of my training. It was top shelf. If he trained everyone the way he trained me, there is no way to tell how many lives and dollars have been saved. Thanks, Tony. I remember the Funky Munky just about every time I shift into high range. And I smile thinking about that as I shift.

A squall line is fast approaching from the northwest. We and the storms are probably moving toward one another at about the same speed. This kind of storm system lives quickly and violently. They can easily roll a bigtruck. Even a loaded one. I have dealt with them on sailboats in the past, and have a very healthy respect for their ability to ruin my day. Whether at sea, or on the road, there are only two things that can be done in the path of these things: run, or secure for heavy weather. I think we can beat the storms along the interstate. I think we will be safely on their other side when they cross the interstate. I decide to run for it. Trainer thinks I am just driving. He doesn't know I'm taking a chance. He doesn't know anything about sailboats either.

We skirt the edge of the blackness, barely beat it across the interstate, get a serious wind blast on our side, and it rocks us heavily for several miles. I wouldn't want to be deadheading about now. If we were, I would not be racing the storms across Nebraska. I would stop at a rest area and sit it out. Big Blue might still be blown over, but with much less tragic results. I would secure for heavy weather, and about all I can do to secure for heavy weather in a bigtruck is park it off the road such that the only damage done will be to the rig alone. Not the rig and a car full of innocents.

Well past the storms, but still able to see them crossing the trail behind us, we stop for a late lunch at a mom'n'pop sandwich shop. A big one. The sandwiches are good, but I am most impressed by the flies.

Gadzillions of them. Inside, outside, snackbar, restrooms, soda fountain. Everywhere. It is difficult to eat without getting one, or two, in my mouth. I figure it is less infested in the truck. I say so, Trainer agrees, and we go there to eat, and when we open the doors to get in, a few thousand get in with us. It must be like insect heaven. All the donut crumbs on the floor from past interstate feasts, sugary coffee rings on the dash, sticky soda cans. They will not leave. We open the doors to shoo them out, and they fly right back in. I don't know what the deal is. Truckflies. They're in here, and we got 'em.

It is an exercise in futility, and I catch on quickly. Shake my sandwich occasionally. Trainer is losing ground over there. Fanning and waving arms. Snatching bites. Expending more calories than he is gaining. For the nutritional value and caloric expense, he may as well let the flies have the sandwich. It's a pretty good show, so I just watch and say nothing. Trainer looks at me from the second chair chewing a mouthful, flapping his burly arm at offenders, holding his fly-garnished sandwich in the other hand, and grins a crumby grin at me. Says he don't mind the flies eatin' a little or even gettin' a sip of root beer, but standin' on his glasses so he can't see ain't gonna work. Sure enough, a couple of flies are hiking around on the lenses of his glasses. Trainer just doesn't have enough hands.

Some of the more streetwise flies get a few bites of sandwich, buzz around, and locate a hideout in the cab. No point in risking a life in the crowd. They figure they'll wait till the feeding frenzy is over. Zip in and get leftovers. It's a good plan. There is plenty on the floor. Maybe they know it's a truck. Maybe they know the truck will leave. Maybe they know there will be a steady supply of grub in the truck. Maybe they know it's a moveable feast.

The ride across the western Nebraska plain is uneventful, except the occasional stowaway whizzing by, and Trainer takes the wheel at a rest stop just into Wyoming. We are rolling along at speed, and a loud pop comes from the rear of the trailer. Loud enough both of us hear it over everything else. I jump to look in the mirror and see a 10-foot strip of retread roll from beneath the trailer and flop onto the roadway some distance behind us. Other trucks steering gently to miss it. No swerving in a bigtruck. Trainer cannot see what has happened from his mirror, so I relay that information to him. He groans. Immediate CB response from the cheap seats behind us. I believe some drivers have the steering wheel in one hand and the microphone in the other just waiting for the chance to get on the airwaves. Any chance will do and this is a valid one, so we instantly hear the heat. Trainer steers for a convenient exit onto a county road so we can assess the damage.

Drivers call the strips of retread "gators" and will use any safe maneuver to avoid one in the road. They caution one another on the CB about gators in terms of size and lane location along the highways. I think they are known as gators because when the strip of retread is laid flat on the road surface, it looks like a partially submerged alligator, and from a distance in most any configuration they look like an alligator that's crawled onto the shoulder. A gator weighs anywhere between 10 and 100 pounds, depending on how big it is and how much tread is on it when it separates, and bad things can happen when they are picked up by a bigtruck's tires. An airborne gator in interstate traffic is a real problem. They take out windshields, remove the plastic fronts of cars, they can knock a motorcyclist from his machine, and flailing around beneath trailers they can rip away the trailer brake air lines. The drivers behind us do not want to hit that gator if they can possibly avoid it. It's a big one.

Safely off the interstate, Trainer gets on the quailcall to alert HQ as to the nature of the problem and see what resolution they will offer. We are some miles from anywhere and it is unlikely there will be any road service dudes to come fix it while we set up the grill, or get a nap. We are probably going to have to take the mountainous problem to a tire Mohammed in a repair Mecca. Trainer wrestles with that while I go to the rear of the trailer to inspect collateral damage. The gator came from the number 14 tire, which is the outside right-side first row of the tandems looking toward the front of the trailer. I crawl beneath the trailer and inspect the air hoses, support brackets, and air tank. We are lucky; though the tire casing hangs in rags from the rim, my untrained eyes see no major damage done to other parts.

I report to Trainer all is well beneath the trailer, but the tire casing is in tatters. He says we have been told via the quailcall to take the trailer to Rawlins and have the trailer inspected and the tire replaced, so get in and let's go. Okay.

Trainer sets out at a glacial pace right into a one-lane construction zone. Soon we have traffic backed up for hundreds of yards, but can go no faster for the fear of another tire failure. We don't want to be at speed if another tire goes, especially in a construction zone. The folks behind us will just have to wait. For nearly 20 miles. We make absolutely no friends along the way. I turn the CB off and ride. Trainer is stressed enough without the string of insults. I doubt many of those things would be said face to face. I imagine in close quarters few, if any, would dare say anything they thought may offend my hulking buddy. He could hurt someone badly, and without the intent to do that kind of harm. I can imagine, no I can't imagine, what might happen to an offender if he were angry or stressed. I put on the FM radio for some wayback country music. I mean, *way* back country music. Like banjo and bass fiddle and hambone jugband racket. I didn't know they ever recorded that kind of thing. This is going to make a slow trip even worse, but it is all I can tune in, certainly beats the CB content, and we have heard every tape we have at least a dozen times.

What seems like hours later, we limp into the designated facility, in this case one of a chain of truck stops, pull into the tire service area, and get out for a meal, a shower, and to do some laundry while we wait. The truck being down long enough to replace a tire will give us time to do all that. At dinner, steak and loaded potato, Trainer decides we may as well stay the night. He has a movie he's wanted to watch and I want to finish Crichton tonight. See how things work out for the professor. I never did figure out what became of the cop and the physician in the first chapter. I think the author forgot about them. Or I missed that part, or the pages were gone, or something.

— — —

The Wyoming sun is up at 6 A.M. and so am I. Wake Trainer with the light curtains, get ready and hike over for coffee, and watch the morning blossom as we sit and do the logs. We will get as close as we can today to Calidamfornia, but several mountain ranges are in the path, so the going will be slow. No big deal, just part of the trip. The whole secret is steady rolling. Keep the left door closed and the hammer down. That is the paraphrased philosophy. So we do that, and it is not as easy as it sounds.

The temptation to stop is strong for a newbie. Just to get out of the truck and walk a minute; not used to the confines of the truck and the constant motion. The veteran drivers don't let it bother them as much. It is there for them, like everyone else, but they understand if the wheels don't roll, no money gets in the pocket, and after many thousands of miles, they work out a system for themselves regarding when and how long to break. If they have to be out here, they may as well make as much as they can, and that means moving freight as far and as fast as possible. Minimize the frequency and duration of the stops.

Lots of road construction going into Salt Lake City, and the commercial traffic is heavy. Bigtrucks all in a row. Three bicyclists far from anywhere on the interstate shoulder. I cannot imagine where they have been or where they may be going. I comment on that to Trainer and he says Sturgis is happening not far from here, but he thinks they use motorcycles there.

The CB yakking is getting ugly what with the traffic, the subsequent slowdown, and drivers in a hurry behind us in the line of trucks. I have determined many bigtruck mishaps are the result of the verbally strong berating the constitutionally weak. One driver goading another into a hurry via the radio. The weak one crumbles under pressure and overextends himself. Too fast for conditions. That's what the paperwork will say. The abusive one will drive on as if he had nothing to do with it, nor will he think he did. Sociopaths are like that. They don't see a problem with what they do.

Through Salt Lake City and across the Salt Desert, pass the Utah tree again in that salt desert, up the hill at Wendover, through the Pequop and onto the high chaparral of Nevada. A couple of drivers get into it on the CB about Wendover and whether it is in Nevada or Utah. Rude comments about one another's education level, particularly in the geographies. One says his dispatch told him to stop in Wendover, Utah, for something. The other says he has stopped in Wendover ten thousand times at the casinos, and casinos are illegal in Utah on account of the Mormons. Says the Mormons have to drive to Nevada to gamble now. That they did it to themselves. Trainer howls. I figure what state Wendover may be in is a valid issue and may have two correct answers, so I break out the atlas to solve the problem, for my own edification if not everyone else's.

Turns out Wendover is actually one metro area divided politically. Wendover is in Utah. West Wendover, or what is locally known as West Wendover, is in Nevada. The state line divides the metroplex into those entities. Wendover Street is in Nevada, and the same street continuing across the line and into Utah is known as Main Street. The casinos are in West Wendover. Everyone is a winner. That's what I got from the atlas, anyway.

We have a fuel stop slated for Carlin, Nevada, and it is close enough to quitting time for Trainer to say he wants to dig in for the evening and try his luck with the slot machines inside the truck stop. Says he needs some vacation money. I tell him with that plan, what vacation money he has right now is likely to stay in Carlin. Good thing I'm not an oddsmaker. While I scrape entomology specimens from the windshield and top off the diesel tanks, Trainer goes inside to potty and brings back a bucket of quarters. That sucker won $45 on his way to the men's room. Dammitboy, he says, I'm goin' to Cozumel.

We opt for dinner with an international flavor. I look across the road into town and see an Italian restaurant. Trainer says he could do some spaghetti about now, and we hoof across the dusty road into a rainstorm that is not. It is late in the afternoon, early evening actually, and the sun's rays coming from behind the horizon cause the wispy rainbands falling from the high clouds to glow. The rain dissipates and evaporates long before it hits the ground. Absolutely beautiful. Long, wavy strands like blue-blond hair sunlit from behind hanging beneath the clouds. I can almost see it move in the wind as it falls and thins to nothing high above the desert. The relative humidity must be near zero. Nature rarely wastes effort, and I wonder at the apparent futility of this phenomenon.

Spaghetti in Nevada. Now there's an indication we are moving toward the global village. Trainer says who'da thunk it. We get inside and order the meal, and it is pretty good. Not like MamaMia's, but better than I would have thunk. Local grandpa chasing local grandson around the tables. Old fella never had a chance. Best act I've seen lately. Back to the truck laughing about grandkids and kids in general, and decided to make an early evening of it. We still have ice cream in our CARE bag.

We settle in for the evening, Trainer in his bunk with a movie and myself with a bargain bookstore copy of *Paris Trout* as the Nevada night comes onto us.

The quailcall beeps some time later, and Trainer leaps from his bunk and the movie to grab the keyboard. I'm still amazed by this man's agility in proportion to his size. He reads aloud we have to repower another load and get it to Los Angeles by 6 A.M. tomorrow. We have to go to Battle Mountain and meet the other driver there. Trainer cranks off a message and sits by, staring into the early-evening lights, his evening trashed. Now, instead of a comfortable evening at home, we get to drive all night. Trainer says he's going to call HQ and see what's up.

I get the truck ready to roll, stowing gear and checking stuff in and outside the tractor; things I would ordinarily do in the morning walkaround. Trainer returns and says let's roll, we gotta haul it. He is hot. Huffs around and finally takes the wheel, as I collapse into the second chair, get the radios on, buckle up, and crank off a couple of macros on the quailcall indicating we know what is expected of us, and what we are about to do as we set out for Battle Mountain.

The lights of Carlin disappear in my mirror, and we ride in silence. Trainer is not happy. Messes up his whole damschedule he says. He is missing his movie and had looked forward to that. It is like getting home and getting comfortable only to be called back to work, I think.

Someplace between where we were and where we are going, I see what looks to be an abandoned camper shell with a person outside it sitting in what is left of a lawn chair. Small fire going. Possibly cooking something, I can't tell for sure. This person is on the high chapparal, miles from anywhere, apparently living in something that blew off a pickup, or was thrown out there. I think on that for a while as we go completely past him, and wonder at what brought him here, to this end. How and where does he get his food and drink? I know there is no possible way he can be happy, unless he is less than stable, having come from such a cornucopia as our society, and finally decide he must have come here to wait on the Reaper, not be a problem for anyone, and do as best he can while he is here, waiting. I will come back this way again and he will not be here, nor will his little camper. I will wonder what happened to him, and hope some mercy was involved in whatever end came to him. To live alone is a choice we make sometimes for a reason, but to live lonely, even with someone, is a kind of living death. To be both alone *and* lonely is more than a person should have to deal with, and I hope that wasn't his fate.

We arrive in Battle Mountain to the siren call of the local cathouse on the CB announcing services available, pull into the designated meeting place at this truck stop, idling along, and there sits a company driver in his tractor I had seen in the Carlin truck stop. I look around thinking I have missed some other company truck in my initial scan of the lot. The one we are supposed to repower. No way it could be this guy unless he just got sick, or got an emergency call from home. He just left Carlin a few hours ago. I saw him. I grab the keyboard to verify the tractor number and sure enough, it *is* him. I tell Trainer as much. We pull up beside him and he gets out to greet us. Young guy. We get out. Says he's out of hours to drive and can't get the load to the customer on time.

I look at Trainer. Trainer looks at me puzzled, and directs his attention to the other driver. Didn't you know you were about to be out of hours? Yep. Why didn't you stay in Carlin? Better whorehouse here. If I gotta be shut down, I want to be shut down here.

I walk away. I do not want to see what is about to happen. Trainer does not like his movies interrupted by idiots looking for whorehouses.

Back at the truck, I do some cipherin' and conclude we have gained enough hours on our trip this far to be able to run the repowered load legally. Teams can do that, gain time on a load, driving in shifts like they do. This guy is solo and has run himself out of hours. That means he told dispatch he had hours enough to run the load when he didn't, or he had the hours but not sense enough to use them driving. Now HQ wants us to cover for the guy. Keep the customer's load on time.

I break out the atlas and do some preliminary calculations for the repower trip while Trainer abuses the cathouse connoisseur in the parking lot beneath the bright lights. I see the kid cringing under Trainer's roaring, looking for all the world like he wants to run, but has nowhere to go in this vastness. It is a long way across that plain to a mountain, and the kid knows he'd never make it. Angry giants are difficult to avoid in a flat desert.

Based on what I'm seeing in the projected figures, we have the hours on our logs to run the load, but we do not have the time on the clock. California is a 55-MPH state for bigtrucks, and we have serious mountains to cross. The distance from here to Los Angeles is too great, the terrain too rugged, and I do not see how we can get the load to the customer on time safely and legally. I hop out and catch Trainer who is walking to the fuel desk for some coffee, before he kills someone, in this crisp and starry, starry night in Nevada. I catch up and tell him what I have found. He listens carefully and brightens at the magic word. Safety. He knows how to use it, too.

He heads for the phone bank inside the building. I walk back to the truck and climb into the second chair, relieved for some reason. Maybe because Trainer will get us out of the repower with the ammo I just gave him. Maybe because he didn't kill the other driver. I hate subpoenas. But maybe because I just don't want to ride all night. Sleep would be better.

Trainer beelines straight for the tractor with his coffee from the convenience store part of the stop, and says we do not have to repower the load. The guilty party will suffer the consequences, and the customer knows the load will be late. None of that fixes a late load, it just keeps everyone aware of what is happening. Late loads are not good. If the merchandise is not available to the customer, the customer will not purchase at the receiver, or worse, go elsewhere. And the trucking company that was supposed to get it there on time will be the whipping boy, and should be. End result is, the trucking company may lose an account. Everyone involved in a late load loses, and this one was lost because a driver didn't plan his trip properly, or wasted his time, or both. It will hit him in the pocketbook as what is known as a service failure. He now has to run his own load, and it will get to the receiver late. He will get another, later, appointment there, like whenever the receiver can get to him. More downtime. He will not get his bonus this quarter, and that bonus can be nice, like in the four-figure category of nice. It will hurt, and he will remember it.

We are going to keep our ice cream and take it to Union City, and we will dig in here for the night. Trainer positions us for that in the wide-open lot, and we resume our evening at home. Book and movie. Trainer has the CB on, volume down. Another cathouse ad. I swear, this thing gets a little more useless every day.

Up at dawn, roust Trainer and in for coffee. He says he can smell the buffet in Reno from here. I wouldn't doubt that. He is a trencherman extraordinaire, and can do some damage at the steam tables.

I do a walk around the truck in the cool early light, like every morning, looking for anything bent, broken, loose, or leaking, and in doing so, I find a little swallow or swift-type bird plastered to the grille. Desiccated. I peel him off and think how I drove through a flock of them just outside Salt Lake City yesterday. They were chasing bugs I guess, and this one was not paying attention. He was either an inexperienced or careless flier. Probably both. Young and intent on the bug. I feel really bad suddenly, having taken the life of such a magical creature as can fly, and hold it in my hand for a morbid look. I remember driving into the cloud of them, but not being concerned. I know swifts are capable aerobats. I mean, dang, those birds can pick a bug out of the air with their beak at near Mach 1, and would surely be able to see and avoid something the size of a truck clunking along at 65 MPH. I thought they all got away. This one didn't, and paid with his life for an error in judgment. I guess I didn't see the thing in my walkaround last night as we left Carlin, because it was getting dark, or I would have felt badly about it then, instead of going on a guilt trip right off the bat this morning. I would already be over it by now.

About break time, I pull off the interstate into a rest stop with a sweeping vista. I get out and walk and look around while Trainer takes a break, and I note a snake identification chart on the bulletin board in a closed glass case out front. Another sign says watch for them. I imagine some guy all in a rush, racing into a stall to take care of an impending gastrointestinal disaster, getting all situated and hearing this buzzing sound behind and below him on the floor of the stall. And no snake identification chart handy. It's hanging on the wall outside in a glass case. He wouldn't know whether he could safely beat on the snake to make it go away. Beat on it with what, I guess is the next question. Toilet paper is about all that is in the stalls that can be dislodged. Might possibly use that little cardboard tube that is in the roll. Maybe that's why the ID chart is outside in the glass bulletin board case. Classic case of a little information is a dangerous thing. Don't want a rest-stopper hammering on a snake that might not take it lying down, so to speak, after a poorly, or hurriedly done comparative analysis. Some of these venomous desert critters get upset pretty easy. Plus, no telling where the poor schmuck would be bitten, sitting there with his pants down. Even if he managed to make the 100-plus-mile trip to the hospital alive, he may die on the table while the doctors and nurses are busy rolling around on the floor. That all just goes to show that there is a reason for everything. Even the location of snake I.D. charts.

Just outside Sparks there is a traffic snarl at a construction zone, so I pass some time scanning the radio for a decent station. Like I am going to find one out here. The scanner stops on a deep cut from a wayback Keith Richards album. This is no ordinary radio station from Reno/Carson City, and we settle in for a slow ride and rock awhile. Excellent radio from some waycool, and seldom heard on the airwaves, rare sixties to nineties albums and CDs. The construction zone going is slow so we have the windows down for a change of atmosphere, and the fresh Sierra Nevada air is flowing across the cab. Let it out. Let it in . . . hey, Jude.

Poking along, I think back on a scene in the last truck stop fast-food spot we'd been in for a greaseburger and thought at length on how some people knew early on what career path they would take, and set out on that path. How the remainder of us just kinda wind up with a job that pays the bills, so we stay and do that, or something else we fall into, for a working lifetime. And how easy it must be for some women with no way out but to become prostitutes. Of one kind or another. I saw what I think was one in that fast-food place with what I assumed was her daughter. I sat and looked at the pair from a distance and wondered what set of circumstances brought the woman to that end. She was pretty, in a plain sort of way, and could have done better, and I could have been wrong about her career choice, but I'll bet I'm not. She ate in a tense conversation with her daughter, some difference of opinion on something, and it was messing up their lunch. I wonder if the daughter, who looked to be early teens, knew what her mother did to pay the bills. I wonder if it mattered to the daughter, or the mother. I wonder if they had a home, or if they were waiting for a john to come and get her, or them. I wonder how all this would affect the outcome of the daughter's life. I wonder if anyone in the room cared but me. I wonder if I am right about any of that. The woman might have been a senator, or an attorney, both entirely different kinds of prostitutes. I come back to the traffic jam and move forward a couple of feet.

Trainer says we'll stop at a truck stop near here so he can take care of some personal business, maybe wait out this traffic and accomplish something in the bargain. We are not making the best time anyway, he says. I agree and he directs us off the packed interstate. I think he needs to check on the vacation preparations, and maybe I can find something to munch on in there.

We pull into the busy lot and he bails out to go across the lot and inside the building. I sit with the truck, windows down in this spectacular Sierra morning, and take in the local goings-on.

The truck stop, most any truck stop really, is a haven for all kinds of people and skills. This one is fenced all around the lot, like many inner-city truck stops, and seems secure enough. It is also broad daylight. That helps a little with the peace of mind in any city. Truck stops are interstate transportation centers and, as such, attract all manner of people involved in the execution, maintenance, and support of interstate commerce. Some of the support mechanisms are legal and some are not. Some of the personnel involved in the support mechanisms are legal and some are not. Some of the items for sale are legal and some are not. Some of the purveyors of these goods gain legal access to the grounds and some don't. This place has a backside fence to keep the rabble that frequents the apartments next door from getting into the truck stop parking lot. That fence has an electronically controlled egress gate. The rabble simply hangs outside the gate until a truck triggers the sensor from the inside. They walk in as the truck goes out. They bring in the goods, or bads, as the case may be, sell whatever it is, and leave the same way with the money. I continue to be impressed with any kind of service industry and its creativity. If there is a need, someone will fill that need. I do not know of a thing that is not available either immediately or by special order from a truck stop, or the parking lot if the proper connections are made. They are little business communities consisting of a few corporate entities housed legally under the roof of the place, and many sole proprietorships, some legal and some not, hanging out in the parking lot. Classic free enterprise, and it abhors a vacuum.

Trainer is taking more time than I thought he might, so I decide on a walking tour of the place and maybe a look-see inside. There might even be a hot dog in there with my name on it. The mental graphic of a hot dog that has the letters PHIL scorched into it causes me to laugh out loud. A guy walking past me as I laugh looks kinda wary as he makes a wider arc around me than he had planned.

About the only place to park, as I could see it, is near the rear of the lot, and that makes for a long walk to the building. We gotta do what we gotta do. Problem is, if Trainer comes back to the same spot looking for the truck, it will not be there. Oh, well. Maybe I'll see him inside and head him off. It is his truck, after all, and he should probably be kept up to speed on where it is at any given time. I try to keep from scaring more people as I go.

Walking to the main building, I pass the rows of idling trucks decorated with colors and names and shiny stuff, and I note the degree to which these machines have been personalized. These trucks are the property of over-the-road drivers, literally in some cases, and are the product of those drivers' visions. Many drivers have anthropomorphized their trucks to the point of naming them. These are more than machines. Out here and far from home, the truck is mistress, best friend, bodyguard, kindred spirit, working partner, and in some cases, projection of self. Some have names set in different script, large and small, on the larger panels of the truck. Some have so much chrome trim it is difficult to say what color they are. Stuffed animals on the dash. Live animals on the dash. That cat must weigh 25 pounds. One truck has a few small potted plants on the dash-top. Lights. Some have dozens of lights added on. The trucks with many additional lights and gobs of chrome are known as chicken trucks, and there's a bunch of them here. Very few trucks are box stock, even the company trucks, since most everyone personalizes their truck to one degree or another. Mementoes from home and loved ones decorate the interior. Airbrush mural of a woman covers the side of a sleeper. Stickers with witticisms and profanity hanging in the top of the windshield, and the peeper window on the passenger door bottom. It is illegal to put anything in that little window or to block the line of sight out that window. It is there to let the driver see what is in the blind spot at the right front wheel of the tractor. Think about that when you are rolling down the bigroad looking at the teddy bear stuffed into that peeper. The driver can't see you. Or your car. Bad teddy bear.

I wander around inside, find a hot dog, doesn't have my name on it, and get on back to the truck, dribbling mustard and onions as I go. Didn't see Trainer. I hope he is not wandering around the parking lot looking for his truck. I'll just wait here and see what happens when I bite this dog, as Trainer says.

Listening to the radio and groovin' on a weekday afternoon, I am trying to decide whether or not this mustard will come out of an expensive golf shirt, and what to do if I am going to try to save it. Trainer shows up in a tizzy. Someone inside told him the interstate is closed just the other side of the California line because of the smoke creating visibility problems. What smoke? That smoke. I thought that was clouds. It is clouds; clouds of smoke. Dang, that must be a serious fire. Yup.

There are some fires burning just south of the passes, and the smoke is thick enough to cause the authorities to route traffic off the interstate. That means we can cross the pass, but we will have to detour onto a lesser road and be slowed down in the process. Trainer doesn't like that prospect, but we have no real choice. This is the only way across the mountains for a hundred miles in any direction.

The diesel grinds up the Nevada side of the pass and eastbound CB traffic confirms the road closure and subsequent detour. The smoke hangs high over the Sierras, and the fire becomes real right at the top. I can smell it. Soon enough I can see it. I have never been this close to a forest fire before. It presents an element of danger and I am more aware of my surroundings. These forests will burn. And it takes decades for them to recover. The fires will eventually come as high up as we are presently and leave a charred landscape, a moonscape really. I will see that in a trip across these mountains some weeks from now.

There are pumper trucks in the parking lot of a hotel/ski lift at the top of Donner Pass filling big bags of water for the helicopters to carry to the site of the fire and dump. I don't know whether it does any good, but apparently someone thinks so. Doesn't seem like that bag of water beneath the helicopters will do much in the face of a fire that is shutting down traffic. Maybe it makes someone feel like they are at least doing something. And no, they don't fill the bags with water dipped from the ocean and catch up the unfortunate scuba diver or killer whale or shrimp boat. Too far to the ocean from the forests and back, or they probably would.

Trainer follows traffic being detoured off the interstate and onto a secondary road that parallels the interstate some miles north. California Highway 20 at Yuba City begins a long, slow decline that approximates the drop on the interstate, it just doesn't look like it or feel like it, so deep in the woods, and the going is slower, it being a two-lane road. We don't realize the rate of descent at this point, but we are about to. It is sneaky, and neither of us is paying much attention. Sightseeing on my part, and lack of attention to detail on Trainer's part, worried about the out-of-route miles we are traveling, rather than driving here and now.

The ride is scenic. Spectacular vistas across the valleys. Ponderosa pines hundreds of feet high. Alpine meadows and rocky, pine-scented canyons. Some places we go up, and some places we go down. It is a sixth-gear climb from Boomtown to where we are in the Sierras. We are at the top. That means we are going to start down pretty soon. The scenery and the two-lane road have conspired to create an illusion of grade stability. The traffic is heavy, it being an interstate volume compressed into two lanes of country road, but it is moving along steadily in the smoke-scented woods. There are houses along here occasionally and not nearly as nice as I would have suspected. I would think real estate in this part of California would be outrageous. More so than the usual outrageous real estate prices in California. That would seem to dictate expensive houses. That isn't what I see. The only thing a few places along here need is a couple of pink flamingoes in the yard. The real cheap plastic ones.

What I do see is a gradual descent beginning. It has been a little up and a little down to this point. Trainer sees it as well, about the time I do. I say nothing and note our following distance on this tree-lined, shoulderless, heavily traveled two-lane road. I notice the decline has become steeper quickly. I notice Trainer has noticed. He is braking and I stop sightseeing to sit up and look in the mirror. Smoke from the tandems. Thin and wispy, but smoke. The brakes are already hot. Again. We have a different trailer now than the one Trainer cooked the brakes on, but the tractor brakes are the same ones he smoked the last time we were in California. This is not good. Refried brakes.

We are rolling down a two-lane shoulderless blacktop at 50 MPH in bumper-to-bumper traffic and the tandem brakes are smoking already. I mention that to Trainer as casually as I can over the cab noise. I think he has already seen it in his mirror and was hoping I wouldn't see it in mine. We have a problem. So do the people in front of us. They just don't know it yet.

I can picture the headlines now. And imagine the photographs.

I scan every foot of shoulderless road for a place to put 70 feet of brakeless truck and am about to tell Trainer, who is reliving a nightmare, to shut it down in the lane we travel and we will deal with the traffic and tickets and cursings because we are out of time and brakes and probably luck. The brakes are smoking heavily. I can't see the tandems for the smoke, and the drives look like a cartoon of a smoking wheel. The brakes are fading, and I can see the strain on Trainer's face. Sweat pours from beneath his cap and drops onto his tank top. Both hands on the wheel and eyes looking for a place to stop. I say nothing. He is doing all he possibly can. I don't know if the truck would stop quickly enough to hit a pullout now anyway. I look out the window and think I would probably survive a jump, because in the past few seconds we have reached the point the truck may not stop, period. Anywhere. I think I could probably pull both brake knobs on the dash and lock the wheels. That would probably cause the truck to jackknife and almost certainly roll over. But it would stop. Probably. Would it stop on the road, though, is the question. And how many oncoming cars would we take out, is the second question. But that would be better than rolling downhill brakeless smashing cars until we finally stacked enough of them under us to stop the roll, or going over the rail and taking out who know how many houses down the hill, kids playing in the yards, and folks inside doing whatever. I don't want to make this decision. I don't want to have to do this. I will give myself ten seconds to see what happens. Maybe a roving band of angels will show up and stop the truck for the want of anything better to do. Maybe a superhuman effort on Trainer's part will be the deciding factor. Maybe this is just a dream and I'll wake in my own bed. But, that isn't likely. Seconds ticking away, brakes getting hotter. He can't let off the brakes or we will speed up. This is bad. I do not see any positive conclusion to this right now.

The traffic is heavy going opposite. We will kill lots of them in either scenario. The cars are just feet in front of us. Not car lengths. Feet. I can see the kids through the back windshield playing in the back seat of the car in front of us. They have no idea they are about to die in a pile of ice cream. I was told as a child too much ice cream is not good for you. I see now that was a kind of inadvertent truth. I am resolved. This is about to happen and there is nothing I can do to stop it. Even if I pull the brake knobs, people will die. Us included. Probably us. I don't have the nerve to jump, and I don't have enough sense to close my eyes. And I can't help anyone. Not even myself. I sit forward to reach for the knobs. Trainer doesn't know I am about to do it. He would disagree with that tactic, but I think it is the best thing to do. The argument would be short-lived, like us, and whomsoever is in the slide path, once I pull those knobs. The drive and tandem brakes will lock, hopefully, if they are not completely glazed, and we will either skid to a standstill with lots of blown tires in one of the lanes or go completely out of control when the trailer jackknifes and comes around into oncoming traffic. The steering wheel will only be something for Trainer to hang on to. It will serve no directional purpose once the wheels lock and the tires begin to skid.

Rounding a curve, and ready to grab the brake knobs now, I look and not 100 yards down the slope the road widens into four lanes and a broad concrete shoulder. That roving band of angels must have just put it there. Trainer sees it as well. I hope we have enough brakes to shut down completely if we can get to the shoulder, because there is a traffic light and a four-lane intersection just past where the road widens. It will be close and we still may not force the truck to stop on the shoulder, and only heaven knows what will happen if we go into that intersection on a red light with no brakes and then into the town. Cars are parked in the street and along the curbs.

Nothing to do now but wait. The cars in front of us have pulled ahead some, and there is some space we can use now. Very little. Certainly not enough if something happens ahead to cause the cars in our lane to stop. Trainer is totally focused and his brow is soaked with sweat, looking straight ahead. There is nothing but the road for Trainer, and how to best get off it. I see he has determined the best course is to put it into the ditch on the right, if the faded brakes don't stop us in time, so he steers that way. I agree. It is all we can do now to protect the blissfully unaware motoring public. I don't want to die here, but I don't want to live knowing others died in my stead if we take out that intersection and go into town with no brakes. Trainer is literally standing on the pedal, and I have never heard brakes make the noise they are making now. It is like an anguished, howling groan and the truck is vibrating badly, as though the tractor itself is fearful it may not be able to stop the load. I can do nothing, not a thing, from the second seat. I am struck by how calm I am. Trainer seems to be, as well, though he is still standing on the brake pedal. We have done all we can do, and sad as that is, it may not be enough. So this may be the end of the line. No fear. Really. Not for ourselves. We made an error in judgment at the top of the mountain, and now someone may have to pay for that error. We choose us to pay if someone has to. All we can do now is wait to see whether we stop or die in the crash.

It is a sight, I'm certain. A bigtruck in heavy car traffic, smoke pouring from beneath, heading for the ditch. I hope I live to tell about this.

The road is cut into a hillside. We will cross the shoulder, jump the ditch, and smack a dirt wall if we don't get shut down. I wonder how hard we will hit it and if the trailer will crush us. Trainer and I will stop before the trailer does. I put my hand on the door lever in anticipation of jumping before the trailer runs us down at the wall, but I know I will not jump. I just feel better holding the lever. Like there is still one more thing I can do to survive this, no matter how bad it gets. That I am not completely out of options.

The brakes are as loud as a jet engine, and I hate it that will be my last memory, if it is. I wanted to go out listening to "Amazing Grace", not "Glazing Brakes".

The engine has been roaring in near redline conditions and is backing down some now, the brakes are making that unholy squealing and groaning, and they are smoking but still barely holding us, and we at long last shudder to a slow stop on the shoulder, five feet away from, and at an angle to, the dirt wall of the hillside. It is an uneasy stop. Like we may start moving again. The brakes must be gone completely. We are less than 100 yards from a very busy intersection. I look out the windshield at the sign that proclaims the Nevada City limits. It is right by my window. My hands hurt and I look down to see they both have cramps from holding the chair arms so tightly. I thought I had my right hand on the door lever. My mouth is dry. Both my feet are flat on the floor. I was helping Trainer brake, I guess. We both sit looking out the windshield as another envelope of caustic smoke overtakes the cab.

Both of us snap to the danger simultaneously.

We bail and Trainer grabs the fire extinguisher on his way out. I break right and he breaks left. Running to the rear of the trailer and looking at the drives as we go past to check for a brake fire that would quickly become a tire fire, I have to go wide to avoid the billowing smoke riding the thermals off the brakes, boiling around the trailer bottom in a peculiar lumpy pattern I have seen on cloud bottoms before, then racing up the side of the trailer in a streamy sheet into the already hazy and smoky California sky. This is bad and fire is a real possibility. I envision a forestry chopper dumping a bag of water on us as I run alongside the trailer. There is no fire at this point from what I can see at the tandems, and no reason to disconnect the trailer. So I just back away from the smoke and wait to see what happens next. If fire does break out, I think we will be able to get the tractor away from the trailer when that happens. Right now, there is no point. Both the tractor *and* trailer brakes are likely to burst into flames.

Traffic is flowing by quickly now, but giving us a wide berth, due in large measure to Trainer's antics on the roadway, and not the thick gray smoke alone. I can't tell whether he is flapping his arms to fan the brakes cool or clearing the smoke so he can see the drums or trying to lift off or what. It is a good show once I realize the danger of fire is past. A huge man flailing around a smoking truck in a tank top and shorts and knee-high socks. It comes to me that it is a venting mechanism. Trainer is furious with himself and is homicidal, and maybe suicidal. He is trying to release his frustration and not kill anyone. Himself included. Possibly me. I decide to stay quiet and on this side of the trailer till he calms himself. More flapping and railing.

Nothing to do again but wait, this time in a much more comfortable mental state. The danger is past. The truck is stopped, everyone is alive, and the brakes are not aflame. I look at the majestic surroundings and wonder about trees. How they go about their life's work alone, pumping water from the earth to the sky and unencumbered by other trees' problems. They live peaceably in large groups. No apparent irritation with one another. Same neighbor for years. No fussing or fighting or talking bad about one another. I see the pale, unfocused sky in the early afternoon showcasing the sun in its brilliance, and decide there is only one thing I can do among these peaceable ancient ones. I have to determine whether or not the coconut overpowers the raspberry in my last pint of ice cream.

Sitting in the shade of the towering conifers on the curb in shorts and mustard-stained golf shirt eating raspberry coconut, with a plastic spoon I stole from a Wendy's, on a lovely Sierra afternoon watching a broken man wander around a smoking truck. We are alive, and so is everyone else, the cool of the shade and ice cream soothes me somehow, and my life is good again. I lean back and reflect on all those things, letting the ice cream melt slowly in my mouth. To save and savor it, I think. It is good to be alive. I savor that, too.

Traffic going by, honks and shoots peace signs and thumbs up. Lots of smiles and nods and shouts of "DUDE !!" But what else can I really do? And the answer is: nothing. Wait and enjoy. The brakes, if there are any, have to cool. Trainer is just settling down. I'll bet he has run around that truck thirty times. I relax, eat a little at a time, and watch.

I sit on the curb and scrape the last of the liquid from the bottom of the paper can with the spoon. We need some special tool for that last little bit in the bottom corners. Imagine if you added it all up, how much ice cream gets thrown out, hiding in the bottom of the carton like that. I compensate by licking the spoon and holding the container at an angle above my open mouth hoping to get the very last of it dripping out. Wait a minute. They do make a tool. A soda straw, and I think about that as I put the lid back on the container. I'll need to steal some of them from Wendy's next time I'm in.

After a while, the brake smoke is reduced to a thread, but heat waves still shimmer from the drums. Depending on the weather conditions, it can take 20 hours for the brakes to completely cool. Trainer is getting antsy. He comes over to my shade and says he will be fired for this. I sit in silence. At length I say they will never know unless you tell them. Let's do like you did the last time you smoked the brakes and just roll with 'em after they cool for an hour or so. Nothing bad happened, and we are at the bottom of this hill anyway, just like last time you did this. Go through Auburn, get back on the interstate and into Sacramento. It is not a dangerous grade, and if we let the brakes cool some, we'll be okay. However, no more hills until we get the brakes inspected at the first available shop.

Knowing I have just lived dangerously, I wait for the effect, acting nonchalant, but looking to make certain my escape path is clear, should I need it.

Trainer sees an out, even though he knows I am gouging him, and agrees. Sits down with me for a while, looking around nervously. Like he is waiting for something to happen. Someone will see him or something. Turn him in for sitting on the curb. He makes me uncomfortable, looking at my empty ice cream container, and I say let's go ahead and leave now, but be careful. We have no heavy-duty brakes for the moment. The brakes will still work, like any friction device, but will not stand any abuse at all. He jumps to his feet and says let's go.

We roll very carefully toward the interstate, giving every vehicle plenty of room. Trainer drives. I'm not about to take the rap for a collision knowing the brakes are thermo'd.

We manage to get to our now regular steak'n'shrimp stop without further mishap, and he still doesn't have a mechanic look at the brakes. I make some noise, but he does not want to call HQ, tell them he has made the same mistake twice, and get authorization for the dollars to pay a tech to look at the brakes. Doesn't want to pay for it himself, either. So it doesn't get done. Now the tractor brakes have been smoked twice, and the next guy that pulls this trailer after we drop it, or trade it, has no idea the brakes are toast. I just mentally shake my head and think there is little I can do that will improve things. I'll just live with it, I guess. And hope my conscience is okay with what I may hear later about this trailer.

A good meal and a good shower make my life better, but no less guilt-ridden, so I head on back to the truck and finish up that *Titanic* video I've been working on for about a week while visions of smoking brakes dance in Trainer's sleeping head. Stress zonked him, I suppose. And the brakes will cool substantially overnight in the chilly air.

Up early and off to Oakland, but not before sitting in traffic and tilting at a few windmills in the fog. They stand tall and spin regally in the misty breeze atop their mountain stronghold, damp and glistening in the morning light, all in a row. Most of them look like huge airplane propellers revolving atop a colossal golf tee. Some of the other windmills have vertical vanes and look like a gigantic barber pole rotating slowly in the wind. More twisting than rotating, really. Some of the windmills are broken and parts litter the mountainside. Big parts. Maybe they are waiting to be repaired. Maybe they have been cannibalized to repair others. Whatever the case, it looks ratty. Junked-up mountainside, and that flies into the face of the whole case for a cleaner planet using wind power to generate electricity. Looks like a good start, but someone dropped the ball. Maybe the windmill electric service isn't profitable yet. Wind is fickle stuff. But still, it seems like they could at least get the trash off the mountainside in the interest of thinking green and promoting clean energy.

We work our way through the Bay Area traffic, that moves right along comparatively, and get to the drop, which is a cold storage distribution center. Ice cream warehouses are cold. Real cold. Generally about 20 below, since ice cream starts to soften at about zero. I get down from the truck and hike around inside the place. I have never seen that much ice cream in one place, or had to wear that many clothes inside. Lots of ice cream in there. Lots of it.

We sent in the requisite messages to HQ regarding our recently unloaded status and we received a message right back to deadhead over to a local food manufacturer for a load of beef jerky. We have no more than rolled to a stop at the place than Trainer zips in and scoops a can of jerky from the managers. I am thinking it will last us awhile, a kind of health snack for the road. He eats the entire can's contents in the three-hour period we sit and wait to be loaded. I get one piece. It's good, though.

Waiting is part of truckdriving. Wait to be unloaded. Wait to be loaded. Wait in traffic. Wait in the repair shop. We don't drive as much as I'd like. We wait. We are waiting now, and I have my bare feet out the window soaking in the warm California sun while AC/DC provides the lunch background. I see some red berries on the bushes in the fence and they turn out to be cherries. We rinse them off in a coffee cup full of ice water, spit the pit, and we get dessert. Tart, but good. Bag of Jolly Ranchers, leftover stale Bugles, and cherries right off the tree. Lunch for a couple of interstate vagabonds. Wash that down with a soda, and boogie with some vintage ZZ Top, a homegrown Texas band that makes about as much music as three people can. Trainer likes ZZ Top. Trainer is nearly deaf. We have a first-rate stereo system in the tractor. I stuff pieces of toilet paper in my ears and munch away on the rubbery Bugles. I jot earplugs again onto my mental list of things to bring back in the second phase of training. Lots of bees buzzing around in and out of the tractor. Maybe they will scare away that last Nebraska fly. Maybe the fly is not the same gender as the bees. Maybe they will mate and the offspring beefly will swarm over the California fruitscape and decimate the pomegranate crop or something.

It would be our fault.

Lots of people walking by and in the area, Trainer waving at them all, because every girl's crazy about a sharp-dressed man. I lay back watching the locals run around in a San Jose parking lot, and am drifting toward a siesta. This truckdriving thing suits my biorhythm. Naps on the job, in the middle of the day. I put the arms of the first chair down into place in the event I doze off. What with the door open and my feet propped into the window, it would be a long way to the asphalt if I nod off and fall from the chair.

Finally loaded, Trainer takes the wheel and we motor out to the interstate and hammer down for the nearest scale, to see what we weigh, then on to Bakersfield. Jerky isn't real heavy, dehydrated like it is, so we should have no weight problem. This load of jerky is going to North Carolina to enhance the diets of the folks around Asheville, and Trainer wants to stay the night at his favorite Bakersfield truck stop and eat at his favorite Bakersfield restaurant and leave for Carolina around 4:30 tomorrow morning. I'm okay with that. We can get across the SoCal desert in the dark and I won't miss anything, having seen the California desert already. I don't want to travel country I haven't seen yet in the dark. Might miss something. He wants to get this load delivered, get back to Dallas to meet his wife, and get going on that vacation. Dammitboy, Mexico's waitin', he says.

We roll into his favorite Bakersfield truck stop, eat at his favorite Bakersfield restaurant, get a shower and hit the bunk early, so we can be gone early. It is another simple plan.

The alarm causes me to attach myself to the ceiling of the sleeper about 4 A.M. I let go, fall back, and lie there confused and sleepy, trying to figure out what happened and what that noise is. Trainer must have fixed the banshee. Dang, why did I go along with this?

Get up, and head for the coffee bar after my morning routine, mechanical now, and stagger back. Still dark. This is messing with my circadian rhythm, which is different than my biorhythm. Biorhythm is still okay. Climb back in and sit in the first chair. Trainer is in a classic case of stage four sleep. There is no daylight to wake him, so I'll have to do it manually. Opening the light curtains will do no good. I'll let him sleep till I am ready to go. He is not gonna like that, but I want to get some things done before he gets up and wrinkles my operation here. Make some notes and catch up on my journal, drink a little coffee, and get at least a partial day plan together. I know he'll want to hear one. Get my logbook done so he can match his to it, that sort of thing. Peacefully. Quietly. No sudden noises or stressful racket. As soon as he is awake, generally, we have everything on that can be turned on. He likes stuff to be on. I like stuff to be off. Let him sleep. I need the quiet for now.

Logbook updated, I notice the quailcall message light is blinking, and I see that since it is dark in here, except for the instrument lights and the one spotlight directly over my left shoulder. The spotlight is on so I can see what I am doing without turning on the cab lights. We turn the beeper off at night, so just the light blinks on the quailcall if we get a message, and the beeper doesn't roust us in the middle of our DOT-mandated sleep. That the light is blinking is probably not good; the message may be several hours old. One of my daily jobs is to turn up the beeper as soon as I get up every morning, so by habit, I do it now, not thinking. I punch up the message and see we have been told to re-power a load in Kingman, Arizona. All the beeping as I scroll through the messages to get all the pertinents for the repower has awakened the sleeping ogre. After a struggle with the bedclothes, Trainer is sitting on the edge of his bunk looking confused, and asking what the hell am I doing ready to drive in the middle of the night. He looks at me with incredulity when I tell him we have been told to repower a load. Where, he wants to know. What. When. I tell him I'm trying to gather all that and to go get some coffee, that it will be dawn soon, but put some shorts on first. He jumps up, bops his head on the ceiling of the forward part of the cab, and lets fly a string of words I have never heard before. I was in the Navy and I never heard those words. He sails out the door, in his shorts and tank top and kneehighs, and double-times to the coffee bar. Rubbing his head. I think it is early and he doesn't like repowers and he cracked his head sleepwalking and it may be a long morning. I watch him hitch up his shorts as he stumbles to the coffee bar. Drops his mug in the gravel. He let go of it to pull up his shorts. I grin and go back to my work.

Kingman is on our planned route from the original trip plan I made yesterday, it is only a few hours away, and repowering a trailer there shouldn't be problem. It is a load of nectarines going to Tennessee. I plan a route to the new dropsite while waiting on Trainer and send in the necessary macros to let HQ know we understand what is expected of us. All set. I sit in the first chair sipping my coffee and look out the window into the darkness waiting on Trainer. Big Blue idles steadily, waiting on both of us.

Trainer strolls across the lot, opens the passenger door, hops in and says whassup. Better mood now. Coffee helps. I get him up to speed and he says it botches his whole Carolina plan. Says these damrepowers; you never know how damlong you'll have to wait for the other damdriver to meet yer ass. We might be stuck there all damday. In damKingman, Aridamzona. Huffs and gazes out the window into the predawn darkness.

Well, it seemed like he was in a better mood there for a minute.

We set out on the road. The California highway number 58 goes up, almost straight up, from the fertile valley to Tehachapi and onto a dry plain, past some more windmills at the top of a little climb, then goes onto a high chaparral and makes a turn into a town called Mojave. Mojave, California.

I don't know whether the town created the airbase at Edwards or the airbase created the town, if either, but I can say this much: Mojave, California, at the break of day, is the most depressing place I have yet seen on this planet, aside from the garbage dump in Mexico City.

I understand Edwards was the place to be if you were a pilot in the fifties and early sixties. NASA, the rocket rides and very fast airplanes. The space program was being built, and the builders walked these streets. Lots of it was top secret, brass was everywhere, the ground floor was being laid, and the best we had were doing the best they could. Right here. The fastest men alive came to this town. Every pilot in the world wanted to be at Edwards, and if they were good enough, they were here. A town founded on testosterone and jet fuel.

But, that was then.

Mojave's glory days are gone. Way gone. Maybe the town has always looked like this. Maybe it never really was a shiny, happy town. Maybe there never were any glory days for the town itself. Maybe the glitz was at the air base, or Rosamond, and never made it to the town of Mojave. But, probably not. The talent that put this place on the lips of the space world would have left its mark on the nearest water hole. That would have been Mojave, California. I would like to have seen it at the height of its importance. All the future astronauts in their Corvette convertibles cruising the Friday night streets and the brand-new tail-finned, chrome-bumpered V8s rumbling to the market, wives shopping for the family in their sundresses and white high heels and hurrying home beneath their husbands' coming and going jetplanes to catch "I Love Lucy" and get dinner on the table. Just like June Cleaver. I'll bet the place was something then. A picture of the military wild bunch and a slice of Americana we are not likely to see again. Postwar economy booming, X-15s streaking across the desert sky, JFK and Jackie living in Camelot, and we were going to send someone to the moon, Alice. Times were good, and looked back on by those that were there as the best in their lives, I imagine.

What I see now, as I look out the window passing through Mojave, is a semirenovated ghost town. A lived-in ghost town. Not even a shadow of its former self, if it ever was its former self. Abandoned storefronts. Deserted gasoline station on a corner downtown. I'll bet Chuck Yeager bought some gas there. Dust has accumulated in rippled piles on the curbs and drifts aimlessly around in the road. Houses the color of the dust, poorly kept. The yard area nothing more than raked dust. The place looks deserted. A sandblasted, sand-colored, tattered and trashed little desert town. Maybe it is just the early hour. Maybe the town will wake up and shake itself off. Add some color maybe, and develop a pulse. Clean up a little. Get ready for the day. The space race started here, man. Damn. Somebody do something.

Rolling out of town, the early sunlight splashing into the windshield illuminates a scrub desert festooned with discarded plastic grocery bags, litter of all kinds, and airplane hulks. There is not a single bush above knee high as far as I can see, and most of them have some piece of litter attached and twirling or flapping in the breeze. There are a couple of houses on the edge of town that make an attempt to rise above the standard, but even so, I cannot imagine waking here and looking onto this windblown trash-collecting desolation more than once. I cannot imagine living here. Maybe it is just a bad first impression. But it stays with me for some time as I settle into the granny lane at 55 and think on it. How part of our culture builds something, another uses it and discards it when it has served its purpose. Shrink-wrapped, freeze-dried, hermetically sealed, microwaveable, add water, heat and throw what's left away when you're done. Disposable dishes, diapers, cars, marriages. In this case, an entire town. Pump money, men, and material into it, suck it all out and let the husk blow away. Maybe we really are consumers. We consume stuff. Like towns.

The ride up the hill through the unusual cactus/palmetto trees east of Mojave and across the naked, barren mountains, scenic, in a plain ol' mountain sort of way, to Needles and the Arizona border, is quiet except the truck noise. Even the CB is silent. I feel pretty silent until we round the corner and drop onto the bridge that divides Arizona and California.

The Colorado River above Lake Havasu glitters on the desert border of Arizona like a living liquid jewel and from the bridge, a white V-shaped wake behind a ski boat contrasts sharply with the darkly emerald water. Almost like absinthe, but clear green around the edges, the white sand showing through. Beautiful. I am struck by this land of defined contrasts. The barrenness of the desert and the life around the river. The faded pastels of the desert and the rich, sparkly, gemlike colors of the wide Colorado. The flatness of the desert plain and the ragged peaks of the mountains that surround the area. The sharp points of the mocha mountains against the sapphire sky near Kingman. The sky here is not a deep blue like the one I see over my ocean at home, but a paler shade, maybe made so by the dust aloft. The jagged peaks to my right seem out of place here somehow. Mountains that young and spiky should be in some geologically new area. Most of this place has had time to weather considerably over the eons to a smoothness, though still rugged, but these bristling peaks are either recent or really resistant to wear. They just don't seem to fit into the landscape, like they were added on, or scraps left behind. An afterthought maybe, hurriedly whipped up, or possibly leftovers from some other projects, piled here and forgotten.

We get to Kingman and roll into the appointed truck stop. Our re-power is here already. Kind of a miracle, Trainer says. As he sees us from the window, our company brother is coming out from the sandwich shop to meet us. He's been waiting. I back in, and we shut down and get out into the heat. He and Trainer talk trucks and look around the inside of the truck stop, and I manage to get a letter, written earlier, mailed out and order a sandwich while all that is happening. The sandwich shop is manned and womanned by one guy and two girls, and the guy is being playfully harassed by both the girls and seems to be making better sandwiches for it. He is paying more attention to their attention than the quantity of stuff going onto the sandwich. The meat and cheese is piled so high on the bread, the guy is having a tough time getting it folded and cut, laughing and defending himself. I'm not complaining. He's happy and I am, too. Both of us for different reasons.

Trainer sees my sandwich as I take a seat at the table where the two of them landed, decides it is a bargain and he wants one. So he walks over to the sandwich shop just as the excitement has died, the guy is gone, and Trainer gets the company spec'd sandwich. He watches wistfully as a metered amount of meat, cheese, and goodies are placed on his sandwich, and pays up. Mopes over to the table and good-naturedly hollers he wuz robbed, and they like the trainee better and he can prove it by the size of the sandwich the trainee got. Lookitat, he says.

We finish our meals and sodas and discussion regarding the sons-abitches that run the trucking industry, and wander into the heat to exchange trailers and paperwork. He will hook up to ours and vice versa. We know it is a load of nectarines and we know it is going to Tennessee, but we didn't know the load was almost 300 pounds overweight. The guy probably didn't know he would be repowered by a team, and never thought to say anything. I know the trailer is overweight from looking at the scale ticket in the paperwork for his load. That's not good. I tell Trainer that is the case. This guy is solo and almost 300 pounds overweight. We are a team and have two people and the gear, food, and drinks for two people aboard. That could put us 500 or 600 pounds overweight. Maybe closer to 700 pounds. That could be serious. We may get by the individual states' scales being a couple of hundred pounds overweight, but not much more. They'll write that little bit off to scaling differences. Sometimes. Depends on whether or not the DOT guy had a fight with his wife or girlfriend before he left for work at the coop.

Worse, we just fueled right here before we traded trailers. We now have 1,200 pounds of fuel aboard and that is our only variable insofar as weight goes. We can coordinate our fuel stops with the weigh station locations such that we cross the scales with near empty fuel tanks to compensate for an overweight trailer. Then fuel as soon as we can after we cross the scales. We can't fill up completely, or we may not be able to burn enough fuel to offset the trailer weight before we hit the next scale, but the atlas shows the locations of the coops and with some basic math, we know how about how much fuel to load. It's a hassle, but it's about the only way to run an overweight load and not get ticketed. Then we hope we don't hit a traveling scale like some states have. Can't plan for those, and the DOT knows that. That is one of the reasons they have those mobile scale units. Catch overweight trucks sneaking through and around the coops. Those diesel bears are pretty sneaky themselves. That's what drivers call DOT agents. Dieselbears, or dieselcops. Additionally, so you'll know, state troopers are known in CB parlance as full-grown bears because they can write DOT tickets and are *the* authority on the bigroad, county sheriffs are countymounties, border patrol agents are borderbears, and metro police are localbears, citybears, or babybears. All those deeply thought-out witticisms stem from the Smokey the Bear hat many police agencies wear.

And, so you'll know, Texas Rangers are not referred to as any kind of bear. I am told drivers refer to them as Rangers . . . and drivers say "Sir" a lot in any conversation with, or about, a Ranger.

After some discussion Trainer and I determine we can slide the tandems to spread the weight around, but that will not reduce the total tonnage. There is just no way to get the load legal. We use the certified automatic truck scale, called a CAT scale, to weigh the load and get an axled-out reading at the truck stop. We need to know how heavy we are before we get onto the road and cross a state scale. Scale ticket says we are 700 and a few pounds over. Not good. We call HQ and are told to run with it. Once the dispatchers are brought into the loop and tell us to pull it, we are relieved of the responsibility, and the company will pay the overweight fines we incur, if any. It is not a moving violation and doesn't count toward the driver's license points, so everything is cool from the responsibility standpoint once we are told to run with it. But, still, getting a DOT ticket is several different kinds of not good. One of the problems is that now they have a reason to DOT, or inspect in detail, the entire rig. Front bumper to back bumper. With screwdrivers and wrenches and real live mechanical inspectors that know what to look for. Even if nothing is found, which is unlikely, which is another ticket or tickets, the driver is still down for many hours, and those inspections count as on-duty time. Lose a day's driving, and the hours, sitting in a coop DOT lot getting inspected. No restaurant, no shower. And a day behind schedule. We don't want any of those things to happen to us, so we want to be as legal as we can, however illegally we have to do it.

Northern Arizona is greener, higher, and has more trees than southern Arizona. The air is cool and has the scent of junipers and pine in the Kaibab forest, so I let the window down a little. There are thunderstorms around and the road is wet. The rain gives the pine-scented air a freshness, and I let the window down a little more to appreciate it all. More thunderstorms and rain-that-doesn't-get-to-the-ground all the way to New Mexico. The vistas across the way, decorated by the different colors of blue clouds and rain, are spectacular. It is very pretty up here. Trainer says there is a truck stop in New Mexico so big it must be seen to be believed, and we will stay there this very night. Okay.

Near Jamestown, which is near Grants, New Mexico, is the truck stop so big it has to be seen to be believed. Big enough it has its own refinery, and it is arranged like a mall. Many different food outlets and services and shops. I don't know if the one in Iowa is bigger or not, but this one is much better organized, better laid out and more appealing. We get a shower in the lounge area and a meal in the restaurant, then head out to the truck and bed down. It was a long run today from Bakersfield, we didn't play around much, and the bunk feels good. No television for Trainer tonight. No reading for me. I don't think I moved all night.

Death, and his little brother, Sleep, were cruising New Mexico, and Sleep found us. Luckily. I wish I could take credit for that Death/Sleep phrase, but I believe it was the Roman poet, Virgil, that gave that to Posterity.

I awaken in the cool August dawn high in the mesa country of New Mexico. My window is open and the cool air flows in and over me. Matter of fact, it isn't cool, it is cold air. I languish, wrapped in my multicolored Mexican blanket, and opt for a snooze. Trainer is gagging and snorting beneath me. I opt to let him sleep as well.

I regain consciousness shortly and rouse myself to rouse Trainer and get the day going. Open the curtains with my foot and let the sunshine in. Grumbling and snorting. Mucous sounds. Rummaging sounds and the crackle of cigarette packs being crushed and flung around. Huffing. Tractor rocks. Lighter clicks, scratches, and poofs. The first chair hisses and squeals in protest. Window hums down. Mug chase. Tractor rocks and door slams. They're off. A trainer and his mug, into the dazzling mesa-framed morning.

Not far behind, I get to the restaurant, locate Trainer, and suggest a decent breakfast. He concurs and heads immediately for the buffet. I catch the scent of homemade tortillas and follow in his tracks. Few breadstuffs are as good, if they are done correctly.

Refried beans, potatoes, bacon, and tortillas. All fried. All perfectly fried. We eat in muffled growls and grumbles, like a couple of jungle cats, snarling and swiping at the tortilla bowl. Territorial/food/male thing. We are sitting by a huge window, the clear light of a gorgeous Southwestern day breaking across the tone-on-tone mesas in the distance, and I am topping off my saturated-fat saturated meal with the same brand of coffee I use at home. Rich and flavorful, and the very thing to finish a good NewMex breakfast. We have had two weeks of fast food, snack food, packaged food, a rare decent meal, and no TexMex at all. Trainer is taking full advantage of the situation. He is returning from his third trip to the steam table. I made a blue moon second trip myself. Almost never happens. Trainer makes them sorry about the all-you-can-eat deal most places we stop, but I seldom go for seconds. The two of us probably average out. I pay the extra buck or two for the buffet so I can pick and choose, rather than be limited to rigid menu selections. If I want a pound of bacon, I get that at a buffet. It so happens today, I want a hot, butter-fried tortilla smeared with a layer of refritos, then a sprinkling of fried potatoes topped with several strips of fried salted bacon, rolled into a burrito and washed down with some hand-picked mountain-grown coffee fresh ground just a few minutes ago. Princes don't live as well as I do. We finish up and lean back to look at one another across the mess on the table. Trainer curls his lip at me. I open my mouth still full of beans and potatoes and show it to him. He winces and looks out the window.

We pay up and moan and groan our way to the truck. Somewhere along the route, we go back in for coffee. Since it was so good, I tell Trainer I'm going back in and tank up. He spins on his heels and walks beside me. We must look the pair. I am tall and thin, golf shirt and golf shorts guy. Trainer is taller and not thin, training shorts and tank top kind of guy. Leather NFL cap. Never comes off. I think he even showers with it on. I don't think either of us fit the truckdriver image well. But that's okay. Few people I see do. Not many of the American Cowboy types left out here.

If the coffee had not been so good, I would have said oh well, and gone on without it; however, in this case, I hate to pass on the opportunity to have more of my favorite. We get back to the restaurant, Trainer figuring we will get it free, our having just paid up and they will remember us, and I present my mug and schmooze a minute. The American Indian lady takes the mug, washes it, warms it with hot water, fills it with that specific coffee, asks about sugar and cream, stirs it carefully, snaps the lid back on, and hands it to me with the lovely white smile only a dark-skinned woman has. I accept with a bow and a smile. She shakes her magnificent black mane, looks demure, and waves me away. Trainer steps up and shoves his mug onto the counter and stands back. The woman takes his mug, fills it, hands it back, and walks away. Trainer looks at me. I look at Trainer. He says he don't unnerstand it. I tell him he looks married. He says yeah, that's probly it, and let's go. Burnin' daylight.

I first came to this area as a boy on vacation with my family and have been enamored of it since. The colors of the landscape and the shape of it, I think, are what attract me. Long vistas and the layered effect a distance has on the mesas; how big the sky is. It seems far to anywhere from here. Most things, here, once you get away from the cities, seem to fit. Few things look added on, the buildings and what. Most houses look like a part of the landscape, or maybe they are just coated with the land-scape and that's why they look a part of it. Whatever the case, the ar-chitecture, for the most part, suits the geography around here. Like things just grew from the ground. Frank Lloyd Wright would have ap-proved. He liked stuff that blended in. I do, too. I don't like his chairs, though. They look uncomfortable. But, that's okay, I was told once he said that he liked the look of his Prairie-style furniture, but he wouldn't want to sit in one of his chairs for long, that they are probably uncom-fortable. That could be good. Get the most uncomfortable furniture I can in my house, and maybe people won't stay long. I'll get a leather re-cliner for me. Maybe one of these Kenworth seats. They are pretty dang comfortable once I get them adjusted to suit me.

Hammer down, shifter in the money hole, yardsticks flying past, that's what drivers call milemarkers, eastward into the New Mexican morning we ride. Nectarines hot on our tail. I am liking the drive and the truck is its usual dependable self, the engine steadily rumbling, the turbocharger singing, and the transmission whining. The tires hiss along the blacktop, the 65-MPH wind roars past the windows, and the wheel is steady in my hands. I don't know that I was born for this, but it sure is easy to believe that here and now. The morning sun and Albu-querque are coming at me headlong and Trainer snoozes a little in the second seat, off and on, but I say nothing. He needs the rest, or his body wouldn't ask for it. And I think sleep is the only respite he gets from whatever it is that occupies his thoughts more and more these days.

The eastbound ride on Interstate 40 into Albuquerque is impressive in the daylight, but is really something to see in the darkness when the city is arrayed in its lights. The city sits between a mountain range on the east and a high plain on the west, sort of in a bowl for all practical pur-poses, and the air quality expresses that. Kinda hazy already this morn-ing. We have to stop here to get a produce check at a branch shop of the company that made the refrigeration unit for our trailer. Same thing we did in El Paso. Produce checks amount to third-party verification the temperature in the trailer is in the range specified by the shipper, and most shippers require at least one stop, most times two, on a cross-country trip. The technician gets a temperature probe into the produce and looks at some data the refrigeration unit stores, then translates that information into a readable form and faxes his findings to the shipper, carrier, and receiver. Produce is essentially killed when it is harvested, cut off from its life source, be that tree or root. The stuff starts to die immediately, like anything removed from its nourishment, and begins the decomposition process. The reefer unit's purpose is to slow that process by reducing the temperature of the produce to just above freezing. The object of the game is to get it as close to freezing as possible without actually doing that—the theory being the colder it is, the slower the decay process and fresher the stuff will be in the market. It works, too. The crisp lettuce in the markets today was picked in Mexico 10 days ago. Harvested, crated, stored, bagged, shipped, received, unpacked, washed, repacked in smaller bags, shipped to market, received, unbagged, and put on display in the produce section with amazingly little spoilage. The produce check alerts the interested parties if something is not kosher temperaturewise, and at that point the receiver has the option to reject the load.

If that happens, the carrier, our company, eats the produce, so to speak. Our insurance company pays the shipper for the load and it is then donated to a local charity that can use it. What the haves don't want, we give to the have-nots. Makes us haves feel better as an economic group. Like we really helped them out. Give them our substandard produce. Let them eat produce.

That probably is not the way to look at it, but I felt sarcastic and bitter for a moment as I was thinking about economic segregation and all. Sometimes I'm like that. I'm not really sure why.

Zip through town on the interstate, which is being redone in ochre trestles and turquoise trim to better blend with the landscape, and work our way through the construction zone traffic to the shop that will do the produce check. The freeway design and color scheme really are attractive and should get some envirodesign award. Though many cities have done very well at improving the gray slab approach to roadways, Albuquerque has it hands down insofar as I'm concerned. Salt Lake City did a nice job with the Olympic motifs in the underpasses, and several cities have some generic geometrics that mimic snowcapped mountains on the retaining walls, but Albuquerque is the only city I've seen that has gone to the extent of color-coordinating the cement and supporting structures for their part of the interstate. Way cool. Frank would have approved that as well, I think.

Trainer once lived in the "big A," as he calls it, and says this is the land of entrapment. He had a job here making so little he couldn't afford to move back to Texas, the blessed land of the fortunate, and his home forevermore. Puts his hand over his heart when he says "Texas." But, as the result of his having lived here, he knows the area where the service shop is that will do our produce check. That's good. In this maze of construction and narrow lanes and dead ends, having a guide is good. We find the place, and in making a tight turn, I hit one of the steer tires on the curb. That is a big no–no in itself, and on top of that, the bounce from the wheel dropping off the curb onto the pavement causes the television to unseat, and it falls from the shelf onto the floor, a drop of some four feet. Hearing the crash and seeing the television flopping around on the deck, about all we can do is look at one another, strapped into our chairs like we are. Can't stop here, in the middle of the street. I continue to drive around the corner and into the lot next to the produce check shop, and shut down.

It is cool here, more so than the season would suggest, so I opt for coffee at the snack counter rather than the ice-cold soda I'd wanted, plus I hate to watch a grown man grieve. I locate the service tech and snack counter while Trainer sits in the cab and mourns the television. No broken glass, but a really expensive-sounding rattle is coming from it as Trainer picks it from the floor.

On the road again. Back through the lunch traffic and out the east side of town to begin the climb up the Sandias, which is a sixth-gear struggle, overloaded with nectarines. The diesel hammering overpowers all the other sounds and it fills the cab with a staccato racketing. I don't know whether or not I like it, but the engine makes that sound every time it has to pull hard, and it has become the indication to me the Cummins is working at, or near, its limit. IthinkIcan, IthinkIcan, IthinkIcan.

It is a long ride up the hill, and there is a ski lodge at the top. In looking down, I guess if the snow was heavy enough, a person could just ski right into town. Environmentally friendly, and fun as well. Maybe a ski lift from downtown to the top of the hill would encourage that. Save on some of this pollution.

Down the hill on the other side, and we settle into the ride to Tucumcari and Amarillo. This stretch of interstate is along the old Route 66 made famous in song and film. Get your kicks on the mother road from Chicago to Los Angeles. We run parallel to much of it and have for some portion of the trip. Some of the old roadway still exists in the form of access roads for the interstate and main streets in the small towns, and a lot of it is on private lands behind fences. Many of the original bridges and viaducts are still around and still in use, but look small and narrow compared to the ones built for the interstate. Some of these remnants are heralded by official state signs, and some are pointed out by hand-painted signs advertising tourist traps. I guess people really stop at those places. Cars are there. See the live coyote, and get a free arrowhead.

On our way to lunch in Amarillo, we roll across northeastern New Mexico and the terrain begins a change from mountains and big mesas to long, lower mesas and a high plain with small box canyons, orange and red and gray and rocky. The sky seems big here as well, and the clouds are high and wispy. Condensed vapor trails from the jets mark up the sky, and the sparc beauty of that sky and the wispy clouds is ruined somehow, as though it was incidentally vandalized. High-altitude smog, I guess. Or graffiti, maybe, depending on the pilot's creativity.

Trainer is complaining of a gastric emergency and needs to stop at the next suitable facility. This is serious. I recall the trash-can thing some days ago, and start to scan the horizon and road signs for any indication of such a place. The trash can has its limit. Sure enough, and right on cue, a rest area shows up. Just a mile or so. We slow to exit and I whip into a truck parking space. Trainer sails out and double-times to the building. I shut the truck down and get out to do an en route inspection, just to see if anything is bent, broken, loose, or leaking. Or gone. It's a good excuse to get out of the truck for a little bit. My ankles are not as swollen as they have been, and I think maybe the increased stopping events and walking more when we are stopped, has helped some. My ankles are always normal sized after having slept, and I suppose lying down has a lot to do with it. Everything is fine in the mornings. They just swell a little during the day.

The midday is temperate and clear, so I walk toward the edge of the place, set on a small cliff, and look onto the broad landscape. Everything seems far from up here. Maybe because I can see far from here. Standing on the edge, a sudden shiver from nowhere causes me to take hold of myself, and I recall what a friend said years ago, that it's because a ghost walked through you. That could be true out here. I'll bet there are lots of them around, and no place to go. It is just too far to anywhere.

Back in the truck and rolling, I am disappointed in leaving this country and going onto the high plains and the eventual drop into the notsofaroff Mississippi River watershed. There is something in this country, as desolate as it is, that attracts me, still. I don't know if it is the wide vistas, or the colors, or the shape of the land or the huge sky or the lack of persons per square mile that causes me to want to be here. I know we are arboreal creatures, at home in the forest. Shelter, food and water at hand. I know our kind is comfortable in the forest's abundance and that even a modern human can probably make do in a forest. Scratch out an existence. We are supposed to be in a forest, it is where we do our best work, exploiting the available resources in the shelter the trees give us. But there is something about the high plains desert. Maybe it's the number of unimpeded miles I can rack up. Bigger paycheck. But I don't think that's it, really. I can't figure it out, but I am content here, with the nothingness, the big sky, the geography, and the ghosts busying themselves with walking through folks at rest areas.

— — —

Texas. Cadillac Ranch. Rusty cars buried nose-first up to the wind-shield at an angle in the plowed dirt some distance from the roadway. There is a path beaten out to them and around them by the tourists walking from the pavement out to the photo op. Eccentric oilman, I am told. No place but Texas. Oddly there is a leaning water tower just down the road as well. Lots of stuff at an angle around Amarillo. Must be the incessant wind.

Great conversation with the local college kids at a handy burger stand over an al fresco lunch, homemade mustarddripping greasycheesy and fatsoaked, saltcaked fries. Said they'd never talked to a trucker before. I thought how they still hadn't. That they thought truckers were big and mean and dirty. Good thing Trainer is having a nap.

We have to stop for fuel soon and Trainer says we need to go to a fuel stop he knows about to do that, plus he wants to drive. Wants to get to Arkansas before we shut down for the night. Says he wants to get this load delivered and get to his Mexico vacation. Trainer is getting in a hurry. Bad juju. Arkansas is a long way from Amarillo, and hurrying in a bigtruck is not good. Matter of fact, that I think about it, we have been hurrying since we left San Jose. I hadn't noticed until now. We pull into the fuel stop to a busy CB radio.

The usual network of service providers for the trucking industry is here. Restaurants, hair salons, commercial women, chrome polish salesmen, detailing services, airbrush artists, knife salesmen, CB shop, all advertising their respective capabilities and competing for airtime and dollars. Trucking has generated lots of jobs for nondrivers. Some of the drivers have their own slant, and hawk overages from their loads, extra parts and pieces for trucks and trailers, and offer to sell or trade videos and CDs. One is taking bets on a dogfight set for later some-where in the area. One is selling 100-pound bags of potatoes left over from a delivered load for $5 a bag. Capitalism at its simple best. No in-sider trading or market manipulation here. Just goods and services for dollars. We buy some fuel, grab a snack and ice-cold fountain drink, and head into the late afternoon for Arkansas, a determined vacationer at the wheel.

There is a dark row of puffy thunderstorms on the northern horizon, and should they loom larger, I get the feeling we may have a rough ride through Oklahoma, world-famous for fierce storms, if we don't beat them to their arrival at the interstate, and get on the other side of them. Maybe we can do that. The Oklahoma border is not far.

Borders are peculiar places. I have crossed many in different parts of our planet and have to say it is most pleasant, no, transparent, in our country. Most times, I don't even know it happened except for the sign. Even in a commercial vehicle, the only reason to stop is a scale, or port of entry, and that may be deep into the state. It is painless. We have forty-eight contiguous states, each with their own legislature, police force, army, governor, and sovereignty, yet we trust one another. We don't fear aggression from another state. We have unfortified boundaries. We share a currency and an economy. We share political parties and religions. We wander freely from one state to another. I can move to Florida tomorrow if I want. No passport, no nothing. Change of driver's license is about all. Fill out a change of address form at the post office. It is a great country. Truly great, to have the freedoms we have, mobility chief among them for a driver.

It is not so in other countries, including those with states. Crossing a border, even state to state, involves at least a small delay and minor inspection. In some cases, it involves a big delay and a big inspection. In other cases, crossing a border is a days-long and paperwork-intense process. We blow past the Welcome to Oklahoma sign. I mentally salute and thank George Washington et al. for lives well spent. Two hundred years later, I enjoy the fruits of their labors, and having taken the time years ago to dig into the lives of the men that built this country, I was taken completely aback at what it cost them to give us freedom. They ruined their lives for it. Sacrificed friends, family, and fortunes for it. We were born with it, cost us nothing thanks to those men, and the

Fourth of July means something to me above and beyond a day off and some fireworks. And so does crossing a state border unchallenged. I can do it because of them, their efforts, and the nearly unbelievable personal prices they paid to build a land of the free.

More south of the storms now, it looks like we will outrun them, and Trainer drives into the night. I ride and munch and watch the flashes of light illuminate the growing clouds far north of us. The storms strengthen and rage. There is a beauty in that rage, and like any cruel spectator sport, the person who sees the beauty is usually not involved in the raging. It is a spellbinding, awesome thing, to see something superior unrestrained in its violent splendor. We are drawn to watch such things for some reason, glad we are not involved, but wanting to see. I know the things beneath those storms are living in fear of what damage may be done, or has been done, but my vantage point offers only the wonder of a spectacular light show in the northern sky. Can't even hear the thunder. Far from harm, un-afraid, and witness to one of Nature's impressive, vicious tantrums in the dark of the Oklahoma night. I count myself a lucky man. Again.

We get into Oklahoma City around 11 P.M. to fuel in a classy truck stop. Classy in this context means new. Not a renovated dump . . . new. Brand-new. Almost makes me feel part of society again. Maybe I'm far-ther gone than I think, if that is all it takes. Been on the road a couple of weeks now, and I may be falling fast.

The fueling event itself is a multifaceted operation; then on top of that, there are several ways to buy the fuel. Cash will work, credit cards will get it, purchase orders will do, individual arrangements happen, and there is a type of card we use that direct-bills the company that is-sued the card. In our case the card-issuing company owns the trucks we drive, so several things are neatly packaged for us and fuel purchases are one of those things. Gotta pull in just right since there is not a lot of extra space on either side once we are between the pumps. A foot or so makes the difference in how accessible everything may be, and whether a pump gets hit or not.

Buying fuel in our case, with a company-issued card, is sort of like getting gas at the local convenience store. Pull up, get out of the car, and stick the card in the card reader on the pump, answer a few questions, and the petrol flows. In a bigtruck the process is the same, just more involved since we are using someone else's money. There is a keypad attached to every master pump, and that is where the requested information is keyed into the system that controls the fuel access, so when the card is swiped, the prompts start. Enter tractor number, trailer number, hub mileage, driver's license number and state, tractor license plate number, trailer number. Select tractor fuel, reefer fuel, or both. Do you want to buy oil or supplies? Do you want a cash advance? Then the command to dispense fuel and see attendant inside for receipt. Just to get the pump turned on.

The master pump triggers the slave pump on the passenger's side so that two pumps will fill the two tanks. There is an equalizer hose connecting the truck's tanks, but two pumps fill the tanks much quicker, each blowing about a gallon of diesel per second into the tanks, like I said before. Top off the passenger side, replace the nozzle, put the screwcap onto the tank, then go back around to the driver's side and top that tank off, then shut down the pump. Climb back in and pull the truck forward so the reefer tank can be filled, then stop, set the brakes again, and get out to fill that one. That tank is a lot smaller, usually only 50 gallons, some smaller than that, and doesn't take as long to fill. The reefer gets diesel fuel that is not taxed at the same rate as tractor fuel. It is the same fuel, you can't tell the difference, so there are drivers out there that siphon fuel from the reefer tank to the saddletanks to improve their miles per gallon in the tractor. That is a real good way to get fired, for a couple of reasons. One, it is a federal offense to burn untaxed fuel in a road tractor, and no company wants the feds rifling the office paperwork, no telling what else they'll find; and two, the driver is essentially stealing a miles-per-gallon bonus from his company. But it still happens, and people still get fired. Some get in seriously deep guacamole, depending on the quantity and/or duration of the offense(s) and what the G-men want to do about it.

Cap the reefer tank, turn off the pump and replace the nozzle, pull up far enough so another truck can get to the pumps, set the brakes, and go in to sign for the fuel. This part ain't like the family wagon. Done quickly, it takes about 15 minutes to fill from near empty. Fooling around, it can take half an hour.

Inside the fuel desk, on this about-to-be-stormy Oklahoma night, the storms having nearly caught up to us, there is a 17-, or maybe 18-year-old whore at the end of the counter with a friend. Friend is dumping her off for the night's take. The kid already looks haggard and shopworn. Maybe it's the hour, but I don't think so, to be so young, she has lots of hard miles on her, and is typical of the lot-lizard class of hookers that frequent truck-stop parking lots. Tattoos, eyebrow rings, tongue pegs, skimpy clothes. She looks at me as I sign for the fuel. I look back. She glances away. I turn to walk out, and she moves quickly to catch me at the inside door of the airlock. She looks up at me and asks do I want some company. I look deep into her eyes for any sign of anything, and say I have a daughter older than she even might be. She laughs bitterly, looks away, and says she hears that shit all the time. We stare at one another for an uncomfortable second or two, then she turns and walks through the doors to begin her business day in the middle of the night. I stand still holding the door handle and watch her go, thinking on how she *is* someone's daughter. The storms are close enough for the lightning to illuminate the parking lot in reflected flashes, like a filtered strobe as the hard-bitten womanchild disappears into the rows of idling chrome and candyapple tractors to earn her living in the anonymous never-never land of truck stops and interstate drivers. No one is who they say they are, no one is here for long, and no one cares.

Another driver wanders around munching a candy bar he hasn't paid for yet. He saw part of that. Says it's sad. She could at least be a truckdriver if she really wants to get screwed a lot and badly. Waves the

candy bar around to punctuate. I get out the door and into the truck to
find a parking place so the guy behind us at the pumps can get in to sign
his bill. I wonder about the kid, and what she thinks about life in general, and what brought her to this end, and how can that much go wrong
in 18 years.

Still thinking, more worrying really, about the kid, there are some
mean men out here, I await my turn at a shower. I stroll over to the row
of televisions that line the upper shelf on the back wall of the place and
they are all tuned to the weather channel, which is the case in most
places. Weather is a big factor in truckdriving, so most stops have that
information readily available in some form or another, and there is a
channel on television devoted entirely to the weather. It is an axiom in
this craft that one should know the weather conditions down the road
for safety's sake if not the impact on trip planning and delivery times. It
is good to know what to expect, especially in the winter. So, we pay a lot
of attention to the weather channel in the places we stop, and here in
this place there is a red and yellow line southwest to northeast across
Oklahoma bearing down on us in that stutter-step radar loop they run
during rough weather. Trainer studies the images for a minute and announces we will stay the night here. I agree. I look once more to see a
satellite view of the tropics and note a hurricane churning the Gulf.
This is not good. I have a house on a back bay, and no time to get it
ready for a hurricane. To get a house ready for a hurricane, you have to
be there. Windows to protect, yard items to secure, and trees to trim.
I'm headed to Tennessee. The local thunderstorms have lost some pri-
ority all of a sudden.

There are few things like being in the upper berth of a tractor's
condo during a gusty thunderstorm to bring on thoughts of unprotected
houses in hurricanes. The wind is strong enough to rock the cab uncomfortably, and I don't know whether or not the rattling on the side and
roof is rain or hail or both. Whatever, it is noisy enough to cause a fitful
sleep for a while, till it settles down to a patter, and I drift away thinking
about a girl I know who just bought a house about a mile from the ocean.

The morning comes in all its glory, shiny and new from the rain-washing, and coffeed up, we set out on the bigroad for a lunch buffet Trainer knows not far from Little Rock. Says the food is upper end of mediocre, but the price is right and you can eat all you want. Two major plusses for Trainer.

Central Oklahoma is unremarkable and we motor through hayfields and pastures until we get to a roadside park where the Oklahoma Highway Patrol has set up a portable scale and DOT inspection station. I didn't know Oklahoma did that. A big portable sign directs us off the roadway and into that picnic area. We wait in a short line for our turn on the scales and to see whether or not we will be inspected, and inch along. I finally get to the officer and he steps up, looks in and says have a nice day, then directs us around the scales and inspection station, toward the interstate. Surprised, I drive past the row of trucks pulled off to be scaled, and more to be inspected, look at Trainer, and ask what happened. Trainer says he don't know but don't slow down. I go up the gears, take the access ramp onto the bigroad, and set out for the Little Rock buffet. Trainer looks hungry. I feel relieved. I really didn't want being overweight to bring on a long delay in the form of a roadside DOT inspection. Those are long and ugly. Those DOT guys have an eight-hour shift to do and they are in no hurry as they take parts off and look at different things. A driver can be down all day, like we talked about earlier. That would have been my first DOT ticket, and I wonder what caused the trooper to wave us on. He knows reefer trucks are most likely at the weight limit, or over it. Trainer says it is because I am wearing a shirt with a collar on it. He says it seriously enough, I believe it. Mentally adding to that comment, I think we look rested, clean, and neat, our truck is one of a national fleet known for being well maintained, and those things indicate, or contraindicate, an inspection. Or maybe the guy is in a good mood, and he possibly recognized a fellow Okie. Whatever the reason, we slid our extra thousand pounds of nectarines smooth by a roadside scale, and that is about a once in a lifetime experience.

I have learned to shift the gears properly, and it is a concert of motion that gives me a satisfaction every time I shift all ten without clashing the transmission. There is a process of shifting the gears called
"floating" wherein the clutch is used from a dead stop only, not as part
of the shifting event. Most seasoned drivers float the gears in an effort to
save time and fuel in getting the truck to roadspeed, and the likelihood
of missing a shift is reduced which adds a safety factor. My shifting capability will not allow that technique at this stage of my development,
but it will come with time. A conscientious trainer would not allow a
midterm trainee to float the gears anyway. In such a green state of capability, that trainee would not instantly know what to do in the event of a
missed shift, and the truck would lose roadspeed quickly, to the point of
being a hazard on the interstate. We don't want to do that.

Oklahoma goes by my windows for a while, nondescript but pleasant country. Houses, farms, and fields. Driver going westbound talking
on the CB to someone going his way about his hometime. Fishin' with
the kids in Alabam'. Glad to get back onto the boulevard, but misses the
wife and young 'uns. We pass through the conversation, and the radio
settles back into its low-frequency buzz. I know Trainer is thinking
about his home, having listened. I can hear it in the silence. I think on
how trucking is not a career for a family man. Just not home enough.

Oklahoma looks homey. In fact, it is my original home. I was born just
south of here, and my parents live in that same area, and once I take note
of that, I decide to call a little later, since I can't drive the truck to visit.
We wouldn't be paid for the miles, and worse, we would be penalized.

Drivers are paid by the mile, and not necessarily for every mile they
drive. There is an industry standard that is used to calculate the number of miles that exist between the shipper of the goods and the receiver
of those goods. All trucking companies use that standard, unless the
driver is paid by the number of hub miles. The number of miles indicated by the standard may or may not be what the truck travels to get
from one place to the other. Most of times it is not. Usually the truck
goes more miles than the standard dictates, and those miles are termed

"out of route" miles. Most companies allow 4 to 10 percent out-of-route miles on each trip from shipper to receiver for fueling, food stops, produce checks, detours, using a loop instead of the city route, and getting lost. Anything more, without a good reason, and the driver not only doesn't get paid for those miles, he or she may have to reimburse the company for the expense of traveling those miles. And bigtrucks don't run cheap.

Sometimes the standard allows more miles than the truck actually travels, and the driver is paid for miles not driven. That's good. It isn't a regular occurrence, but it happens. A device called a Hubometer monitors and displays the miles the wheels actually cover, and it is attached to a drive axle on the tractor, usually on the driver's side. That way, the driver can get out and have that information close by for whatever the occasion. The device is a super-accurate odometer, tamperproof and lovingly referred to as a "hub." The mileage on the hub is reported regularly at fuel stops, by the fuel pump transaction, daily e-mail reports from the truck quailcall, and repair authorizations, among other things, and the company tracks that by the tractor, and with a little basic math, HQ knows how many miles the truck has been driven at most any given time. Pretty simple, really.

The cell phone call is cheaper all around. My parents are fine, and wonder where I may be. They wonder from time to time. They have traveled a great deal in their lives and like to hear about such things as happen on the road, or at least act like it, and I stay more in touch with them on the road than when I am home. My life out here is not cluttered with the demands on my time that my home life has. Big Blue rumbles on, past those houses, farms, and fields.

Another border painlessly crossed. I see there is a lot of swampland in Arkansas, and those Arkies grow a lot of rice where there is no swamp, per se. I had no idea either of those things existed this far north. I had Arkansas envisioned as something else and had never seen this side of it. I could wake up here and think I was in coastal Louisiana. Lots of mosquitoes hereabouts and we are certainly taking out a bunch of them.

In one area just now, where there were cows in the soggy lowlands, I guess the little suckers had been feasting on the beef; we drove through a cloud of mosquitoes that hit the windshield like red raindrops. Must have been hundreds plastered on the glass in just a few seconds.

The wipers just smear the bug parts and blood, and the washers take several attempts to get the biomuck wiped away to the place I can see well enough to continue. I had thought to pull over and clean the windshield, knowing the critters would gum up the blades, but the glass is so pasted with them I have no choice but to scrape some off with the wipers so I can see well enough to get off the road. Dammit. It makes a huge, smeared red mess for a few seconds and then begins to clear up once the windshield washer solvent kicks in, and we are left with only a crust of carcasses and clots and windshield soap at the ends of the wiper tracks. Nasty looking. Still some streaks of bugstuff on the windshield. Yuck.

We get to the buffet in time for lunch, and Trainer hurts 'em. I don't do too badly myself this blue moon, and tank up on the buttery rolls. Breadhead, y'know. This is gonna hurt. We both weeble back to the truck and hit the bunks for an hour. We look like a couple of dog ticks. Air conditioner feels good blowing on me, and it is easy to float away.

Short nap, power nap Trainer calls them, and we are heading east for Memphis. There is a brake check, and we sit for more than 45 minutes, then see a Medivac chopper go over and land somewhere down the road on the westbound side of the interstate. The CB misinformation has everything from blazing cars with fatalities to a guy changing a flat on the shoulder and two kids flying a kite creating the backup.

Turns out to be a major accident, and as we creep by with the lookylews, I see a bigtruck has hit a pickup square in the arse. The rear axle of the pickup is on the roadway and the badly crumpled body of the pickup is on the shoulder some distance from the axle, like 40 or 50 feet distant. Tremendous impact, obviously, and if there is anything good about this, it is that the pickup didn't roll under the tractor. I hope no one was killed, but it looks bad. Real bad. Bad enough someone gets a helicopter ride. I silently ask whatever Power is out there to look after the victims. I don't know if that helps, but it is all I can do from here, and makes me feel a little less helpless at times like this. Careless, sleepy, distracted, and drunk car drivers. Bigtruck drivers too, unfortunately, and I wonder which one caused this wreck. I am still amazed there are no more accidents than there are. Maybe that Power really does watch over kids, drunks, and fools. Or some of them anyway. Apparently not all of them.

We move slowly past in a conversationless tractor cab and listen to the staticky garble of the CB commentators, both of us sobered by this incident for us, and tragedy for others. Lives are ruined, and ours are made more aware. As Trainer and I go by the scene, we are both thinking the same things. Torn for those we see and mindful it wasn't us or ours this time.

Traffic spreads out a little past that, and we regain roadspeed heading east to our fuel stop in West Memphis where I mistake the entrance to the fried chicken place for the entrance to the truck stop. They are right next to one another. I wheel right into the parking lot with 70 feet of truck and realize too late what has happened. Trainer is livid, the chickenstore patrons mortified and the other drivers coming out the truck stop are on the CB like a pack of jackals. It's a hoot. Missed by one driveway. I sit and look around for a second and realize someone knew this would happen because there is a connection between the two parking lots and if I drive straight for it and go sharp, or buttonhook, a right, I can get out of here without tearing down phone lines and light poles, or crushing a four-wheeler. Things are good. Seeing that out is like realizing the lion is nearly on you and there is one more bullet. If you miss, you're dead.

So it is with me, I have one shot at getting us out of the chickenstore parking lot and if I blow it, we will have to back out and that means stopping interstate frontage road traffic. The police will be everywhere and Trainer will imagine more of his career slipping away. It is a serious predicament, but I feel no pressure once I see the option. I somehow know I can do this, but I also realize if I muff it, traffic will be tied up for hours, this place will not sell a single piece of chicken at the drive-thru, and HQ will defecate. Trainer wants to not be here. I see what I need to do, and with a few inches to spare, it'll work if I do it right. Shove Blue into second gear and start fighting the steering wheel. Watch those tandems and the poles and the cars and the buildings and the overhead wires. People stop to watch, noses pressed to glass, from inside the chicken store and cars along the roadway. Not to mention my peers lined up for the show across the lawn at the truck stop I was aiming for. Must be a hundred pair of eyeballs trained on this truck.

I pull it off. It would make a good training video: How not to get into the chickenstore parking lot and how to get out if you do. Much hand-clapping and laughing and head-shaking from all quarters as we roll out and away uneventfully.

All the excitement past, we get fueled and make our way into the town of West Memphis and move in the flow of bridge traffic across the mighty Mississippi. This is one deep and wide river. Through Memphis, home of Beale Street, Elvis, and the Delta blues, onto the flatness of western Tennessee, which steadily becomes more like the Tennessee mountains and forests sold on travel pamphlets as we motor along the way to Nashville. That's where we will head south to drop our nectarines, and near, well, kinda near some old stomping grounds for myself.

In a past life, I lived as a contractor in the nuclear industry and as such, was lucky enough to get an assignment to the Watts Bar facility in the Tennessee River Valley. I stayed the hot summer, colorful autumn, and snowy winter in a rented cabin along the shore of Watts Bar Lake near a town called Ten Mile, and it ranks still as one of the best chapters of my life. I spent my time semi-alone, Thoreau-like, hiking the Cumberlands, Chilhowees, and Appalachians, going into civilization only for supplies or my regular meeting with contemporaries on frosty Tuesday nights across the mountains in the comfortable restaurant of a friend, raising our glasses to those unable to be with us. Those ribeyes were good, and the times were as well. I think on those days regularly and fondly, and the company of good friends that would warm my winter nights.

So, I enjoy coming here when I can. We are not really near the area, but it is good to be in this part of Tennessee. Kinda feels like I'm almost home again. I won't be getting much closer than I am this trip, but I may be back this way later in the training process, and hopefully I'll get a little closer. See how the 'hood has changed, if at all. This part of Tennessee doesn't get very involved in the headlong rush to oblivion, and I think that is one of the things I like most about it, natural beauty not even mentioned.

I spent some time in that sabbatical developing a semi-skill with a friend's camera, and when I had exposed several rolls of film, I would make the trip into a larger town some distance away to have the shots developed in the photo department of a discount store. Many times the same girl would be there to handle the process and we struck up a casual relationship over a period of time, to the point we could ask questions about one another. She knew I was not from the area, and asked me what I did for a living. I told her and she said it sounded interesting what with all the travel and seeing new things. I, in turn, and in making conversation, asked her where she had been and wonders she had seen. She said she had never left Loudon County, Tennessee. Surprised, I asked why. Said there was no reason to leave.

In thinking about it later, she was correct. There was no reason for her to leave. She had the mountains, lakes, forests, rivers, waterfalls, and four distinct seasons. Family all here as well. Might seem shallow to some, but having ranged far and wide in my fairytale life on this blue planet, I think I could find happiness in Loudon County, Tennessee, much like herself.

Oddly, I knew of two other people that worked on my project at the nuclear facility that had never left Rhea County, Tennessee, up to that point in their lives, and may not have left yet. Folks just don't seem to have reason to leave the ancestral grounds in Tennessee, unless it is to volunteer for a fight at the Alamo in the Texas territory. And I am happy there were itchy-footed folks that liked a good scuffle living in Tennessee about the 1830s. Were it not for Tennessee, there might not be a Texas. Might still be Mexico.

Nashville has a simple, but attractive skyline, and is the ballyhooed playground and home of the country music elite. It is a surprisingly cosmopolitan city for all that, so don't come here thinking to see a bunch of hicks or hayseeds. Don't have any of those here, but they do have the exit we are looking for just a little way down the interstate.

We take a southern route a little to the east of town and head south toward the distribution center waiting for our nectarines. It is a nice evening, and I feel like I'm home somehow. Trainer feels good, too. It is kind of amazing how attitudes are contagious sometimes. It feels good to feel good. I look over at Trainer and grin. He looks back, shakes his head, and laughs that goofy hawhawhaw. We roll down the road to our stop, the early lights of Nashville in the vibrating mirrors.

Aristotle was right about lots of things, and one of the most profound, and true, is the observation that the only constant is change. In my mindless enjoyment of the situation, I've forgotten we are in a machine. Aristotle also observed the more complicated the machine, the more subject it is to failure. We are in a complicated machine, the "change" constant is in the equation, and the prophesy lands on us unannounced.

A loud pop interrupts my meditation and instinctively, I look in my mirror. The pop came from behind me, and the mirror is the best way to see what is behind me. Trainer does the same. He sees nothing; I see baseball-sized chunks of rubber flying from beneath the trailer tandems and say as much to Trainer. There is no reason to stop and create a traffic situation, so we slow a little and look intently for a truck stop of any kind preferably, and any place to pull off the highway secondarily.

No more than a mile, and we see a billboard touting one of our favorite brands of truck stops. It is only a couple of miles down the road. That's good. These nectarines are mostly water, and that makes them heavy. We need eight tires back there carrying an equal share of the load. Not seven overloaded ones. In a situation like this, if we lose another due to overloading, we could lose them all. One at a time, and in quick succession. Not likely, but it has happened, and I don't want to be a part of that.

Tense moments until we exit, and get pointed to the tire shop part of the facility. Very little conversation. Just focused driving and mental handwringing. A lot of people's safety is at stake here. Again.

The facility we luck onto is one of a nationwide chain and, as such, has predictable services, so we are confident we will not be out of action long. We roll into the large lot and idle toward the repair shop. I get on the quailcall and request authorization for the tire replacement while Trainer checks out the area from the cab of Big Blue. He says it looks like a good restaurant in there. I say that's a burger shop, as I type the message to HQ. He says yeah, it looks like they got good damburgers in that burger restaurant in there. How can you tell? You just can.

He probably really can.

The response is quick in coming, and it is, of course, an approval for a tire purchase. The company I have chosen to drive with is very safety conscious, and spares no reasonable expense to maintain their trucks. They are acutely aware that a maintained truck is both safe and productive. I like that, and it is one of the two main reasons I will stay with them for most of my driving career. They don't mess around with safety issues.

I guide Blue's nose into the tire repair bay of the service shop and Trainer says he needs to get a bite or two, and to come on in after I take care of the tire, that I need to learn how to do all that stuff anyway. He sails out the cab door and is gone. I set the brakes and get out to arrange the replacement. The man says give him an hour and he'll have it ready to go. Time enough for a burger, I am thinking. A still, small voice tells me to get a shower while we are down. I ignore it and lube up my arteries in the burgerbar with the available time.

That hour passes by and we get back to the truck, which has a new tire, and we are ready to get on the bigroad. Sign some papers in the shop so everyone gets paid, and head south to our stop and hope we can drop the trailer early, since it is not due till morning, and we can go get a decent night's sleep in a truck stop. Maybe we won't have to lay around a distribution center parking lot all night waiting to unload, and have no coffee in the morning. I know it may not work out that way, but it is a pleasant thought, and it could happen.

Rolling along the countryside and following relatively simple directions makes for a pleasant trip, but that's not always the case. This place will be easy to find because it is a distribution center in the middle of agricultural land. It'll stick out like a sore something or other. Pop right up out of the landscape. Big concrete and steel building surrounded by acres of concrete parking lot. Can't miss it. Especially in the dark. It will be lit by gadzillions of candlepower. We'll see the glow long before we get there. It will be the only thing glowing after dark around these parts. Unless they built another nuke plant hereabouts.

Ridin' and guidin' along the interstate with the a/c, FM, and CB blasting, watching the land go by the windows, is a very enjoyable part of truck driving. This is a beautiful country with beautiful things in it. The pattern of life on a cross-country trip is relaxing and predictable. Get up about daylight, grab a newspaper and coffee, get the paperwork for the day done, and drive till we are ready to stop. Pull into a secure facility, usually a truck stop, and shut down for the night. Get a hot meal and a shower, read a little, call home, catch the 10 o'clock news, and get into the bunk. Do it again tomorrow. The days lose their names, and the date is only important for the paperwork. For a solo driver, it takes about six days, depending on the weather, road conditions, and the delivery date, to drive from California to Maine. A good team can run it in three days with time to spare on the third day. It is a pleasant way to make a hundred-and-a-half a day. Dress like you want. Break when you want. No boss watching every move every minute. Just move the freight from one side of the country to the other on time.

But, the two end processes, pickup and delivery, are headaches for an over-the-road driver. There are dedicated runs, where the driver picks up and delivers to the same places day after day, year after year. They know what lane to get into, where to exit, and what roads to take to make their scheduled stops. Those are like real jobs, though, and the essence of cross-country driving is lost. Same route every day, or week or whatever. Knowing where you are going is the only advantage I see to that, aside from more plannable and regular hometime. And to a family guy, those are reasons enough to do that. Forty-eight-state and international drivers don't get either of those. When they'll get home is a toss-up between the availability of freight going toward home and a sympathetic dispatcher.

Over-the-road drivers rarely get to pick up or deliver at the same places. It is the nature of the business. The coordinating of the loads and keeping the truck moving and that law of large numbers says a given driver won't get to the same places very often. So the driver finds him/herself trying to find these pickup and delivery places. Many things conspire to prevent that, and the first is bad directions.

Most trucking companies have one of several available mainframe programs accessible through the quailcall that will provide directions to shipper or receiver. Just scroll through the macros and stop on the I-need-directions screen, punch in a couple of characters, and hit the "send" button. A few seconds later, the screen beeps and the directions to the facility from a major highway are right there. Problem is, the directions were put in there by a driver most times *after* he/she managed to find their own way to that facility. They don't always remember accurately, or they may have taken a really roundabout route to get where they are. Sometimes they leave out a phrase, or a turn, or a road. Sometimes they came in from the north, and we are coming in from the south. Their left turn is now our right. There is another program that uses GPS coordinates. It looks at where the truck is, where the driver wants to be, and selects the shortest route. Sometimes it will send a driver right down a no-truck route in an effort to be mileage efficient. Even if all those things are okay, there are other problems.

Storms plaster snow and ice onto road signs. Which one of these eleven exits is the right one? Kids take street signs. Adult street-maintenance workers take street signs. It just isn't there to see. Driver misses the turn, and who knows how far that driver will go before the stark realization this ain't the right way comes along. Bigtrucks knock signs down on corners at intersections. Bushes and trees hide signs. In Quebec, all the road signs are in French. Try that in a blizzard, in the dark, or both. Car drivers cut bigtrucks off—zip into the exit lane from behind and won't move forward or back, or zip onto the access lane and won't move onto the expressway. Driver misses exit. That brings on a host of other problems, some of which we have talked about.

Sometimes, based on funktified directions in the macro that don't make a lot of sense, it is deemed facile to call the facility and get it from the horse's mouth, or the other end of the horse, depending on who answers the phone. I am constantly confounded by people who work in these places and don't know how to tell someone else to get there. They go to that place every workday but they do not know the names of the streets, they don't know which exit to take, they do not know east from west. But they are not as bad as the ones that don't know and think they do. Those offenders sound very matter-of-fact and cocksure of themselves. It is easy to believe them. It is easy to get lost behind those nondirections. Nearly unfixably lost.

Unfixably lost is a bad thing to have happen in unfamiliar cities. In some cities a driver is semicomfortable. He may know an interstate or two, or a loop or a spur, and, armed with one or two of those, can make his way back to the state of being found from the state of being lost. But, getting lost, or turned around, or missing a turn in an unfamiliar city is not so easily remedied. The driver may drive miles to find a place to turn around. Even then, the driver has to go back beyond the missed turn, make another turn somewhere, and come back where he began and start over. Having that happen is a scary and unnerving experience, and drivers start doing dumb stuff to get out of that situation. It is very easy to logic-out the cloverleaf solution where the driver solves a wrong turn, or missed turn or exit, by getting off on the next exit and looping under the freeway to go back the way he came. Get off. Stop at end of ramp.

Set up to turn left. Hope it is an overpass, but it may be an underpass, if he thinks that far ahead. Make the turn and start toward the underpass, if that's what it is. The clearance sign says 12 feet and 2 inches. The trailer is 13 feet 6 inches from the road surface to top of the box. The trailer will be topped if the truck continues. Driver has to stop, call police, and get them to direct traffic while the truck is backed out of the underpass. If the driver sees that low-clearance sign in time to stop. Some don't. Just as bad, it could be the low clearance is a reason that road is not a truck route. That happens, which is another problem all by itself: Being lost, trying to turn around, and getting onto a no-truck route. Then, finding out the hard way why it is a no-truck route.

The driver is like a drowning person trying to get air; they just want to get back onto the bigroad, and will do nearly anything to get back where they can breathe. There is a measure of comfort on the interstate. They may still be lost, but the problems they would encounter on city streets are removed from the mix.

Drivers do really dumb and dangerous things like U-turns trying to correct a missed turn or exit. That sets the stage for a rununder. They'll stretch the trailer across the road to make that U-turn. Anything to get back to the interstate where they feel safe. It is easy to panic and do the things a panicked person does to fix what is wrong. There is no measure of reason put to the dogged determination of a lost and panicky driver trying to get back on the bigroad. The situation is highly stressful for the driver, and very dangerous for the motoring public.

All these things can and do happen to drivers who miss their turns. Sometimes the situation can be corrected just by going around the block. But it's rare. Pickups and deliveries are the bane of a driver's existence, and can eclipse nearly all the fun of the whole cross-country experience. Particularly if it involves a missed or wrong turn, for whatever reason up to and especially including bad directions. Drivers depend on signs and directions for a successful connection to shipper or receiver. Without them, or the ability to see and read those signs, things get bad fast. For everyone around that truck.

We don't have that problem in this instance. The place is easy to find in the middle of rural Tennessee, like I figured it would be, and as we exit the highway, Trainer says he's pretty sure they'll let us drop the trailer. We slow for the gate and hiss to a stop exactly where the sign says to stop. Steer tires right on the painted line.

Trainer unclimbs the truck and goes inside the door with a sign that says, "Drivers stay in your trucks." Trainer gets involved in a discussion with two thin and elderly gate guards. He is three times their individual sizes and contained in a glass building about 10 feet by 10 feet. He looks like a bear in a glass cage with two storks.

He comes back out and says we are early and we can't drop the trailer. We have to wait until our appointment time. That would be 5 A.M. Okay, will they let us park inside the compound where our load is secure and we have access to the driver's lounge and the other facilities in there? No. Okay, is there a place to park for the night around here? Park along the access road to the place back the way we came. Just don't block the incoming traffic . . . That's what they said.

I point to the shoulder of the asphalt road in the dark. Over there? Yup. I'm not comfortable with that. We could be hit, and it would be our fault. We are not supposed to park on the shoulder. The trailer could be broken into, this is not a secure area. We need to get to a secure place, like a truck stop. Protect us and the load. Nope. The closest one is the place that put our tire on two hours back. Mmmm. He's right. That would put us seriously out of route, and cost us two hours there and two hours back, taking four hours' sleep out of our night. Unsatisfactory.

Trainer says park it on the shoulder. What if the shoulder is soft? No answer. Okay. It's your truck. I clutch and shift into second gear. Big Blue lurches forward. I am going to drive inside the compound to turn around. Doing so out here is impossible. It is a two-lane road and the guardshack is in the middle. I drive by the storks and they look up at me, I think put off by my audacity in driving in without permission. Trainer looks at them as well. We are all looking at one another as we go by. They know what we are doing. They see it a dozen times a day. They just want to register disapproval. Petty people in minor authority. I think it was Chief Joseph who said true strength is gentle. Geezer types need to widen their horizons by reading a little Native American philosophy while they sit around in guardshacks. Do something besides jerk drivers around.

I get the rig turned around inside the fenced compound on the concrete acreage there and drive back out the gate past the guardshack onto the entry road about a klick or so, then notice a perpendicular apron I hadn't seen coming in and decide that will be better than parking on the entry road itself. I make the turn and spin the trailer on the tandems so I can set up to back straight in and leave some room for the next guy. Trainer sits in silence. Looking out the windows into the darkness. He doesn't relish spending the night here anymore than I do. I leave one set of wheels per axle on the pavement just in case the shoulder is soft, for traction to get back onto the road, and so I don't get far enough over to cause a rollover if those wheels sink in during the night. We sit and stare after I set the brakes. I am the first to set about getting into the bunk, Trainer still staring out the window. We sit at a serious angle from level because of the shoulder grade, so much so that I spend most of the night holding the grabrail of the bunk to keep from sliding to the passenger side of the bunk now become the bottom. No shower, either. I knew back at the repair stop I should have taken a shower but instead got the burger. Failed once again to listen to the voices.

Five A.M. rolls around finally, to put an end to the slanted half-sleep, and the new crew of gate guards let us in to be unloaded. I'm thinking I'll just get some more sleep while all that happens. Trainer says let's make the bucks and unload these nectarines ourselves. I point out he is either a greedy capitalist, or a guy needing vacation money. He says no, it's his wife. She's a greedy capitalist *and* wants the vacation money. I like his wife, and in her interest, I reluctantly climb into my denim jumpsuit I brought along for just such foolishness and go along with him into the cold storage facility that must cover 40 acres, no kidding.

It is huge. And cold. Not nearly as cold as an ice cream storage place, but still, I don't have enough clothes on.

We unloaded 2,400 cases of nectarines in two hours. Forty dollars an hour to suffer this abuse. I will be sore for days. I don't think we have enough aspirin in the truck to fix this.

Done, I start in about being up since five and having no coffee, and being forced to unload nectarines in the freezer before daylight. Trainer says they always have coffee in the driver's lounge and I can get some there. I say I don't want coffee from a nasty, unkept twelve-cup coffeemaker in a flimsy eight-ounce Styrofoam cup, I am a recently paid man with cash money in hand and I can have what I want and I want good coffee made by coffee drinkers at a reputable establishment and I can afford that now, so let's be about it . . . Jocko.

Trainer looks down at me and squinches up his eye just before he roars with laughter. I stand my ground in mock defiance. He stops laughing and glares down at me in the same tone. I inch closer. He says he ain't goin' anywhere with me in that faggit jumpsoot, an' I'm the biggest asshole he ever knew. Says I'm an asshole, too. I tell him he's already called me an asshole. Says that's okay, that I'm a big enough asshole to be called an asshole twice. Flounces around and heads for the truck. He probably needs cigarettes anyway, or he wouldn't give in that easily.

We go back the way we came last night and stop into a big convenience store that has a space big enough to park a truck for a minute to get coffee and, I knew it, cigarettes. Trainer says damgood thing he needed cigarettes as we emerge into the early morning from the store. I agree it is and say I'd have been all over him like cheap underwear had he not stopped for my coffee. I notice he says all this with a cup of coffee in his hand.

We need to do the logs.

When I return to the store to get my extra-large cup refilled, a young black woman is cleaning one of the commercial coffeemakers, her back to me and singing soprano in a quiet voice like some women do when they work, and I stop behind her a few feet so she can't see me, be surprised, and possibly stop the charming melody.

She is alone in her work at the bar, the morning rush probably not what a regular truck stop would have, and, busily cleaning, she sings unaware of my presence and puts her quiet spirit into it. Softly, but clear and rich, she works her magic for both of us. She is where she is, and I am taken back to the kitchen of my childhood and hear my grandmother's soft singing, once more, as she washed the dishes, or folded the towels so long ago. Just for a moment I am with my grandmother in the summer kitchen of the old house, and then I am whisked back, listening to this girl's unheralded talent. It is absolutely enchanting, to hear a woman's voice, when she thinks she is alone, and lets her heart sing, unafraid of ridicule. *Encanta*. I listen, afraid to move, that the spell would be broken, a few feet behind her.

She turns in her work, shortly, sees me, and stops in midword, wide-eyed, and looks straight at me. Face frozen. Caught. Embarrassed at having shown that secret side of herself. I say that was beautiful. She looks down. I say I am glad there are women that still would sing when they work, that it reminds me of my grandmother. She says thank you. I tell her the pleasure is mine, to have taken that little break with her. She hurries away into the back. I feel bad for having embarrassed her, but I smile at how I know she will get over it and be the better for knowing someone appreciated her voice. Satchmo was right. What a wonderful world. Of the planets out there, I am glad I got to spend some time on this one, with people like that. I do not know her name, only her face and her song, and both of them in my album now; she sings for me still, sometimes. I have been given some truly fabulous gifts, and sometimes I get them out and look at them again, and am reminded of how and where and from whom I got them. Her voice and her song are among my favorites.

I get back to the truck, thinking on all these things, and send a message to HQ that we are empty and need a load. Message comes back it may be a while, to go to the facility that replaced our tire and wait there. Okay. That's a good place to be, and I need to do some laundry anyway.

We climb in and crank up. Trainer wants to drive. I am okay with that, too. I'll just drink my coffee, made with a song, and see the sights on the way.

Southern Tennessee, early Sunday morning, good company and good coffee. Trainer and I yack back and forth about things in general. How life is mostly what we make it and partly what other people make it, and the sonsabitches that run the trucking industry.

I still do not believe they pay me for this.

Back where we had the tire replaced—actually, both tires on that set of duals because one was bigger than the other, and the DOT says both tires on the dual rims have to be the same size. The DOT doesn't spend a whole lot of time explaining their rules, but when a rule is presented, it is usually to prevent history from repeating itself. That may have been history repeating itself when our tire blew. Whatever happened back when to cause the DOT to lay out that rule, may have happened to us. Our blown tire was the biggest of the two and may have been carrying an unfair share of the load. Stressed, maybe, it popped. Both tires on a set of duals need to be the same size. Whoever changed that tire on the trailer before we picked it up in Kingman didn't know about, or maybe care about, the DOT rule regarding tire sizes and just put on whatever they felt like putting on the rim. Maybe it was midnight and that was the closest thing the place had to the right size. But probably not. These are common-sized tires, and most reputable places would have many this size. Someone just didn't care and because of that, our tire blew. DOT knew it would.

Arriving, Trainer sets the brakes, we look at one another, and Trainer hollers breakfast. So, we go into the restaurant and order a down-home, Southern-fried, gravy-topped, butter-soaked meal with a sugar-frosted donut to finish it off, and slop down the last of it with some of the best coffee I've had since that cup earlier this morning.

We sit picking our teeth and sipping the coffee, looking out the window at the interstate and the sparse traffic going by. I see one sizable bacon rind in the stack of greasy dishes on the table and use the last crust of butter-sopped toast to wrap it and dip that morsel into the last spot of buttered, salted grits and savor the last bite I can scrounge from this repast. Got about half my fourth or fifth cup of coffee left, and that'll be about right. Trainer watches me and says I'll probably have a heart attack before I'm 50 eating like that. I say I'd rather drop dead face-first into my plate of steak and mashed potatoes at 60 than live to be a hundred eating rice cakes and drinking low-fat milk. Besides, you ate the same stuff and twice as much. He says yeah, but he ain't worried about food killing him, it's cigarettes he's worried about. Said the wife told him if cigarettes get any higher priced and he don't quit, he's dead meat. Smokin' up the grandkids' Christmas money.

Last of the coffee gone, Trainer says he needs a nap while we wait to be dispatched. That moving his jaw muscles to eat that much food makes him tired. It almost makes sense. I need to do some laundry, so we head back to the truck in the now-warm morning. Trainer for his nap and me for my laundry bag and some quarters, wondering if I'll have time to finish before we get a dispatch. We only have an hour to ac- knowledge a load when we are sent one via the quailcall before dispatch gives it to someone else, so we have to be ready to roll when we get a load assignment, or at least have them think we are ready to roll.

In the truck, I had no more than thought about that, when the quailcall beeps and the message says no load until tomorrow morning. Cool. We have the day off. Plenty of time to do the stuff we need to do. Laundry, housecleaning, snoozing, read, watch movies, call home, and wander around the 'hood. Eat some more.

All those things get done, and it is dinner time. Chicken-fried steak, salted, buttered mashed potatoes, salted, buttered corn on the cob, pep- pered sawmill gravy, buttered biscuits topped with sugared, caffeinated iced tea for dinner at the local pub. We struggle back to the truck to sleep it off.

I wake nine uninterrupted hours later at dawn on Monday morning.

I know today will be a busy day, so I decide to wake Trainer and get things happening. I lie curled up in my sheet and think we will have to get a load, get over to wherever it may be, get hooked up, get it scaled, and get rolling. All that takes time, and the earlier we get our morning routine out of the way, the faster we will be able to respond to the load assignment when we get it. So, I don't let us sleep in, and open the light curtains with my foot, and listen to Trainer get motivated. The usual stuff with the usual sounds. Shortly, I get up and take advantage of my few minutes alone in my routine, and follow him to the coffee bar.

Inside, he says we need a load this morning, that laying around is for rich folks. I whip out a dollar for two cups of coffee, Trainer grabs a box of donuts and we start back for the truck where a waiting message from HQ instructs us to go to a nearby chicken processing plant to pick up a frozen load of luckless birds that will never know about their trip to Oregon, although they will ride with us only as far as Dallas. Someone else will get them to their final destination. Meanwhile, we gotta be there by 10 A.M. to pick them up. While Trainer sends in the proper responses, I go back for seconds at the coffee bar. Twenty-five cents this time.

When I get back to the truck, Trainer is sitting in the first chair and ready to go. Trainer says he wants to drive this morning, that it is such a beautiful day. Okay. I'll just sip this coffee, read the paper, and watch the Tennessee video tour out the window.

Keeping up with the news is no problem on the road. Televisions are on at most places we stop, tuned to a news or weather channel, and I learned long ago that *USA Today* is the newspaper for someone who travels a great deal. Problem is, with that paper, Friday is the last edition until Monday morning. I like a paper every day. With new news in it. Not rereading Friday's paper. But today is not Friday, and a lot has happened over the weekend, so the paper is thicker than usual. I'll grab one to go.

It really is a beautiful day, and I climb into the second seat to watch the countryside go by and navigate to the pickup point for Trainer between sections of the paper. I sip my coffee, read and ride in silence through the same territory we traveled yesterday. It seems different to me somehow this morning. More alive, maybe since we will be leaving here soon and off toward home. The first few minutes or the beginnings of a journey are always exciting in an anticipative sort of way. The thought of leaving where I am, and going somewhere else, especially home, and I sit in that expectation as I take my coffee and relax in the second seat. I watch Trainer out the corner of my eye so he doesn't know I am watching which will cause him to do things like he's being watched. I like the way he is when he is driving and thinking whatever it is he is thinking. He is comfortable with driving and is as relaxed as I am, or as relaxed as he can be while he is driving. I smile to myself, look out onto Tennessee, and unfold the paper.

I know we are about to come into the town where we will pick up our load, so I get out the atlas and the directions to the shipper from the quailcall so we won't be caught unaware as we get close. I recite the directions for Trainer and he nods in agreement, says he recognizes those directions and thinks he has been here before. Says he won't know for sure until we get closer. I call out the street names and intersections to watch for as we approach them. Trainer says he has been here before, but is not sure how to get there from here. We come to a T-shaped intersection and the directions are vague, so Trainer decides to wing it and go forth on memory alone. Dam them directions. I say I have no idea what to do, why don't we use my cell phone and call. He says he thinks he knows where to go, we'll call if he gets lost. Okay.

We move through town in the bigtruck. It is an old and long-established town, like many in this part of the nation, and as the result of that turn he guessed at, we are now in the middle of it. The streets are from the early part of the century. I know this because the dates carved into the arches of the brick and stone buildings are from the turn of the century. The date on one is 1902. The street was here then. We are on it now. In a 40-ton truck. I am almost afraid to look at the signs along the sidewalk for fear one will say no trucks. DOT ticket. The streets are narrow and the storefronts are right on the curb, and I hope some little old lady doesn't step too far out the door of some establishment and into our path. I cringe a little mentally and hope we get through town quickly. Reminds me of the ride through Laredo, but with brick streets, and no trees.

Trainer is getting a little crimped and says we musta made a wrong turn. He keeps driving. Slowly. I just look over at him and say nothing.

The street curves gradually to the point I am almost unaware it is happening until I see the sun is no longer on our left side. It is more behind us now, and is moving around to Trainer's side of the truck. We are making a gentle circle and have moved a little away from the heart of downtown. The road is a little wider, and the wires are a little higher above us. I have no idea where we are now. We are so far off the directions we were given I have no reference point, no benchmark. The only thing we can do at this point is call the facility and ask how to get there from whatever street we are on and hope the person on the other end knows where this street is. I say as much to Trainer and he agrees. I punch up the phone number to the shipper we were given in the directions on the quailcall. I dial it in and make the call. Recording comes on and says that number is no longer in service.

I send a message to HQ and request a working phone number. We wait. Nothing. Nothing for a while. I send another message. We are rolling all this time. Probably getting farther from our destination. I don't know. Maybe we are getting closer. Trainer drives, puzzled and wracking his faulty memory.

At length Trainer says he has been to this facility and this is not the way to it. We need to turn around. Once he realizes we have missed the turn, or made the wrong turn, he almost immediately becomes agitated. Very unlike him. I watch from the comfortable distance of the second seat.

We roll along a two-lane road looking for a place to turn the truck around. We need a big parking lot or paved area or hard dirt. Some area large enough and hard enough to support the weight of the rig. We are riding along and looking. Trainer's frustration is beginning to feed on itself. He is nowhere near out of control, but he is very out of character. I've not seen him like this before. He blames the directions. He blames the missing sign. He blames me for not watching. I let him rant till he burns out and then let him simmer a little.

In his tantrum, he has missed an opportunity to turn around. We blew right past a gravel parking lot plenty big enough. I saw it. He saw it and missed it. He knows he missed it, but will not acknowledge it.

We are coming up on another gravel lot in front of a country store kind of place, not yet open at this hour. No low hanging wires, or things to prevent us going in and turning around. I point it out to Trainer, and say we are now about 20 miles out of route and we should take advantage of that parking lot before we get to Cuba. He looks askance through his glasses at me, safely ensconced out of arm's reach in my chair, and bursts into laughter at himself and my comment.

Calmed now, he says he just wants to get home and get on to his vacation. The whole family is going and he just wants to get back to his house and get to Mexico and get to vacationin'. I grin and agree. We could use the break. As much as I like him, we need to spend some time out of the truck, or at least some time from beneath one another's feet. If he is going to be this touchy about a relatively minor thing, dang, get the man a vacation.

Relatively minor thing.

Relatively minor, as compared to say, asteroid/planet collisions. Practically speaking, there is nothing minor about missing a turn or an exit in a bigtruck. We talked about that a little while ago. If that happens, it is usually the problem of the day. No city, county, state, or province will allow a U-turn in a bigtruck. The fines are huge, and the companies will usually fire the driver that does it because the danger it presents in the form of a potential rununder is obvious and unforgivable. But stressed, lost, panicked, late, and tired drivers do it anyway. They fall victim to a twisted logic that says take the chance, cut your losses, and get out of that game. Most get away with it. Some don't, and the price is high for the losers.

In one of our orientation classes, we heard from a semireputable source, a stressed driver missed his exit and decided to save the out-of-route miles and time on an interstate by doing a U-turn across the median. That alone is illegal. That little shell or gravel crossover is for emergency or official use only. He compounded the mistake by doing it in a bigtruck. Gonna save some time. So he pulled into that crossover and drove his rig onto the interstate going the opposite way in the predawn of a weekend morning. While he was stretched across the travel lanes making that turn, a bus full of gamblers headed for the casinos went through his trailer. Most of the bus riders died. The lawsuit was such that the trucking company was left uninsurable and, as a result, closed their doors. Twenty-five people lost their lives and 2,500 people lost their jobs because a panicked driver did a U-turn on a dark interstate. Missing a turn or an exit is a relatively minor problem. Right.

I grab the cell phone and call the new number we were given for the shipper along with our load assignment. Trainer brings the truck to a standstill in the gravel lot till we get oriented. It will calm him a little. I suggest he get a snack while I call. There is no one here anyway. The place is not open yet. We are not being rushed to leave. He agrees, and rummages the cooler. The phone is ringing on the other end.

I get a receptionist and her English is better than my Spanish, so we settle on English. I ask how to get where she is from where we are. Turns out we are only a few miles away. We follow her directions, which involves a tour of a different part of town, and turn at the places she said to turn. Just like that, we drive right into the environmentally correct chicken processing plant. Right on time. Love these cell phones.

I hop out of the truck and trot over to the guardshack, notes in hand, expecting to drop our empty trailer and hook up to our trailer full of chicken so we can hotfoot it to Texas and get on to our respective vacations. Before Trainer has another meltdown. I'm a happy guy; I'm going home, too. While Trainer is on vacation, I'll take one as well. The current plan is to take our individual vacations and meet back in the company yard to complete the last two weeks of my training. I could go back and get another trainer so my training period would be uninterrupted and be done by the time Trainer gets back from Mexico. But I like him and he hasn't seriously threatened to kill me yet; I really don't want to break in another trainer and the company is okay with that, so I'll just take some time away myself. When we get back to the yard. With these chickens.

I bounce into the guardshack all excited about getting the load and getting on the road to the yard, show the pickup numbers and appointment numbers to the guard, and stand back smiling and thinking how we should be out of here in half an hour. Headed for Texas. See the kids and a little Mexican cutie I know. Yard probably needs mowing as well, but that's okay. I have a brand-new lawnmower I have been wanting to test-drive.

Deadpan guard shoves the notebook back across the counter and says pull in and park over there until your load is ready.

Whaddaya mean till the load is ready? Ten. The load is supposed to be ready at 10 A.M. Says that right here, 10 A.M. Monday morning. That's today. It is 10. We give you an empty trailer, and you give us a trailer full of dead chickens that need a ride to Oregon. Drop and hook. Drop the empty and hook to the full one. Ten o'clock Monday. Right here. Have a look at these pickup numbers, pal. And I shove the papers back at him across the counter.

I am usually pretty resolute and not easily frustrated and rarely get mouthy with things out of someone else's control. But now, I want to go home, too. And this trailerload of chickens is the ticket home for me.

I want to get hooked up and rolling. I am surprised at my attitude, especially since I know this guard can't fix that. It isn't his call. I immediately try to lighten up, and say nothing further after roughing the fellow up, but I'm still not happy about the whole thing. The guard is getting shaky. I guess he's had to deal with disappointed drivers before.

Guard bucks up, stands tall, and says our load is a live load. Not a drop and hook. We have to wait with the empty trailer until the chicken-shipping department is ready to load it. His voice is still a little shaky. I am staring him straight in the eye. Pull in and park over there and somebody will be out later to tell ya when we are ready to load ya. Right over there. Park over there. He goes back to shuffling some papers and looks away. Pretending to ignore me. Dang. Okay. I don't want to make this worse than it already is by abusing the poor old guard. It isn't his fault the chicken-shippers can't operate on a schedule of their own design.

I turn and walk out the door of the little air-conditioned glass enclosure to break the news to Trainer. I walk along head down and dragging my toes. Trainer is not amused. What's wrong? I tell him. He says we ain't waitin'. We don't wait for no damchickens. He whips off about ten nastygrams to HQ on the quailcall and grabs my cell phone for the coup de grace. He'll show 'em. We ain't waitin' for no stinkin' chickens. Voice on the other end at HQ stops him in midsentence. Silenced, he holds the phone away from his ear. I can hear the voice from outside the cab. Puts the phone back to his head. Yep. Okay. We'll do 'er. Roger and out. Clicks the little clamshell phone closed. Looks at me through his glasses. Where wuz we s'posed to park?

The facility is a nice one on the outside. Clean. Neat. Landscaped. Blends well with the surrounding area. Trainer sets out to find the potty, and I climb behind the wheel to park Big Blue. I drive around back to turn around and sit for a minute waiting on Trainer, but the morning sun is shining into the cab through the windshield and heating things up. The a/c is struggling. I decide to drive around to the west side and get into the shade provided by the building. It is three or four levels high and pretty good sized so the shade is substantial. I find a spot and back in. Set the brakes, idle the engine, and let the a/c do what it can to cool the cab. It is warming up nicely out, and the fresh push of cool air from the vents feels good.

Trainer gets back, says it's gonna be a long wait and wake him when it's over. I tell him I'm abandoning ship. I sail out the door to look around a little. I don't like the idea of sitting in the cab for any length of time. I stay in it enough. It is a beautiful day and I think I need to snoop around. Beautiful country to snoop in as well.

Off the cement area where we parked, there is a maintained grassy area to the south and east and west of the plant, I guess they cut the trees back so the woods would not be right at the edge of the lot. Kinda gives the place a little depth and breadth. There are dozens of butter-flies and dragonflies flitting around in the sunny meadow several acres big, bordered by the trees. Butterflies looking for flowers and there are many out there, and dragonflies looking for 'skeeters. Haven't seen or felt any of them, so, good job dragonflies.

In the folkloric environment I was lucky enough to be raised in, dragonflies were known to be snake doctors, and could heal most snake illnesses; also they could also sting a human horribly, anyone quick enough to catch one. I never saw it done—catching one, but as children, my friends and I wondered if they would really sting, so we avoided them. I always thought they were pretty, though, and I liked the way they would glide around. Kinda like a little biplane. Farther down the educational road, I know that not only do dragonflies not sting, but they eat critters that do. However, they prefer mosquitoes. Eat them by the hundreds. That alone puts them right at the top of my favorite insects list since I live on the Gulf Coast, famed for trophy mosquitoes. Go dragonflies.

I sat in my back yard late one September afternoon and watched a swarm of dragonflies moving above me about 25 feet that took nearly 10 minutes to pass. Not a thick swarm, but a steady procession that num-bered in the thousands. I just happened to look up at the twilight sky and notice their silent sojourn. No telling how long they had been pass-ing by before I looked up to see them. Squadrons of them cruising southwest just above the tallow trees. Memorable thing for me, being a fan of dragonflies. A neighbor of mine was over at the time, enjoying the late afternoon in a lawn chair, and when I pointed them out, he won-dered aloud what all them durn bugs was and where was they goin'?

The minimeadow has a gentle grade that slopes down to a line of trees that sit lower than they should from where I am. Like they are in a ditch or something, and in looking closer, I note a river down there. I can see it through the trees. I walk down and across the field and down the grade to early morning in the Duck River Valley. Must flow right through town. Good canoeing, probably, or kayaking. Clear, green water. Gravel and sand bottom. Leopard frogs. Small fish darting around. Couple of newts in the shady, shadowy, shallow water. Looking across the river, there are clouds of bugs whirling above the slow-moving surface of the river near the middle. Not far to the other side. I think I could throw a rock across it. The sunlight refracted through the gossamer wings of the bug whirlpool causes those wings to fairly glow, and as quickly as the bugs are whirling it looks like a living thing made from whirling bugs. The air is still and cool down here. Standing here looking upon this scene, I am tempted to wade out a little, barefoot, and feel the bottom, like I would have done as a boy. I decide not to and I'm not sure why. I think because I really don't want to do that right now. I walk/climb back up the bank a little and go some distance upstream where I see a little alluvial fan created by a small stream flowing into the river. Just a little stream, but I think I'll follow it up from the river and see where it goes. Check it out. This is a real change from my regular routine and I want to not waste the opportunity to change my daily modus operandi. Kinda appeals to my stifled explorer within, and I don't have to get too far from civilization. Daytime explorer. At night, I want a shower, a hot meal, and a soft bed. All of that in my own house, preferably, but I'll settle for a four-star hotel when I'm away exploring. Or in this case, a Kenworth sleeper.

The stream, actually a brook, is a textbook babbling one. Clear and fast. Little waterfalls, six inches or so. Fast, clear water rolling over stones laying in a little gash in the earth probably two feet across and eight or ten inches deep. I follow it from the bank of the river up the minimeadow right to the discharge drain at the chicken plant. The burbling stream I follow is conditioned chickenwater. My first take is the chickenwater is cleaner than the river water. I can't speak micro-biologically or chemically, but just from what I see, this water is clean. In gumshoeing around the source, this discharge is far from being foul, really it is clean and odorless. The brook/discharge chute rolls and boils and falls to the river through the little streambed cut for it in the Kelly green meadow and drains right into the river. In fact, where it mingles with the river, the cleaner discharge water creates crystal-clear eddies in the green river water. I'm impressed. Science improves nature. Right here in Tennessee. Mulling that over, I am here at the plant anyway, so I walk around the corner to the small parking lot just big enough for a single file of trailers and find Trainer right where I left him. Snoozing off the donuts. It is easy to do. Warm summer morning, a/c blowing a cool breeze in the sleeper, Cummins idling and rattling away. He is full of pastry. I look around and decide to leave him alone. I am not into waking large furry mammals. I think I'll walk back to my newfound wilderness to see the slow-moving translucent green water on its timeless way to the sea. I will wadefish in molecules of this river someday after it flows into the sea, when the tide brings it into the backbay flats of my beloved Gulf Coast, and think on how I knew this water when we were younger and in Tennessee.

Turtles getting some UV exposure on a big log near the opposite bank. The sun is beaming onto my side of the river and the other side is shaded out to about where the turtles are roasting. I step out of the shadows onto the riverbank and the turtles splash into the water. Messed up the tanning session. I think turtles may be among those animals that have to warm up to digest their food, so I may have messed up a digestion session. A couple of them bob up a few yards downstream and float along with the walking speed current. They look angry. I sit and watch. Some birds, swifts maybe, swoop along the surface of the river and into the whirlpools of insects. Small fish sifting the gravel on the bottom and sampling the surface stuff. A little newt or salamander of some kind squiggles by, in no particular hurry. I see nothing hurries much around here. The river makes no sound as it moves by, unhurried. Jillions of tons of water moving by and not a sound. Birds call in the trees, critters skitter across the surface of the water and hop around the edges of the river. A little splash here and a little splash there. Survival movements. Big ones after the little ones. But the river itself makes no sound, at least that I can hear. I am struck by that somehow.

I suddenly don't care if it takes all day to load the trailer. I'm okay with that. Of a sudden.

The sun has climbed a bit higher and has begun to warm the canyon a little. There was a wispy mist just above the water when I came down here earlier, and it is gone now. I'm still not sure how this dew point and humidity stuff all ties together. I thought I knew once, but it gets re-explained to me every so often and then I understand it a little less. As long as we don't stay fogged in, I'm not going to worry about it all, because the canyon has warmed to the point I feel like I'll do that barefoot wade I didn't do a while ago. Seems like it would feel good about now. Get these shoes off and wade out there a little on this lovely riverside morning.

The bottom is just like I figured. Gravelly, sandy mud. Gooshy enough to goosh up between my toes. Feels cool and grainy, and it's like I just shaved 40 years off my life with two barefoot steps into a river. Like a kid, I stand in the river, taking in a different feeling, both physical and mental.

I stand amid a relentless force and wonder at the power of it even knee deep. This stuff wears away mountains. I wonder what would happen if I just stood here for a small piece of eternity. Would I wear away at the knees? Fall over like Ozymandias? How long would it take? I wade out to a gravel bar just beneath the surface. These structures are called "spits" in Alaska. Just so you'll know. Looks like something higher up the food chain than a crawfish had a snack before I got here. The water is about ankle deep here on the spit and gets greener and darker as I look toward the depths of the middle. Not so translucent. Probably a big ol' catfish down there.

I stand on the gravel bar, alone for all the world amid this flow, in the warm sun, looking up from the spit, past the tree-rimmed banks into the sky. I am the only one here. I know around the bend upstream there is a town, and up the hill is a chicken processing plant, and downstream is probably a neighborhood and a strip mall, but here and now, it is only me, these creatures great and small, and the ancient river. I look around to take it all in, down here in this small canyon, and keep it for my mental screensaver. Nothing has changed here for tens of thousands of years. The riverbed has probably moved around a little and carved a new path every few thousand years, but the darting fish, amphibians bouncing around, and birds chirping away in the trees are the same kind that have been here since before any human stood in this river. Hopefully with more companies like this chicken-killing operation looking out for the environment, someone centuries down the road will be able to wade out to this bar and see things like I am seeing it now and the way those things have always been. We care less and less about the planet in the headlong rush to commerce. I see the results of it alongside the roads every day, and it is refreshing to be in a place like this.

Coming back to where I am, it dawns on me Trainer may be snoozing and possibly missed the call on the CB that we should back into the dock and be loaded. I probably should go check on that. I have spent the morning in this river bottom and it is past noon now, so I would do well to see what is going on up the hill in civilization.

Walking back across the sundrenched meadow, I am stirring up bugs galore. Siesta time for bugs, I guess, napping in the grass. Across the parking lot to the idling tractor that hasn't moved since it was parked. I figure Trainer is not to be disturbed, and I know I can get the same information, actually better, from the girls in the shipping office. So, I start over to the shipping office, head down against the midday glare. Sunglasses are in the truck. Didn't need 'em earlier, or down in the river bottom. Shady and cool there.

The girls say it will be a while, probably tonight, before they start to load us. A little shocked, I ask what happened and one says it is a staffing problem. Bunch of people called in sick. So the loading is slow. Okay. She says it with kind of an attitude, and I start away, but turn back and say I don't mean to be pushy and just wanted to know if we missed our call to the dock. She softens a little and says she meant no offense, that most truckers get mad when they are told they have to wait, so she was just getting the first lick in. I said waiting is part of truckdriving ordinarily, but we were supposed to be a drop and hook. She says she wished all truckers felt that way, about the waiting anyway, and sorry about your drop and hook mix-up. So we look at one another until it gets uncomfortable. I thank her for the information and head for the door. Staffing problems.

All the personnel problems that exist in any company plague shippers, too. Carriers know production and staffing problems create logjams and backlogs and they log that information, so carriers have developed a process for repeat or serious offenders that load late. The carrier either penalizes the shipper or refuses the load if the shipper fools around with a waiting truck. Waiting trucks don't make money for the carrier. The trucks have to roll or no one makes money, like we talked about before. The process for penalizing a late loader is called different things by different carriers, has different acronyms in different companies, but all of those terms amount to the same thing, a loaded departure deadline, and it is usually within a few hours of the scheduled pickup time, or loading time. In our company's case, it is six hours from the agreed-upon contract time for the shipper. We will be considerably past that if we aren't loaded until tonight. It's gonna be expensive because the penalty goes up by the hour until we are loaded and leaving the facility, unless some brother-in-law arrangement is made to circumvent the agreement. And that could have happened. These chicken-killers are part of a national chain and therefore a big account for my company, so there is probably some latitude here. Gotta kiss up to the money if you want to get ahead.

Oh well. It is about late lunch time, and I figure on a dagwood made with stuff from the refrigerator in the truck; some olives and sundried, oil-soaked tomatoes for effect. Chips'n'hotsauce and an ice-cold soda. Maybe break out a lawn chair, sit in the shade by the river, enjoy a meal and a nap. Can't drive, so I'll just make the best of it. I hike across the lot, warmer and brighter now, pop open the rider door, and jump into the second seat. Trainer is awake and watching a movie on the 13-inch AC/DC TV/VCR. Good picture. I guess he fixed it after that curb in Albuquerque. Or the burnt offerings and incantations worked.

I announce my lunch plans and he looks at me. Yer one of them conversationists ain'cha. Wanna be outside all the damtime. Huggin' trees and lookin' fer striped owls and blond fish. That's conservationist, and those are *spotted* owls and *blind* fish. And yeah, I guess I am. You want a sandwich or no. Yup. You make 'em different with that bread in the middle.

Lunch is on, and I am out. Trainer is munching away on his dagwood engrossed in his movie. A/C blasting, aliens blowing stuff up, diesel clattering at an idle. Man, I hear that enough. Where's my lawn chair.

Lawn chair under my arm, hauling my sandwich and soda, I must look like Carmen Miranda's hat as I walk across the breezy meadow in the early-afternoon sun, stirring butterflies and dragonflies as I go. Lunch date with Mother Nature. Nothing like a good meal with a beautiful woman.

Comfy now, in the shady glade 10 feet from the lazy river, I enjoy my sandwich and soda, kick back in the lawn chair, and slip into a long nap. The gentle breeze, the chorus of birds, and the dappling shade cast their spell and I relax with it. This is one cool job.

Rustled awake by a strong breeze in the leaves, I open my eyes and look around. The shadows are longer by some, but it isn't late, maybe middle of the afternoon. I settle back and drift away again, like a leaf down the river.

Some time later, a bird lands on my chair, and upon my waking from that fluttering of feathers, he flits away into the safety of the branches above to check me out. Must not be afraid of people. I sleepily wonder if that is because people are so common down here, and the thing has lost its fear, or the bird has never seen a human, and doesn't know we kill things for most any reason, and gadzillions of his kinfolk are losing their lives a hundred yards from here. I look around and sit still, not taking long to reconnect behind that nap, and decide to go back up the hill to check on our progress in the shipping office. Not so much because I want to, just that it seems like the thing to do at this point.

Drop the lawn chair off at the truck, doggedly idling away, put the trash from lunch in the proper receptacle by the building, and stop inside the shipping office. New crew aboard. Must be the second shift. I ask about us and our schedule. New girl says it will probably be around midnight before we are loaded. Well, okay. Not much I can do about that. I'll just go out to see if Trainer is still conscious. He will be hot when I tell him about the new loading plans. I can't wait.

Back at the truck, Trainer is blacked out, so I shrug it off and decide I may head back to explore more of the river bottom. Or maybe not.

A canyon of sorts is just to our west from the parking lot, and since I have seen the river, at least one part of it, I'm thinking I'll just ease over and have a look at the canyon what with all this newfound time I have.

The rocky wash down into the canyon is much steeper than the riverbank, and the canyon is more a miniature gorge cut into the soft dirt down to a slate bedrock. I am noticing all this as I climb carefully down, rock to rock. Hope one of these units doesn't tilt or move as I put my weight on it. I have never ridden a rockslide before, and I don't want to do that today. The gorge is about 25 or 30 feet wide and 10 to 15 feet deep, depending on the undulations of the slate bed. It has a stair-stepped rocky bottom with little 6-inch waterfalls every 30 feet or so that pour into pools of cold, clear green water about a foot deep. Frogs, minnow, crawfish, and salamanders zipping around in the crystalline water. Same things as in the river. Water things can see three directions. I didn't know that until I really got serious about fishing years ago. In clear water, they can see all around them, and some can even see behind themselves. They can see the bottom of the pool reflected from the bottom of the surface, and they can see through the surface to what is above it. I think they see me and freak, hence all the zipping around. Things were probably pretty calm before I got here, and I hate to think my presence messes up the natural order of things. I'd like things a little better sometimes if I weren't noticed, maybe get a more realistic picture of what goes on when I'm not around.

I look at the mossy rock plates on the floor of the canyon, cool water bubbling over them, and think about walking around barefoot again, mainly because I don't want to get my shoes wet. It is going to be slick walking on the rocks, shoes or none. Just have to be careful.

I wander and wonder in the canyon, barefoot and careful most of the afternoon, walking first upstream, then down again to where the canyon stream converges with the river, and think how I am the only person ever here, or at least the first person to inspect the exposed tree roots eroded from the canyon walls, flaky stone ledges along the wall, and dodge the harmless water snakes.

Having been soaked for the past couple of hours, my feet are wrinkly and numb from the cold, so I step more than carefully for the lack of feeling and the slick rocks. It is beautiful here, like a photograph on an insurance company calendar—speckledy sunlight through the breezy leaves livening up the walls of the canyon, and dancing around on the water. A lovely afternoon well spent, even if it were my last, and it goes quickly, like good things do.

I hate to go, but it is late, the sun is no longer beaming down here and soon the creatures of the night will come, and I don't want to be down here with some of them. So, I wade back to my shoes, get them on, and climb back up the rock pile and onto the lawn of the chicken plant. It is late afternoon, almost twilight, and I want to get my chair and watch evening come to the meadow.

The meadow has no direct sun now, shaded by the western trees, but it is aglow from the sunset reflected by some stately thunderclouds immediately east of us. A soft light comes down at a sharp angle from the wrong direction, and the effect is like an Impressionist painting. The insects settled in for the evening come back out to do insect stuff in the new light, but seem disoriented and confused by this opportunity. Much erratic fluttering. The storm clouds change from white to peach to rose to pale blue to gray, and the reflected light diminishes in intensity according to the cloud's color. It comes to me, as I sit, that there was no specific Garden of Eden. It was the whole planet. The whole thing is the Garden.

Lightning flashes in the east, beneath the clouds and far behind the trees, and before long the quiet, low thunder ambles by. No threat, just a gentle shower for the Garden over there somewhere, and the clouds fade into the coming darkness.

— — —

Light gone, and the show over, I fold the lawn chair back into the bag and stow it in the side locker just as the parking lot sodium lamps pop on. It is an ugly light, and I am put off by it. Fake. Phony. Contrived. Impotent compared to the sun and its daylight.

Civilization and Creation side by side. I am standing in the orange glare of artificial lighting one hundred yards from pristine country. Lights beat back the night here at the chicken plant, like it does in cities and towns and waysides everywhere. We try to re-create the day with the same poor results any imitation produces. Some light we have so we can see what we are doing in the dark. Headlights, baseball fields, police helicopters. But as I go about the country, I think most electric light I see just expresses a fear of the dark of some kind, ranging from terror to trivial. There is something in us that is afraid of the dark, maybe not the dark so much as what is in it, or what we can't see in it, so we try to make the dark go away. And we are doing a pretty good job overall, I guess. I read recently they are not able to use a couple of big telescopes now because of light pollution. The glow of the lights from the cities is so bright the telescopes can't pick up the faint stars anymore.

Not much to do outside now, night and all, so I think I'll take a tour of the chicken plant inside. I have seen several truckloads of chickens in small cages go around back in my walking about today. No chickens come out. Like a chicken roach motel, or chicken Hotel California. Chickens check in, don't check out.

I found long ago that the absolute best way to snoop is to ask for the men's room. It is an innocent and reasonable request and works most times for most places. So, I ask the gate guard. Not the same one from the last shift. He says go in that door and go this way and then that way or something like that, and I say okay, thanks a bunch, and go inside the building. It has a nice entry. I'll bet the chickens don't get to see this part. I am imagining a Larson cartoon here somehow. Past the offices, deserted now at this hour, to a double door, make a couple of turns, through another couple of doors, and farther along I hear the

mechanized sounds of a production line. Or destruction line. I'm getting close. It looks kinda blue-collar along here. Lockers, hat racks.
Turn another corner, and the air is getting more damp as I approach
the fogged-up, sloppy-fitted plastic-slat double doors at the end of the
passageway. It is noisy and damp as I approach to look inside. Shout-
ing above the noise behind the door. Hissing sounds, and splashing.
The floor is progressively greasier and smelly. Not a bad smell, just
smelly. I can see outlines of things behind the door through the plastic
slats. I sneak up to the door and open it just a little, so I can see inside
the production area.

It does smell in here. Pressure-washing dead chickens, I guess.
There is a mist in the air and the floor is shiny wet. I don't step in. This
is close enough. Two migrant workers brush past me and say nothing. I
look around. What a process. Hi-tech chicken prep. The scene and
sounds remind me of one of those apocalypse movies. I expect a red-
eyed robot to loom from the fog. Maybe from the mist behind that vat
near the middle of the room. Lots of chicken carcasses. Probably lots of
chicken souls for the soup floating around in there.

I back out, satisfied I don't want to see more, and retrace my steps
along the slippery utility-tiled hall to cleaner pastures, so to speak. I
used to like chicken. I manage to get out the way I came. It is good to be
out of there, in the quiet of the night. Even if I'm in an artificially lit
parking lot. I am reminded of what a friend said years ago that food is
nasty. I am inclined at this point to agree, based on what I have seen, and
decide to swear off chicken. For a while. Till I want some wonton.

The truck has moved. It is in one of the dock doors. Trainer is at the
wheel. Reading. He has several books aboard, but this is the first time I
have actually seen him busy reading. He looks up from his book as I get
closer to the truck.

I climb into the cab and flop into the second seat. The chair hisses
and Trainer says where ya been, and I say a chicken holocaust. He looks
back to his book and says yeah, it's bad in there, that we are being loaded
with some victims now. I say we are a chicken hearse and we should

drive with our lights on. Trainer looks at me over his glasses. Chewing on something. I hope it isn't chicken. Goes back to his book.

I don't feel like doing anything else now, so I sit and look around from the cab and get tired of that really quickly because it is dark out. Nothing to see. Trainer still reading. I get up from the chair and get into my bunk and just lay on top of it. On my festive Mexican blanket. The Cummins rattling and the a/c blowing on me take their toll, and I nod off. A forklift occasionally rolls into the trailer and the truck shakes like a wet dog. I wake to the jostling and roll over. Happens several times at irregular intervals. Hard to sleep like that. So I just snooze between the shaking events. After a while, no more shaking. I am awake at irregular intervals now expecting to be shaken. Frustrated and pissy, I get back into the second seat. That all took about two hours. Trainer looks over at me. I look back. A guy comes up to his window and I say there is a guy coming up to your window. Trainer looks out and rolls the window down. The guy says yer loaded, go into the shipping office to get yer bills. Trainer says nothing and rolls the window up. I say pull out and I'll close the doors, and I'll go get the seals and bills. I open the door and climb out. Trainer puts the truck into second gear and the cab rocks as the engine's torque twists the suspension in moving the load away from the dock. I'll just wait right here until the end of the trailer comes by, then close the doors when Trainer stops.

The doors have to be closed just so, there being several latches on the sealing mechanism, and they have to be properly secured, or the air-tight seal will leak. Don't want that; at below-freezing temperatures like the reefer can generate, the humidity will cause the leaking seal to ice up and freeze the door shut. Closing up a trailer is not as easy as it sounds, and there are improperly closed doors rolling down the high-way out there right this very second. Drivers in a hurry, raining or cold or rushed by the shipper or not paying attention or whatever. I am none of those things currently, and therefore take my time and effort to en-sure the doors are properly closed, my wanting to develop good habits in this sort of thing. I have to do that, being a creature of habit like I am.

Train myself properly or I will do things sloppily. I know that about myself, so no big deal.

I head over to the shipping office and pick up the bills and get a different kind of seal for the trailer door. A seal, in this case, is a plastic or metal strap that fits through the hasp on the trailer doors after they have been properly closed. It has a number several digits long embossed or stamped on it, and that number is on the bill of lading that goes with the driver. That is so the receiver will know what seal number left the shipper attached to the trailer. If the seal number on the trailer is different than the seal number on the bill when the load gets to the receiver, something is wrong. There is no way to get a properly placed seal out of a hasp without breaking it, and everyone in the trucking industry knows that. Therefore, if the seal on the door is not intact when the load arrives at the receiver, someone may have been into the load, and the receiver is not going to be happy about that. Someone may have added to, or most likely, taken from, the load the receiver paid for. Because of those things, the seal number must be checked against the seal number on the bill before the load leaves the shipper, not somewhere down the road. So I do that, and take the seal out to put it on the trailer. The numbers match. Good to go.

Trainer informs me he wants to drive all night to compensate for having been down all day. He slept all day, but I don't know if I'm comfortable with him driving all night. I voice my concerns. I'm thinking we should bed down in a truck stop tonight. It is near 11 P.M. I don't care what who says and what studies have been done, people start shutting down mentally and physically after midnight. Even if they have slept a big chunk of the day. Trainer says he knows what he can do. I say I'm sure you do, but I don't want your biological clock to catch up to you at three in the morning, while I'm sleeping my life away, literally. He huffs up.

Besides all that, I don't know whether or not I will like bouncing around in a sleeper all night.

I take the wheel and drive to Nashville, where Trainer decides he will take the first chair. I tell Trainer as we exit the freeway, I don't like this and you know it's dangerous. We have plenty of time on the load and it is not necessary to push this hard. We can sleep comfortably in that truck stop right there. He says he is wide awake and can drive all night. I recite the corporate policy regarding driving after 3 A.M. That immediately offends his office of trainer and I realize too late that was not the card to play here. Trainer jumps right into the decision-maker mode. Gonna drive all night. More informative than angry, I say flatly I simply don't trust his wee-hours driving ability. That isn't the right approach either. My judgment must be failing at this hour. He is more determined now and will show me he can drive all night if it kills us. I decide I am too tired to argue, that my responses are exacerbating the situation, and I don't want to risk further determination on Trainer's part with thoughtless comments. I just get up from the second seat and collapse into the bottom bunk. That is Trainer's bunk, but company rules state no one can be in the upper bunk when the truck is in motion. It is a good rule. In the event of a rollover, the top of the condo is almost always badly mangled or even crushed. That's where the upper bunk is.

Trainer goes up the gears in the access lane to Interstate 40 west, and aims for Arkansas. I am too tired to care now. I won't know if we crash anyway. I hope.

Tossed around in the bunk to the point I am floating above it much of the time, actually thrown into the air several times in rapid succession, my first waking thought is we are off the road. The bedclothes seem to be alive and won't let me go; struggling violently to get free, I know I must get into the cab, but don't know why. It is as though my survival depends on it, like I have to make it to the surface to breathe, I absolutely must get through the light curtain and into the second chair. The bouncing is more rapid now, with cursing from the cab side of the curtain. The tractor is rocking so violently I cannot stand. I am panic-stricken and finally fight my way free of the sheets and rip aside the light curtain so I can see the last few seconds of my life come through the windshield. I knew this would happen. Damn those cruise controls.

As much by accident as purpose, in my semiconscious stumbling, I land on my butt in the second chair to look across and see Trainer with an easy grip on the wheel and munching some kind of something. Jaw muscles alternately contracting and relaxing. Staring at me through his glasses. Expressionless. Bouncing easily with the truck as it bounces along the interstate. Trainer reads my incredulous face and says dam them Arkansas roads. State ain't got no money to fix 'em, and caused him to spill his drink. Been like this for years. Reaches for the Styrofoam cup in the holder and swills down the last of what coffee hasn't sloshed from it. I allow myself to move with the chair, bouncing and rocking in sync with the oscillator, looking around in nothing but Donald Duck boxers and bed hair in the first light of dawn rolling along I-40 west, not sure whether I am panicked or relieved or both or should I even care.

My body is shot full of adrenaline, and probably some other pretty powerful hormones that have it ready to leap tall buildings in a single bound, but my brain is still fogged in. I am glad to be alive, I think. I think I think, therefore I think I am. Carpe diem. Carpe the chair arm before I am unseated. I just ride and hang on. Maybe I'll wake up in a minute. Then I'll try to figure out what is happening.

Trainer looks at me and rolls his eyes. This road is seriously rough. The bucking is not as intense now, but it is still bad. I realize I have no coffee. I have had a real busy morning so far, and some coffee would be a good antidote for it. I sit and look at Trainer and say coffee. Trainer flips on the turn signal with a knowing smile. Exit and coffee coming up. I guess he drove all night and didn't kill us. Or maybe he did, and this is driver hell: rough road and no coffee.

As soon as I am confident I can, I stand and grab every available handhold on my way back to the condo to get dressed. Good thing I don't have to pee. I should have to. But I don't. Maybe I don't have to pee for a reason. Maybe I have done that already in the panic earlier. I grab the crotch of my boxers. Nope. Dry. Good. I didn't want to have to check the bunk. It belongs to Trainer.

I manage to get into my clothes despite the lurching, rolling, pitching and yawing tractor by lying on my back in the bottom bunk and wiggling into them. Standing in the condo is out of the question.

Flop back into the second seat just as we come to the end of the exit ramp. Spray my face and hair with water bottle. It is just past dawn as we make the turn and creep to the truck stop for some coffee and a break.

Trainer says let's get the coffee and catch up on our logs and roll, that his vacation starts tomorrow. It is our last day on the road for a while, we'll be in Texas soon, where we will go our separate ways for about 10 days. The coffee bar is busy, and I walk behind Trainer up to where he stops, holds up his huge arms, and says to about a dozen people, Move Away From The Coffee Bar. They look up, everyone laughs from a lot to a little, but they move aside. They don't know if he was kidding. He is not smiling. I shoot in through an opening and grab a 20-ouncer while everyone is confused and milling.

Coffee in hand, I wander over to the row of televisions tuned to the weather channel and see Hurricane Chantal hammering the tip of the Yucatan. I look and see Trainer by the pastry cabinet, bag and forceps in hand. Looking. I wonder should I show him the storm. I don't want to be the bearer of bad tidings, but I don't want a bunch of vacation money wasted either. I decide to go get him and tell him he needs to see this. I'm a little leery of rattling him during the donut-stalking mode. Stealth and ambush are everything if you want a trophy.

Gripping his bag of donuts, Trainer cruises over to the wall filled with televisions. Several rows high and several televisions on each row. Must be thirty of them, from 9 inches to probably 19 inches, different brands—all on the weather channel. This must be the way a fly sees things through compound eyes. Trainer snaps to what is happening in Cozumel. He thinks for a few seconds and says no problem, it will have moved away by the time he gets there tomorrow night. It comes to me that people from north Texas don't know a lot about hurricanes.

I sip my coffee and look at the satellite track on the television. Hurricanes are serious business. I have been through three of them ashore, one of them on a motorcycle in Mexico and Belize. They eye of Alicia came within ten miles of me in 1983, and stalled for six hours just after dark.

The wind carried away an official speed indicator at 135 MPH a couple of hours into those six about half a mile from where I was. That still stands as one of the longest nights I have ever lived. A person that makes it through a category three or higher storm usually doesn't want to repeat the experience, especially coastal dwellers like me. It is real scary stuff once a person realizes they are no longer in control of what is happening. People from upstate, on the other hand, get nothing more than a good drenching and a bluster from the storms once they move inland, the source of their strength lost. Hurricanes need a hot ocean to really get going, and once they move ashore, they weaken quickly and break into bands of thunderstorms and some wind. For those reasons, the populace some distance away from the coast have little respect and fear of hurricanes. Matter of fact, that time of the year, those folks need the rain. They like hurricane leftovers. Trainer just doesn't see a problem.

We walk back to Big Blue and climb in with our respective goodies. My coffee and Trainer's pastry bag.

There are lots of trucks here, most all of them having stayed the night, and the drivers are beginning to awaken and get ready for work. I have my log done in no time, because I slept, sort of, for several hours. Trainer, on the other hand, is trying to figure his out since he drove most of the night and through the hours of 3 and 7 A.M. where we have been told not to drive. The so-called danger zone, and the numbers seem to bear that out. A big percentage of the fatal truck accidents happen in that time frame. Our company says don't drive those hours unless we have a delivery in those hours. That way we shouldn't be driving far. We don't have a delivery in those hours today. Trainer is just in a hurry. Now he has to massage a logbook, or get hollered at by the compliance department for driving in the no-no zone. But, after some attempts to manipulate the numbers, his integrity is maintained and he opts for the beating rather than cheat on a log. He knows as well, the compliance guys and girls would most likely catch it anyway, if he did. They are pretty sharp and know what to look for, and Trainer is not a very good liar.

The compliance department at HQ is responsible for the logbook legalities. That group oversees the adjustments and accuracy and corrections of the logbooks, so that if the DOT guys show up, all is kosher. That the logs are legal and make sense. The compliance department can, and will, keep a driver from leaving the yard to correct or explain an entry. They don't play. Not even a little bit. We do not want to cross swords with these people. Do it legal and no problem, and the easiest way to log our time is go by the rules and log it like we do it. Just graph what we do and when we do it. Simple enough. We know the hours of service rule that says how many hours a day we can do what. All drivers do. The DOT makes certain any driver that gets into any interstate truck has a fundamental understanding of those rules. They hold the driver's employer responsible. Some drivers just choose to not concern themselves. The employer then holds that driver responsible. When we ignore a part of that DOT thing, we can expect the compliance department to land on us pretty hard. Trainer knows he messed up. Drove when he shouldn't have. I'll just stay out of it. I was sleeping, like I was supposed to be, during those hours, so I have nothing to explain.

I turn my attention to the goings-on in the parking lot. Looking out the windshield at the drivers going to and from the convenience store in the truck stop, getting coffee, breakfast stuff, cigarettes. Some are solo drivers and most are well kept and ready for the day. Others, a small percentage, are not. It is easy to see who maintains their personal standards even through the early-morning attitudes, even though mornings are not usually a good time to get an accurate portrait of a person. Some people walking to and from out there are male-female teams, or married couples. Same thing. Most well kept, a very few others not so well kept.

I watch one small couple in particular walk past the nose of the tractor, hand-in-hand in the early light, obviously just getting involved in the day. Fiftyish. Ragged husk of a man, cigarette between the smoke-stained fingers of his loose hand. Small man, probably five foot five, maybe five six. Greasy, rumpled plaid shirt and jeans. Greasy, like unwashed greasy. Scraggly, wiry salt-and-pepper hair pulled into a tangled knot at the back of his head. Long, loose, feathery strands of hair waving around in the air, Medusa-like.

His measured stride is like that of a surveyor, or landsman of some type accustomed to walking some distance. Not an unsteady or tentative walk, and it is done in western boots so old the toes are turned up and the heels are rounded. His other leathery hand is clutching the hand of the woman working at staying beside him. Hers is a practiced move as well. She has developed her moves to suit his, and it is automatic now. She doesn't even know she is working at it. She is some neater and better kept, clearly makes an effort to be a woman, but is far from eyecatching. Nonetheless, she is devoted to her man, steps right beside him and is plainly going under with him. She has the faded look of a housewife with no house. But then, in some fairness, maybe she isn't a morning person, and I'm reading this whole thing all wrong.

They climb into a raggedy old cab-over tractor hooked to a flatbed trailer with curled, loose boards in the deck. Blue-white smoke chuffs from the stack as the engine stirs awake. Owner/operators. They are not company drivers. They own the rig and hire out to whomever needs a load hauled. They work through brokers or word-of-mouth, or if their equipment will meet a company's standards, owners drive for companies like ours. The old tractor and trailer tell me the owners don't drive for a company. I don't think a front-line company would hire that rig. They must be straight contractors for brokers.

I don't know what happens to old, worn-out truckdrivers, and their women, when their old, worn-out trucks die, but I hope there is something for them. Some place for them to go. Something they can do. Not a handout, or a free ride, they don't want that, but some place that will let them work for their wage till they don't need it anymore, for whatever reason. They don't look like folks that would take something gratis. They just made some bad decisions somewhere back along their road, and we don't live in a very forgiving society. If one of us falls, the rest of the herd just steps over him. Sometimes on him. Or her. No one is likely to help them get back on their feet, so I hope they don't fall any farther than they have.

But again, I could be wrong. They might own this truck stop and just came out to move some old truck that's been sitting there for a month.

Back on the interstate. Bigtruck on the bigroad in the bighole. Going home. We are in high spirits and will be back in Texas this very afternoon. Trainer is ready for his vacation, and I am ready for my time away. Arkansas moves past my window in the early sunlight. It has rained heavily here recently and there are places flooded. I see a big sailboat in a small lake. How did that happen?

Texas has a really hip welcome station as we enter the state from Arkansas, and it is time for a break anyway, though Trainer is getting ready to get out and run the rest of the way to the yard if I don't hurry back. Says he wants to see Mama and the kids and grandkids. Then go to Mexico. I tell him Mama and Mexico will be there when he gets to them, I gotta pee, and I head out. He's ready to be there. I think he is already there, he's just waiting for his body to catch up. But that's okay, I do the same thing sometimes.

Rolling into our corporate town, the traffic is no more than usual, though Trainer says it is absolutely horrible. I recall Houston traffic for him, and he agrees this part of Texas ain't so bad after all. We exit the loop around town and roll down the last few miles to the yard for a perfect eighteen-point landing, and a big sign out in front of the compound welcomes us back.

It is good to be back.

We turn off the boulevard and onto the apron of the driveway, stop at the gate to be checked in, and I see other trainers and their trainees getting ready to leave. I was there three weeks ago. I remember how I felt as I drove out that very driveway right there. The one that trainee is driving out now. I see the look on his face. I know how he feels. Class is over, and now it's him and the truck. For him, this really is where the rubber meets the road. Easy part is over. Class is out, films are finished, and the exams begin. One a day for the remainder of a driver's career.

Lots of neophytes worry about getting past their commercial operator's license test, and think that once they do, the hard part is behind them. One of my instructors in driving school said not to worry about the commercial examination, that we would pass it or we wouldn't. That the real test starts every day when you pull into traffic and it is over every night when you shut down and haven't killed anyone. You passed. Tomorrow will be another test. I never heard anything more true, now that I have been there.

Trainer says at a roar, we're here, we are back. I concur, and feel like a chapter of my life has just closed. Like something is over, and I'm not sure if that is good. I am glad to be heading for home soon, but I feel like I was cut short or something was left undone. Like this is not all there is. It is an odd feeling, and I don't know what is causing it. Trainer says he'll be in Mexico tomorrow night. I smile and cheer him on, getting him primed for a good time. I don't want a hurricane to mess up his vacation. He's been looking forward to this for three weeks. I hope his wife feels well enough to enjoy it. I know he will not have a good time if she doesn't.

The place does look good, in the late-afternoon light, and I see my cranberry/plum/purple/maroon, no one can agree what color it is, pickup parked in the employee parking lot. Dusty and rain-streaked. Waiting. Faithfully, for three weeks. Some things can be depended on. For a while anyway.

Much business going on in the yard with the arrivals and departures of over-the-road drivers, and the general beehive-type activity the place has on a weekday. This is HQ as well, so there is some sense of establishment here, like what is done does not go unnoticed, an importance, but it is relaxed enough no one really gets tightened up about it. We will drop our trailer full of chickens in a part of the yard reserved for loaded trailers and since HQ now knows we are here, or at least the computer does because the guard told it, that trailer will sit for minutes or hours until an outbound driver is ready to roll and is assigned that trailer, whereupon he or she will hook up and leave with it. We will drop the trailer after we go through a special service bay in the maintenance facility where some inspectors will look the truck and trailer over for anything bent, broken, loose, or leaking that would cause the tractor or trailer to be regarded unsafe, or unroadworthy. They will see what fell off or wore out while we were on the road, make a note of it, and pass that information on to the maintenance department which will deal with what is found here.

Should anything be found, or reported by the driver, that trailer or tractor will be red-tagged and put out of service, and Trainer says they always find some damreason to put you out of service in this damsafety inspection. That tractor or trailer will be put on a list of equipment needing attention, and prioritized according to the time left before the delivery date and type of goods, particularly in the case of the trailer. It is a good system and keeps the machines safe and ready to roll. Trainer says you can use it to your advantage too, if you want some time away, just give them a list of stuff you think is wrong with your truck. They will look into it, and it could take days. Meanwhile, you're at home.

Sure enough, the trailer and tractor are red-tagged. I don't know what they found on either of them. They don't say much, so I don't ask. I guess they know what they are looking for, and I'm outta here for 10 days anyway.

We pull out of the inspection lane and drop the trailer in the area for loaded trailers, called "hot" trailers for their need to go, and almost immediately a small maintenance tractor called a yarddog grabs it up and takes off to one of the trailer repair bays so repair guys can address the red tags on it. When that is done, another driver will take it and go on to Oregon. Move the freight. Driver in, driver out.

We idle the tractor over to an area reserved for drivers loading and unloading their stuff from tractors that abuts the fenced employee parking lot. Makes it easier to haul the gear to and from, and Trainer starts unloading his stuff. I will stay in the tractor one more night since it is a six-hour drive to my house on the coast from here. It is late, and I have seen enough interstate for one day.

Trainer gets gone after a handshake and an agreement to rejoin here in 10 days. I wish him well on his vacation and watch him go. I return to the truck, get my gear, and go into the driver's lounge for my shower.

Back at the truck, I think I will go down the road and get a meal, since I am all clean now, and would enjoy a good roadhouse steak. Dinner alone, but I'm okay with that. I need a little time alone now, after all that togetherness, and welcome the solitude. That won't last long. I will be home tomorrow for some more togetherness, but a different kind of togetherness. Family and close friends. The steak is excellent, so is the loaded baked potato. It is good to be back in Texas.

Back to the truck and my now-familiar bunk. It feels good, the grumbling Cummins has become the background music for my every moment in the truck. I am thinking I will not be able to sleep well without it for a couple of nights once I get home. And I am probably going to shout unnecessarily for a while.

Daylight finds me awake and ready to get on the road south to my coast. In my life's travels, I have seen many beautiful places, and many pleasant climates. I don't know why I keep coming back to the Texas Gulf Coast with its 90-degree temperatures and 90 percent humidity, 90 percent of the time, but I do. Maybe it is the food. Maybe it is the proximity of fine speckled trout fishing in the endless grassy flats along the coastal bend. Maybe it is my home and I just accept that somewhere in the back of my brain. Maybe because a lifetime of acquaintances and friends and family, close and extended, is there. Maybe it is because I know where everything I need is located. I don't have to send in for directions on a quailcall, or risk missing a turn. I don't know what the reason is. But I do know I am about to saddle up and leave here to go there. I have moved my gear earlier from the tractor to my pickup, gassed and ready, and I leave its little cranberry self idling at the gate with the a/c roaring. It feels strange to drive the little truck around the parking lot, after driving so many thousands of miles in Big Blue. The controls don't feel right somehow. Not enough gears, and the steering wheel is too small. I don't sit high enough. It feels like I am sitting in a kiddie car.

As I walk back to Big Blue for the last of the little things, like my coffee mug, I think about how it is a handsome truck. It looks big and strong and it is, but it is a nice-looking tractor on top of that. It is still idling. I left the a/c on while I was in and out so I wouldn't melt. I climb in, sit down in the first chair, hold the wheel in my hands and look around, the interior strangely empty and spare. Like it might echo if I spoke. It doesn't look like our truck anymore, with stuff hanging everywhere, cramped and crowded. I sit still and think about a few of the things that happened in here the last three weeks, and see mental video-clips of the trip back and forth across the country, and hear faintly the laughs and shouted conversations. I am a richer man for it all.

I slowly and consciously switch the ignition off, and the 425-horsepower Cummins clatters and rattles and shakes to a dead stop for the first time in several days.

I'm headed home.

# WEEK Four

I SPEND A THOROUGHLY ENJOYABLE TIME AT HOME, DOING THE yard before the rain, fishing a little, working on the house, but not preparing for a hurricane. Chantal trashed the Yucatan, curved north, and became a problem for other folks. A tropical depression did develop offshore, then moved over our part of the coast and parked itself there. It rained 22 inches in six days according to the gauge in my backyard. That sounds like a lot, and it is, but I live in a subtropical climate and several inches of rain at a time is not uncommon. It does, however, create problems when it rains several inches a day several days in a row, like it tends to do in a slow-moving tropical depression.

My homeland is flat; the highest surface around is a freeway overpass, and once the ground is saturated there is no downhill place for the excess water to go. Neighborhoods flood first, since the earth that would normally soak up the water is covered by concrete and roofs, and there are usually a few shopping carts plugging up the storm sewers in the cities. The rain stacks up as runoff, and we have some pretty serious flooding. Not vicious raging floods, but a slow-and-steady rising water that disrupts lives just the same. And we had that near my place. Many had to leave their homes as the result of that flooding, but mine is built on a mound of dirt for that very reason. There was a foot of water in my driveway after an overnight downpour. Happens a couple of times a year. My house on the mound of dirt becomes an island.

In addition to the runoff problem, the grass grows much faster with the warm nights and soaked soil, and since the earth is so soggy, mowing is out of the question. The grass gets knee-high in a few days. Clouds of mosquitoes and floating mounds of fire ants looking for higher ground. It's a good time for me to leave.

I get up Monday morning, bid my adieus, and hit the road for north-central Texas. Today is the day I will meet Trainer, fresh from vacation in Mexico, and we will begin the final phase of my over-the-road training. I am not as excited as I was during the first phase, and I don't know why. I think it may be that I have an acclimation to it now, and the newness of driving is not what it was. But it will be good to see Trainer, and to be on the road again. It is still new enough that leaving to do it some more is pleasant.

I get to the company yard, strangely deserted for a Monday, and realize it is Labor Day, the offices are closed and nothing is going to happen for us today. I call Trainer at his home, and after some pleasantries, I tell him there is no one to assign us a truck, so I will drive another two-and-a-half hours to spend the remainder of the day and tonight with my parents. He says no problem, come on over and stay at his house rather than drive any farther. I thank him sincerely, but would like to see my parents. He says he understands and cautions me to be careful. I tell him I will meet him here at the yard tomorrow at noon, if that suits him. He says that'll be fine, 'bye.

I set out for my parents' house to have what is left of the holiday with them, after I call to warn them I am coming.

My parents run kind of a high-class flophouse for friends and family. The house is old and big and comfortable, my mother has it furnished like a centerfold for *Southern Living*, and most of the visitors have lived at least a part of their life in it, so there is a homey feeling there. It is as common to find someone at my parent's house for the weekend as not, and they wouldn't have it any other way, I don't think. They are extraordinary people with a wide circle of friends and family and almost-relatives, collected over a lifetime of being and going and doing, and they are a pleasure to be around. Segments of that circle are in and out regularly, so it does not surprise me to find I just missed a family member and yet another is slated for a visit later in the week. But for now, I have them to myself. Almost.

A distant relative just called to invite us all to his house on the lake for a Labor Day backyard barbecue and ice cream social. My mother accepts and we look out the window to see one of those ol'-fashioned Oklahoma thunderstorms coming down the gravel road. It stomps around for nearly an hour, and the fear is the event may be canceled. A phone call says no way, come on down, we'll just do the ice cream and pie inside. Be here when the weather lets up a little. Okay. So we do that, and I meet another long-lost relative and his wife at that gathering. I didn't know I was related to so many people. A good time is had by all, and we leave late for my parents' house to sit and talk for a couple of hours over more pie and coffee. I shower and get into bed. The same bed I slept in as a boy, in the same room. And they say you can never go home.

Up early and coffee on the deck, goodbyes and hugs, and I set out for the yard and a meeting with Trainer. I am ready to get on the road now, to travel some more. I am looking forward to it as I drive along sipping the last homemade coffee I will have for a while—two weeks, at least. I also came away with one of my favorite childhood treats. My mother makes a kind of chocolate-covered toffee bar I always knew as a brownie. Though adulthood has changed my tastes for many things, those brownies are not one of the things for which I have lost a taste. My mother gave me a bag of them for the road because she knows that.

I am also a lover of bread. The closer to homemade, the better. My mother makes homemade bread, without a breadmaker. As in, by hand. I have a loaf of that as well.

My dad was quite the seafood chef when he lived on the coast, and my mother would let him have the kitchen when he decided it was his turn to do the honors, but he doesn't cook much now, since he doesn't have a group to cook for regularly, and spends his time in the garden and his workshop. There is a pecan tree, spreading over his workshop and my mother's paint studio, that produces outstanding nuts and has for my lifetime. In the gardening effort, Dad gathers the pecans in the autumn to use for whatever. He has some of last year's crop bagged for me, and I have them, too. Big take for a one-niter, and I ride down the road looking and remembering and munching.

I decide to go out of town this morning by a different route, through the Kiamichi River bottom, and by part of the old farmstead. I have not been there in years, and am surprised by what I see.

Progress has come to this part of Oklahoma. Since no one was interested in continuing the family farm after my grandfather died, it was just left to go to seed when the cattle were sold. The meadows grew up with weeds for the lack of cultivation and no cattle mowing them down one bite at a time. We would go back out there on occasion to fish or to hunt quail during a holiday stay, but other than that, no one paid much attention to it. The farm had just always been part of us, and I assumed it always would be. That it would just be there, like it always had been, maintained or not.

My parents retired comfortably, and did not need the money, but they realized the farm would be a white-elephant farm if they died and didn't dispose of it. All the heirs live far from the place, so my folks and aunt and uncle decided to solve that problem before it became one. It was a wise move, but the results of that sale surprised me. Not upset me, just surprised me. Like Aristotle, I understand things change, and this is as good an example of that as I have seen all morning.

As I drive by on the now-paved state highway that essentially bisects the place, one of the fields that held my favorite fishing pond, and where I learned to shoot a rifle, has become the site of a wastewater treatment plant. Across the road, where the old ranch house stood, is now an implement barn. Just south of that shiny sheet-metal structure, where one of the old corrals had been, is a dirt oval racetrack complete with bleachers. Dang. What a difference a decade makes. What a difference a *century* makes. My great-grandfather and his sons cleared this land a hundred years ago, with axes and saws and mule teams. They moved those rocks into that pile right there by the fence. I guess someone will move that pile somewhere else one day, possibly not knowing the stones have laid there untouched for more than one hundred summers.

Ah, well. That's what I get for moving to the city. Shoulda stayed on the farm . . . but then, maybe not, I'd probably wish I had moved to the city.


I drive into the company yard about noon minus a couple of brownies and most of the loaf of bread. Locate Trainer at the office that issues truck keys, and he says we got a diffcrent tractor than the one we had. Okay. Trainer says let's split up to find it, so we start our separate ways and I stop and say hey, what happens when we find it? He looks at me not understanding. I say I might get lost so let's go look for it like a team, because now we are one. He chuckles and says okay, let's go.

This company, like many, uses a fleet arrangement with the manufacturer and therefore all the tractors are identical in appearance. There may be differences under the hood depending on what engine configuration the purchasing company would like to try for power and fuel economy, but that's about all, except for the manufacturers' model ycar differences. Most trucking companies develop a color scheme and logo, then stay with them for the brand recognition their trucks receive, so outwardly, they look the same.

So it is with our new—to us—tractor. It looks just like Big Blue, so we have to look for it by tractor number, painted on the sides of the condo. We find our new tractor out on the edge of the yard, parked in a neat row of other tractors, and the driver's window is plastered with red tags. It needs front-end work, tires, and a headlight. Trainer says it needs a windshield as well. Lookitat chip right there.

It is out of service, and Trainer is at first put out, but I say what are you going on about? You get to go back home till maintenance gets it ready. He says yeah, that's right. Says it looks like it may rain anyway, and we don't want to leave in the rain.

I take Trainer home, and move my gear into the truck. On the way back I stop off to get a burrito and soda at a fastMex place. I will stay in the truck until the shop gets the tractor ready to go, so I get a shower in the driver's lounge building, and visit with a couple of my trainee buddies for half an hour. Coming out, I see it has started to rain a little. Kinda pecking on the roof of the condo as I get in and get comfy. Suits my mood. I was ready to roll. Now we are shut down until maintenance gets to us. Oh, well. Just some more waiting, I guess. I plug an alientype movie into the TV/VCR and settle in for a night at home. I wish he'd get a wider selection of movies.

About ten thirty P.M., a guy walks up to the door, sees me inside, and hollers they are ready to replace the tires. I say okay, I will move the truck over to the tire shop, and he says okay, he will meet me there. So I crank up and slip the tractor into second gear, the cab torques up, and I idle over to the tire shop and drive inside the building, leaving wet tire tracks and dripping rain all over the concrete floor. Makes big puddles everywhere these guys have to lay in. I wouldn't like that, but it doesn't seem to bother them.

I climb out and stand around while the crew jacks up the cab and changes the steer tires, and lets it back down. It takes them one-and-a-half hours to change two tires and a headlight. Late shift. No hurry. No bosses watching them. I get back in when the guy says yer done, and idle back to the spot I had before and back into it.

Plug my movie back in and watch it until the credits roll, and hit the bunk. I wake up about every hour. Different truck, different noises. I'll get used to them.

Up at 7:00 A.M., out to my pickup, and drive down to the corner market for some coffee and a newspaper. Back to the truck, flop into the second seat, drink my coffee, and scan the bold print in the paper, looking for something that interests me. Read a few columns, and decide it is time to get Trainer. So I go do that.

I get to his house—in a well-kept neighborhood, old trees lining the broken concrete streets, the houses are from the midseventies probably, but well maintained—and Trainer is not quite ready to go. Out walking his grandson. Cute kid. They look meant for one another. Diapered toddler reaching as high as he can to take the finger of Trainer bent over to offer it, walking along the sidewalk in the cool of the morning. I get to his driveway and pull in to wait for them. Trainer's wife resting in the shade, an ample and gracious woman, offers me coffee and a seat. I accept both, and we talk about things in general while Trainer enjoys these last few minutes of this morning with Grandson. It is a pleasure for me to watch such a thing. It does me a kind of good to know there are still grandparents like I had.

Trainer says we need to pack up and go, so he bids his wife and grandson g'bye after we have my pickup stuffed with his gear. I have not seen so much, and wonder how he will get it all into the truck. I guess he knows what he's doing, and he's pretty good at getting a bunch of stuff into a little area. He tells his wife he'll be back in a couple of weeks, and she says she'll be waiting, like she always is.

We are driving back to the yard along the interstate, and a police car pulls alongside and makes that obnoxious electronic squawk. Trainer says slow down, he wants to tell us something, and rolls down the window on his side. The officer shouts that a bag blew out a little way back. Trainer says okay, thanks, and the officer pulls away. We pull over. Trainer goes through the load of stuff in the bed of my pickup and says he ain't missin' nothin'. Musta been a mistake. Probly blew out of another truck. Okay.

I figure as we unload the stuff at the bigtruck we'll find what is missing.

Back at the yard and unloading the stuff, Trainer says he has everything. I think he probably does. He is stuffing an entire pickup-load of whatever is in those bags into the truck. Amazing. He does not waste a single cubic inch. He may have some other issues, but Trainer can organize a truck cab. I just stay out of the way and haul bags to him from the pickup. He is inside and putting it away, singing some song about getting out of jail and his mama getting runned over by a train at the very top of his lungs and way out of key.

After the last bag, I stick my head in to look around, and it looks like home again, Trainer busily setting out air freshener, cleaning the windows, and making his bunk.

It is about lunchtime and he says let's go get a burger. Triple-decker at Trainer's favorite burger place just down the road. It is good and greasy. Just the way we like 'em. Iced tea, lemonade, and back to the yard.

No one has come for the truck to get it into the repair shop, so Trainer goes over to the shop and gets on the manager about that and the fact he wants a new windshield in his truck, that one has a big chip in it and he ain't driving it like that. The manager says okay, but the truck will be down a flat twenty-four hours for the windshield sealant to cure. Whaddaya mean? The windshield will leak if the tractor is moved during the curing process. Trainer looks at me. I look at Trainer. Manager walks away.

Nothing to do now but wait since they say it will be later today before the front end and windshield can be repaired. I take Trainer home again, since there is no reason for both of us to be here. I can stay with the truck. All by myself.

Coming back to the yard later, I see a big black trash bag on the side of the freeway about where the officer hailed us. Trainer said he wasn't missing anything, and that is a big bag so he certainly would know if he was missing something that size, so I don't risk stopping on the shoulder to get it.

Get out to the discount bookstore for the want of anything else to do, and grab a couple of novels for 99 cents. Good, cheap entertainment. Head on over to the deep-discount store for road goodies, water and munchies and soda, and get trapped in the store by a thunderstorm. Wandering around, I buy some more stuff while I wait out the storm. This has to be some marketing plan. Maybe they just play a thunder recording into the sound system and spray water onto the doors of the place to make us *think* it is storming out. Nothing would surprise me now in the science of customer manipulation.

Finally get out after the storm, and go to the mall for a new cell phone face. It looks like the Texas flag. Now *that* is desperate for things to do. All that activity pretty much uses up the day, so I motor back to the yard after a stop at a taco stand. Good, greasy and salty.

Shower at the lounge, chili-cheese-onion dog and soda for dinner, and still the truck has not moved. No one from maintenance has come for the truck. It is the second shift in the shop, and I know my attitude will not improve their performance, that they will move at their own pace, so I just settle in for another night in the yard.

About 9:00 P.M., I can stand it no longer and climb out to climb on someone about what I see as a total lack of concern about our truck. Our truck now, not Trainer's truck. I am assuming some ownership as the result of my being the advocate for repair. I tell the guy in the office we need our repairs completed and we need to roll. If these trucks don't pull freight, there will be no need for a maintenance department. He listens patiently and says we'll getcha first thing in the morning. He is apparently accustomed to pissy drivers. Pleasant fellow.

Okay. In the morning. Seven A.M.. Sharp. Okay. Seven A.M. Okay. We'll get you rolling.

In my perfect little world, everything is as it should be now that I have brought closure to this event. I have the promise of satisfaction from a manager. I smile mentally at having negotiated a settlement, and walk away supremely confident all our problems are behind us.

In the truck watching another alien movie. I must have completely run out of things to do. Eating chocolate grahams and drinking diet soda. My longtime buddy says if you drink a diet soda, it cancels out all the calories in what you're eating. Something snitched from another's plate has no calories either, he tells me. Aliens all over this poor guy in the movie. I see a flash of light in the sunroof and note another Red River Valley thunderstorm bearing down on me, so I just turn everything off and climb into my bunk for a good sleep in the rain. Or at least

I hope it is a thunderstorm and not a UFO booming and flashing around the truck.

Next day, same/same. Up early for coffee and a paper at the convenience store down the road, so I'll be done and waiting while the windshield is repaired. Trainer will be proud of me.

Everything is soaked from the storms last night. Greens the place right up. Need to be back around seven, like the guy said, to make sure all those repairs happen. So I am off to the coffee and newspaper store.

Eight A.M. and nothing. Done with my coffee and paper, I go into the maintenance shop to see what the holdup could be and am told no problem, we are next. Okay. I've heard that story. I decide to go get Trainer and bring him back to put some heat on the shop, irritated at having been taken in so easily by the night manager. I want to see some blood now. Preferably the night manager's, but any maintenance manager's blood will do at this point.

On the way back from his house, we slow alongside the freeway and I show Trainer the bag, still there, down the grade, and he says pull over and he'll go get it and see what it is. He comes back up the hill and says Yup, it's his mattress pad an' it's a good thing we stopped. How could you not have missed your mattress pad? Dunno.

Back at the yard, mattress pad installed, Trainer goes to the shop and lets 'em have it. He's got them lined up against the wall outside the day manager's door. He ain't drivin' that damtruck with a damchip the size of a dime in the wiper path, and that's the way that is and he's been waitin' three days to get that done among other things, so get on the dam stick and get the ****ing windshield replaced . . . NOW.

He glares at them a moment for effect. No one moves. No one breathes while he scans each face for signs of defiance. No one looks defiant. No one says a word.

We walk out, me giggling mentally.

Two hours later, sitting in the truck getting little adjustments made to the radios, still no call to the shop for a windshield. Trainer has had it. He takes off for the second floor of the office complex. Gonna get some highlevel backing, and get the windshield replaced. I hang out at the taco truck that has pulled into the parking lot, visit a little, and get a soda. Wait on Trainer while he is roughing up the suits in the executive suites upstairs.

Trainer comes back across the yard and says let's go get a load. What about the windshield? Ain't gonna be no windshield. Gotta drive it like it is. There ain't no cracks coming out of the chip so they ain't gonna replace it. We need ta roll. Gotta make some money.

I am moving at a fast walk to stay with him. He's angry. Not good.

It is 4:30 in the hot afternoon, and the guy at the dispatch window says the only thing he has is a load of chicken that needs to be picked up in Center, Texas, and taken to Corrine, Utah. Trainer says we'll take it. Dispatch says take an empty to trade for the loaded one in Center, and the load is ours.

We hike out to the tractor and climb in, crank it up and idle over to the part of the yard with the empty trailers in it. We survey the row of trailers like we know what we are looking for, and I ask what are we looking for, in the way of an empty trailer. Trainer says we need just the right one, that chicken plants are persnickety about trailers, gotta be clean and shiny. I just sit and watch as the selection is made. There is something about that one that catches Trainer's eye, and he sets the tractor up to back under the apron.

Suspensionwise, there are basically two kinds of trailers: spring-ride and air-ride. Spring-ride trailers have heavy leaf springs attached to the tandems, the carriage, and trailer frame. It is a time-tested setup, but being direct-contact and metal-to-metal, they ride rough. The stuff inside the trailer takes a beating, especially on a bad stretch of road.

Air-ride trailers have an airbag design that lets the trailer sit on at least four air cushions, that take nearly all the abuse, and the goods arrive none the worse for the trip. Another distinct advantage is for the driver: air-ride trailers pull so well, except for the weight, it is hard to tell they are back there. The just kinda float along, and take a lot of the jerking motion out of the rough roads. The one he has picked is an air-ride. That's good.

We hook up and close the doors, those moves being better polished at this stage of my training, idle to the gate, and the gate guard logs us out and Trainer says, here comes two more weeks on the road as he turns left onto the boulevard and we make our way to the loop around the city. We are going to Center with a chipped windshield to get some chickens. We are about to be a chicken truck. Again. We must eat one helluva lot of chicken in this country. Seems like every other load we haul is chicken.

It is a nice ride and a pleasant afternoon across north Texas and through the pine forests. It is good to be back on the road, the drive made even better by the clean air left behind a row of afternoon show-ers. I tell Trainer it is good that we were not caught in the rain because we have a big chip in the wiper path of the windshield. He looks over at me and tries desperately to control himself. I waited until he was calmed, and restrained by a seatbelt. And made certain I was not in arm's way, so to speak. I couldn't help it.

The chicken-processing plant in Center has our trailer preloaded and ready to go, when we get there after dark, so we drop the empty and I set up to back under the loaded trailer apron. Trainer said he drove from the yard to here, and said I should drive to our planned stop out-side Marshall. I can do that, and we trade chairs, and Trainer gets out to supervise the hookup.

I back under the trailer apron and in hooking up, it doesn't feel right for some reason. I am not sure what is wrong, but something is not right. I get out with a flashlight, it is dark now, and go under the trailer to look into the fifth wheel notch, and see the kingpin is not seated behind the wedge bar; it is on top of the wedge bar. It is a highhook. My first experience with that, and I caught it right here. I am proud of myself for having done so, and Trainer stands some distance away in the dark hollering what the hell is the holdup. I come from beneath the apron and tell him I am going to pull away from the trailer, that the yarddog left the landing gear too tall and the trailer apron is too high for the fifth wheel, and the kingpin won't seat. Trainer says that happens all the time here, and he'll get the gate guard to call the yarddog and have him lower the trailer apron. I wait and pat myself on the back. I do not have the feeling I got lucky; I knew something wasn't right. I think I have the knack, but I caution myself to not rely on it. I paid attention to the red flag that went up mentally when things weren't feeling right, and that was a bigger factor than the knack.

There is a saying among the bluewater sailors that the time to reef the sails is when the thought first occurs, and that is good advice. That wisdom could easily be expanded to cover driving as well as many other parts of my existence. The time to check on something is when the mental red flag goes up. Those red flags are indicators one of our self-defense mechanisms uses to let us know something isn't like it should be. We don't pay a lot of attention sometimes, and bad things happen as the result. I sometimes pay attention to my quiet warnings from within. Not often, but sometimes. Depends on what they are warning me about.

In a past life, there were a couple of phrases that really caused me to cringe. One was "team of experts." Man, there is no end to the problems a team of experts can deliver. They bring with them the other phrases I came to really hate hearing: would have, could have, and should have. A team of experts is really good at telling the victims they would have, could have, and should have. That brings us back to the highhook. I did not want to get into a "should have" situation, so I stopped at the mental red flag, and doing that prevented a calamity. That incident, allowed to play out, would have cost Trainer his job certainly, and myself, being a trainee, would have been brought back to the yard and a decision made there. Most likely termination. The sonsabitches that run the trucking industry do not play when the topic is highhooks.

We finally get hooked properly, and make our way out of the chicken plant. It is late, we are tired, but it is not far to our overnight stop near Marshall, and that will put us on the interstate first thing in the morning.

The road from Center to Marshall is a good one, and the ride is quick and quiet. We don't say a lot when we are tired. It is too difficult to talk over the engine and windnoise. We just ride and look and wait.

Wait for the truck stop to get here. First nights on the road are always an adjustment after hometime. Circadian rhythm has to get in sync with the interstate signs, I suppose.

The place Trainer has chosen is a long-established, genuine old-time truck stop like the ones that come to mind when someone says truck stop, but it is a welcome sight to us as we pull in and park on the edge of the muddy lot, it having rained here earlier. There is a restaurant glassed into the front of the building, and the lights inside beckon Trainer. He says let's have a midnight snack. Sounds good to me, as long as it isn't chicken, and I agree to go along. We make our way across the soggy sand-and-shell lot to the paved lot that surrounds the business area. It is warm here, even for midnight.

Inside is a long row of red vinyl-upholstered chrome stools attached to the floor in front of a long Formica-topped serving bar. Diner-style right out of the fifties. I like it. Then I think how this is not the product of some interior designer, this place *is* from the fifties. Those are the original furnishings, but well cared for. Trainer selects a stool right in the middle of the row. I take a seat one over, to give the man some shoulder room. The girl comes along and pours coffee into cups already at the place mats and says how ya doin'. Trainer says good and he wants some gravy and biscuits. She looks at me and I say make it two, so she smiles and heads to the back and shouts something at the cook about bricks and mud on her way down the counter flipping cups over and pouring coffee.

Trainer and I head back to the truck stuffed and tired. Morning will be here soon, and I have to go back in and get a shower. Should have done that when I went in for the coffee and biscuits.

I wake at about 6:00 A.M., get Trainer going, and follow him in for coffee. Again. Back to do the logs and plan the trip we are about to embark upon. I wake a little at a time today for some reason. Like stairsteps or something. Never had that happen before. Most of times, I wake in a gradual crescendo. Slowly, but smoothly. Trip plan. Gotta plan the trip. Get a grip on consciousness here and tune in.

A trip plan, officially, is a list of projected arrivals and departures for food, fuel, and overnight stops along a selected route that must be sent in to HQ until the company is okay with a new driver's ability to determine about when and where he or she will be. That tells the company whether or not the driver can budget his or her time. And that tells the company whether or not the loads that driver pulls will get to the destination as scheduled. That tells a company whether or not a new driver should be retained or let go.

All new drivers have to send in a trip plan until that driver's fleet supervisor is convinced the driver can manage his or her time. I haven't seen much use for one past that. There is a school of thought out there that says always plan your trip. That way you'll always know about where you should be. I guess that is one way to look at it, but I am not much of one to keep to a schedule of any kind, having seen people in my past wind up in dire straits over trying to stay on a schedule. I think a driver, or anyone for that matter, should do all he safely can every day and enjoy the cushion at the end of the trip, or project, or day, that comes with doing that. Don't waste time and get hung up in this schedule thing. Sticking to a schedule can actually slow a driver down, by having him or her stop before it is necessary, to stay on that schedule.

Anyway, at the beginning of each trip the green drivers have to send that trip plan in via the quailcall to HQ, where it is filed away, and at the end of the trip it is matched against when and where the truck really stopped and started, based on the quailcall pings, and the results are judged yes he can do what he says in the plan, or no he can't do what he says.

After a few reality checks, the trip plans get a lot more accurate, and there is a point in the driver's development where he or she is no longer required to send them in, as I said earlier. At that point, the company knows the driver understands his limits and governing factors in ETAs, like traffic, weather, road construction, and fuel mileage, or by then knows he never will.

We don't have to do that trip plan thing officially because we have Trainer. The company is confident he is competent at trip planning. So, as soon as we get a load assignment, I become responsible for planning the route and stops for fuel and breaks, and overnight stops as well. Trainer will determine whether or not I know how to plan a trip properly and that will keep me from having to do the trip plan routine for the folks at HQ after I leave his tutelage. Maybe. If I show him I can bracket my time to suit him, and demonstrate a modicum of ability at trip planning, and if HQ agrees.

Basically what I do to create a trip plan is lay a straightedge across a map of the forty-eight states from where we are to where we are going and select the interstates that best parallel that straightedge. Then, in the atlas, I go to each state we will cross and look for low clearances, restricted routes for trucks, loops around cities and warnings of any kind. I look for timesinks as well: two-lane roads that will slow us down, and metro areas. Obviously we want to stay on the interstates for the limited public access and relatively high-speed one-way traffic, but they do not always go the way we want to go. A second choice is the U.S. highway system, but many of them go through towns and burgs and hamlets, and that seriously reduces our average speed. On the interstates, we average 60 to 63 MPH if we keep our stops short and infrequent. On the U.S. highways highlighted in yellow, the ones bigtrucks can go on, and on the secondary routes, that number is cut in half. Towns. Traffic. Traffic lights. Speed limits. Stop signs. I want to use interstates if I can.

Then I go back to the continental map armed with MPH and MPG figures and determine where a given number of driving hours will put us. I mark those spots on the map. Based on current fuel levels and consumption, I know we get 6 MPG at an average, and I plug those numbers into a basic equation. That tells me where we will need fuel, and I mark those spots. I try to coordinate breaks for meals and showers with fuel stops in the interest of time conservation. Consolidate everything I can into one stop, and that is usually pretty easy. When we eat, sleep, shower, call home and break is a little bit flexible. When the truck needs fuel is not.

Running out of fuel in one of these babies is a $300 and hours-long mistake. On top of that the driver will be forever branded by his peers as plagued with Dumbass disease. Running out of fuel in a bigtruck is not a distinction to have on a résumé.

All that done, I present the plan to Trainer for his perusal and approval. He usually rubberstamps it and says let's do it. The first one or two I did got some pretty harsh scrutiny, but now he just asks did ya plan the trip and where are we stoppin' at tonight. It heartens me he is confident in my ability. And so it is today. He sees me with the atlas and city maps and truck stop guide and list of company-specified fuel stops spread all over my side of the truck as he drinks his coffee and smokes with the windows down, and leaves me to my work.

Just as I am done, he looks and says ain'cha done yet? Yeah, I am done, and we stop tonight in Jamestown, near Grants, New Mexico. He says Grants, New Mexico. Accent on the Grants and Mexico. He's thinking buffet. Tonight and tomorrow morning.

I get the books put away and tell him to get out of my chair. He says okay and moves his stuff to the second seat, and I move mine to the first seat. We idle out of the muddy lot, coffeed up and happy, gear up for the day's ride, get to roadspeed in the bighole, and settle into the tempo of the joints in the interstate pavement. It is a sort of clacketyclack the pavement joints cause the tires to make, as though they were counting cadence for us. The metronome for our days and nights. Always there, on the bigroad. Like the sounds of the wind and the engine.

The tractor we have been assigned is going to take some getting used to, as we said on the farm. The turbocharger has a distinct and irritating whine that changes with the engine RPMs. The shoulder belt on the driver's side left a diagonal grease stripe across the front of my shirt yesterday, I hate nasty seat belts, and I swear the steer tires are square. Gotta be something wrong with them. That or the trailer is loaded wrong. Maybe both.

To avoid trashing more clothes, I peel off about three paper towels and wrap them around the shoulder belt to keep them from rubbing

more grime into another shirt. Trainer rolls his eyes and says this ain't
no fashion show out here, let's burn some diesel.

We need to scale the load even though we know it is light. The bill
says we have a partial load of select chicken parts and they are probably
going to wind up in high-end restaurants in the Salt Lake City area, and
therefore, we don't have a full trailer. A full-service truck stop is advertised on a billboard at the next exit, and Trainer says let's get off and get
some more coffee and scale these chickens. So we do that, not so much
to ascertain what we weigh, but where the weight is. We know we don't
have a full trailer and therefore we know we do not have a general overweight problem, but depending on how the trailer is loaded, we could
have an axle weight problem. There may be more weight on one set of
axles than we could shift by sliding the tandems and fifth wheel, and the
only way to fix that is load the trailer correctly. We would have to go all
the way back to the chicken plant for them to fix it, so we don't want to
go too far before we scale the load.

The scale ticket axles out the weight, and we see the trailer has been
what is called nose-loaded. All the weight is forward in the trailer. Not
much we can do about it now, nor do we have to, it is legal, but all the
load's weight is over the drives. Very little is on the tandems, and that is
why the steer tires feel square. The load is pressing down on the drives
and taking some of the weight of the tractor off the steer tires. Kinda
seesawing the tractor. Very few tires are perfectly round, but under a
load, they are mashed pretty flat and roll fairly smoothly. Without that
load, or in our case, partly unloaded by the trailer's tendency to lift the
steers, the out-of-round tires can assume their innate shape more easily.
Makes the front-end ride a little bumpy.

Fortunately, we can solve that problem in this specific instance, by
unlocking the mechanism that attaches the fifth wheel to the frame and
moving it forward a couple of spaces. Doing that moves the load's
weight more forward on the tractor frame and helps hold the front of
the tractor down. That will improve the quality of the ride and the overall balance of the rig. Much safer as well.

Back in, fresh coffee, axled out and rolling. It is a beautiful morning, and the ride is much better now. The front tires feel round, and it is much easier to steer confidently. I no longer feel as though I am merely aiming the truck.

West across north-central Texas, and the wind begins about Fort Worth. Serious wind, about 30 to 35 knots. It has been from the south and on our side most of the morning, but has moved more to the southwest and hitting us on the left side at about a 45-degree angle. This would be what is called a close reach on a sailboat, and it is a rough point of sail. The boat pitches and pounds into the waves, spray blows around the bow and into the cockpit. Minus the spray, it isn't much better in a bigtruck. The cab rocks heavily in the gusts, but the chickens hold us down.

The weather has been clear from Marshall, but a dust storm kicked up by the wind near Henrietta slows progress considerably. My first inclination is to turn on the windshield wipers, but that's not the right thing to do in a dust storm. The wipers act like big emery boards and scrape the glass all up. I resist the urge, knowing what will happen, but it is still hard to see, so I compensate by slowing down to buy some time if I need it. Trainer is fidgety. He is trying to decide if it is bad enough to stop, and hoping we get through it before he wishes we had.

Getting beyond all that, and fairly quickly, it being as local as it was, I notice three white crosses in the median on US 287 outside the city limits of Wichita Falls. Three of them. Most of a family gone. Maybe a part of three families. I don't know which. We see lots of crosses, mostly single ones, sometimes a pair, rarely more than two. Three are here against the blue-black clouds in the western sky as we climb the hill, and then set against the green of the median as our vantage point changes at the top. I am overwhelmed by the enormity of the loss. I don't even want to imagine it.

I see many crosses along the roads we travel, and I am always sobered by what they represent. A life lost. Someone, though, cared enough about that life to erect a memorial to the person that lived it and,

in most cases, maintain that memorial. Though death is surely a part of
life, there are some limits to its acceptability, the way I see it.

Parents should go first and in their due time; but parents should
leave, and not be taken. Parents should also not have to bury their children. Those should be the rules. When things happen otherwise, the
feeling of loss is compounded and we are driven to look for answers, and
sometimes there are none we can accept. All we can do at that point is
memorialize that life and learn to live without them. It helps somehow
to build a monument to the lost, no matter how small. It is the last thing
we can do for them. It may be the last thing we can do for ourselves, and
maybe we don't do it as much for them as for ourselves.

Farmers plowing dry panhandle dirt, and the resulting dust blowing for miles across Texas in the wind. These guys didn't learn a thing
from the dust bowl. A windmill every so often, is a reminder there is little surface water here. Many of them are long broken and dilapidated,
like the sunset pictures in brochures. Another relic of another age.
Some, very few, work just fine, spinning fast in this gale, and have water
tanks beside them for the livestock.

Lots of cratered houses and barns here, in this part of the state. I
go along and wonder who lived in them and worked in them and think
of the seasons they must have seen. Happy houses, I hope, in their day.
Old trees in the yard, untrimmed and overgrown, some dead and the
bark weathered from them. Few things are as stark to me as a dead tree
without bark, gray and lifeless. The tragic ruins of a magnificent soil
anchor, air filter and water pump. No leaves, and they don't sway in the
wind, graceful, like a living tree does. A tree corpse standing there,
naked, stiff, and forsaken, reaching to the sky with spindly, broken
branches for some mercy of some kind from some One. An ignoble end
to a life of service to man and beast and planet.

Clouds have overrun the sky along the way to our Amarillo fuel stop
and, hopefully, lunch when we get there. They are lowering and threatening ugly weather, the wind steadily increasing as we go. Sure enough,

the rain comes along in blustery downpours. Bands of heavy rains separated by windy spaces as we go west.

There is a little town alongside US 287 called Estelline, and a little to the north of it is a bridge over the Prairie Dog Town Fork of the Red River. It is the longest name for a river I ever saw posted on an official sign. And the most red-orange riverbanks I ever saw. This land is really red when it is wet, and the shallow, but fast-moving water beneath the bridge is just as red as the land. Hard to tell what is river and what is bank; the river looks like liquid land flowing beneath the bridge in waves that don't move as the water rolls over obstacles on the sandy bottom. Kayakers know those as "standing waves." Rocks and irregularities in the river bottom make it do that. Looks kinda neat, like roller-coaster cars going over the high and low places on the wild track.

North of the bridge is a marker for a trail into the Palo Duro Canyon. I make a mental note to come back here one day and maybe walk around some. It looks like a place I might want to see at walking speed.

There are two trucks off the road in separate places between Estelline and Memphis. Wind got them. No skid marks. Both of them empty, foolishly deadheading at speed in the wind. Carelessness. They should have stopped and waited it out, but hurried on hoping to get away clean. Now look at them, lucky to be alive, standing at the troopers' cruisers explaining what happened, both in separate places. Troopers already know what happened. They are just happy no one is hurt, writing and listening to the driver concoct some story to exonerate themselves. The ticket will say "too fast for conditions," and the tow truck bill will be staggering this far out of the way.

There is heavy wind and a wet road all the way to Amarillo, where we pull into a busy truck stop. Some drivers fueling and some just ducking out of the waves of storms. It is a good chance to get a nap or shower or do some laundry or call home or whatever can be done waiting out the weather. No one likes driving in nasty weather, so any prudent driver having a time frame that will allow it, takes the safe way out and stays parked. There is no reason to expose themselves unnecessarily, and they may as well use the time wisely. We don't have that luxury. No extra time on this load, but we are heavy enough to stay stable, so we will drive on.

In what has become the second phase of my training, we are being dispatched like a team, and expected to perform like one. Run the truck as long and as far as we can safely and legally. If the weather were dangerous, we would certainly shut down. I don't think either of us awakened this morning intent on killing ourselves or anyone else. Our company is not wild about ugly weather either. They can, and do on occasion, request via the quailcall that drivers seek shelter in conditions the safety department feels may be, or may get to be, dangerous, and they monitor those events closely and carefully. But neither myself nor Trainer feels the weather is likely to be dangerous, and we don't concern ourselves beyond getting what amounts to a pit stop. We just drive with that much more attention to doing things by the training book.

Ordinarily, the training process, detailed in that book, is a continual thing. When the trainer and the trainee leave the yard, they do not return until the road training is complete, some five to six weeks. It is a long time so close, and serves at least three distinct purposes.

First and by far foremost, it gets the freight moved. That is the sole purpose of a truck and trailer. There is no other reason for its existence. They, the corporate henchmen, can look at it, or sell the program, or romanticize it or present it any way they want, in any favorable light possible to the potential recruit, but the truck serves one primary purpose: it moves freight. Everything else is a distant second and third and so on. Everything.

Secondarily, the training period gets a team into a tractor. Now the truck can go twice as far in a day as a solo driver can. That means faster delivery. Carriers can sell nothing above and beyond the competition but delivery times, and since every one of them sells transportation, the quicker the better. Merchandise lumbering across the country behind a solo driver is not being sold in a market. It has to be in a place the customer can get to it. Teams can get it there twice as fast. The road training process guarantees a certain number of teams get on the road in a regular pattern at regular intervals. Team training is good for business, and there is nothing wrong with that. It is a sound and productive plan. It works to several ends, and all of them provide employment in several sectors of the economy.

Thirdly, the over-the-road training weeds out the people that really don't want to do this for a living. A month and a half away from mama and the kids is not for everyone. It is like sales, in that anyone can do it, but it is not for everyone. The industry has a near 100 percent turnover for that reason. But to make any real profit at all, a tractor has to move freight about 7,000 miles a month, so most companies want a driver to stay out as long as possible. Move the freight. The bare minimum is two weeks. It takes that long for a solo driver to get out of the yard, make one run coast to coast and a couple of cross-country trips, then get routed back to the yard. No forty-eight-state company I know about will accept less than two weeks out. Most want five or six weeks out, but they rarely get it. The average is three weeks. Most drivers can get in a couple of coast-to-coast trips in three weeks, and that makes a reasonable paycheck for both parties.

The other side of that hometime coin is that the driver is not making any money laying around the house. He has to be behind the wheel to get paid. So the driver is torn between the money away and the honey at home. It is a tradeoff, and a hard choice to make, that choice to get back into the truck, and leave mama and the babies in the mirror. Some driver, somewhere, is making that decision right now. The wife is being brave, the kids are waving 'bye Daddy, and he is fighting the urge to stay and see about that job down at the hardware store. It happens to him every three or four weeks.

We get our tractor fueled, a triple-decked sandwich apiece for ourselves, store-bought too, and ease back onto the highway. In this case, we just came onto I-40 west from US 287, and west of Amarillo the rain has become so heavy many cars have pulled onto the shoulder to sit it out. That is dangerous as well. In getting onto the shoulder because they cannot see to drive in the rain, they put themselves into position to be hit by someone getting onto the shoulder that cannot see in the rain. I have often wondered about the logic in that, if there is any.

Some distance west of Amarillo, we leave the rain behind us and get into the brilliant pale blue sky and panoramic vistas of the Texas panhandle, along with some cooler air, and I see the ragged little pieces of gray and black clouds, left over from the front, riding the north wind trying to catch up to the storms. Like little whatevers trying to catch up to the herd. The fresh wind rocks the truck occasionally as we roll toward the sunset. The air is a little cooler as I feel the windshield, maybe not a whole lot, but every degree down from 100 helps. We rise onto the Llano Estecado, and the altitude gained helps a little as well. Matter of fact, it is pretty pleasant out there now.

Llano Estecado means "staked plain" in the Spanish language, and that is what Francisco Vasquez de Coronado called it when he and his men walked across it in about 1652 on their way to Kansas, as I recall. It is some of the most geographically flat land on the planet, or so the girl in the New Mexico rest area tells me when I pop in and take a little break there to get the free coffee. She says the plain starts in Texas where she lives. You live in Texas and work in a rest area in New Mexico? Yep. Okay. I love this country. I like the rest area, too. It has a Route 66 theme. And free coffee. And the folks there know a lot about staked plains and Route 66.

Tucumcari is up next, citywise.

Along the interstate past Tucumcari is a little town with a name made famous by tequila. It sits on both sides of the interstate like two dilapidated strip malls made of long-retired school buses and homemade shops, deserted way back. Corrugated tin and sunburned lumber held together by the red earth plastered onto them. I wonder why it doesn't wash off in the rain and snowmelt. Maybe it does and they just put more back on. An apparently abandoned red brick adobe-covered house, windows and people long gone, the bare earth floor stomped shiny by tens of thousands of footsteps reflecting the late sunlight through a missing window. Cedar and juniper dotting the landscape that stretches away to the blue mesas far to the north and west. Desolate land around a desolate little railroad water stop from back in the days. They sort of fit together. People must be here, I just don't see them. There are goats in a way-too-small pen by the train tracks. Someone must be caring for them. We pass through the place in a matter of seconds. It and its history, whatever that is, are behind us in a moment. Probably someone's bones out there that lived their life in that little town.

About here on I-40, the signs touting the old route US 66 begin to pop up and get more frequent as we go west to Albuquerque. It seems at one point, the landscape is completely occluded by a near endless hedge of billboards touting restaurants, hotels, diesel, casinos, free arrowheads, and expensive Indian blankets all using Route 66 as a common denominator. Mute hucksters blocking out the scenery, bright lit and pushing back the gathering darkness on the high plains.

The CB is getting noisy. There are a couple of motor homes locked in a two-lane standoff struggling up the hill a klick or so ahead of us, and the drivers in the bigtrucks stacking up behind them are getting rowdy on the airwaves. Trainer tunes in, but says nothing.

I personally think motor-home drivers, while not the fastest, are among the most courteous people out here, and tell Trainer as much. He says yeah, that's true.

We are driving into one of those beautiful whole-spectrum sunsets the dry northwest winds produce, and Trainer says we need to stop in Clines Corner for a snack. I think the signs got him. He certainly has no interest in the colors of the sunset.

As it gets later, and darker, I notice our right headlight is shaky, or at least the beam in front of the truck is, and that leads me to think the headlight is not secure in its socket. I make a point of that to Trainer and he says yeah, that he dropped one of the rim screws at the last rest stop when he put a new sealed beam unit in, and he looked but he couldn't find it. The parking lot and the screw were the same color. I had wondered what he was doing with the hood tilted forward when I came out with my free coffee from the Texas girl in the New Mexico rest stop. I should have known something bad had happened, or was about to, what with the hood up. Hoods being up are rarely a good sign.

No problem, he says, we'll get another one when we stop in Clines Corner. Says everybody has damheadlight rim screws, 'cause they're so easy to lose in rest stops.

We get to Clines Corner, and they have no headlight rim screws, but they do have some duct tape. I get some and show Trainer how to tighten a loose headlight with the tape. He is unimpressed and says it'll do until we can get a screw. I agree. This stuff is good for patching nearly anything. Space shuttle probably has a roll or two aboard.

As we work in the dark parking lot, it is surprisingly cold out in the wind for this time of year. I guess I'm not used to cool weather in September, or that little front was stronger than I thought. I shiver a little and think how I may soon wish I had brought more clothes. Or maybe not more clothes, but some for cooler weather. That is one thing about traveling the country I will never get accustomed to for the time I will drive: the near-constant climate changes as we go about the country. Hot to cold, high altitude to low, moist to dry. My body will never get to the place it makes easy adjustments. Goose down jacket and hot cereal in the morning, iced tea and shorts by afternoon. Soggy hair in the coastal fog in the morning, lips chapped by nightfall on the Nevada desert. I just don't think my body was designed for dramatic atmospheric changes.

Back onto the road for Albuquerque. Coming into the city after dark from the east is impressive, dropping down from the Sandias into the pool of light at the bottom of the hill that is Albuquerque, but it is not as impressive as coming into the city from the west after dark on a clear night. The long, gradual slope from the west lets the show last for a while coming I-40 eastbound. Still, on a westbound ride, it is nice until we get down to the bottom, into the business district, and then it is just another city at night. Traffic and construction and detours. We make our way through and I look for the exit to our fuel stop, right downtown. The stop is near the intersection, or interchange rather, for two major commercial arteries, I-40 and I-25, which cross paths in downtown

Albuquerque. Like most established cities trying to update their infrastructure with all the traffic coming and going, Albuquerque has been
paralyzed by that effort alone, with two interstates adding to the confusion. What a mess. I didn't know there were this many orange barrels
outside Chicago, and almost all of them are in our way.

We negotiate all that and manage to get into a way-too-small truck
stop for fuel and a hot dog. I wish the corporate powers would use a little consideration instead of the price of fuel alone in determining the
fuel stops. Some of these places are not the easiest to access, in addition
to wasting time, and getting to them radically increases the risk of a collision. Snaking around a downtown construction zone is a great way to
crunch a bigtruck or trailer. Seems like a real expensive process to save
a penny a gallon, but I guess someone in some cubicle somewhere in the
bowels of HQ figures it is dollars-effective in the big picture.

Working our way out of the snarled traffic through downtown Albuquerque to get back onto the interstate going west for the long climb
out of the valley, Trainer at the wheel. Big Blue Two strains against the
gravity-powered chickens up the gradual incline that seems to end in
the night sky far ahead. I look back on Albuquerque, or the lights of it,
in the mirror, *encanta* by the sight. It isn't like watching it in the windshield, but it is like they are worth the effort of watching them in the
mirror, with my head, neck, and back all twisted out of shape to get the
proper angle for the reflection. The windshield view would really be
something. Panoramic electric spiderweb, I'll bet.

Those dang hot dogs just didn't do it for me, and I begin to whine
about it over the engine and windnoise. Trainer just drives and looks at
me askance, from behind his glasses. I kinda like his glasses. They look
like a two-piece windshield on an old pickup truck. That sort of image
fits him. Uncomplicated and just off the farm, honest and dependable.
Overalls and a straw hat would suit the man.

I decide we need more to eat just about the time we crest the rise
and Albuquerque disappears behind the ridge, and the starry New
Mexico night covers us from horizon to horizon. The lights from the

dash illuminate Trainer's steady face, driving. Doing his job with a determination to do it well. I like it. And that inspires me to dig into the pantry and spread some sausage and cheese and crackers onto the top of the cooler between the chairs and create some hors d'oeuvres, interstate style, in the soft light of the instrument cluster. One for me and one for Trainer, one at a time until all the crackers are gone, and that takes a while. I think we are past the point of being not hungry, we are eating now for something to do as we ride along and munch. Doesn't really matter, we ate all the crackers. We either have to stop eating or go with just the sausage and cheese. I decide on just the sausage and cheese. We are in it this deep, might as well finish the stuff off. Trainer doesn't notice there is no cracker. Or if he does, he says nothing about it. He just takes the stack of sausage and cheese and packs it in, chewing and driving. He doesn't care what it is. We finish off the sausage, then the cheese, and settle in for the ride to our overnight stop in Jamestown, New Mexico. We have stayed at this place before.

The sign that heralds the truck stop alongside the interstate is visible for miles. It, like everything else about this travel stop, is huge. There must be several hundred thousand light bulbs in that computer-controlled billboard. A miracle of modern technology in the high-desert night beckoning the roadweary. That would be us.

We pull in, park, shut down, go in and get a shower, and climb into the bunks. It is too cold to open the windows for the fresh air, but I don't care. Give me some sleep. Eating sausage and cheese and crackers all night makes me tired, apparently. Trainer doesn't want the buffet, says we'll get it in the morning. He must not feel well.

I don't remember putting my bags on the second seat, but I guess I did. There they are, as I pull the light curtain back with my foot and the New Mexico morning floods the cab. Trainer grunts and starts his morning operation. Hacking. Rustling bedclothes and cigarette packs. Scratching lighter flint. Squeaking, hissing chair. Mug bouncing around on the dash. Door opens, cab rocks, door slams. Quiet returns to the cab. I get up and get about my business in my cherished time alone first thing in this shiny morning.

Coffee, breakfast buffet, just as good as it was the last time we were here, and back to the truck. Do the logs, and Trainer is acting a little strange, so I send him out to call his wife, and he does that while I finish my log and drink some coffee in peace, languishing in the cool morning light of the high country. It is beautiful here, and like I said before, I have thought so my whole life.

The planned route will take us through part of the Navajo reservation in northwestern New Mexico. I was here many years ago, as a contractor in the San Juan coal-fired power facility between Farmington and Shiprock. I spent a year hereabouts and took my weekends to see the sights and look up the local past, and this part of America has some celebrated chronology. The Anasazi were here, the Pueblos and cliff dwellers, Spanish conquistadors, priests and desperadoes, Apache warriors. They were all here and left their mark, then passed into the pages of history. Soon the current natives will be famous for the casino business. There are several nice ones along the interstate, and if these folks aren't famous for their hospitality at this point, they will be. They are quiet, warm, and easy to deal with.

Trainer gets back and climbs in, much the better for the phone call, and I bail out for one more mug of my very brand of coffee, then see a fellow inside I went to driving school with, so we talk shop a minute, and I say I'm off, we wish one another well, and I get back to the truck. Climb in and Trainer says let's go, we ain't makin' any money sittin' here. I just look at him, look out the window, and grin. Never lets up.

I shove the shifter into second gear, the tractor torques, and we idle toward the parking lot exit and the road to Gallup.

Gallup was a major trading center for tooled silver in recent years, and may still be. Matter of fact, the present site of Gallup is the ancient site of what was thought to be Cibola, the storied city of gold the conquistadors desperately wanted. Coronado came here looking for it, and found nothing more than a small pueblo. He either didn't know about, or didn't care about, the silver, apparently. The high-desert Indians are among the elite metalsmiths in the world, and with their own style as well, bold and assertive. Their work ranges from some of the most gaudy jewelry available to some of the finest details imaginable, but they are most famous for the showy, heavy silver rings and bracelets and squash necklaces. Beautiful work, and most of the local artisans still bring their products to merchants in Gallup, I'm told. The interstate goes just north of the old downtown area where all the silver shops were along the main street. It is not a problem to get there; I can see it from here as we roar along the elevated interstate looking for our exit. But I don't know if the silver shops are still there. I don't have the time to look.

Shortly, we peel off onto US 666 north to Shiprock in the early light and the bleakness of northwestern New Mexico. The road is rough, but the drive is nice. I was told once there were more people killed on US 666 per mile than any other highway in the country. It could well be true, and not just because of the highway number. This is a very long, straight trip on a rough two-lane road, and in the dark or snow or ice, it must be a deadly ride. But, for now, it is pleasant and I sip the last of my coffee and watch a majestic landscape go past. Early desert sun and shadows and colors. Trainer likes the desert early, and rides comfortably in the second seat watching the scenery go by his window.

I ride and think about what all has happened here in the last fifteen or twenty thousand years, about the ancients and what may have happened to them. I think about the Spanish that traipsed through here looking for gold, missing the silver, and passing out diseases five hundred years ago. I think about how this land is holy to the aborigines, and here we are driving a 40-ton truck through it. I see lots of revered places as we go by. Places I had forgotten about.

When I was here years ago, there was a Navajo fellow I got along with, and over a period of time and several Sunday afternoon trips, he showed me some of those places and let me in on some of the tribal lore. I pass a few of those places again today as we go toward Shiprock, which is among the most sacred of those sites, and think on what causes a place to become hallowed ground. Or, in most cases, a hallowed height. Viewing a mountain or a plateau or mesa from a certain angle, I can see how people might think the way they did, and some still do. Some of the legends and beliefs are plausible. Those places are difficult climbs, impossible climbs back when, and I can see even a modern climber regarding it as a spiritual experience, especially if the summit is attained. Just standing on the plain looking up at the height and sheer sides of some respected peaks lends a great deal of credence to believing the gods live there, on so lofty a place, unreachable by mere mortals. Some of the beliefs would be easy conclusions to derive from what is here.

We cross another state border at Colorado and still another into Utah, and stop for coffee in Monticello in a windstorm. Dust everywhere, it is difficult just to get the tractor door open. Then, once I get it open, the wind has it at an angle and I can't get it closed. Wind and dust whipping the stuff inside all around like tempest in a big teapot. Trainer bellowing something I can't hear in the maelstrom. I feel like Dorothy must have felt trying to get the storm cellar door open in the wind, and start to laugh, but realize there is nothing funny about this. The cab will be in a shamble when we get back and no telling what important papers are blowing out the other side. I manage to close the door finally, by leaning into it, and run for the building I hope is in that direction, and I swear a woman on a bicycle rides past me. Miss Gulch, I'll bet.

I get into the little convenience store about the same time Trainer makes it, and we look at one another for a second and he starts to laugh, and that's a good sign. We get the coffee, ask about the wind, and the lady says she hasn't seen it like this in her time here. Doesn't know what the deal is. Clear sky, but lots of wind and plenty of dust to blow around. We jump out the door and head for the truck at doubletime. I am glad once again for the interference-fit lids on coffee cups as I run and hope I don't crash into the side of the truck, not seeing it in this dust.

The wind and dust settle down some as we get onto US 191 and go north. It is a must-see for rockhounds and geotypes. Beautiful wind-and-water-carved canyons and cliffs. It is surprisingly cool outside.

Maybe it is autumn here. Autumn where I live usually arrives in late Oc-
tober, if there is an autumn that year.

Sometimes, on the coast, the weather is warm all the way through
December and a cold front blows in and freezes everything for a day or
two, seldom longer. Problem is, we go from shorts and polo shirts, to
coats in one day. That kind of temperature drop kills all the leaves and
they just turn black and fall off the trees, when a frost comes on the
heels of summer like that. Generally speaking, autumn on the coast is
nothing more than the temperature going from the midnineties to the
midseventies, and drizzly rain instead of thunderstorms.

Some years, the tallow trees put on a spectacular show, and when
they do, I would match them against any autumn foliage anywhere for
color and photo ops. Tallow trees are the predominant tree along the
coastal plains in the area where I live, and are not really trees, I think,
but big bushes with a trunk. They don't get real tall, 30 feet maybe at
the highest, and they don't leaf out like regular trees. The leaves are in
tufted groups along the twisted branches, and in the autumn the things
look as though they are holding out bouquets of red, orange, and yellow
flowers for the end of summer. Beautiful, especially in groups or thick-
ets. The ever-present coastal breeze causes the leaves to oscillate and
produces a kaleidoscope effect, the colored leaves flipping front to back.

Anyway, there are not a lot of trees out here to indicate the onset of
autumn, what few I see are conifers, but it is definitely cooler than I
think September should be, and the rock formations and cliff sculp-
tures make up for the lack of trees, colorwise. I wonder how it is that the
erosive forces concentrate on one part of the cliff to scour a cave from
it. Maybe the rock there isn't as hard for some reason as the rest. Better
still, there is a place along here where someone has built a house inside
the formation. Charges folks to see it. Hole in the rock. Free enterprise,
again, at its basic best.

Getting into Moab, a little more than halfway to our intersection
with I-70, is a disillusioning experience from the south. Ratty, shabby,
dusty, everything for sale. Broken fences and cars. Sad looking. Not

what I expect from a tourist trap/outdoor mecca. It must look better covered in snow.

Downtown Moab is completely different. Touristy, boutiquey, up-scaley. Tummytucked and facelifted old buildings. High-rent shoppes. Gucci-shod, Rolexed hikertypes with shopping bags walking the sidewalk and crossing the street at very human-friendly intersections. I like it. It is quaint and feels like money. I'll bet it is nice in the winter, all the snowbunnies hopping around with diamonds dripping off their fingers.

Passing all the eateries inspires me to create a dagwood with chips'n'hotsauce and a soda. Trainer believes he'll have one as well. So, I whip out a couple on the top of the cooler as we set out for the Utah hinterlands, frozen chickens right behind us. The king of sandwiches for a couple of princes of the road. Trainer says gimme a soda with that, and supersize it. Okay.

We get out of the badlands—so named, I understand, because it was hard to get through them before we had cars and highways—and onto a sort of plain, and soon we arrive at the intersection of US 191 and I-70. It is in the middle of nowhere, literally, and looks like the set for some movie. Two roads intersecting. Nothing else. It seems like something is waiting to happen here. Crossroads of some kind. Has a suspense about it.

Interstate 70 is a busy place today, and we settle into the ride west along the base of a mesa, actually the Tavaputs Plateau, for miles. Many miles. The talus of the mesa is light colored, so much so that it reflects the sunlight and is a distraction, and the edge of the plateau looks like where the earth just broke like a cookie and rose up a few hundred feet to sort of parallel the interstate, rough along the edge, like a broken cookie would be.

We turn off onto US 6 north after a little while and soon are going along the edge of the Price River. The river is picturesque in its canyon, green water boiling over small submerged rocks and eddying around big ones. There is easy access to the river almost anywhere along here, the sign says it is stocked with trout, and it is a sparkling morning. Strangely, there are no fishermen. None. I cannot imagine having a place like this to play and not taking full advantage of it. The river is undisturbed by man. Now, anyway. The scenery alone is worth the price of admission, much less a river stocked with fish. I shout over the engine noise at Trainer that is amazing. He yells back whaddaya mean, that's crazy?

Trainer had a good time in Mexico, but on one of his water-sport adventures he got water in his ear that won't come out. His good ear. He misunderstands almost everything now, and it is difficult to communicate at all. Deaf in one ear and can't hear with the other, no kidding. He has to be looking at me to understand what I am saying, and when the cab noise is factored in I may as well say nothing—does no good. He is good-natured about being hearing impaired, and lets it all roll off him, but I have resigned myself to life alone until he can hear better. I guess the water will eventually leak out one of the holes in his head.

Meanwhile, I will just keep my thoughts to myself to minimize confusion, and that doesn't always help. Sometimes, out of nowhere, he will look at me and holler "WHAT?" Then he stares at me for a few seconds, waiting for a response. That brings on body language that doesn't always make sense. Shrugs and looks and gestures. More confusion. More gestures.

We are climbing up to Soldier Summit, about 10,000 feet high, and at the top is a little convenience store and Trainer shouts he wants to drive down the west slope, so I pull into the parking lot. I know better than to argue, nothing will be gained, so I bring us into the truck parking area. I need to empty and clean my relief bottle anyway while Trainer gets a soda, or whatever it is he has to have.

Back in the truck after a rest stop, and Trainer glides down the mountain without incident. I am comfortable with my ability to bring a bigtruck down a mountain, because I have spent so much time coaching Trainer with what I learned in class, reading from the book and being in the truck coming down a hill. It is no real matter to me, I mean, I would like to do it, but it is not worth the argument. Let Trainer do it and feel better about himself. I am okay with that. I need that sometimes myself, but I don't risk other people's lives doing it, and I guess that is what I am doing—letting Trainer risk my life to feel better. We both know he is not very good at descents, and this is a dandy. I'll just buckle up and keep the door unlocked. Then I think how that doesn't make any sense at all.

There is a device on some tractors called a jake brake that helps in a descent, but it makes a loud rattling sound as it racks the exhaust pipes. It uses the engine's compression to assist the drive-wheel brakes in slowing the truck on a downhill run. We don't have one on this truck, but it would be nice, because I personally think any help coming down a mountain is always welcome. Someone somewhere in the cranium of HQ doesn't think that way, though, because we don't have one. Maybe because so many drivers misuse them. The device is only necessary when descending a sharp grade where the brakes are taking a beating, like down a steep mountain, and many drivers use them in cities and towns for nothing more than the shock effect the noise has on the locals. Legislative bodies know that and have made it an offense to use one in many city limits. The very drivers that abuse the jake are the ones put off by the prohibition in some places, totally oblivious to the proposition there is not likely to be a hill requiring a jake in a town or city. All of that matters little to us; we don't have one.

The drive down through the Uinta Forest is pretty and pretty uneventful, and we roll into Springville, then on to Provo and Salt Lake City. This is one of the very few times I will go through S.L.C. and not stop for something. We cruise right through and head north on Interstate 15, as I watch the planes come and go from the airport.

I go along the interstate wondering about things in general, and riding shotgun for Trainer in case of bandits. Absolutely prepared to defend our load of dead, frozen chickens with a cell call to 911 should we be accosted. This is the West. Anything could happen.

As I ride, I see many things from my place up here. I can see down into cars. I can see what people are doing in those cars. Someone could tell me the things they see in cars and had I not driven a bigtruck, I would listen politely, but would not begin to believe them.

For me, it is difficult to comprehend what I see going on in some cases. I guess the law of large numbers plays into car ownership as well, in that there are a certain number of idiots and experimenters and generally not-normal people out there, and some of them have cars. Some of them are on interstates at any given time in those cars. I think I seem to be there when they are. Now that I think on it, I guess it is no real wonder some truckdrivers go off the road. They may be watching the antics going on in a car.

What I am watching right now concerns me more than anything else I see, and I see it more often than I think I should, looking down from my chair. A couple driving along, sitting on opposite sides of the car, looking in opposite directions, living opposite lives, and wondering if they've made a mistake. I don't have to hear it spoken, I can see it. It is obvious. They wish they were somewhere else, maybe with someone else. And maybe that happens down the road for some of them. Trapped is a bad place to be, and it looks as though some of them are just pacing the mental cage. I see the disillusionment on their faces. I see it on lots of faces looking out the windows as they go by. Lots of them.

I am looking out the window at the north side of Salt Lake City and trying to decide how much more it can grow and which way. The lake itself is on the west side, and the Wasatch mountains are on the east. I guess it can go no way but north or south or up.

Salt Lake City. It shouldn't require a lot of deep thought to determine how that particular place got its name, and as we go through many cities and towns and places with unusual and colorful names, I think on how the place may have gotten its name. What Cheer, Iowa. Toad Suck Park, Arkansas. Cut'n'shoot, Texas. Sore Finger Road, Arizona. Hungry Mother Park, Virginia. Eastaboga, Alabama. Say that one real fast several times. Almost like a chant of some kind, has a tempo to it, and it is the sort of thing that gets stuck in one's head all day.

Some American cities are known by name worldwide, and they don't need states behind them. New York City. Los Angeles. San Francisco. Chicago. Most anyone in any civilized country has heard those names.

They may not know exactly where those cities are, but they do know they are famous American cities. They may or may not know what state that city is in. Doesn't really matter. They know the name and the connotation.

Some cities call different things to mind at the mere mention of their name. Tombstone. Key West. Santa Fe. Cities like those have a personality or fame that precedes them. An aura, maybe. We associate those cities with some thing or some feeling or atmosphere or person-ality we have heard they have.

But, we are about to go into the one city that stands apart namewise from the hundreds of others in this vast land. Its name conjures all that is good in a place to be, or it does for me at least. Hope, satisfaction, comfort, plenty, and everything a person might need, summed up in a name. The word itself is pretty and pleasant to say: Bountiful. It is just north of Salt Lake City, and it sounds like a good place to be.

Kalispell, Tohajiilee, Two Guns, Two Arrows, Cloudcroft, Yakima, Pierre, Watertown, Birmingham, Orlando, Cape Fear, Coos Bay, Kingston . . . Bountiful. The most comfortable name for a city I have seen or heard at this point in my travels.

Our exit is not far, and I have focused my attentions on my duties as second-seat navigator just long enough to realize we have been given bad directions—by another driver from our own company, no less. I come to that a little too late. Our exit is upon us, Trainer merrily takes it, certain I know what I'm doing, and I am about to have to guess. Which way to go at the stop sign at the bottom of the exit ramp. Right or left. I have a fifty-fifty shot at success. Straight ahead is not an op-tion. This is a T-type intersection; there ain't no straight ahead. Trainer has no idea I have no idea which way to go. He is confidently gearing down for the stop sign. If I whip out maps and atlases and directions from the quailcall, he will have a seizure. He positively hates it when he is the victim of bad planning on my part. I will have to tell the truth and say I relied on someone else's directions rather than call in and verify their accuracy. I got these off the quailcall from a driver that didn't know north from south or highway 13 from 31. I just assumed he, being a driver himself, would know the proper route and be able to get it down accurately. Assumed. Again. I would think I would not be assuming things this far down life's path. That I would have learned long ago.

If I sit still and guess correctly, no one will be the wiser. Nothing will be lost, and my rep as a detailed navigator will be intact. The worst that could happen would be we go the wrong way and Trainer has to find a place to turn around and we lose some time. Rather than be accurate, get out the map, and take my medicine, I guess I'll guess. I opt for deception, hoping that guess is the correct fifty-fifty. We pull up to the stop sign and Trainer looks over at me. I very confidently say go right. He makes the turn and we head into the sun, visors down.

About two miles down the road, the signs for our destination begin to pop up. Trainer looks at me and grins. I smile, and I think how he has no idea. Then it comes to me he has no idea.

I feel bad suddenly, for having been so treacherous as to not attend the details of my duties, double-check things, and possibly risking Trainer having to turn this thing around in some little lot we may have found, and deceptive at having taken advantage of his faith in me, unjustified like it obviously is. Sometimes I don't think much of myself, and this is one of those times. Trainer is babbling merrily about some incident on vacation, happy we are at our destination on time and safe, and I am sitting here looking out the window feeling absolutely filthy about having done that to him, even though the outcome is okay and he never knew anything about it. That will become one of my pet driving peeves, having bad directions given to me, and I just now did it to him. Purposefully led him to think I knew what I was doing. Luck alone saw it through. Dammit, why did I do that to him?

We pull into the facility, a huge one, dozens of acres of concrete and a metal building that covers more acres in the middle of the concrete. The sun is getting low above the mountains to the west, and as Trainer parks to go in for further instructions, I get out the chips'n'hotsauce to make myself feel better. Trainer gets back just about the time the top of the cooler is set for two and says that's good, and thanks fer gettin' out the food. It just makes me feel worse. He can be so pleasant and inno-cent sometimes.

He climbs in and says it'll be a little while, and we may as well take it easy till they get to us. I agree and offer him a chip loaded with pi-cante. Disappears instantly. The picante makes him think of Mexico and his vacation, and he regales me with tales of Mexican sunshine and water and food and fun. He roars above the engine idle and his deafness, about his time there and how he enjoyed it. I sit three feet away directly in front of him. It is like sitting in front of a megaphone spraying small chunks of tortillas. I try to not hold onto the arm of the chair in the blast of noise and crumbs.

Looks like the receiving department may be a little slow, so after we clean up the mess from the chipfest, I take a book and go sit outside in the Utah afternoon to trim my nails and read a little. My nails are a lit-tle longer than I like, and get dirt beneath them easily because of that. I hate dirty nails, mine or anyone else's. And another thing . . . I hate dirty teeth, mine or anyone else's. That is the first thing I see in another human. Their teeth.

What did I do with that book? Where is my lawn chair? Why am I thinking about other people's teeth?

The air is very dry here, the driest place I think we have been. I don't know what the relative humidity is in this area, but it has to be low. My skin gets real scaly real quick here, as opposed to other dry places. Taking hot showers probably doesn't do my skin much good, ei-ther. I notice all this trimming my nails. I can get out of the locale to ease the dryness thing, but I am not likely to back off the hot showers very far. I like the way I feel after a hot shower, hot being a relative term. Re-ally warm is probably a better description. I look forward to that shower every day; a sort of reward for making it to the end of the day. I rank a good, really warm shower right in there with bluewater fishing, a good meal, and high-quality sex. Problem is, everything is a trade-off. Blue-water fishing trips are expensive. A good meal brings on some calories. Sex involves dealing with another person. Really warm showers damage skin to one degree or another. A case in point: I know a girl at home who takes showers so hot, she has scarred the skin across the top of her back and shoulders. She still does it anyway. She is a shining example of the fact we will do some things, no matter what the consequences.

Anyway, between the showers and lack of humidity, my skin is registering a complaint. I need some lotion or something. I am beginning to look like an alligator suitcase. I don't have this problem on the coast, the air *is* the lotion. Soaking-wet sea breezes. It is so humid, there is no room in the air for more moisture, so the least effort brings on saturating perspiration. We do not worry about dry skin on the coast. I read once that Houston is the most air-conditioned city in the world per square foot, as much to dry the air as cool it, probably.

Trainer ambles back from inside and shows up just in time to inspect my toenails after the clipjob. I went ahead and trimmed them as well as my fingernails. He says I'll probably mess up my nails unloading the trailer. I say what? He says we have to unload the trailer. You and me? Yup. I don't want to unload the trailer. Okay, I'll do it myself. Dang. Guilt trip. Trainer walks off to get his cold weather gear, and I don't want to feel guilty about something else I did to him, so I follow shortly to get mine. I would get along more comfortably without a conscience. I wonder if they are removable, like gallbladders or hemorrhoids or appendixes.

Man, it is cold in here, and 350 boxes of frozen chicken later we are done. Boxes of frozen chickens are heavy. We make $30 apiece for an hour's work. Bad bargain. Freezing cold, heavy boxes, no hand truck. Thirty dollars. Apiece. Unloading dead chickens. Man. Damn. I just want to drive the truck, not unload the trailers.

Back to the truck to send away messages we are empty and ready for a load. We stow everything in anticipation of a quick assignment, and I get back into the first chair to move the truck away from the dock so we can close the swingdoors and let someone else in that dock door to be unloaded. Or to unload themselves. Shouldn't be long now before we get a load assignment. The dispatchers are usually pretty quick about it, because the freight needs to move. Still, receivers and shippers are not real accommodating when it comes to leaving empty trucks lying around since they take up a lot of room, especially in large groups, so Trainer trots over to the guardshack to ask permission to hang out and wait for a load. They say okay, but just for a little while, and we move to an out-of-the-way part of the lot.

I set up to back into a space and put the transmission in reverse, let out the clutch, and the cab torques up, but we go nowhere. I let off the clutch and the cabs sinks back down. I think we are wedged against something I didn't see as I was setting up for the backing operation. Light pole maybe. Please don't let it be the front end of a truck I didn't see back there. I am almost afraid to go look, and Trainer bails out his side to go see what is keeping us from going backward. I set the brakes, or think I do, and climb down my side to go back and have a look. Really, the brakes are already set and I just don't know it yet.

We find nothing behind the trailer, and see nothing under the wheels as we walk back to our individual sides of the tractor. Odd.

I climb back into the first chair and there is not much of a hiss when I release the parking brakes by pushing in the knob on the dash. That is odd as well. Further, the light hiss becomes nearly inaudible, as it should, but doesn't stop, as it should. Continuous faint hiss. Air leak. Tractor brakes. I look at the gauge for the primary tank and it shows 55 pounds. It should be 90 to 120 pounds of air pressure. What we have currently is barely enough to keep the brake shoes pushed off the drum and allow us to move. And that pressure just built up as it sat still and we looked for whatever we thought I hit backing up.

Nothing was hit in backing, and simply put, I drained the air tank of what little it had gained on the leak in the system by using the brakes in going across the lot and setting up to back. The tractor brakes were trying to set for the want of air pressure. That's why the cab torqued like it did when I let the clutch out. The engine was trying to turn a braked axle, and the brakes will win that struggle every time. Lucky I didn't break something.

Now I know what the problem is, and set about locating it. I can hear the hiss faintly, but Trainer cannot hear it at all. He can't hear anything less than a scream. He doesn't know what to do but stay right with me in the search for the source of the hissing. Supervising, I suppose. Some minutes later, and outside, I find it in a valve just above the front drive axle. Small, but serious. The brakes would be applied as though the pedal were pressed down if the valve fails completely on the highway. Failed trailer brakes are one thing; the driver can usually drag a locked trailer off the road with the inertia of roadspeed. But failed tractor brakes are not something a driver can work around. The truck begins to skid as if the brakes were slammed on, and usually jackknifes when the trailer takes control as it tries to go past the tractor. The trailer will do that because the tandems are not braking, and it happens so suddenly there is little that can be done.

We have a problem. We are in a part of the country that has several mountain ranges, and going downhill we will be using the brakes. The valve will leak and we will run out of air in the tanks going down one of these hills. It will be unpleasant. I tell Trainer as much, and hike away to the facilities in the driver's lounge to use the facilities while he taps out a message on the quailcall to the maintenance department outlining the situation. He couldn't hear it, but when I pointed out that valve and said it was the culprit, he understood. Said he'd be in the lounge in a minute, he wanted to get a couple of messages off.

As I walk into the lounge, there is a young couple and a retirement-aged fellow already there. I assess them as I walk for the men's room, and figure the old guy is either about to retire from driving or a well-dressed cowboy just starting his driving career having retired from the military, maybe. Has that disciplined look, clean-cut and well maintained. The young ones across the room have the bedraggled look road-weary drivers get in the beginning, before they learn to manage their time. They are guaranteed newbies. I get into the men's room and take care of my business there, then go back out in the lounge to chill a minute and let Trainer catch up. We need to be out of the truck for a while anyway. Change of atmosphere. See some new faces. Check my zipper, make sure I pulled it up, as I walk into the bright lounge.

The old fella nods his head at me and says nothing. The young couple looks at me and the girl smiles; the young man looks at me expressionless, waiting for me to make the first move, or no move at all. I smile back at her, look at him, and say howyadoin'. He perks up and says good, thanky. I ask have they been waiting long and he says naw, not really. That they just came in. She chimes in and says it is their first real delivery, that they have just come out of training and this is the end of their first load. She looks at him and says she is proud of her husband for getting it here on time. I smile and agree it is a good thing to get into that habit. She says she has figgered it up and her husband will make near $40,000 in a year's time, an' ain't nobody in their whole fam'ly ever made that much money an' they get to travel all over together jus' like a vacation. I ask where they are from, and he starts to say something but she cuts him off and says Miss'ssippi. He looks at her like he knew the answer to that question, but says nothing, just looks back at me and nods his head. Smart man.

We talk awhile and the young man says it was real nice talkin' to ya, but we gotta get rollin', and she waves 'bye as they walk out the door. I look at the older man and he looks at me and says he hopes the best for them. I agree and ask where he is headed. He says home, that it is his last time out. He is waiting for a load assignment that will take him to his company's yard, and he is hangin' up his spurs. Givin' back his keys. I ask did he have a good career, and was driving the right choice for him. He thought a second and said yeah, that it had been good to his family, and it was the right thing for him to do. There were no jobs in his part of West Virginia back then, he had no trade, and he didn't want his new family to do without. I understand by his response he had asked himself that many times in 35 years. Said he made a good living and his family had things others back there didn't have. Just weren't any jobs back then. Said he and his wife talked it over, her pregnant, and he responded to a newspaper ad, and was driving the next week. He sent the money home and she did for the kids, and others they could help, and now the house is paid off and the kids are all gone, and he can get a good retirement, so he would like to spend what Christmases and Thanksgivings he has left with her. That she is a good woman and deserved better than what she got. Says he's gonna make it up to her as best he can, if you can make up 35 years of missed anniversaries and birthdays.

He crushed his cigarette and looked out the window.

I sit a moment looking at him as he stares out the window. He is already on the mental road home, and already mentally retired. Just waiting for that last load assignment, and his gold watch. I look at him carefully, and I know he has the answer to every driving question I may have.

There is a wealth of information in this man, if I can just get to it. I don't know how to do that, so I just ask him straight out, if he had one piece of advice to give, and only one, what would it be. He looks at me again, pauses, and says he never was in a wreck, never laid one over, never went off the road, that he never even scratched a fender. I look at him absolutely amazed. He is telling the truth. To have such a record is phenomenal. Virtually impossible. He is referencing probably two-and-a-half, maybe three million highway miles in all kinds of weather, dozens of thousands of backings, tens of thousands of parking lots, and innumerable opportunities to wrinkle a truck. But I see in his countenance he is not lying. He did it. I ask him how.

It was another answer he thought out years ago. He looks up and says, you just have to care . . . and I am suddenly aware I have been given the key. The key to lots of things. He is right. You do just have to care. And that is really the deciding factor in getting anything right. Caring that it is done, and done properly. The man said you just have to care.

I think on the irony, or chance, or kismet, or fate, or fortune, or whatever, if anything, that caused a couple on their first trip out to be in the same place with a driver on his last run. I don't think they ever spoke to one another. Strange, how that sort of thing happens. The rookies walked by an encyclopedia, and obviously didn't recognize it as an encyclopedia. Or didn't care. He knew what the next 30 years holds for them. He watched them go by and didn't say a thing to them. I wonder why. Maybe he saw they didn't care. Or maybe he knew they wouldn't understand. Maybe he doesn't offer unsolicited advice. I wonder at how we do that to one another. So much could be saved.

Trainer pops in and says we have been instructed to go to the nearest truck stop with a repair facility. In my lack of understanding, and faith the professionals at HQ would steer us right, I agree with that. Trainer does as well. Go to a truck stop with a repair facility. It is the wrong thing to do. The right thing to do, I will find later, is stay parked and have road rescue come to us. Never drive an unsafe truck anywhere even if the company maintenance group says to do that. The potential for disaster looms, and the final responsibility for the fallout rests comfortably on the driver's head. The driver sits at the controls. Not a VP at HQ, nor a dispatcher nor the second-floor janitor. The driver causes the truck to move or sit still. The driver is responsible for the damage done. "They," whosoever passes judgment on the incident, will say the driver knew the equipment was faulty, and drove the truck anyway. And "they" will be correct.

We set out, in our ignorance, for the nearest truck stop with a repair shop in a bigtruck with faulty tractor brakes. In looking back, I don't believe I did that without questioning the whole process. But, I did.

Trainer at the wheel. I am okay with that. Says he wants to drive in case of emergency. He also tells me he thinks the truck is not new. That he noticed some loose dash screws before we left the yard, and tightened them himself, and that he thought he heard a leak behind the dash as well, but it stopped, so he didn't worry about it. He thinks the wind leaks, and they are bad, at the door seals especially, the air leaks, loose dash screws, and the loose headlight rim are all related, that this truck may be a repaired crash.

Well, that's just great, here we are motoring across the country in a sloppily resurrected wreck. Maybe. Trainer now says that, at that point, he ran out of air in Albuquerque holding the brakes down at a traffic light, but didn't think anything about it, that he had used the brakes a lot in the surrounding construction and he thought he had just used up all the air. So he didn't say anything. Figured it was a self-solving problem. And sure enough, when we got back onto the interstate, the pressure built back up.

I'm thinking yeah, the compressor running at roadspeed will keep up with a small leak, and we are not using the brakes on the interstate. The gauges would show plenty of air pressure. So here we are shut down away from help because you didn't want to take the time to get this thing repaired on the way. You knew it would slow us down. We just drove halfway across the country in a tractor with a brake-line air leak because you didn't want to stop. But I don't say anything. I just think it. I could be wrong. Could be. But, I think he knew about the air leak all along. He just hoped it would go away, or the world would end before it became a real problem, and we would continue racking up the miles meantime.

Trainer has an idiosyncrasy that is proving to be a problem. He is results motivated, but not plan guided. He generally has only one plan: get there ASAP, and nothing substantial for a contingency plan. If plan A falls through, then plan B is to panic and push himself harder. Like working himself into a sweat with no direction will make things better. End result is the goal is not achieved, or luck sees it through. And luck is pretty flimsy stuff to rely on.

That puts us here, looking for a place to solve a problem that could have been done relatively painlessly at any one of a dozen Kenworth dealers we passed along the way. Just didn't want to take the time to do that.

What would have taken three hours, properly addressed, is about to take three full days.

So, we get onto the interstate, me looking for a truck stop with a repair shop in the guide, and we happen upon one so new it isn't yet in the guide. This is good. It also has a repair facility right across the road. That's even better. Several eateries around the area, easy walking distance. We'll take it.

Trainer exits the interstate and rolls right into the parking lot and pulls up near the edge of the lot in the back of the place, kind of out of the way, us knowing we may be here several hours before the repairs can be made. Engine idling, we roll down the windows to enjoy the late-afternoon coolness, and decide what to do for dinner while we crank out a message to HQ indicating we are shut down in a safe place and a repair facility is nearby. Looks like soda, hot dogs, and peanut-butter crackers for dindin, since neither of us want fast food, again, and we are both too lazy to walk a block to a restaurant. We break out the picnic gear and spend a pleasant dusk grilling, and into the cool evening munching and talking.

HQ sends a quailcall and says road service will be along in about an hour. Good. We can get on to our next load. That'll give me time to get a shower as well. We haven't bought fuel, so I have to pay for a shower. Five bucks. The showers are nice because the place is brandnew, and I take advantage of the seemingly endless supply of hot water. I get my five dollars' worth in soap and water alone. Money can't buy the feeling a warm soaking gives me, but we've talked about that.

I figure the repairs are probably made by the time I will get back to the truck, Trainer will shower up, and we will motor right out of this town and get another load going another direction to another town.

Trainer is sitting in the truck that was surely repaired whilst I showered, and he is surely ready to clean up and roll. I know how he is. Miles equal money.

I climb in and toss my gear on my bunk and flop into the second seat. Trainer looks over and looks back out the windshield. I say nothing. I look at my watch and see it is 1:30 A.M.. Trainer says let's get bedded down, the repair guy never showed. A little put off, I say no matter; I am sleepy anyway after the warmth of the shower, and the length of the day. Trainer says maybe tomorrow. The quailcall beeps. Message says the reason road service didn't show is they didn't have the part we need and can't get it till Monday. I look at Trainer and Trainer looks at me. How do they know what part we need? We told them. We did? In the first message. How can that be? We don't know what part we need. Yeah, we do. No we don't, we are guessing; repairdudes will decide what part we need, there are probably several different things that could be wrong with that valve, and there may be several different kinds of that valve. Nope, already told 'em. I don't think you understand. Yep, I do. Let's get some sleep. Okay.

I climb into my bunk and open the windows. Nice and cool. I am clean and comfortable in my Mexican blanket. The Utah stars speckle the sky above the truck, and the lights in the Wasatch twinkle faintly. Little houses up there, I guess. I drift away looking out the window, thinking about a what a friend had said. Like Neil Young, I am hoping it was a lie.

Six-thirty finds me blinking awake and squinting at the light in my face. Didn't close the light curtain last night. Trainer gurgles regularly below me. I realize our situation and roll over with my back to the light for a little more snoozing. No reason to get up early on Saturday, particularly if we can't go anywhere. We'll just hang around the house today. Nap is the first order.

Middle of the morning finds me in the bunk looking out the window at a sunny day in Utah. I need to do some laundry and this might just be the right time to do that. I see no reason to wake Trainer, but I know he will wake when I get down and rock the cab getting my laundry and heading out to the washing machines and coffee bar. I accept the responsibility and the consequences. Bad as I hate laundry day, this has to be done. I am wearing my last clean underwear.

Laundry is empty and I make relatively quick work of a much-despised project with some coffee and a few chapters of *Paris Trout*. Nice and quiet here. No competition for the machines. No television running laff tracks, but I have to say, again, most sitcoms need them. Anyway, it is quiet here except for the machines running. I glance up occasionally from the book to watch the dryer tumble the clothes. I wonder why I do that. I don't know if I am staring or looking. Whichever, they shouldn't put glass doors in those things. It distracts simple minds.

Really, it is strangely quiet hereabouts. Most truck stops are not bustling on Saturday mornings, but they are usually a little livelier than this. Maybe it is so new no one has it on their list of favorite places to stay. Interstate drivers are creatures of habit like anyone else. They develop preferences based on what criteria a particular place satisfies. I like this one now for the new and uncrowded laundry. Coffee bar is nice, as well, so I will stop here again for those two qualities alone.

Nearly lunchtime when I get back to the truck, get my cleaned and folded clothes into my locker, and Trainer says let's do lunch, bails out the door, and I hear him in the side locker dragging out the picnic stuff we put away last night. I sense a pleasant, unhurried afternoon coming along, and sure enough, it will be. Trainer is resigned to staying put till Monday and settles into the groove of waiting. I didn't think he would handle all this downtime well, but looks like he has accepted it. That alone will make the waiting easier. He isn't hyperactive, but he is into racking up the miles, like I said earlier, and that kind of person is generally not good at waiting.

We are set up in the shade provided by the trailer on the asphalt lot, pretty much to ourselves, stretched out in chaises that fold into a bag, and we are stuffed with grilled sausagesbecomehotdogs. Dang, those things are good. Mustard, onions, and dill relish. I think I ate three of them. Trainer is zonked after his half dozen, bubbling and snarkling, slack-jawed in his chair. It is cool here in the shade of the trailer and the breeze is dry as kindling. Even if the temperature were higher, I don't think a person would have to worry about sweating. I am not worried about a thing, sweating included, so it is a good chance for a nap.

An hour or so later, judging from the angle of the shadows now, I wake to look around and notice the ancient, rounded hills to our north have taken on some character in the afternoon sun. They are big for hills, but not to the point one could accurately call them mountains, and have ravines washed into them that develop shades and depth in the slanted light.

E. Hemingway once wrote a short story about some people at a bar in Africa discussing and finally arguing about the nature of some hills they could see from that bar and whether or not the row of hills in question looked like elephants holding one another's tail in trunk as they walked across the plain. I think he would have thought that about these hills. Hills like elephants.

To the east are the Wasatch, spectacular in their purple mountainous majesty, already starting to take on the fall colors that will add splash to the Olympics. Looks like a patchwork quilt laid across the peaks. I guess that happened already since it is cooler up there, and probably sacred, so the peaks get preferential treatment. That brings another thought to mind.

I have an acquaintance who practices a religion based on the North American Plains Indians' way of worship. I find myself interested, but not enough to get involved, in their approach to the connection between Earth and Man, the health of one being tied to the health of the other, and how all life is sacred. They may have to take a life to sustain their own, but the giver of that life is exalted by the taker of it. They dance and sing and eat and have ceremonies public and private to celebrate the mystic part of that animal's existence, or the place it was taken, or both. They do not, and did not, appear to indiscriminately kill things. Except people. I don't think many of the American Indian tribes spent a lot of time socializing or moralizing. Actually, I think they were pretty bad about killing one another. Anyway, warfare aside, I admire any culture that understands and honors the providers of the things those cultures have. Water, fire and food, scenery.

Some of the stuff they come off with is not in keeping with what initially seems like a reasonable form of worship, like fooling around with live rattlesnakes, but by and large, those religions make about as much sense as any other, have a lot more respect for our planet, and create much less pollution and waste than modern church Dumpsters. So, I guess what aggravates me, and caused that outburst, is the fact I can see radio towers on the tops of a couple of those peaks. The aboriginals thought that place significant, and we come along and put a metal tower on their hallowed ground. Just doesn't seem right somehow. I mean, we wouldn't want someone who kicked our ass to the point of extermination sticking some hideous-looking communications device on top of one of our centuries-old cathedrals, I'll bet.

One of the things we have in abundance here is flies. I don't think even nature-based religions have much good to say about flies. This is nearly as bad as that sandwich shop in Kansas. They are everywhere all the time. Not in huge clouds, like Kansas, but one right after another. One is on Trainer's nose. I wonder if it would cost me my life to see if I could snick it off there with this rolled-up newspaper. Better not. The day is going along nicely without that, and here comes a game warden in a state pickup. It would probably lead to some kind of assault charge—either me for whapping Trainer in the face with a newspaper, or him for bolting from his nap and beating me to a glob of protoplasm before he awakened enough to stop himself. And for all I know, flies are protected by game wardens just like antelope or rainbow trout. Game Warden would see everything.

He pulls up and looks out the window at us spread out on the pavement like this is a roadside park and we have set up camp. Window comes down electrically. Smooth, not jerky as it would be had he rolled it down by hand. He looks me in the eye, and reaches onto the seat for something. I am thinking we are about to be cited for some health code violation. There are a couple of sausages rolling around on the pavement near the barbecue pit. Drops of suddenly highly visible mustard dot the pavement. Trainer's shirt looks like a picnic tablecloth, stains and chunks of condiments stuck to it. Game Warden moves beside the steering wheel and holds a small watermelon out the window. Says this is the perfect dessert for a hot dog dinner. Suspicion gone, I laugh and agree. We talk a minute, and he says this is his first nonconfrontational situation with a trucker. Says we are not so bad after all, regular guys really, and I say it is my first discussion of any kind with a game warden and I'm favorably impressed. We laugh, he tells me to drive safe, and I thank him for the melon. He drives away, and I stand holding our dessert just in time to see a couple walk past the nose of the tractor and spy the grill. There are several crispy sausages still on it and the coals are still hot enough to warm them. The guy asks do we have any extry, knowing well we do, and the girl pops him on the shoulder for having done it. I smile and say hurry up, we are about to have dessert.

Another fellow dropped in for the last of the burnt sausage and bread, and a girl showed up and got the last piece of the watermelon. We sit in a circle, some on the pavement, our group having grown still more, sodas and bags of chips appearing from nowhere, Trainer wide awake now, and I listen to tales of the road and past good times for two hours till the late sun's rays dictate other things to do. Trainer is in fair form, as the oldest and most experienced driver, and with the best stories. I sit and listen along with the others to hair-raising tales of fast trucks, wrecks, and cops, and running scales on snowy nights. It is a very pleasant afternoon, and I am glad to be here and a part of it.

Trainer says to the group, at length, we need to clean the house, so get yer stuff and get out of our way, we got work to do. Drivers getting up and cleaning up and gathering gear, handshakes and thankyees all around, and they are gone like a swarm of bees.

Trainer and I open up the tractor, every door and window, and get down to some serious cleaning inside. We take out everything, we sweep under everything, we wipe everything down, put it all back, and flop into the first and second seat. He is not getting any more caffeine or sugar today. It is about shower time anyway. Still some daylight left, and I'll use it getting clean and back to dig in and finish *Trout* tonight.

Clean up, call home, get a fountain soda, and get back just as darkness catches me. Trainer is in the shower now. He'll be hot about the five dollars. Sure enough, he's back shortly and hollering about the high price of gettin' by.

Near bunktime, I turn to the last page of *Paris Trout* and read it, wondering what goes through the minds of writers, and put everything away. Trainer covered up and snoring, I turn off the alien attack video, and climb under my fiesta blanket and think about the day. It is cool here and we don't need the a/c, so we will sleep without the engine's grumble tonight because it burns about a gallon per hour at idle and we want to save what fuel we can. No reason to waste it. Trainer's apnea will have to do for white noise.

# WEEK Five

DAYLIGHT WAKES ME, I WAKE TRAINER, AND COFFEE DOWN, Trainer swaps messages back and forth with HQ on the quailcall regarding the brake part. Trainer is not happy and is getting restless. This is not good. Flies buzzing in and out the windows. I have the windows down in the cab and open in the condo because it is 48 degrees outside, but I am comfortable in the sunlight in shorts and a gulf shirt. At home, the humidity and 48 degrees would be miserable. Trainer is visibly angry with what he perceives as being left out to dry by the weekend maintenance group, and says they just plain don't give a shit, and storms off to the convenience-store part of the truck stop.

I look around the tractor and see a couple of drivers taking their dogs out to give a shit. They could at least have the dog go on the grass, or someplace other than the parking lot where other drivers have to walk in the dark. I have yet to step in it, so to speak, at least in a truck stop lot, but that is because I know it is out there waiting for me. I see these inconsiderate people letting their dogs do their dog business in the lots every day. Some of the dogs are small, and probably don't leave much to worry about, but I think dog poo is one of those things that doesn't need to be doled out in quantity to get the job done. A little goes

303

a long way. On the other hand, in walking to and from on the parking lots, I see piles of poo that cause me to wonder whether or not someone has a gorilla in a truck nearby. I hear drivers talking to one another about their pets and saying how the dog is like a child to them, and I am sure that is true, but would that same driver let one of his kids defecate in the parking lot? Probably not.

Trainer comes back and says he's had it with this waitin' stuff, we're goin' across the street to the repair shop and get this damthing fixed. Okay. I reach into the refrigerator to grab a soda for the ride across the street, and notice it is not as cool as it should be. I look and see the little reefer is not making its usual humming sound. Trainer gruffs around in the first seat getting ready for takeoff, turns on the ignition, and hits the starter. Nothing. Not even a click. He looks at me. For some reason, I am thinking there is a connection between the not-socool soda in my hand and the truck not starting. He tries again. Same result. He looks at me again. Like I can fix it. I look back. I look at the soda. Blue Two is dead.

He hops out and whips open the hood. Like he is going to fix this thing with no tools, or diagnose what ails it. It must just make him feel better. I sip my lukecool soda and look on, acting interested. I don't have the feeblest idea what most of that stuff is under the hood, much less what it does or how to fix any of it.

He hops back in and says the battery must be dead. Probably. Whaddaya mean probly. I mean the soda is not cold. Whaddaya mean the soda ain't cold. I mean the refrigerator most likely drained the battery since we have not run the engine in two days and the refrigerator sucks on the battery constantly. Oh . . . yeah, I think I did that once before when I was shut down. Long time ago.

I look across the lot to see a local service truck doing something on another tractor. He is most likely set up for jump-starting bigtrucks; I say as much to Trainer and offer to go get him. Trainer says do it, and I set out.

Sure enough, the guy says he can do that and will, in just a minute. I hike back to the truck and Trainer says that's good, how much will he charge? I didn't think to ask, but does it really matter? We have to have it done. Trainer looks at me like I have no business sense at all. I say he is already here and will not charge us a service call for that, in addition to what he will charge to hook up to the battery. Calling out another service truck will be an additional charge. Yeah, you're right.

Serviceman drives over and gets out. We get out. Trainer says what is this gonna cost. Serviceman says if it is just a direct connection to the posts under the hood, nothing, since he was already here doing another job. But if he has to crawl around looking for a place to connect, since the batteries are under the cab, it'll be $45. Trainer says we got them posts right here, and points to a spot where they were on our last tractor. We are all looking at the blank space. There are none on this tractor. He was thinking this truck would have them as well. No such luck. Serviceman looks at the place where the posts would be and says he'll need to first find the batteries and then hook up to them, and it'll be $45. Trainer looks at me like will I pay for it, and I say just write a company check. That's what we call a particular type of payment method available to all companies, and our company chooses to use that pay type. Trainer brightens and says yeah.

The truck is running shortly and the check changes hands, and we are all better educated about refrigerators and idling engines. Trainer says let's get over to the repair facility and get this done.

We do that, and the repair shop diagnoses the same problem we knew we had all along: leaking air valve above the differential. They think they have the part, but turns out that is not the right one. Apparently there are several versions of the valve. I look at Trainer and silently say I told you so. He looks at me and silently says you'd better watch your mouth. They can get one from Salt Lake City tomorrow, but that is the soonest we can hope for repair and they are really sorry for that. Trainer says okay, let's order it now and we'll be back tomorrow to get it installed, that we are staying just across the street.

Drive back across the street and return to a spot near the one we had, and park for the night again. There is one of those sausages still rolling around the lot. Even the seagulls won't eat it. Seagulls in Utah. Somebody help me with that.

Park and go in for a shower. The girls here know me now, and the shower is free. So is the coffee in the mornings. I hike back to the truck, get in and get situated for another alien-genre movie. Sunday night at the truck stop.

Monday dawns and Trainer is up. I watch and sip my coffee as he sets about getting the regular weekday crew at HQ involved in our problem, since he is firmly convinced the weekend gang does nothing to help anyone.

And it looks like he may be right. The maintenance supervisor at HQ says he'll find the part and fly it to us UPS today if he has to. Trainer triumphantly says let's go to breakfast.

Sure enough, after messages are exchanged on the quailcall, and some time passes while we hang out and walk around the neighborhood to see what's happening, we get a message indicating the part has been found in Salt Lake City and will be here in four hours, and then we can get rolling. We are instructed to take the truck across the street to the repair facility and wait for the part to arrive. So we do that.

The hills like elephants are still there this morning, and the sun is barely from behind the Wasatch as we go across the road to the shop, pick a spot in the parking area, and back in to wait for the part to arrive. Trainer goes in to talk, and I break out a lawn chair and climb in for a nap, out by the trailer in the warm sunlight. I am kinda getting used to being shut down, and on salary it isn't so bad.

We mess around all day long, not just four hours, at the shop across the street from where we have messed around at the truck stop for the weekend. The view of the Wasatch Mountains is great here, we are very nearly at the base of them, I'm in the shade of the trailer midday, and I nap, off and on, most of the afternoon between sips of lemonade from a bottle. It seems like there is a little more gone from that bottle each time I wake than when I put it down to nap. I hope evaporation is the culprit and not that dog chewing on a soda straw over there.

Near dark the part arrives and we have to unhook from the trailer to take the tractor into the shop; the tractor and trailer connected won't fit inside the shop. So we do that. I would have stayed in the chair, but it is getting a little nippy so I just ride along into the shop, stay in the tractor, and munch some stale tortilla chips while the repairmen take the back of the tractor apart. Trainer gets out to socialize. AC/DC belts out a tune on the radio playing in the shop. I munch and watch and wonder if I'd marry for the money. They finish the job at 9 P.M.

I send a message requesting a load and am told by the night dispatch guy to go back to the truck stop and stay the night, that there is nothing we can haul available at this particular time. Probably something tomorrow, maybe in Idaho.

Trainer will be livid. He is just getting back to the truck after signing all the purchase orders and filling out receipts. Our company will pay the bill later through an electronic invoicing system, so we pay nothing up front. I show him the discussion thread on the quailcall.

He reads messages one by one until he gets to the last one. Drops the keyboard into his chair and looks at me. Has a look of absolute disbelief on his face. Says nothing. He cranks up the engine and we idle back to the trailer and hook up, then drive across the road to our spot at the truck stop. Trainer turns off the engine. I turn off the refrigerator. Trainer shoots out of his chair and climbs into his bunk and is snoring and fizzing in less than a minute. I still have my seat belt on.

I get out for my phone call and shower, (get another free one, the girls know my kids now), back to the truck in the very-cool-for-this-time-of-year Utah night. The shadowy Wasatch in the starlight distract me as I walk. I am ready to go home for some reason. Very unlike me to want to do that out of the blue, like it seems to come. I don't often get homesick. Maybe three times in my life, and I am not now, I just feel like I need to be home. I get in and crank up the engine. Let it idle tonight. Maybe charge up the battery, or at least keep it from discharging. I sit behind the wheel and look into the darkness for a while, thinking about things in general, and still wanting to be home for some reason. The feeling will not leave me and I can't put my finger on why.

I undress and climb into my bunk, and will be asleep in minutes. Trainer has been out for a while, and is making all kinds of upper respiratory noises. Dry air gets to him too, I guess.

I awake to the sound of air hissing. I jump out of the bunk and hit the floor, two steps forward and start scanning gauges. I still hear it. The gauges tell me nothing extraordinary. I flop into the first seat and it stops. I get up and it starts again. Sit down, it stops. I look under the chair, and the air-supply hose to the bladders in the seat has a leaking union. It is so loose, I can tighten it with nothing more than my fingers. Trainer is most likely right about this truck being a wreck. The shop didn't tighten the hose union when they replaced the seat. That is the only reason the coupling on a poly hose would leak—that it wasn't tightened in the first place. These brass and plastic coupling things will not vibrate loose, properly installed.

Well, it is nearly time to get up anyway, the sky is glowing behind the Wasatch. Trainer snoozing. He knows I am awake to handle the quailcall and he knows we have no load assignment, and both those things make his getting up totally unnecessary. I head out for coffee and the bathroom. I have been living in a truck stop parking lot for days, and have gotten acclimated to this regular procession of meals and showers and full nights of sleep. Kinda like it. It just doesn't pay much in Trainer's case, his paycheck being dependent on the number of miles we run every day. I'm on salary, so I can afford to like it.

Back to the truck, and I pass Trainer heading to the bathroom and coffee bar. We make a wide circle around one another in mock confrontation. I get in and sit down and break out the log to catch up. We will most likely roll in a little while, and we don't want to leave with the logs not updated. I have the windows down and the fresh morning air drifting through the cab. I get it all done except the date. I have to look it up on the calendar. I place the numbers in the blocks at the top of the page: 09/11/01.

The day is gorgeous and I am ready to get gone. Quailcall beeps, and dispatch says we have a load of french fries to pick up in Idaho, but does not tell us when to be there. So we'll just wait for further information in the barrage of messages that will follow regarding this load we are about to go get. I am sitting in the second seat and am about to put my log away when a tractor fresh from the road pulls in tight beside us, windows down. The driver hollers at me through the open windows: Didja hear that New York City and Washington, D.C. are being bombed? What? Yeah, turn the radio on and listen. I can see he is serious. I click on the FM radio for the first time in days, and the announcer is talking about the explosions in the World Trade Center towers. I change stations. Same thing. I look back at the truck and the driver is already out and heading for the convenience store. And a phone, I'll bet.

Trainer comes across the lot, and as he gets to the tractor he hollers, turn on the TV, New York is being attacked. I don't know what to think as I turn on the TV and see one building burning and a plane fly into the second one. We watch in horrified silence as the buildings burn and fall. People are running around the truck stop, lining up at the phones. No one knows what is next, or how long it will last, and they are afraid. Calling home makes them feel better, I guess. I grab the cell phone and call home myself. I am not sure I believe what I just saw. Then it comes to me that this is no sensational advertisement or some adaptation of Orson Welles's reading of *War of the Worlds*, and I think how some radical's ass is in a meat grinder now. We may be a nation of overfed TVzombies, but it doesn't pay to attack our cities.

A message comes on the quailcall for us to fuel and remain where we are until we get further instructions. Says nothing about the situation we are watching. I guess they figured we already knew what is going on.

Well, we *don't* know what is going on. I don't think anyone does, but with full tanks, fuel will not be an issue should we have to respond to most any assignment from our company or another agency. We don't really need to fuel, our tanks are full anyway.

We wait in the truck glued to the television news. It is all we can do. Look and listen. We watch the little dots fall down the sides of the buildings, thinking they are chunks of building. Turns out later those little dots were people who chose to jump rather than burn. I can't imagine having to make that decision, ever. These people just got to work and were slammed with this.

The buildings collapse, and those left inside go down with them. Countless tons of concrete, and people, falling a thousand feet. I think about how I was there just days ago. I think about the black girl under the awning and her brilliant smile and how pretty she was then and there. I think about the leggy Italian beauty in the white skirt on the esplanade, smiling and popping her gum. I hope neither of them were involved. They are the only two people I knew in New York that may have been in one of the Towers, and not that the loss of anyone else is any less, just that it would have been more personal if one or both of them were gone. I don't know what to do. No one does. We watch and wait, disbelieving, stunned at the loss of life we know has taken place in that cloud of smoke and concrete. This can't be real. Surely, a talking head will come on the screen in a minute and say it was a movie trailer or something accidentally put on the air, and this is all a huge mistake, and they are really sorry for the confusion. Surely that will happen.

But it doesn't.

The morning drags on, the minutes become hours, and I slowly come to the realization it is not a broadcast error. We all wait for whatever is next. Time passes unnoticed, and it looks as though that may be the end of the attack for a while, so the news focus turns to replays and interviews and shocking pictures of the aftermath. We watch in anger and denial. The quailcall beeps.

HQ has determined, through whatever channels they have, that it is safe to go on with the day's business, and for us that means getting to Idaho for some frozen french fries.

Silently we get the truck ready to go, packing away gear, securing other gear, and shifting into gear. Other trucks are beginning to leave as well, so I guess the various companies have decided it is still business as usual. It seems cold to me at first, but as the day wears on and the damage and intent is assessed, it seems the proper course to take. The whole intent and purpose of the attack was to disrupt our flow, to knock us off balance. We have to show them, whoever "them" is, we are still on our feet. Later the country will see it was the right thing to do, as callous as it appears to us all initially.

The ride to Idaho's Snake River Valley is quiet between us, but we have the FM and CB on, and are listening to both. A lot of really intelligent conversation on the CB, and some incredibly lame stuff on the FM. Those call-in/talk shows need to broaden their respondent base. Same people every hour, seems like. I guess everyone has to deal with something like the attack in their own way, and making a fool of oneself ranting on the airwaves is one way of doing that.

Southern Idaho is pretty nondescript, but pleasant, rolling hills and flat river valleys. Potato-related businesses everywhere. Trainer and I agree CNN has the best radio presence, so we settle on them for the news updates, and there are many. They don't appear to sensationalize it like some of the others, and stick with reporting only what they know for certain, the anchors quizzing the reporters for verification. I will come to admire Peter Jennings for that same thing as the days go on, and become aware of just what an accurate newsman he is. No fluff nor pap. I watch him grill a couple of reporters who bring him half-baked stories. I think other reporters see what happens as well, and decide to dig a little deeper before they jump on camera for their 15 minutes beneath his polished gaze. I notice a distinct change in the reporting style of subsequent stories after he nails a couple for sloppy information. The man demands credibility. Never knew much about him, or cared, before this happened, but I come away deeply impressed with his professionalism as the days pass, and his determination to stay with it until we get some answers. I hear he's a Canadian, by the way.

We get to the shipper in Burley, Idaho and pick up our load; everyone we deal with is completely somber, and has no real interest in

anything. Radios tuned to news stations everywhere we stop on our way
to our regular overnight hideaway in Wyoming, the donut place.

Most afternoons in this part of the nation, the blue sky has at least
one or two condensate trails left by the airliners crisscrossing the upper
levels. Not today. For the first time in our history, the FAA issues a no-
fly order for commercial aviation. All the airliners are grounded. The
azure sky is clean, but starkly so.

We arrive in Wyoming and settle in for the night. This day is over
for us. For others, more personally involved, it is the beginning of a life-
long nightmare. For the country, it is the beginning of a different kind
of war. We have suffered losses in our homeland at the hands of a for-
eign enemy, and we may again. That hasn't happened in a couple of
hundred years, and we are not sure how to deal with that. The people, I
mean. I guess the military has a plan, but plain folks, like us, are a little
jumpy and vengeful.

Up at dawn and rolling, and again, western Wyoming doesn't fail to
impress me. I ride even more defensive of my country, thinking on what
has happened, and the landscape I travel. We roll through the scenery
and mountains and valleys and forests, and finally level out on the high
plains of eastern Wyoming and Nebraska. It is pretty impressive how fast
sodas go flat at higher altitudes, and I think about that to get my brain
doing something besides wondering what will follow this attack. Drinking the soda is like sipping cough syrup, once the bubbles are gone.

We listen to the radio again, most of the day, like everyone else I
suppose, and the rehash and the experts and the chest-thumping and
the calls for revenge. I still don't know what to think about any of it.
Trainer offers his opinion, which amounts to a good carpet-bombing of
any country that allows people to tie a turban on their head, and any one
of them "stan" countries: Pakistan, Afghanistan, Kurdistan, Turkestan.
Any of them dam heatheren countries.

Still have a Salt Lake City fly buzzing around in here. Lands on my
soda can. Doesn't know it is diet, and has no sugar—and no bubbles.
Maybe the fly is on a diet, and just lucked out, sodawise, and happens to

like flat diet soda. I look around out the window and see where Nebraska needs a little rain. It was a lot greener the last time we were here.

Trainer says he believes we will stay the night in his old haunt. I think he means the place where he muffed the backing lesson. Turns out he does. We exit the freeway and pull in to fuel and shower and eat and get to sleep early. Both of us a little stressed about a lot of things that didn't bother us before. Me, anyway. Trainer, bless his oxhead, always has a concern about home, but for me, it is the first time I am not comfortable with what is going on, and my not being at home. It isn't like I could do anything to protect my people if I were there, just that I would feel more fulfilled in my role as protector-general if I were close to them.

Up early, coffee and rolling, no food in the truck. We usually eat out in the evening when we stop, but having sandwich stuff in the tractor is a timesaver when the munchies drop by. Trainer says he knows of a deep-discount store not far from here where we will stop for goodies. I have only had one cup of coffee this morning, since we needed to get on the road, and Trainer promised to stop and get another when I finished the first one. Says this place has good coffee and we can restock the pantry as well. I am okay with that. He wanted to drive this morning for some reason. We are in no hurry and he doesn't drive one bit faster than I drive. He can't—the governor, in a corporate fuel conservation effort, only allows us 65 MPH. I don't know what his problem is. Maybe it is the same as mine, and he just has to feel like he is doing something, or he starts to feel like he is not accomplishing anything. Sitting idle in the second seat isn't what he needs to be doing, maybe.

We stop and get the stuff; I get another cup of houseblend, and take the wheel. Back on the road. Our drop is an underground storage facility in an old quarry in the Show Me state of Missouri. It is dusty and unusual. I understand there are many around the country, but this is the first one I have seen. If it weren't for the dust, as fine as flour, a couple of inches thick on the floor of the canyon outside the place, it would be pretty neat. The dust is so fine that the slightest disturbance produces a gray-white cloud of the stuff. I think it is some kind of limestone dust.

The trees are coated with a thickness of it, and so is everything else. The tractors with weedburners raise clouds of the dust, the exhaust pressure literally blasting the powder into the air to hang there. It isn't heavy enough to come back down of its own accord, and with no breeze at all in this hole, and a dozen trucks moving around, the dust becomes more of a fog than anything. I don't think even rain would wash this stuff out of the sky. We nap and munch and read and talk for hours, waiting our turn to go in and be unloaded. I turn on the washers and wipers every so often to create a sludge on the windshield and hope the wipers are strong enough to scrape it away before it overcomes them. What a mess. I can't think of a single thing that would cause me to get out of this truck and into the dust storm outside. Nothing.

At 1:30 A.M. we finally get our opportunity to take our load down into the caves and the tunnels, and I am impressed. There is actually quite a bit of room down here, and I would not know I was underground except for the rough rock wall, and the occasional pillar of stone left as a support. The grade going down is sharp, and the turns are tight, but turnable. We get offloaded and pull out through the tunnels and climb back out to the dusty crater and go out the dusty gateway, the dusty guard waving us on. We are headed to the nearest truck stop for the night. Both of us are a lot tired and a little dusty. Trainer sends in message we are unloaded and going to sleep for the night, that we will accept a load in the morning. HQ says no problem, get some sleep.

I awaken late and look out the window to see the sun well on its way across the sky. My watch shows nine o'clock in the morning. I kick open the curtain and the sun comes in for Trainer. He is up in a flash and at the keyboard hammering out a message, I suppose to notify HQ we are ready for a load. Then he is out for coffee and a smoke. I go into my regular routine and follow shortly. The truck stop is old-line, but well decorated and neat and colorful. Lots of Native American trinkets. Wolf and eagle pictures superimposed on humans and vice versa. Medicine wheels. The lady at the register is wearing some handcrafted things, and we talk a little. There is some Carlos Nakai on the speakers. His work lends some ambiance to the place, along with the crafts, and I feel all right at having coffee with a shamanwoman in her lodge this morning. Maybe the spirits are benevolent, or she can cause them to be that way, and the day will be good.

Trainer is in the truck and ready to go, says we are to pick up a load of chickens just around the corner in Monett. I climb in and we take off for the chicken plant right downtown. It is a nice ride to the turn-of-the-century agricultural town, with many refurbished houses along the highway. Very pleasant countryside early in the misty morning. We rumble by, and I look to see all I can. Old tractors and implements, redone barns and sheds. Manicured lawns and tree-lined limestone caliche driveways. Americana. White picket fences and all. I could live here, too.

The chicken plant is right downtown and actually sort of blends in. We pull in and are told our load will not be ready till tomorrow. Trainer says What? Tomorrow. Drop your trailer and we will load it when we have time.

Trainer is beside himself. So, I take immediate control and say let's go get some breakfast and find a place to park. But I have to let HQ know we will bobtail to a truck stop and wait there. Truck stops have more facilities than chicken plant parking lots. Trainer is too put out to argue. He just follows me back to the truck to unhook. So we do that after getting on the CB, asking around, and finding out about a little backwater truck stop with good food and clean showers not far down the road.

We get there and Trainer gets fed, and life is better for both him and myself. Biscuits the size of burger buns and peppered sawmill gravy. Greasy buttered hash browns fried just right and coffee to flush it down. Good stuff, especially in view of last night's lack of a real meal, though neither of us was hungry at the time.

This load of chicken is going to a drop in Spokane and a drop in Seattle, if it ever gets loaded. That's not a problem. The problem is, that's a two-day run there, a day total to offload, part of a day's wait for another load assignment, and a two-day run back to Texas. That is another week on the road. My training period is over today. I now have 35 days in the saddle of a bigtruck, no longer a trainee, and am eligible for pay by the mile. Trainer calls HQ for dispensation. HQ says my options are: go to Seattle on salary, wait here to repower a load going to Texas, or get on a train and come to the yard to be assigned my own tractor. I think a very short time and say we'll take the load to Seattle. Trainer beams and says all right. He cranks off a note to HQ saying so. Problem solved. But we still have to wait for the trailer to be loaded. Separate problem.

We are parked at the very rear of the lot of a small truck stop by a barn and in front of a stable with a couple of horses wandering around in the enclosed lot. Breakfast was good, so I decide the thing for me to do is to relax in the shade of the barn in a lawn chair, while Trainer gets his nap in. So, I get a chair out of the locker and get set up to do that. It is a cool morning with a light breeze, the sky is that Midwest blue, and the puffy clouds move airily across the sky, no threat at all. All is well in my little corner, though I haven't forgotten all is not well in lots of corners.

Reading a pulp novel, very unlike me, I take a break and sit for a moment just to take note of my surroundings. Crickets chirping and butterflies heading south, stopping by a clump of Queen Anne's lace for a late breakfast by the barbed-wire fence that encloses the horse stable. Big black-and-yellow swallowtail is just magnificent, and probably the size of a small coffee saucer. Grasshoppers buzzing around. The two horses in the stable lot are pictures of the species. Ropy muscles rippling beneath chestnut coats shining in the sunlight. The premier track-and-field athlete of the animal world. Nothing on the prairie would be a match for them, set free. They nicker and play about the lot, well fed and sheltered. None of the worries of their plains-dwelling ancestors. None of the freedoms, either.

Martin house overrun by sparrows. Sparrows . . . we called them townbirds as children, and they are actually a type of finch, not a sparrow at all. But, they are prolific, and beat the martins to this bird condo. It is a pretty ugly disagreement. The martins are better fliers, but the finches are more tenacious. Looks like the martin house will have new tenants next year. I thought the time for martins to migrate would be past by now. Maybe they are some of the crop of kids that just don't want to leave home. Go sparrows.

Trainer awakes and immediately gets restless. Says we need to go to town for supplies and laundry anyway. He's right about that. Catching up on the laundry and laying in a few supplies wouldn't hurt us. It is a long ride to Seattle from here, weather this time of year could bring on anything, and being snowed in, or iced in, at a rest stop or mountain pass with no food in the tractor is not a pleasant experience, I'll wager. I will find later in my driving career I was correct.

Laundry bag is getting bigger as well, so without further ado we pack up and bobtail into town.

We pull into a strip center with a supermarket for the goodies and I hike over to the dollar market for some laundry detergent and ask the checkout girl for directions to the nearest laundry. She describes a circuitous route through town to the one she uses. I'll take it, and those two bags of chocolate chip cookies right there.

Across town to the laundry and sure enough, it is a comfy place. The proprietor makes us feel right to home, even though we have taken up five of his parking spaces out by the street. He is a closet driverwannabe, like so many of us. Just like to try driving one of those things one time. What's it like, fellas, going all over the place? Do ya meet a lot of people? See a lot of stuff? What state has the best scenery? What city has the worst traffic? Have ya seen the Pacific Ocean? Do ya stay the night in motels?

The television is on in the corner, and it is showing the beginnings of the cleanup effort at the place they now call Ground Zero. That is some stretch of the term's accepted usage in the nuclear fission field, in which it denotes the geography directly below the blast of a thermonuclear explosion. It kinda fits, I guess: the damage, at least to those two buildings, wouldn't be much worse. We watch and comment on the situation and the agonizing search for survivors, while the bad guys dance in the streets half a world away. And I am struck that this is all done in the name of a god, and that god was credited and praised for the successful attack. I fail to make any connection with any religion that causes harm to another. I further fail to regard any faction that willfully causes hurt to another as any kind of religion. And I don't think any real god takes sides when his/her children squabble, much less blesses one killing another.

They say it is the work of extremists. Religious extremists. I hear that word a lot these days. Extreme. Extreme games. Extreme sports. Extreme video. What I see in those cases is not extreme; it is reckless. There is a difference between extreme and reckless, and this is a good example. This is not the work of religious extremists. There is no such thing. It is the work of reckless homicidal self-destructive maniacs, apparently motivated by a charismatic madman. If that is true, then we can add his name to a long list of charismatic madmen that brought ruin to their faithful, because that is what will happen.

The clothes are done, and we say our thankyous and gather our stuff. We got chicken to haul. Maybe. If it's loaded yet.

Another stop at the local discount store for some antibiotics and razors. No connection, just some stuff we used up along the way. I don't spend a lot of time messing around in the place; I want to get the trailer and get rolling. Get this training business behind me, and get home. Trainer wants to get home as well. We both want to get home, but for different reasons. Maybe I should have taken that train.

Back to the chicken plant, and our trailer is in one of the doors being loaded, so we think the best and decide the load will be ready by the time we have a meal. There is a Chinese restaurant near here and we walk over for the buffet. There is a pizza place nearby, but the buffet is finished there. Trainer wants a buffet. Looks like Chinese is the one, and it has some pizza in it. Chinese pizza. Culture blending.

Buffet behind us, we wander back to the chicken plant in the hope our trailer will be ready, and sure enough, there it sits. But there is a problem. In my looking around the trailer, making certain it is ready to go, I notice the temperature display on the reefer unit shows an interior reading of 70 degrees. That must be wrong. There is frozen chicken in the trailer, or supposed-to-be frozen chicken. It will not be frozen long at 70 degrees. I think there must be something wrong with the display.

There is no way the loaders would have put frozen chicken in a trailer that warm. But, I'll check the inspection door at the rear of the trailer. There is a thermometer there as well. Getting there, I see I don't need to check the door, there is chicken juice dropping out the drains in the back of the trailer. The chicken is thawing. I trot back up to the refrigeration unit and set the thermostat to 20 degrees. It kicks on immediately. I don't believe the idiots did that, but they did. Someone set the thermostat at 70 degrees with a trailer two-thirds full of frozen chicken. I am angry and take off to find the guard, who should have seen something, if it were done with malice, and get someone to find out what is going on. Not only is our trailer not cooled, it is not completely loaded. I am thinking I never saw a place of business this inefficient.

The guard says he saw no one near that trailer, then gets a supervisor on the phone and I ask him what the deal is. He says not only is the trailer not ready to go yet, but that it was probably another driver mad at our company that reset the thermostat. None of his people would do that. I tell him that's what I'd say in his position. He doesn't think that's funny. I want to know why our trailer isn't ready. This is the end of the second day we have waited for a load here. He says he's just behind, some of his personnel didn't show up. I tell him that's what I'd say. He hangs up. I call him back. He's brainless enough to answer. When will the trailer be ready? Maybe sometime tomorrow. Well, that just ain't good enough, I want it NOW. He slams his phone down. Might have really slammed it. There is no dial tone on my end. Oh, well.

He's just a little huffy, and I sort of enjoy hassling him, I think because he so quickly put his employees' mistake onto a phantom menace. There are no less than fifty trailers in that lot. Why would someone single out that trailer? With a guard watching? And the answer is: they wouldn't. The loader dudes just didn't properly set the reefer unit after they loaded the trailer. Didn't care.

I decide the thing to do is call HQ and tell them what has happened insofar as the trailer temperature thing goes. So, I do that, adding that I have no idea how long the trailer thermostat was set on 70 degrees. After some discussion and a three-way call to the customer, the decision is made to run with the load as is. That the chicken probably didn't completely thaw, and no matter if it did. The receiver still wants it. Okay.

I was taught in the military to not make command decisions in the field, so I still don't do that. I was also taught by the military to take a buddy on a dangerous mission, so I still do that. This thawed-chicken thing looked like a decision to be made by command, and I can think of no better buddy than the customer service rep at HQ. That deal is done, the onus is off myself and Trainer, and we will leave with semifrozen chickens tomorrow. Hopefully. I wonder about the departure deadline fine, and hope it is a dandy. That'll show that wise-ass chickenmanager. I should have asked about it when I was on the phone to HQ.

I hike back to the tractor and tell Trainer what I did and that we have to wait till tomorrow, that the load will not be ready tonight. He looks around and says we'll just stay here. I say no deal, I am going to get a shower tonight, and I am going to have coffee in the morning. He says you're getting spoiled. I tell him I have my priorities in place.

We set out for the truck stop and a shower and a decent night's sleep.

Up early, coffee, logs done, we drive to the chicken plant. The trailer is ready. I didn't think it would be. I thought we would have to wait for a while this morning. We hook up, get the bills of lading, and set out for Spokane. I look at the restored farmhouses on the way to the interstate from town. Excellent work, and historically accurate, looks like. These are not remodeled homes. They look to be authentic turn-of-the-century, and well done.

We head out to Joplin where we will fuel, and I shame Trainer into a shower. He did not take one the entire time in Missouri. He doesn't stink, I just feel like it is time for him to clean up. He does not shame easily. I have to work on him a little.

The weather deteriorates near Kansas City, and begins to rain. I don't like driving in the rain, but it has to be done, so I just slow down and increase my following distance. It is hard enough to stop one of these things on a dry road.

Radio says we have declared war on Afghanistan. I wonder is there enough of Afghanistan to attack after the Russians gave up and moved out some years ago. We pull into a rest stop for a lunch of ham-and-cheese sandwich. It is good to get out of the truck for a few minutes. Most of the time, these days, I am pretty comfortable in the truck, but sometimes it is good to get out and move around some. My ankles still swell on occasion, and getting out some seems to help with that; also lying asleep for several hours helps them return to their normal size. I have yet to figure that out.

We roll through the tall grass prairie for many miles, and I think on how this was Pawnee land a couple of hundred years ago, and I don't know that it has changed a lot landscapewise from the days when fast food meant you had to catch it.

It is cool and foggy and drizzly and raining a little as we roll along Interstate 80 going west, and I feel like a cup of coffee would go good about now, and Trainer has to stop at the men's room anyway. A rest stop is coming up, according to a sign alongside the road, and maybe there is a vending machine there that dispenses coffee. This isn't my usual coffee hour, but with the weather being what it is, a warm drink seems like the thing I need. Vending-machine coffee isn't on my list of waycool things to drink, but you gotta do what you gotta do.

We begin to slow for the exit and pull into the rest area parking lot reserved for bigtrucks, ease into a space, set the brakes, and get out to stretch and move around a little. Trainer heads to the restroom most rikitik. It is kinda comical watching a big guy move so quickly. I look around, and among the vending machines is one that dispenses several different kinds of brewed beverages—tea, coffee, and hot chocolate. At least this row of vending machines is out of the weather. I wait on the old-timer ahead of me to make his selection. Takes him a minute. That's okay. I don't mind the wait, for a couple of reasons. One, I don't know what I want yet, and he probably does. Two, and more importantly, I don't rush old folks. I will be one someday, soon enough, and I already have no patience with someone rushing me to do anything, especially selecting my coffee. Additionally, his generation essentially made the life I lead possible. They fought the World War. They built the industries that give me the things I have. The generated a postwar economy that gave rise to the blue-collar class that provided for me. They had lots of babies. I was one. They made a great country greater.

I'll wait on him.

Vending machines are nonnegotiating. They receive the money and they usually give something in return. Not always. I hope this is one of those reasonable machines. I only have a little change. The old fella gets his, nods his head and smiles on his way by me and back to his car. Carefully dressed gentleman, professional type, walks with that rolling gait 70-year-old knees generate, and disappears from my life. It is only me and the machine now. I put in the money. Cup comes down the chute. Locks into place. Whirring, grinding noises. High-pitched whine. Steamy brown liquid comes out a spout just above the cup. Noises stop. Liquid continues to flow, diminishes some, and slows to a trickle. I reach in and remove the cup from the clamp. It smells like coffee. It sips like coffee. It is coffee. And it isn't bad coffee. I can handle less than perfectly brewed coffee later in the day, but in the mornings, it has to be right. This is fine for now.

Problem is, the cup is paper. It isn't going to keep the stuff warm very long. But in its current just-brewed state, it is too hot to drink. Timing is everything here as well, so the trick is to get it down in the very small time bracket between too hot and too cool. Otherwise, it is an unpleasant experience. I am needing a pleasant experience on this chilly, dreary, blowy, rainy day in the Midwest. The java gods are pleased with my 35-cent offering, and my taste buds are fulfilled this time. I wonder should I tempt those gods and go back for a second cup.

Not this gloomy day, Trainer is already back in the tractor and waiting. He'll wait. He knows. Ah, well, time to roll anyway. He sees the coffee and looks longingly as I get in and buckle up. I silently and obviously move my coffee closer to me. He grins and shifts into second gear. We head back onto the rain-slick highway, tripling our following distance. Foggy, misty, rainy day. The tires hiss loudly, and the rain pelts the condo and windshield. The wipers tick away the afternoon, and the Great Plains go past my window shrouded in a dismal haze.

The spray from the tires in a billowing cloud occludes everything behind us and to the sides behind the drives. Any car that gets into that fog does so at considerable risk. A truckdriver cannot see a car in the spray any easier than the cardriver can see out of it. As a car occasionally comes into the cloud to pass us, I think to myself, but try to communicate with the four-wheeler driver: speed up or slow down, but get out of the spray.

As we roll along the interstate, I look and am impressed by the little towns and farmsteads, even in the rain. I'll bet those Currier and Ives holidays happen here. Bungalow-type houses with picket fences. Big trees in the yards. Gramma and Grampa waiting on the snowy porch for the kids and grandkids on Christmas Eve, the house all aglow. It gives me some kind of comfort to know that this part of our culture is real. That it happens. That the elements for its existence are still out there, and that someone has those things.

We have the FM radio on scan as we move across the Heartland, and happen into the pregame show with the coach of the Kearny Vikings discussing what the rain has done to his gameplan. It is really great to hear such a slant on high school football. He comes across as genuinely interested in the game for the kids' sake. He wants to win, but not at the expense of safety, and there are some potholes in the field. Gonna be full of water. Kids could be hurt. I am impressed, and the show is good as well, but we soon roll out of range, and I hit the scan button wishing I could stay for the game itself. I'll bet it will be a good one, if he decides to play. Muddy field and all that.

Portions of one of the interstate highways south of here run over what was the Trail of Tears. Not everyone coming through this part of the country enjoyed the trip, or listened to the talk shows on the radio. Along about the winter of 1838/39, the whites in the southeastern part of the country were finally able to get rid of them blasted redskins camping all over the Appalachian woodlands. Public pressure caused the Congress to remove the natives to somewhere, anywhere, west of the Mississippi, and, having no arguable choice, Chief John Ross led somewhere between thirteen and seventeen thousand Cherokees from the Carolinas to the promised land of Oklahoma, losing several thousand along the way, the old and young mostly. It was a bad winter for a 1,200-mile hike, and food was short. Those folks walked along the same ground that interstate is cast upon. It is almost a sacrilege to cover a mass grave several hundred miles long with a strip of concrete, and nothing marks the travesty except a little blue highway sign every so often, "Trail of Tears." I guess someone thinks that's enough of a reminder.

The weather begins to back off a little as we roll into a corporate franchise truck stop for the night. Looks like a good place for a shower and a meal, and I'm ready to get this day behind me. Rain all day, and driving in it, makes me more tired than a usual day of driving. I have to be on superalert all the time behind the wheel, and that is very tiring. The concentration is exhausting, and today has been extraordinary in that the rain was with us all the way. Most times, the rain is in one area of the country and we run into or out of it in a few hours, at the longest. Covering 700 or 800 miles a day, sometimes near a thousand, the weather changes regularly for us. Anyway, I am going to make it an early night. After a shower and a surprisingly good steak at the in-house restaurant, Trainer will have to watch alien movies without me.

# WEEK

UP AT 4:30 A.M. LOCAL TIME, FOR SOME REASON WIDE AWAKE, AND I sneak out to get some coffee in the restaurant. I don't know why I arose so early in the day; I may get up to pee in the middle of the night, but usually I go right back to sleep. This morning there is no point in lying around. Sometimes, I wake at an odd hour, and I am as awake as I will be all day, so I may as well get up and get started. Doesn't happen often, maybe three or four times a year. Looks like today is one of those days. Rather than get Trainer up and roll, which I would do if I were solo and had the hours, I decide getting some coffee and an early breakfast is the thing to do. Pass a little time as constructively as I can, and wait on Trainer and daylight.

Trainer wanders by the window on his way to coffee at about the usual time, and happens to look in at me as I watch him go along the sidewalk. He stares at me. I stare back. We stare at one another. He grins like the Cheshire cat—exaggerated grin, I grin back—till all that is left of Trainer as he heads into the convenience store is a toothy smile. I shake my head to snap out of it. I may not be as awake as I think. Way too early. More coffee, please, waitress. And hurry.

Looks like another cool, foggy morning, but so far no rain. That's good. Trainer comes in and has a seat. We discuss the day's plan, and who will do what when. First thing, past breakfast, is to fuel.

Fueled and getting coffee for the road, Trainer says he wants me to drive to Bitter Creek. That's fine. It's a good trip and an easy drive. I wonder what is wrong with Trainer. We have been together long enough now we can read one another fairly well. He will not say anything, but something is bothering him. I don't think it is a home thing; that is chronic among drivers, particularly himself. I think it is something else. I think I figure into it somehow. And he smokes a lot now. Several packs a day. He is getting worse at decision making, and worse still at staying with a decision if he makes one. He will outline a plan for the day, and not stick with the first parts of that plan, and that throws the remainder of the day, and plan, into a tailspin. Makes it difficult for me to know what to expect when I don't know what we are going to do, or what part of the original trip plan he will disregard. All I know is we are going to drive. A lot.

Many years ago I learned that indecision is a killer. It kills people, it kills careers and businesses, it kills relationships, it kills confidence. Make a reasonable decision based upon the best and most complete information available at the time, get to work on it, and live with the benefits or consequences. Some folks have a hard time with the decision-making process. They take too long, or waver, or just back off and let the Fates have it. Some make a decision and get it implemented, only to second- and third-guess themselves, becoming their own worst enemy. Some make a decision and stay with it and suffer through what it brings just to see it through, and that's not the right thing either. Some make a decision, get behind that decision, and do what it takes to make that decision a good one. They understand that a successful choice, a decision, requires commitment and effort. That things don't just happen, they are made to happen. Good decision making and commitment to that decision are critical to any degree of satisfaction with any choice. I don't think Trainer understands any of those things, or if he does, I don't see it.

Trainer smokes and rides, and I drive the morning away, lowering his window a couple of inches as soon as he lights up. I can do that from the first chair. It irks him, but he says nothing. He is busy being indecisive. I think the stress of whatever it is that is bothering him is part of his uncertainty. I think the fact he knows his day is erratic and unpredictable feeds on itself, and in trying to compensate, he becomes that much more unpredictable as the result of second-guessing himself. I just ride and guide, and let him work things out for his ownself, as a buddy of mine would say. He has enough to deal with, and doesn't need me throwing gas on whatever fire he is trying to put out.

From nowhere, he decides it is time for him to drive, and tells me to pull over at the next truck stop or rest stop. Okay.

A rest stop happens to be not far down the road, and I pull into the parking lot and set the brakes. Trainer hops out and heads for the phone bank. I lock the truck, leave it idling, and get out to walk around a little. More to get out of the truck for a while than anything else. I walk into the place and look for the bathroom. I really don't have to look too hard; I have been in this rest stop before. As I go inside to the facilities, I pass the phone bank and there is a driver talking loudly on the phone to his son, apparently. He says, loudly, didja kick his ass, Boy? didja hurt 'im? . . . looking around to see whom might be paying attention to his question. I presume the conversation had to do with football. I stop and look at him for a second, many things running through my head, and I think it sad that the man was so interested in whether or not those things had happened. Not whether the game was a good one, closely matched teams playing their best and right to the wire, but interested in his son hurting someone else, and using the game as an excuse for it, hiding malevolence in the plays. Vicious violence thinly disguised as sportsmanship. I think that sort of thing may be a sad indicator of a lot of problems I see in my travels. Especially road manners. It is certainly a sad commentary on the way some children are raised, and the expectation levels they are given.

Trainer takes longer than usual to get back, so I use the time to make some sandwiches. I have long since become the chef, largely because

Trainer likes the sandwiches I make, and I don't like the thought of
Trainer making my sandwiches with last week's grime and who knows
what else on his hands. Washing his hands just isn't important to him.
Trainer ambles out of the place just as I finish the matching pair of triple-
layered ham-and-Swiss masterpieces. I put his on the first seat, and start
in on mine. All I need is a beer. But that ain't gonna happen. DOT says
the only alcohol on a commercial vehicle legally is sealed into the trailer.
Can't even have some cold remedies aboard because of the alcohol content. No one says anything until a crash happens. Then it doesn't matter
whether the blood alcohol content came from good whiskey or a bottle of
cold or flu medicine. I settle for a diet soda and look longingly at the foam
as I fill the chilled glass. Trainer grabs his sandwich in a swoop and has a
bite out of it before his butt hits the seat. He looks over and grins and
roars this sumbitch is good. Man, I wish he'd get that ear fixed.

The trip across Wyoming is as beautiful as ever, even in the darkness, with the rich textures of the land and the earth colors in the softness of the night lights from the midnight-black sky. Our headlights are
the only connection to the twenty-first century I see out there as the
hours and the miles go past.

Trainer decides to shut down early tonight, and I agree. A shower
and a snack suits me about now, though Trainer has obviously thrown
my trip plan out the window. We exit the interstate and pass a broken
VW bus with a DeadHead sticker on the back windshield, and a road-
pizza coyote just behind it. I wonder if the two are related somehow.

Morning finds us on the interstate west to Salt Lake City. I figure I
could move to Salt Lake City and be home once a week.

The aspens are beginnng to turn, and as we drive through the
canyons cradling Interstate 84, aka the North Bypass, they take on that
golden yellow that makes them famous. Actually, they have been like this
for some distance, and in the breeze that blows through this
canyon/pass, they live up to their quakie moniker. It is something a person would have to see to enjoy the full impact, and I believe that event
alone, seeing a grove of fiery aspens flutter in the wind, would make the

trip worthwhile. So I ride and look, taking full advantage of the opportunity. The fast-flowing shallow river running alongside the road adds more to the experience. Gotta be full of trout. And what a memorable day would be spent in the catching of them, if I had the time. And the fly rod. And the flies. And the skill. River trout fishing is completely different than my usual method of wading the flats for specks or reds. Matterafact, now that I think on it, I probably wouldn't catch a thing in that river. But, I'd still like to try. Just being out there would be good enough for me. The art of the cast, I think, and being a part of the scenery.

The loop/bypass intersects Interstate 15 just north of Salt Lake City near Ogden, and we go north across some seriously barren country and past several abandoned farmsteads into Idaho, which is a little less barren. Lots of wheat and potatoes hereabouts, and not much else. Parallel rows of blond wheat stubble in Zen gravel-garden patterns to suit the rolling landscape. Smell of rotting potatoes every so often. I'm thinking this may be a good place for a vodka mill. Recycle those potatoes.

Near the air base at Mountain Home, we barely skirt a huge thunderstorm I have been watching for some time, and get some of the windshear. There are a couple of tense moments in the cab, as we are thrown about the two lanes of the interstate and it requires both lanes to keep Blue Two on her feet. Moments like these generate a physical reaction, called a puckerfactor. That is when one's anus involuntarily constricts tightly as the result of the fear stimulus. I have heard that in some cases, the effect is great enough to cause the anus to grip the seat covering through one's clothing. That could be about to happen here, at least in my chair. It may have already happened in Trainer's chair, judging from the look on his face.

We both know we are in too deep to stop or get off the road as we are hit by the blast, so the only thing Trainer can do is hold on and try to keep us on the road. Really good thing we are loaded like we are, and we go past the wind by the time Trainer gets back in the granny lane. We both look at one another wide-eyed. Neither of us says a thing. We ride on, and I look in the mirror to see what is going on behind us. Other trucks are there now and having to deal with it as well. Flatbeds have a distinct advantage on windy days, I think—unloaded ones, anyway.

Trainer is cruising along when a car passes us and, like many times in the past, the kids in the back seat bend their arms at the elbow and pump up and down to indicate they want the driver to sound the horn.

That is a clumsy way to say that particular thing. Sound the horn. But how else would I say it? Honk the horn? Air horns don't honk. They blast. Maybe I should have said "blast" the air horn. Anyway, like many times in the past, Trainer grabs the horn honker that swings from the ceiling of the cab and hangs on it for a few seconds. The blast is tremendous, even in the fairly well insulated cab.

I have reservations about a couple of things Trainer does behind the wheel. One of them is honking the air horn. Air horns are loud, and the sound of one is an indicator something is wrong, causing people to look around for the problem. The sound of an air horn really close causes people to panic, thinking something is wrong real close. Air horns are loud and piercing. Folks react first, then look to see what is wrong. That is not good when we are all moving along the interstate at speed. I have cautioned Trainer about that before and the possible consequences. He says no problem, that the cardriver always knows the kids are going to do that, so they shouldn't be surprised.

This specific car swerves wildly, but the driver maintains control and manages to get into the granny lane right in front of us and slow down. Trainer gets on the brakes, and the kids disappear into the back seat. The cardriver pulls onto the shoulder, and we move into the hammer lane to pass. I look into the driver's window as we go by, and the poor woman is beginning to break down emotionally. Trainer doesn't see it, and I look over at him. He knows I have something to say, and looks straight out the windshield. It is enough for me that he knows. I look out the window and he moves back into the granny lane. We drive on.

We shut down for the night and have a sit-down dinner before we shower and get back to the bunk. The meal is great, and the shower tops it off. The bunk feels good, and the Idaho night is short.

— — —

Strong coffee in the morning. We must be getting close to Seattle. There is a cinnamon roll shop in this truck stop, and those delicacies have an aroma unmatched. The temptation is really great, but they are made with eggs, and I want to live for a few more years. I hear Carly Simon singing on a stereo display inside the merchandise area. My body does not like eggs in any shape, form, fashion, or disguise. Dang, those things smell good, but I haven't got time for the pain.

I usually do the first walkaround of the day while Trainer gets his stuff put away and ready to roll, and it is so today. I put all the lights on, including the hazard flashers and headlights, before I walk from front to back on both sides. I look for lights not working, low tires, anything bent, broken, loose, or leaking. Just like I was taught to do it. I look at the internal temperature of the trailer, the refrigeration unit, and the door seals and locks. I do it every time we stop and I do it first thing in the morning, before we set out for the day. That doesn't preclude any problems developing as we roll, but it does let me know now about any existing ones before the DOT guys at a coop let me know. If I find the problem, the offense is free, penaltywise. If the DOT dudes at a coop find it, it is not. DOT tickets for unsafe equipment are no juke. So, I try to find whatever may be bent, broken, loose, leaking, or not working in a daily walkaround.

Today, I find the left trailer blinker is not working. I figure the connection between the tractor and the trailer has just vibrated loose, and continue my walk around the end of the trailer and along the other side. My intent is to disconnect and reconnect the wire from the tractor to the trailer, called a pigtail for its curlicue shape, like a coil spring, hoping that is the problem. I do that when I get to the back of the tractor, and go to the side of the trailer to see what a difference I made. Nothing. Still no work. I go back and wiggle the connection at both the tractor and the trailer to make certain whatever contacts are there are contacted. Nothing.

This is not good, and we are shut down, legally, until we get it repaired. I tell Trainer, getting out for his last cup of coffee, we have no left trailer signal light. He goes to check it out, and wiggles the pigtail on both ends just like I did, with the same effect. Nothing. Says the pigtail is bad, that they sometimes just quit carrying the signal to the trailer and we need a new one. Says I need to go inside and get one. I say no, you need to do that. He says he ain't got no money. I say use the company check. He says oh yeah, he forgot. He hikes in to get a pigtail. Comes out a few minutes later with a new one. I see him coming and remove the old one. Plug the new one in, and the lights come on. We swagger around with our coffee and brag on how we are regular fixit guys. That's good, we can leave now. Legally.

It is now daylight enough we can see without the flashlights, so I go inside and get one more cup of coffee to see me through the morning drive. We will be in Oregon soon, and there is a particular descent there on Interstate 84 known among drivers as "Cabbage." It is steep and curvy, I hear. Trainer says he wants me to drive down. For the experience. I want to be wide awake when that happens.

We listen to the radio as the wheatfields of Idaho go by the windows and the airwave geniuses decide where the terrorists will strike next. Trainer says he thinks the refineries. I say that could be, but most likely our special forces are already way into breaking the back of the terrorists' organization. I recall for Trainer my military days and my very limited experience with our special ops people, and tell him it is not good to have one of those elite groups looking for you. The world just ain't big enough. He laughs and says he hopes so. Before they get the refineries.

Oregon is nice, and we come to the edge of the drop called "Cabbage." I stop at the mandatory brake check on the top of the hill and go through the procedure for adjusting the brakes. They are self-adjusting, but there is a process for making certain that adjustment has happened, so I do that, and come away satisfied the brakes on the truck and trailer are as they should be. Another walkaround, and we start the descent.

I start out in the bottom gear of high range, and it is slow going, but I have to use the brakes very little. Some trucks whiz by and holler on the radio for us to pep it up, but I just ease along and stay in the same gear all the way down. Let them go. They are either not loaded or crazy or really good at this hill. Maybe all of those things.

The ride down proves uneventful, and Trainer is nonplussed, though he never encourages me to speed up. He lets me take all the time I want. I look back in the mirror, near the bottom, and from a distance the thing does look like a head of cabbage. A deeply veined lump of earth with an interstate coming down the side of it.

There is an instructor at the driving school I attended that said a driver can go down a hill too slow many times, but too fast only once. That pearl stuck with me, and I have yet to smoke a brake. I have made many wilder drivers angry for not going fast enough, but I have never hurt anyone, nor damaged any equipment, going too fast. I want to keep it that way. I don't care how many get angry, but I do care how many get hurt.

We get to the straight stretch that drops off the hill, and with Trainer's okay, I let it roll. Kinda like a toboggan run. We are down, and I look over at Trainer, looking out the windshield. He says it was a good job. Thanks. We drive to the next rest stop where he gets out to call his wife. I get out and walk around to metabolize the adrenaline. Things like that don't hit me till they are over. I am not shaken, just excited that I have come down a world-class descent and lived to tell about it. I feel like I have accomplished something on a professional level. Feels good.

We need to get to Spokane, which we do, and drop some of this chicken, then get on to the planned stop in Ellensburg so we can get staged for an early appointment in Seattle. It is a nice ride through a pretty part of the country. I am most impressed by the Columbia River Valley and the wind roaring in the canyon. There are whitecaps on the river, and we go alongside it for some miles. I can tell the river is deep, just by the way the water is colored and the wave patterns. It is wide as well, with steep verdant banks, walls really, going right down into the water. There is no riverbank I can see from here, and that may explain the total lack of boating and people here. That may be a good thing. This is a widely renowned river, and I would hate to think we had managed to trash it like we have some of the other, more easily accessible and placid rivers.

Some places in this country, famed for their beauty and wilderness, need to stay that way. It comforts me somehow, to know that some parts of the country are still unsettled and unpaved. There will be a deep-discount store and a burger joint here soon enough, and the litter will be close behind, so I am glad I have seen this storied river in its pristine state.

There is a bridge we have to cross as we turn to the west and go that way. It is high above the river and offers a great view both up and down the river and the valley it flows through. The wind is a force to be reckoned with, so high in the air like we are on this bridge above the river, but Trainer is ready for it. The wind is steady, with only a few gusts, and we are under control, but there is a lot of lateral pressure. I am surprised at its strength. Amazingly strong wind on this bridge. I wonder aloud if it is always this windy here. Trainer says it is every time he comes here. I didn't think he would hear that. Not that I hoped he wouldn't, just that it never occurred to me he would. Maybe his hearing is coming back.

We get to Ellensburg and stop at a place Trainer knows right by a small river that has a deep look to it. The truck stop is nice, with a sub-sandwich outlet in it and the local bus stop. He picks a place at the rear of the lot and backs in. Says he wants the steak sandwich and a shower and let's turn in early for the ride to Seattle in the morning. I say just give me the shower, I have been eating all day.

Trainer is smoking three-and-a-half packs a day now, and it concerns me as much for my own health as his. What if something happens to him while he is driving? He is way too big and way too old to be smoking like that. Something must be wrong, and he seems really distant these days. I wonder again if it is me or something else, or something else and me. Maybe it is only too much togetherness, and too much notathomeness.

I have been privy to many conversations chaired by drivers of many different skill levels and experience in many different places. One of the things most drivers have to say is don't go team driving with your best friend, that the best friend part will go away after about a month of living so close together. The little things become big things, then out-of-control things. I was told by an instructor in my driving school that most companies like husband-and-wife teams because they are used to living with one another, and know one another relatively closely and well, but marriages that come to drive teams have about a 50 percent survival rate. I have seen, in my limited experience, that to be about right. Being married is one thing, the bigger part of a day apart and the evenings together; but driving as part of a team, they are together 24 hours a day, seven days a week, for weeks at a time, and little things become big ones. Those situations are exaggerated when the two are not married and know little or nothing about one another at the outset. Like myself and Trainer.

Early to bed, no movie or reading for me. I don't think I moved all night.

The meemee goes off at 4:30 A.M., and I land on my feet in the middle of the condo. Trainer got in late and must have set it as I slept. I know I didn't do this to myself. Battery cover, wires, the screaming stops. I glare at Trainer, slack-jawed and drooling and gagging in his bunk. Didn't faze him. Fling the little siren into the locker and get started on my day, my body wide awake and my brain trying to get cranked up.

I don't bother waking Trainer for coffee, thinking he is better off asleep, and get the truck ready to roll by five in the morning. I am sipping my coffee, enjoying the quiet, log done and the walkaround complete, macros sent in to HQ, when Trainer jumps out of the bunk and hollers we are late. I watch him stagger and fall around the condo from my perch in the first chair and savor my coffee. He struggles with the mental haze, the clothes, the confines, and finally collapses into the second chair looking for a lighter. I wait until he settles down and say we are fine, we have six hours to get to Seattle. I point out we are still on Central Standard Time, and the local time is two hours behind. He looks at me like I am a long-lost brother and says yeah, that's right. He hops out the door and strolls to the coffee bar, all the time in the world. I grin and sip and listen to the radio. I spend more time on the news stations now listening to the opinions and reports from the scene of the first attack on American soil since the Civil War. I hear people talk about justice being done.

I have thought on the subject of justice lately, and have come to the conclusion there is no such thing as justice, after the fact. There is only revenge and retribution. Justice, to me, is when the pot is made right again. Simply stated, that just can't happen once the damage is done. There is no putting something back like it was before whatever incident has taken place. There is only some further aggression that makes us feel like we get even with whomsoever did what. Two wrongs. We have chosen to call that justice, and not only in this case of attack, but in most instances I see where the subject of justice is in the conversation. Murder trials, racial discrimination, child abuse. We throw someone in the penitentiary for life, or sue for millions or dissolve a company, or beat the bejesus out of anyone looking like the perpetrator. That isn't justice. It is retribution. The victims are not improved one iota. Yet we come away saying justice was done. No, it wasn't. Maybe we just feel better when someone we feel is guilty is made to suffer to some degree we think adequate, and we call that justice. Still smells like revenge to me.

Justice, if there is such a thing, happens before the time of the offense. The potential offender chooses to not commit that offense. The victim is never a victim. Everyone goes their way, and no one's situation is made worse. Only a potential offender can provide justice. I wonder what we will decide is justice in this case of so many dead, and so many lives laid waste.

Trainer gets back and hollers let's roll, and he wants to drive. Okay, I'll ride. I have never seen the Snoqualmies at daybreak.

Lots of darkness out there, but I know I will see whatever there is to see on the way back later this morning. I'll just navigate and sip my coffee in the darkness and think on what a lucky guy I am for the life I lead and the people I have in it.

It is what we called good daylight in Oklahoma, as Blue Two rumbles onto Mercer Island and we hit the traffic, surprisingly thin for 6:30 A.M. The tunnel must be the one I see in the various car commercials. Nice, clean and well lighted. Traffic is fast, and we get onto the bridge across Lake Washington that heralds the end of Interstate 90, and our trip west. I call out the directions to Trainer as we approach the industrial area near the Sound. I think the fish place is around here somewhere. It was the scene of a human resources video I saw in a past corporate life where the patrons buy a fish and the salesperson flings the fish across the area and another catches it in paper and wraps it. Very impressive, in the video, and the folks who work there appear to be happy in their work and glad to be there throwing fish around. I tell Trainer we need to stop by for the show. He looks at me, looks back out the windshield into the misty morning, and drives on.

I am out of coffee. My cup is empty. In Seattle, coffee capital of the world, and I have none. How can that happen?

Anyway, we get to the row of truck docks where we will drop our chickens, the line of trucks waiting to back in is not long, and I stay with the truck while Trainer goes to find out when and where from the receiving group. We apparently are next, because Trainer is right back and says let's move over there to get backed in. He says for me to back it in while he directs me.

The little lane we have to use to get into the docks is narrow and has cars lining the curbs. There is little space to work in. The dock space is little wider than the trailer is long, so to keep the tractor out of the lane such that other trucks can go by, the trailer has to be backed in straight to the dock, and the tractor left at an angle in the lot, to keep its nose out of the street. The backing operation has to be planned so all that happens.

I get out to look the situation over, and tell Trainer what I want to do. He doesn't argue. Just nods his head and says okay. He gets in the lane to hold back traffic while I set up to back, and I look out the open door because the mirror won't show me what I need to see. Whatever it takes to get where I need to be. Trainer stands between the cars and the front of the tractor, and there is a lot of faith here. If I don't handle the truck carefully and well, Trainer could lose his legs, or worse be killed between the cars and the tractor. I don't know if this is a testament of confidence on Trainer's part, or his just being tired of living.

After much close-quarters maneuvering and steering-wheel turning, I have the trailer in the dock, square with the doors. We are offloaded in minutes. I have not seen so quick a job in my time driving. Trainer goes in to get the paperwork and is told to get the truck out of the dock immediately, and he relays that to me immediately. I get him into the truck and we pull away from the door so another truck can get in. This place is extraordinarily efficient, like they all should be. Probably because the managers are on the dock floor making things happen. The mice can't play here, the cat's not away. Should happen more places; there would be a lot less downtime for drivers.

We pull out and go down the street to look for a place to hide for a while so we can send in the macros to tell HQ we are unloaded and ready for a ride back to Texas. Our next trip will be to the yard, and then home for a week or a little more, before I am assigned my own mule. This will be the last ride with Trainer. We get a message back that it will be an hour or so, and to find a safe place to park in the neighborhood. Like there is a place to park a truck in this warehouse district. They know we have no place to park this thing. To be here in a truck, it had best be unloading or loading. Anywhere else is in the way. Trainer says them sumbitches know that, they just don't want to let us get too damfar out of route if our next pickup is close by. Well, that kinda makes sense from a business standpoint.

Says let's drive over a block or two and see what we can see. So we do that and sure enough, there is a vacant lot near a warehouse. Trainer says pull in there and park while he goes and calls HQ to make certain they know to get us a ride home, and not get stuck with a run to Canada from here. I settle in for a wait, and look around me in the early morning. No coffee. I'm in Seattle, for pity's sake. I don't believe it.

The area is beginning to wake up, and a few people are milling about. Getting out of cars and heading to the office, going about their business, and it comes to me this is where all the leftovers from the sixties went. They must have all come here and had kids with long hair. Most of the males I see, young and old, have seriously long hair. Nothing is wrong with that, just that this is the greatest concentration of longhairs I have seen in years. I see longhaired males every day, but not in any quantity. Here, they are everywhere I look. Like a time warp. Most every male I see looks like a member of Credence Clearwater Revival. Shoulder-length hair, beard, and a plaid flannel shirt.

Grabbing a package of snack crackers for want of anything better to do, I look around from the cab, thinking about going home, and notice a bush along the fence near me and some dark things hanging on the bush. Big bush. Big dark things, look like berries. I get out and walk to them, and see they are berries of some kind. Blackberries maybe, but it is past the season for them. They mature in July where I live. Maybe hereabouts they ripen in September. I hate to pass up the chance for fresh wild blackberries, but I am not sure they are blackberries. The bush is drooping with the weight of them, there are so many, and I can't stand by much longer, blackberries are among my favorite berries. My grandmother would mix blackberries, cream, and sugar for me when I was a child, and there are few things as good, back on the farm.

I figure the worst that could happen, should I try one and they not be blackberries, is, I die. For a good blackberry, the risk is almost worth it. These look really ripe. Soft, just right for picking. Firm enough to not dissolve in my hand, but ripe enough to be sweet. An unripe blackberry is not something to put in one's mouth. Not very tasty.

We had our berry patches pegged timewise, when we were children. We would go day after day to check on the readiness of each patch, and when the time was ripe, as a friend would say, we would stain our hands and tongues purple with the things. Gotta be just right. Black but not ripe, and they are hard and way too tart. Too ripe, and they are way too soft, just turn to juice right in the hand. Had to be careful about snakes, though; according to the old folks, the birds kept an eye on those berries as well, and the snakes kept an eye on the birds. They would lie beneath a bramble in wait to ambush a bird come for some berries. We didn't stick our hand in a bush without looking, but I don't recall ever seeing a snake in our berry patches.

These berries are huge, and there is not likely to be a snake in there. I pluck one off and inspect it and pop it into my mouth. It is a blackberry.

A good one. I spend 15 minutes picking and eating the best-looking ones. My fingers are purple again after all these years. I look at them and think of no less than a hundred things I have done since the last time I looked at my hands stained like this, and little did I know as I last sat stuffed with berries in the Oklahoma sunshine, the next time that would happen, most of a lifetime would be past and I would be standing gray-haired and coffeeless in a misty Seattle morning.

God Almighty, where has my life gone and why did I pay so little attention to the time. It really is later than I think. It is later, much later, than we all think.

The blackberry phenomenon: Stained fingers cause retrospection. And time consciousness.

Trainer shows up and says we are to go back to Ellensburg and wait for further instructions this afternoon. Them damdispatchers. What damdispatchers? We are being picky. We want a ride to Texas. They have to find one for us. Having said that in the damdispatcher's defense, I stand there in the murky Seattle morning licking purple fingertips. Trainer looks at me like I have purple fingers in my mouth.

We set out for Ellensburg through the Snoqualmies.


The Pacific side of the mountains is cloudy and foggy and cool and damp. I can breathe better than I have for days. At the summit the clouds stop, and the sun shines down. Until now I have only seen the weather so sharply contrasted in a storm front.

The girls at the free-coffee booth at the rest stop tell me that is the norm here at the top of the mountains. Cloudy down there, clear up here. Free coffee for a donation. Cookie, too. Helluva deal for a quarter on a mountaintop, sunshine on one side, foggy drizzle on the other, and I can see both. One of the girls says you don't look like a truckdriver. I say I am not a truckdriver. She says I saw you get out of that truck over there. I say I am trying to be a truckdriver, but am not there yet. She looks me up and down and says you are no truckdriver. I look back and say she doesn't look like a person who would give away coffee for a donation. We both laugh, and I head for the truck with my free coffee I got for a quarter.

Trainer says in two months this place will be covered in snow. I do not doubt that. This place looks snowy without the snow. Great conifers with drooping branches, and mountain peaks all around, as though waiting for the snow.

We roll along the edge of the Yakima River in its autumn colors, McCartney's golden willows with their backs to the wind, and I think on what a great fishing river it must be. We pass solitary fishermen here and there, apparently caring more for the being out than the fish, and unless they are hungry, that is the way it should be. I fished for 30 years before I realized that just being in the flats at dawn or dusk was most of the reason I was out there. The art of the cast-and-retrieve is secondary, and the catching of the fish is tertiary and almost incidental. That doesn't diminish the catching of the fish, just that my reasons for going to catch the fish have become more apparent to me.

As we rumble into Ellensburg and the truck stop where we stayed the past night, there is a gravel bank of the river across the road and Trainer announces he will bring his wife here to stay on that riverbank one day. That they will camp out there and stay awhile. I listen and smile and hope he does that. Planning a getaway is a good thing for anyone, and gives us a mental vacation as we go through the process. I think mental vacations offer instant relief and instant gratification with no expense and no vacation-type problems: lost luggage, missed flights, wretched cabbies, overbooked hotel rooms, maxed credit cards.

Trainer says we need to clean the truck out while we wait, and I agree. A general dusting is always in order, and it still amazes me the amount of trash two people generate, or maybe it is the quantity of wrapped and packaged food we eat that amazes me, and the trash is little more than the indicator of that quantity.

Housecleaning done, and lunch behind us. We settle in for an afternoon nap just about the time the quailcall beeps with a message. HQ says deadhead to Ontario, Oregon, for a load of potatoes, drop the empty

trailer and get a loaded one going to Louisiana, and bring it to the yard
on the way. I read it aloud and Trainer grins that toothy grin and hollers
crank 'er up an' let's roll, we're headed fer hometime. I smile to myself
and start getting the gear stowed while Trainer does a walkaround. We
grab a soda from the fountain inside, and the big girl behind the counter
asks Trainer when is he gonna get back this way, and he says how much
fer th' soda and we trot out to the Kenworth. I look at him and laugh, and
he looks back and laughs. We climb in and Trainer says he wants to drive,
so I tuck in and watch the countryside drift by as he does that. There are
autumn colors on this side of the divide; not that the cool green of the
Pacific side is unattractive, just that this side has four seasons.

We ride along the Yakima River several times as it meanders
through its valley, and I am impressed by what a clear and green river it
is. Fisherman casting a fly as we go by. I am envious. Trainer watches me
watch the fisherman set against the water reflecting the afternoon sun.
He thinks there are places I'd rather be than riding right about now, but
he is almost wrong. While it is true I would love to be out there casting,
it is also true I like it here, riding along and seeing what I can see.

Apple trees are smaller than I thought, having passed a couple of or-
chards along here, and the empty trailer behind us doesn't hop around
as badly as one usually does. That is a good thing, because we have quite
a way to go with it. I hope the wind doesn't get any stronger than it is.
I think this is another place the wind blows all the time. Sometimes the
wind makes fly-casting difficult, and I wonder if river fishermen, with
their little flies, have the same problem I have at home with my big ones.
I have been known to crack expensive saltwater flies smooth off the tip-
pet, starting my wrist snap too soon into the everpresent breeze on my
backbays. Pisses me right off.

We get to a place where I can see what I believe to be Mount St.
Helens, and Mount Rainier both at once. I make a note of that to
Trainer and he says he doesn't think so; that can't be Mount St. Helens,
it blew up. I think it is, and Mount Rainier as well. I break out the atlas
to confirm, and I think it all fits together. I'll bet that is what I am seeing.

Trainer is skeptical. We motor on, and I watch the buff-colored hills and rounded mountains go by the window, and I ask what all that greenery on all those acres of trellises might be. Trainer says it is hops, grown here for the beer industry. We go by miles and miles and farm after farm of hops. For some combination of meteorological and geological reasons, this is one of the best places on the planet for hops, I am told.

The countryside not planted in hops is covered by a wheat-colored grass about two feet tall that shows the pattern of the wind moving across it. It may be wheat, we don't know. The hills are covered with it, and it lends a depth to the landscape that bare earth and rocks do not. The grass-covered hills look almost like they are alive as the grass is rippled by the wind, and the effect is impressive.

Across the hills, concentric arcs of the grass are blown down to rise back, and be blown down again. I think I could live out here. It is the outlands for sure, but not desolate, like so many sparsely populated places we see. It is a long ride on a beautiful afternoon through some strangely appealing and spare country. Not much out there now but the rolling hills and the knee-high straw-colored grass undulating in the wind. Cool and dry, and most of an afternoon well spent, riding and looking, and thinking on the Maker of it, Whosoever, or Whatsoever, that may be.

We ease into Ontario, some hours early for our pickup. It is late afternoon, but before the parking rush, so finding a space is relatively easy in the small but well-kept lot at the truck stop. I don't know what Trainer's plans are, and I am past the point letting his indecision keep me from a basic set of objectives like eating and showering, so when we stop, I sail out with my getaway bag and head for the shower and food court. He'll probably take a nap, and that is fine. He has been driving and most likely will want to get started home tonight after we get loaded. And that's fine, too. I'm ready to get back myself.

Cleaned and fed and back at the truck, Trainer is listening to the CB and the parking lot players. I listen in as I stow my gear and flop into the second seat, thinking about a nap as well. There are a couple of hookers advertising their services to the tune of $435 an hour. One driver is laughing so hard he is unintelligible on the radio and gives it up to let another, more controlled, driver take up the cause. Driver says he ain't never seen no dam woman worth that kinda money no matter what she could do. One of the commercial women says he don't have that kind of money anyway and she ain't lookin' fer shoppers, she's lookin' fer buyers, so shut the hell up and get off the radio. Another driver gets on and says he'd be willing to swap a shower ticket for a little bit, and expects her to use that ticket before she comes over. Much hooting and jeering. The whores are indignant. I am laughing along like an idiot. Trainer keys in and says at least they ain't stealin'. Another guy says he ain't so dam sure about that. The amateur prostitutes give up after about two or three more attempts to get their price list reasonable; by then the comic interest is gone, and Trainer announces he is hungry and is going to get something to eat and a nap before we leave at midnight for our pickup. I set the alarm for 11 P.M. and climb into the bunk and open the windows, lay back and stretch out in the cool of the evening coming in my window. I am coming to believe I could not do a nine-to-five job anymore.

That sucker starts chirping right off the bat. Says 11 P.M. Dang. That nap didn't last long. It is dark out and all the trucks are tucked in for the night. Mmmm. The pickup is just a couple of blocks over, and I'm thinking we just go get the load and come back here for the night. Trainer sits up and says he thinks that is a good idea. I know he's tired and sleepy. So we do that; go pick up a loaded trailer and drive right back to the truck stop and even get our same spot back. Trainer wants to fuel and scale the load, but I reason with him we can do that in the morning. Let's sleep while we can. He says yeah, let's do that, and he's back in his bunk before I get the truck shut down.

Up early and get fueled with diesel and coffee, then scale the load. The load is crated potatoes, so this trailer is going to be heavy, and we have to take it through a couple of states that don't mess around with overweight trailers. We get it legal by sliding the tandems and moving some weight onto the steers by shifting the fifth wheel. Perfect. Full of fuel, full of coffee and potatoes, we axle out at 80,000 pounds. Exactly. If Trainer brings a dozen donuts back from the bakery inside, we'll be overweight.

It is surprisingly chilly out this morning. This is only September; what is the deal, I wonder.

We head out of town, windows up and heater on, toward Texas, discussing the virtues of the different kinds of diesel engines. As I drive into the morning, a light frost is disappearing as a mist in the early sunlight, and I am inclined to think I know more about these engines than I do, but I don't overstep my bounds. I tell Trainer that it seems to me the Detroit engines are stronger, but the Cummins engine seems faster. He agrees. I am surprised at that, as irascible as he has been lately, and don't know if he is doing that to placate me, or because it is so, or because he doesn't want to deal with points of view so early. Doesn't really matter, I guess. Just topic for conversation as we zoom along the interstate into the sunlight, sipping coffee and talking at a shout over the wind, road, and engine noise about winds and roads and engine noise.

Back across the same plain of northern Utah we trod before. There is something about this place that makes it different than other wide open places; I'm not sure what it is. There is that old cabin out there, forsaken farmstead really, a not-so-gentle reminder to the rest of us that life in the twenty-first century is good. Life in the last couple of centuries may or may not have been, but one thing is for sure: life wasn't as easy then as it is now, and that abandoned farmhouse is a messenger from the past, if one knows how to read that message.

But, I don't think the weather-beaten ruin is the thing. There are lots of tombstones that resemble tumbledown houses along the plains of the upper northwestern United States telling silent tales of failed dreams and abandoned hopes. All it took was one bad crop or a freak weather condition to decimate a plan, a crop, a farmstead, or even a life. We merely go to the supermarket.

But, that isn't it either, the whatever-it-is that makes this place different.

It isn't the incessant wind, or the long vista across a talused plain rising into the base of the mountains. One could walk all day and still not be near them from here. That isn't it. There are lots of other sweeping vistas out west. It is a feeling here. Not a bad feeling, just a feeling that something is different. Real different.

I knew a girl once who couldn't stand to be where anyone was hurt or suffering. She'd nearly lose control when we would pass a hospital, full of pain and suffering, or come near someone sick or hurt. She really could feel the pain. Not the pain so much as the suffering, and it would cause her to not be in pain, but suffer along. It was real, at least to her. And it was no act. A psychiatrist friend said it was a sympathetic condition. I don't think that is the case here, sympathetic suffering, but there is a feeling about this place. I have been to what I thought was the middle of nowhere, and at the time I believed it was, but there was no feeling like this, even in the middle of nowhere.

That's what it is. No feeling. There is no feeling here. Nothing. There is nothing here. Only the landscape. Devoid of the essence of being. Empty space. That is what it is. It is the only place I have ever been where I felt like this. I want to get out of it, get away; I feel vulnerable, like the nothingness will get me, or something. Even in the comfort of the truck cab being pulled by more than 400 horses, I don't think I can get away quickly enough, and try not to think about it, or feel the nothingness that lives out here and waits for its chance to be nothing to someone.

It is a little early in the day for one, my having seen them mostly in the afternoon, but a dustdevil is whirling across the nothingness sucking up sand and debris and scattering it along. It is far away, probably several miles, but I can see it well enough to see it well even from here in the cab. That is a good indication of the size of the thing. It looks like a tornado, and speaking from past experience, they can demolish a raked hayfield such that it has to be redone, and they can shake a car all about. Not pick it up and toss it away, but rock it uncomfortably. Though it presents no danger to us, I want to get out of its path. It looks as though the thing will cross the road before us if it continues on its present heading, and I don't want to be there when that happens. I comment on that, and Trainer says he has never been across here but once, and that was a couple of days ago, that he didn't see a dustdevil. Three or four months from now, I will be across here again and collide with the biggest one I have ever seen, right about here. I am still not sure how that happened, but I'll talk about that some other time.

Trainer starts hollering about lunch as a city comes into view, and wanting a hot dog. Looks like hot dogs for lunch, and I'm up for that. Trainer likes his with everything behind the counter on it. I want a hot dog one of only two ways: mustard and dill relish, or a chili-cheese-onion dog. I can eat three of either of those, and it sounds good right about now, so we pull into a new truck stop in Ogden to bite some dogs, as Trainer puts it.

Them suckers are good, too. Corn chips and hot dogs and ice-cold soda. I live well. So well, I don't even bitch when Trainer says he wants to drive. I have to change shirts anyway; this one has chili all over the front. Leaky bun. Gravity never takes a break.

We take the canyon road north and east of Salt Lake City, again, and the ride is beautiful. In the afternoon sun, and the canyon breeze, it looks as though red and gold and yellow and orange paint was flung onto the mountains and is still dripping toward the base of those mountains, the leaves changing like they are.

Trainer is coughing. Coughs a lot these days. He smokes a lot, a lot more than he did. And doesn't say much anymore, unless I take the initiative.

I ride and look. We go by some neat little houses and farmlets and ranchitos, and I comment I think I could live along here as well. Trainer says we don't make enough money to live here. That all them computer eggheads that got their asses laid off in Sillycone Valley took the money they made selling their crackerbox houses in Calidamfornia and came here to Utah and drove the price of reasonable real estate sky-high. Says they'd give a quarter million dollars to a farmer for five acres and a shack and never blink, and the damfarmers would run off laffin'. Now the damfarmers ain't laffin' cause their damkids can't afford a house no more and the family farm is gone.

There is a duck perched on a fence post. I have never seen a duck on a fence post in my entire life. Trainer says he can't remember seeing a duck on a fence post either. We go on, beyond that new milestone in our lives.

There, right there, is something I have seen, and seen more often than I want to see, or should see; tandem skid marks leading off the pavement and through a mangled guardrail and over the side of the roadbed, down to whatever is down there. I wonder if the driver was hurt or even lived. Looks like he went to sleep. The skid marks don't start until the edge of the road. He could have been avoiding something in the road, but I'll bet not. This road is straight enough he could have seen it far away even in the night, and had plenty of time to stop or change lanes. He probably dozed off. The twisted guardrail is a silent warning to the wise and wary.

At the very least, he crashed a $150,000 rig and lost a load worth who knows what. At the most he lost all that and his life. I don't like this part of driving, seeing this. But, I like seeing a four-wheeler involved in that same crash even less. Trainer doesn't comment on the crashes and crash sites we see. It is like he wants to ignore them. Not so they will go away, but so they won't remind him of what carelessness brings about. And that's what it is. Carelessness. Not caring that the truck is going too fast for conditions. Not caring that last night's rest wasn't enough. Not caring to inspect the steer tires. Like that driver on his last run said, you have to care.

There are many ups and downs and hills and dales along this road toward Elk Mountain, rock cliffs and what, and the trailer full of potatoes is heavy. The engine has to work hard, hammering away, and the turbocharger works hard with it. Trying to do its job, the turbo screams as we struggle up the hill toward Elk, as it is known on the CB. Almost hurts my ears.

Turbochargers, since I am on that subject, are a good example of energy conservation by reclamation. A turbo is a device attached to the engine that uses spent exhaust gas to compress the intake mixture of air and fuel, and shove an overdose of it into the engine, causing a bigger explosion, thereby gaining power. More fuel, more air in the allotted space. Turbos are much more complicated than that; my explanation is greatly oversimplified, but that is basically the principle. Works, too. Turbos are good things. Problem is, they whine. Supersonically most of the time, the really impressive part of the whine is above the range of human hearing when they are operating properly. But, they are sensitive mechanisms and, operating at the RPM ranges they do, in the tens of thousands, if the least little thing gets out of whack, a wobble in a shaft or a bearing starts to fail, it makes them noisy. Some whistle, some grind, some groan, some rattle, most whine. This one has chosen to whine. Loudly. And when the engine really has to work, like dragging 45,000 pounds of potatoes up the side of a big mountain, it fairly screams. It is a shriek really, and an unnerving one. Something is going very wrong with it very slowly and very noisily. Times like this, I wish it would just go ahead and crater. Be done with it. Get a new one installed, or at least a quieter one.

It is late afternoon, and the Wyoming wind has come to us head-on, and as it goes past the loose door seals and mirrors and windshield eyebrow, it whistles and roars. It has joined a cacophony, a disjointed, unconducted orchestra of whistles, shrieks, hisses, roars, screams, and metallic hammering. The wind, the engine, and the tires. I almost laugh. What an ensemble of noises. No, this is no ensemble, this is a garage band of noises. Trainer looks over and sees me thinking and knows it has to do with the racket, so he smiles and shakes his head and drives on. I don't think he hears half of it, but it seems he is in a better frame of mind now.

Wyoming has a 75 MPH speed limit. Has to have. It is a big state, lots of wide open spaces. Covering that much real estate is time consuming, so the faster a person can go in Wyoming, the better for them. Trucks go fast, too. We kinda talked about fast trucks a little earlier in that there are governed trucks like ours, and ungoverned trucks like some of the ones that go past us. We can't go faster than 65 MPH on flat land even with a tailwind. If we try, there is an electronic device that interferes with the engine's ability to do that. It is called a governor and it turns something off. I'm not sure what it turns off, but the device lets the truck go just so fast, and that's it. We can go faster downhill, but the systems monitor will snitch on us when the information is downloaded upon our return to the yard. That could bring on a meeting with the honchos.

Fast trucks do not have that speed restriction. They can go as fast as they want. Actually, a really fast truck can hang with some pretty fast cars if they have the room to run. And there are drivers out here nervy enough to drive those trucks that way. One is coming up behind us now.

I look in the right-side rearview mirror as we go across the Bar Hat. The interstate drops into a valley and I can see for miles across the floor of the valley and all the way to where it goes up the long hill on the other side. In the mirror I can see a bright yellow long-nose Peterbilt tractor pulling a chrome reefer trailer coming up quickly from behind. In seconds, the length of time it takes to look again out the windshield and return to the mirror to check how far he's advanced, the yellow Pete is thundering by in the hammer lane. Flash of yellow paint, chrome, and noise, and this guy is past us in the matter of a few more seconds. He is getting smaller fast in the windshield as he pulls away from us, and we are doing close to 70 with the downhill pull from the road. He has the hammer to the floor, and I know that because I can smell the raw diesel in his exhaust wafting into the fresh air vent. I look at Trainer, Trainer looks at me. I look again out the windshield. In that length of time the guy is a full quarter mile ahead of us. He is gone, gone as in up the hill and out of the valley in the length of time it takes us to get halfway across.

Trainer says that sonofabitch is doing a hunnertanfifty if he's moving at all. I am inclined to agree. I have never in my life seen a truck moving that fast. Anywhere. Kinda like a duck on a fence post.

The thought that comes to my mind is that he cannot stop the truck inside a mile. All the physical laws are against it. I wonder what he is thinking, or is he so full of adrenaline he isn't thinking at all. I wonder what his last conscious thought would be should a steer tire blow. The guy is a loose cannon. Fortunately, there are few four-wheelers on this stretch of interstate. Mostly bigtrucks. I can't imagine what a four-wheeler would look like after being hit by 40 tons going that fast. I hope some grizzled old prospector doesn't come onto the interstate from a dirt road somewhere in a battered old pickup barely limping along.

Interstate highways are not supposed to have an at-grade intersection. All intersections are supposed to be overpasses or underpasses, and the pavement is supposed to have access lanes to and from those over- and underpasses so old prospectors don't hobble into 70-MPH traffic. I have seen it otherwise in several places. Gravel roads or hayfield roads sneaking onto the interstate shoulder. Not a real road with a name or number, but access just the same. Dangerous access. There is no way to get to roadspeed from those homemade roads, no acceleration lane. Grizzled old prospectors or grizzled old farmers in grizzled old pickups wobbling into interstate traffic moving at interstate speeds. I don't even want to think about it.

We stop at a rest stop after dark for a just-get-out-of-the-truck break, and while Trainer takes the opportunity to make a phone call, I wander around in the windy, cold darkness outside the high-tech facility to become one with the night. We have had the heater on since dark, and both of us like it cool, so it is pretty chilly out. Especially for September. September for me, anyway. The grass is holding on for its life, laid flat by the wind. I turn my back to it like the willows we have seen in our travels. I don't think I'm as graceful, but I'm nearly as tall.

The warm glow of the truck cab beckons, the little interior lights giving it a look of being warm and inviting, so I walk completely around the place for the leg motion, then mosey, like we do in Wyoming, back to it. A car pulls into the parking lot, a little woman gets out, looks at me for a long second, and I can see she doesn't associate me with the truck as I put the key into the door. We lock eyes, she looks away quickly and pulls her jacket around her neck with her fist and scurries into the lit facility. I wonder what she is or was thinking. At least she had the presence of mind to get inside. We are a long way from anywhere, and she let her curiosity override her self-preservation for a moment out here in nowheresville.

I was surprised by how long the second was we looked at one another. That hasn't happened before now. I realize I am standing on the first step of the ladder to the cab and have the door open, looking after her like a bozo. The wind and the cold snap me out of my trance, and I finish the climb and swing into the first chair. Slam the door against the wind, and the sudden quiet inside startles me. There is no noise but the incessant idle of the Cummins and the gentle flow of the fan pushing warm air into the cab. The pulse of the truck, and its breathing. The sounds the mechanical womb makes. I am comforted quickly and calmed by it. I look around and realize how comfortable I have become in so few cubic feet. When it is like this, serene and sheltering, I don't want to get out of it very often. Only when I know I need to walk.

Trainer wanders out of the building, looking at his feet for some reason. He looks up and starts purposefully for the truck; he wants to drive. He is walking toward the driver's side of the truck, head down against the wind. I figured he would want to ride for a while, but I guess not. That's okay. We'll let him drive if he wants. Keeps his brain busy, and that keeps him less crotchety.

He climbs in the driver's door as I move over to the second chair, and announces we will stay in Laramie tonight. Got a good buffet there. Okay. We buckle in, I get a soda and a package of peanut-butter crackers, toss a pack at Trainer, and he shifts the idling engine into second gear as he releases the brakes. The cab torques up as he releases the clutch, and we roll out of the pool of light at the rest area onto the interstate and go up the gears, heading east to the buffet at Laramie in the crystalline Rocky Mountain darkness. This country is spectacular even in the near-black night. I can see how the natives fell into nature worship. Well, worship may be a little strong. Nature reverence is probably more accurate.

I sit back into the second seat to look out the window and enjoy my hermetically sealed, salted and preservative-saturated pre-buffet appetizer, and wonder if the muck between these alleged crackers was ever peanut butter as I listen to more of the radio, on now because Trainer thinks we need to catch up on world events.

The FM radio has harangued us for days now with the attack on New York. No real news, just rehashing and guessing and letting callers-in vent a little. I am taken a little aback by how much anti-Arab sentiment there appears to be. Like all of them are guilty. I am also arching my brow over the abuse heaped onto anyone who speaks against racism and generalizations. I damn sure hope this is the neversatisfied vocal minority and not the vox populi. I reach over and switch it off after a quarter of an hour of opinionated illiterati.

Trainer looks at me and cranks up the CB. He grins. Okay. If it makes him happy.

CB pundits are no better these last few days, the reason and presence of mind apparently gone, but then I think they get their material from the FM talk shows. I wonder if any of them can spell Afghanistan. Or know where it is. One says we need ta jus' kick their ass real good, that it is the only thing them dam ragheads unnerstan'. I'm thinking that in the final analysis, that's all any of us understand. A moderate chimes in and with a comment that the Russians already did that some years back. Diplomat number one says well, we apparently need to do it again. Another voice breaks in and says that is a shallow way to approach this, that the Afghan people are not guilty of this atrocity, that they are too poor to mount such an offensive. That whoever did this has the financial means to do so and we should look for a moneyed operation.

As this discussion unfolds, I am impressed at the depth of knowledge, the critical thinking, and the moderate tone that takes the airwaves truck to truck. Maybe I am wrong. Maybe reason is still out there. I don't know which way the talkers are going, with us or away, and therefore don't know how long I will be able to listen in. The redneck faction is put off at that moderation, and resorts to suggesting expatriation for the moderates and questioning their loyalties. The moderates question the rednecks' understanding of the situation and accuse them of radicalism on the same level as the attackers. The rednecks cannot muster a sane argument and fall to cursing the moderates and accusing them of treason, though none of them can think of the word. The moderates, to keep the discussion pace going, help the rednecks with that word, treason. That really lights up the rednecks, and the accusations of collegedamfaggits and references to feminine anatomy begin to pepper the conversation. The moderates respond by accusing the rednecks of being flag-waving sunshine patriots hiding behind bravado, and ask how many of them would be prepared to send a son to die for American honor. That image is too much for someone who keys a mike to block everyone just about the time we drive out of range. Dang. That was the whole national post-attack emotion in microcosm. I would like to have heard how all that worked out. It may be like one guy on a call-in said, that football season, a few beers, and basketball season, and we, the people, will have forgotten all about it.

Things calm down on the CB as we go along behind the glowing puddle the headlights make for us. I look out the window into the sky and see Hera's Milky Way. I have no idea how many stars are up there, but it is a bright band of stars from the southwest to the northeast across the blackness of the sky here. No light pollution. It is hard to imagine something more impressive or expansive. I am looking at both our history and our future in those stars. Some of the light I am seeing left those stars before I was born. Some of the light from some of those stars left before our kind sprang from whatever matrix was here. The end of some of those stars has already happened. The flash of light from it just isn't here yet. One at a time I guess they will all go out. I hope more are born, and I think they are. I don't know, but I hope so. It would be a shame to lose the beauty of the night, and it become no more than darkness.

The CB's steady crackle is punctuated by a woman's voice. I guess she's been talking and we come into range as we catch up or she goes past the other way. It is a calming influence, most of times, when a female voice is on the radio, in the evenings. Everyone wants to talk to her, as though she were a surrogate wife. They all wait their turn. She talks to everyone, and gets two or three offers of marriage as we go. She does have a sultry quality to her voice. Rich and tenor. Confident and gentle.

And thanks all for the offers, but her husband is driving and she is just the bookkeeper. Everyone laughs in their turn, and thinks him a lucky man. Everyone drives on, better educated and rejected by this queen of the interstate night, as she passes through our lives going along her way. All the drivers will soon, if not already, be thinking of their own women back home, and sure enough the CB talk turns to hometime and Trainer looks over at me and says that's where we are going. Home. Headed to the yard now with these damspuds holdin' us back.

Questions and comments come and go between trucks headed our way and staying with us, about wives and ex-wives and kids and dogs and fishing and hunting, trucks and potatoes and how long ya been out and the sonsabitches that run the trucking industry. Questions and comments pop in occasionally from a driver going the other way, and not in range for long enough to get an answer in lots of cases. It is highly unlikely we will ever see the face of the speaker, yet we are able to talk as though we were at a neighborhood party on a summer afternoon. Casually and comfortably, held inside this brotherhood of the road where being away from home is all we have in absolute common, everyone just wants to get back there, and talking about it helps some, as though we really are there, just for little while.

It comes to me I could be home the night after tomorrow.

I watch the line of trucks go past on the other side of the interstate and count twenty-seven of them single file in one of the lanes. A long, diesel, painted-chrome-metal lighted serpent following the convolutions of the road surface. It is impressive. My dad told me once he was at a rest area in Tennessee one night and saw so many trucks nose to tail that it looked to him like a freight train. I see what he meant. I listen for the CB chatter usually involved in a group setting, but there is surprisingly little. Then I think, in a situation like that, so close to one another, about the only thing a driver has time to do is drive. His whole world is in the taillights of the truck in front of him. It's that lead-dog thing, with the addition of serious consequences for inattention. It is one thing when a sled dog doesn't stop at the same time as the one in front of him, and another when a truck doesn't. The sight of the roadtrain is pretty, though, and something to be seen at night with all the lights and motion. It has the look of an ages-old, but faster and higher-tech procession. A caravan, of sorts.

Diesel camels, braying protests through shiny exhaust stacks, decorated with paint and chrome and lights, heavily laden, rolling single file, traveling far and banded together in this outland for some mutual benefit, along the Silk Road–become–Interstate, bringing rare goods from afar to the busy marketplace, like so many beasts of burden for so many ages, looking for the day's end at some oasis, or caravanserai, that beckons in the night. The principle hasn't changed much in 5,000 years, only the mode of getting things to the market.

All this waxing poetic about going far causes me to think about a fellow I knew, and came to like in my driving schooling, and think about what he said one afternoon as we were walking along the edge of the road near our motel, out for something to eat, it being easier to walk some places in cities than to drive. He said he keeps imagining having his wife and kid with him when he sees those Rocky Mountains in the windshield for the first time, 'cause they ain't been much out of Miss'ssippi.

I hope it happened for him. I liked his country demeanor and forthrightness. I don't think he ever had a dishonest thought in his life, and he believed everyone he met was among the finest of persons. He is a rare man in the business world I come from, and deserves all the good he can get. I don't think I ever met a person from Mississippi I didn't like; one from long ago, in particular. I hope life has been good to her.

The lights of Laramie glow on the horizon, and I feel a good shower and delicious dinner coming on. Trainer says this is the best buffet in the county. We park and shut down, go in and eat, and I don't know about the overall best, but it is one of the biggest, and certainly one of the best managed. We see a couple of drivers from our company at that buffet, so we sit to visit a minute on our way back to the truck, exchanging stories from the road. I can tell a couple of my own now, and we speculate on how the changing seasons, snow and ice mainly, will

affect the driving. Handshakes all around and we leave them to their
dinner and we are off to shower and bunk. Tomorrow will get us close
to the yard, I think. Trainer is getting antsy and I don't know if that is
good or bad. Good that he will drive hard to get there, but bad he may
push himself too hard like before when we were going home. It is a common practice among drivers to do that, and serves no useful purpose.

Some, many really, will drive all day and all night to get home in
the morning, then sleep all day, and awaken at about the same time in the
evening they would get home if they had slept the night and driven the
day. Plus, having slept all day, he will want to be up all night. I don't know
what the numbers are for bigtruck accidents on the way home as compared
to accidents going out or midtrip, but I'd wager they are more common.

Up in the smashing Laramie morning with my teeth chattering from
the cold. I left the window open all night, and my sheet and Mexicano
blanket are no match for the forty-four degree breeze coming in that
pneumonia hole, as a friend calls windows. Trainer sputtering and
wheezing below. I hop up and get my clothes on first, just to get warm.
Climb into the first chair and crank the engine to get the heater going.
Trainer flips up to the side of his bunk, feet on the floor and wrapped
tightly in his blanket looking completely confused. Relax, I am just
going to get it warm in here. He just sits there and says Hell, I'm awake
now, and I say no you're not. I sail out the door for some coffee to warm
me inside and make me feel better about being alive while he figures out
where his clothes are in the pile of coverings on his bunk.

There is a near riot going on inside the fuel desk when I get there.
The sun is not up yet and the place is packed with drivers. The coffee
machine is broken. No free coffee at the fuel desk. Some of these people are angry way out of proportion to the problem. Probably not morning people. I decide this is no place for coffee, and head inside to the
convenience store. Seventy-three cents. It's a crime to charge for coffee,
says one driver in line ahead of me. There are four or five of us more
reasonable drivers in here to get coffee and go about our business rather
than get involved in the hubbub at the fuel desk. Another says it is just

a way to stop giving out free coffee without directly saying so. Another says we should just fill our mugs and leave and see what happens. Well, I was thinking these guys were more reasonable. One says he thinks he'll just hold the tap on the urn and let all the coffee run onto the floor and then they won't have any to sell *or* give away. Another says that is a real good way to get an ass-whippin' early in the morning. I'm thinking just let me pay for my coffee, I don't care if it is five dollars a cup, and let me get out of here before something bad happens.

The weather channel says the wind is 22 MPH this fine cold September morning and it should warm nicely as the sun gets up. I hope so. I have on shorts and a golf shirt. I see Trainer coming in for coffee. It would be wise for the fellow to wait to drain the urn until Trainer gets his mugful, or at least not let Trainer walk in the door to see the last few drops going onto the floor. I don't think ass-whippin' would adequately describe the next event.

We head out, and the truck is in fair form once it gets warmed up. There are many myths associated with these engines that persist even among neophyte drivers to this day, one of which is that diesels smoke. That is only partly true. When a diesel is warmed up, which can take half an hour, tuned properly and not under a strain, the exhaust is invisible. The heat waves are visible because diesel exhaust is hot, but there is no smoke. However, when a cold diesel, and I mean cold like freezing cold, is first cranked, the smoke is a thick and heavy bluish ivory color, from vaporized diesel that didn't burn properly. That soon turns blue, then white, and finally disappears when the engine nears operating temperature. If it smokes any other time, it is an indicator something is wrong. Usually, it is an indicator of poor maintenance, or the engine is simply worn out.

Blue Two is smoking lightly this morning, still, and has been idling for more than a quarter hour. Just slow to warm, I guess. The heater is off now, and the windows partway down; I have come alive and am comfortable in the cool of the morning as I wheel out the lot and onto the feeder to the interstate. The windows come up. Cool air is one thing. Cold 65-MPH wind blasting in is another.

Trainer riding and sipping his coffee looking out the window at the brisk, breaking day. Seems far off lately, and we don't talk a lot anymore. I guess it is a combination of things: his being preoccupied with whatever is happening at home that bothers him, the difficulty in communicating at a comfortable level over the noise, and us having run out of subject matter miles ago. Doesn't make a real difference, I suppose, we are on our way home, and will soon go our separate ways.

We have the Wyoming public radio on and are catching up on the developments that took place in our suddenly smaller world while we slept. The stock prices keep going down, all the experts predicting worldwide calamity. No one is sure what to do, not knowing what will happen. I think I don't understand that. We have never known what was going to happen. That was the whole thing in the stock market. Gamble your money. Hope you pick a winner. The more I hear about the fears, the less I think it may have been a gamble. Maybe some did know who would be a winner. Maybe they are the ones uncertain now. Maybe the rest of us just thought it was a level playing field. That could present a whole new problem in that there has always been an unseen certainty in the market the little guy never knew about, and it is gone now.

The destination is Denver for fuel, and we motor right into the fuel stop, smack downtown, about midmorning. We get out and fuel, and I check the various juices and clean the mirrors and windshield.

The protocol is to fuel, and do those aforementioned things at the same time, then move out of the pump area far enough forward to let the truck behind us get to the pumps. So we do that and go in to sign the fuel bill, get a soda, and come back to move the truck to the parking lot where, once the truck is in a space, the driver can take all the time he wants to do whatever he wants. He isn't in anyone's way.

One truck that pulled away from the pumps just enough to let the guy behind him up to fuel, has been there since *we* fueled. That truck has not moved. The truck behind him has long since fueled and is ready to go, not wanting to park but get on the road again. There are other trucks waiting in line for fuel as well. Even though there are ten or twelve sets of pumps, the lines are two or three trucks long at each. This is a heavily traveled interstate in a big city, and lots of trucks stop here. Once a bigtruck is in line, that is where it is. Unlike a car, the driver can't just ooch over a lane, and get into another line. The only way is forward. No clear-thinking driver would dare back up in a crowded fuel lane. We have had time to fuel, go in, sign the receipt, get a soda and sandwich, wander back out to the parking lot, and get ready to get back on the interstate. Probably 25 minutes. Some tempers are beginning to flare. Trainer says let's get out of here before someone gets his head ripped off. I agree through a mouthful of pigskins, which are a whole lot like chewing fried tissues, I am thinking.

On the road a little while later we hear about the truck stop incident on the CB, and one driver says it was found out the driver of the truck that plugged the fuel island was inside taking a shower. Another driver suggested the guilty driver would need another shower had he, the speaker, been in that line. Lots of laughs and much talk about fuel island etiquette. And I have seen it so. Most of the drivers are very considerate of others in tight places—moreso than I would have thought for the image drivers have (truckers, they are called by anyone other than themselves). The picture isn't one of politeness and courtesy. And maybe it isn't politeness and courtesy alone that I see. Maybe it is just respect, or consideration for a fellow human in a like situation, because we all have been, or will be, in a given situation, if we stay in this craft.

Beautiful afternoon in southern Colorado. HQ changed our route, via the quailcall, to a shorter, more direct route to the yard, and that is okay by the both of us. The problem with that is, we have been routed onto US 287 south to Texas. It is a two-lane road through several widely spaced country towns. Traffic lights and stop signs. Slow four-wheelers and farm implements. Livestock on the highway, possibly to become deadstock, and at considerable expense. That is more than just a little thing.

Some of the country is closed range, meaning the stock has to be fenced in to keep it from wandering. If a cow gets out and is hit by a vehicle, the owner is liable. Parts of Texas are like that. If a cow or horse gets hit, no one will claim ownership of it. No one ever saw that cow before today. That is why lots of farms don't brand their stock any longer. On the other hand, some of the country is open range, meaning there are no fences required and the stock can roam freely. If a cow is hit on a highway in open range, it is the fault of the vehicle operator. He should have been watching for the animal, knowing one could be out there. In that event, since the operator is not going to go far after whacking a 1,000-pound animal with a plastic car, there will be a dozen farmers show up to identify that carcass as the best milk cow they ever owned or heard about, and the reckoned value of that animal suddenly goes up to dollars per pound. And hitting a farm animal in a bigtruck is not much better, damagewise; most all the body panels are plastic or fiberglass to save weight. Gotta be careful in these animal husbandry areas.

Lots of road construction, because the highway is old and exposed to some destructive elements—sun, rain, and ice. It is to the age now where those things have taken a toll, so to keep the locals working, and to improve a major thoroughfare, there is road construction in the months it is feasible. September is one of those months, and we are down to one lane of travel alternating directions. We sit and wait for a string of cars and pickups and straight trucks and bigtrucks to go by and then it is our turn, and we do that several times on our trip across the windy steppes and grasslands Chief Quanah and his famed Comanche warriors patrolled not so long ago. He probably made about as many miles in a day as we are at this rate; maybe more. As told by U.S. cavalrymen, there were no horsemen as skilled as those warriors. None. They could ride and shoot hanging from their mount's side or even beneath them, at a dead run. It must have been a thing to see, the killing aside, and we are right here where it happened. I look around. Like I am going to see one of them.

Toward the south side of Colorado there are some wide open spaces, some of the road is not under construction, and that excellent two-lane road lays across some gently rolling hills. It is too much temptation for some of the wilder drivers. With the construction crews out of the way and no town in sight, they drop the hammer and attempt to recover some time. It is a foolish thing to do, but one swings out from behind us and into the oncoming lane just as an oncoming four-wheeler crests a hill less than a quarter mile ahead. I can see the car, but the passing truck doesn't until he is alongside us. Two bigtrucks side by side on a two-lane road with a car coming head-on. I am doing all our governor will let us do, about 65 MPH, when I take my foot off the accelerator and get onto the brake as hard as I dare. The other truckdriver is not going much faster, having just gotten room to run alongside us, and cannot get around quickly enough. There is no way I can stop, and I know the other driver won't. He is in too deep. He has to break left and go into the ditch or hit the oncoming car. We are down to seconds before impact. I have been programmed to break right always. No matter what, do not go into oncoming traffic. If he does what he should have been trained to do, and breaks right, that is what I will do. I will put Blue Two into the ditch and we will ride it out, or jackknife. Trainer and I will probably die if either of those things happens. The tractor will stop before the trailer does, and that is not conducive to long and happy lives for people in the tractor. It will not be necessary for me to do that if the fool breaks left like he should, having caused this looming disaster. He needs to go in the ditch, no one else. The car driver will then go safely past in his proper lane of travel. The other driver has most likely been trained to break right as well, but he has nothing to lose going left. A crash is imminent. The question is who will suffer. He is already in the oncoming lane. I grip the wheel in anticipation of turning it to the right and hope Trainer survives. He had no part in this and is an innocent bystander about to pay for the bad judgment of a moron. The four-wheeler and its occupants are entirely in the hands of whatever Power may be paying attention. The car looks tiny suddenly, so vulnerable. Like it has no chance whatsoever. And really, it doesn't. A clear lane of travel is all that will save it, or going off the road to avoid a head-on collision.

I see what is about to happen. The truckdriver is not going to give any ground. He is about to do the unthinkable and force the four-wheeler off the road, and that may be the best thing at this point. No telling what will happen if he goes into the left ditch and the auto does, too. If both of them swerve into the ditch at the last second, it will be on the front page tomorrow. I see the four-wheeler starting off the road, gravel flying, and lose sight of it as it goes past the truck at our side and just ahead. It must be in the ditch by now. I hope it is still on its feet. I am furious with the murderous fool at the wheel of the bigtruck and grab the air horn strap and pull hard and long. The horn bellows for what seems like an hour and I let it. His voice comes on the CB with a long and resentful "Heeeeyyy." I grab the mike and let a string of words fly that I didn't realize I remembered regarding his heritage and pedigree and intellectual level. Total silence as we roll along single file; several trucks jammed up behind me as I braked, seeing everything and hearing my tirade as well. He knows he screwed up. And he knows we all saw it. He speeds along ahead of us in silence, trying to get away from the scene of the crime. Like that will absolve him somehow. All the drivers behind him saw what happened. One comes on the radio after an uncomfortable silence and says the four-wheeler got stopped okay out in a field. Took out part of a fence, but otherwise everyone is out and okay.

Trainer looks over at me and looks back out the windshield. I wonder what he is thinking. He never made a sound or a move during those seconds. At least not that I saw, or heard, not that I spent a long time looking at him.

I resolve in the moments that follow that incident to carry with me from this time forward a disposable camera in the door pocket of any tractor I get into, or four-wheeler for that matter. It occurs to me a picture really would be worth a thousand words to the company that owns the truck a fool is driving.

Simply point the camera out the back window of a car, and snap a picture of the truck right on my arse, or running into oncoming traffic, like the moron just did. Wait till he comes around, and he will, then get a shot of the door or side of the condo as he comes alongside. All the information necessary to nail that driver is on the side of the tractor. Company name, address and tractor number, DOT numbers. Send that photograph to the attention of the president of that company with the date and location of the offense and let them clean their own house. And they will.

We roll into a neat little town and get out for a break and a soda. The parking lot is tiny, I am careful pulling in, and don't notice there is no way out the other end. I am not skilled enough at gauging these almost-truck-stops to determine how to approach one with any hope of getting out comfortably. We pull up, and I set the brakes. Trainer says we are stuck. I say not with 425 horsepower. We'll make a hole if we have to. Trainer laughs, and we bail out for a soda and a short break. Maybe a snack. Depends on what they have in there. I need something. I am still shaken with the murdertruck driver. Just need to get out for awhile and get my brain busy doing something else.

I turn the key to switch off the ignition for some reason. I sit in the first chair and look out the windshield at the eastern horizon with the now lifeless wheel in my hands. I have a feeling of some kind and I don't know what it is. Like this is a parting. Like some portion of my life is behind me now. That it will never be like this for me again. Somehow.

I guess I'd better catch up to Trainer.

Back in the truck, and Trainer says he wants to drive. I agree and realize at that point what the deal is: He will drive all night to make it to the yard by morning. He wants to get home. Whatever suits him. It is, after all, his truck, and apparently tonight will be our last night on the road. I guess I was right about that feeling. That was my final turn at the wheel as a trainee, and one with a memorable lesson. I climb into the second seat and tilt it back a little to get comfortable. I suppose I'll just ride.

My on-the-job training is over. I have driven my last mile as a trainee.

Onto US 287 south to the Colorado border. I ride and munch and ride and look. The road is good and the truck is loaded right, and pulling straight behind us, not crabbing to one side because the tandems are twisted, like a couple we have had, and the scenery is nice. There is a row of thunderstorms lined up across the eastern horizon hammering southern Kansas and northern Oklahoma, and I know it is no fun beneath them, but from where I sit, they are beautiful. The late-afternoon sun-light paints them all the red/orange pastels.

There are lots of old towns along the route with lots of old stuff in them. Turn-of-the-century architecture, and a petrified wood house in the middle of one little town. Now, that took some effort. Lots of old mixed with the new. Maize mixed with the corn mixed with the wheat. Not in the same field, but in the same country.

I think about how bigtrucks may be less dangerous with governors all around. Get completely rid of fast trucks, but I haven't thought it through yet, so I would stop short of that recommendation. But it may bear investigation.

Lots of hayfields and some cattle in the late-afternoon sun. Like many things I have seen, it comforts me to know this is here in some intangible manner. Spending part of my life on a family farm gives me an apprecia-tion for continuity, I think. I sit more relaxed—maybe because I am going home, and maybe because life is as it has been, and should be, hereabouts.

It is a two-lane road, and we can see the faces of the oncoming truckdrivers. Trainer is his usual extrovert self and waves at every driver that goes past the other way. The sun is in their eyes. One or two wave back. His optimism is not dimmed, and he believes in the inherent good of every man. He just wants to be part of the culture, to be accepted and recognized by his peers. Like we all do, I suppose.

He coughs a lot, even more the last day or so, and smokes three-and-a-half, maybe four, packs a day. Three-fifty a pack. The setting sun tints the raging thunderheads all the red-spectrum colors, and the lightning flashes are beginning to show in the dimmed clouds. Some of the storms have matured and become dangerous. The tops have gone to that anvil shape they assume when they are nearing the end of their life and col-lapsing into 100-MPH downblasts and driving rain. Others are beginning to build, and are sharp and clear around the edges. It looks like the chemistry that generated the first round is still there and the country-side may be in for it most of the night. I marvel at how good it is to be alive. To be here and see this.

Trainer begins to whistle, not loudly, but audibly. He does that when he is nervous or self-conscious or being nonchalant. I am having to look across the cab in his direction to see the sun color the clouds, and he most likely thinks I am staring at him. As the sun goes down, the clouds go from vermilion to peach to rose to copper to pale green to lavender to gray. I alternate gazes from the clouds on one side to the sunset on the other side. I'll look out my window for the sunset now and again to ease the pressure on Trainer. Maybe he'll stop whistling.

The sunset out my window is hand-painted by some immortal hand or eye. The sun itself sits perfectly on the horizon, tangent, a dozen shades of red, deepest on the bottom. The sky above it goes through the red spectrum from blood red to orange and finally a strip of yellow, then begins the spectrum of blue from turquoise to deep blue directly above us. I move forward in the seat to look out the windshield above to see the color gradient. The sunset changes from glare to haze to glow as I watch, in the span of 15 minutes. The light from the setting sun causes the dust in the air to incandesce, and the sky takes on a life for a moment, and then it is gone. The faint rose-to-blue progression is all that is left. But that is beautiful as well. The storms on my left get bigger and more billowy and more spectacular. And probably more dangerous.

I am lucky enough to be between these magnificent phenomena, with the straw-colored buffalo grass stretching away as far as I can see in any direction. This time of day, this going on around me, I count myself lucky to be alive again, as we roll into Campo. It is an enclave of trees and turn-of-the-century houses I see, as we motor three-quarters of a mile through, and a sign wishes us happy trails when we leave town. Really. The sign says "Happy Trails." And I guess that is what we are having. Happy trails.

Windmills along here on occasion, creaky reminders of the ranching west set against the angry storms to the east, flashing now incessantly with the lightning among the clouds, and inside them. I know that some of the bolts get to the ground and cause havoc, but I can't see those, nor the sheets of rain that must be falling. The arc of the Earth's surface occludes those things. I see only the beauty and the ferocity.

Trainer sees only the highway. All this is lost on him. He is going home.

The next town of any size is Boise City in the Cimarron Strip of Oklahoma. There is a traffic circle in the middle of town where the thoroughfares converge and the kids get together and sit on the tailgates of the farm trucks and do what socializing they can in the cool of the day. I like it. Looks kinda like the things all kids get together to do, but with a farm flavor. Little bit of hay in the bed of one of the pickups. Boys have Western hats on and the girls kinda stick together, all of them on one of the trucks. It is right out of a movie set, and it is another example of the things the Midwest is famous for; Small-town America, and I am glad to know it is there for those that have it. For me, too. I like knowing it is there, sort of a tangible connection I can have with parts of my childhood, that those things and places are still around. For others, maybe, but still there to be had.

Towns have a life like anything else. They are born and live and grow. They mature and get to middle age and start to decline and finally get feeble. Then they die, for all practical purposes. A few people hang on and live out their lives in the old hometown, but the young move away to brighter lights, and take the hope of new vitality for the town with them. I have seen a thousand of those little towns in my travels this past two months. Few things are as desolate, or depressing, as a dying town. Our country was once peppered with small towns that grew up around water holes or train stops or cattle corrals or the only merchant for miles. We now know them only as a part of Americana. Most of us live in, or near, a city, and life there is nothing like a small town.

We have passed through several of them on this road; US 287 is an old highway that connected many of those towns, and this part of the country suffered an exodus during the dust bowl era, and later the post-war industrial days, that left many of the villages little more than ghost towns. Some were abandoned completely. There was just no way to make money once the farming stopped, or went corporate, and people moved away from ancestral farms to earn a living rather than starve at home. It shows even now. It must have been depressing for those left behind, passing by the skeleton of Main Street, waiting for the kids to come home for the holidays, and remembering the good old days when both they and the town were younger, and looked better.

We have rumbled through the architectural bones of many little places that bustled once, during these past weeks, and now we are waiting on Texas to come into the windshield. It isn't far across the Cimarron Strip, and we'll be in the National State of Texas very shortly.

Most states have a sign that rolls out the welcome mat for a traveler, try to make the wayfarer more comfortable, and says goodtaknowya with a peppy motto or neat logo. My chosen state has a rock sitting on the side of the road, with "TEXAS" carved into it. Texas is not into impressing people with sappy slogans. Your ass is in Texas.

A brilliant crescent moon hangs in a turquoise background over the still-red horizon to the west as we ride into the only state that was ever a republic. God bless Texas. The thunderstorms boil and flash in the eastern distance as the darkness comes upon us and the headlights begin to take hold of the highway. Trainer is his concentrating self, forgotten cigarette dangling from his lips, mostly ash now. The dashlights illuminate his face, and I will remember that pose most of all. Burnt-down cigarette dropping ashes onto his tank top, totally focused on the road.

Trainer will drive all night, get lost in downtown Amarillo, become agitated about it, I will guide him out with the atlas, and sit up to ride through the high-plains darkness for a while. Then, I will sleep peacefully, trusting him with my life, in the bottom bunk to wake in the showery dawn, the storms having intercepted us overnight, and sit up to see the early lights of the metroplex on the rain-gray horizon when I open the light curtain. My training is behind me now, as is a chapter of my life; we will soon be back at the yard, and I will be home tonight, and sleep in my own bed.

I will not see Trainer again, or hear about him.

I will have my own tractor, and travel this indescribable continent for more than two years. I will go northern border to southern border and sea to shining sea and along both sides of all the Great Lakes and into Canada many times. I will watch all the seasons come and go through my windshield. I will see ice storms and mountain snow and bitter winter winds. Torrential rain and hail and blazing sun will be my summer companions. Coastal fog, desert dust storms, and Midwest tornadoes will herald the beginnings and ends of those summers. The heavy scent of magnolia and jasmine and honeysuckle will intoxicate my Southern springs, and the aspens and maples and sycamores will color my autumns. The days will lose their names as the weeks on the road become months and the seasons become years; only the date will be important for the paperwork. Where I am and what day it is just won't matter.

Home will become more a place and less a word.

This country and this nation will become more precious to me. I will have been much closer to both of them, and feel it is an honor to be here, with these American peoples, where I roam at will, and I can see the moonrise over New York or sunset over Los Angeles, if I choose, rather than cringing beneath the lash of some sadistic despot.

I will learn to live alone in my tractor those short years, and be comfortable there. I will see the beautiful and the terrible and feel those things, and have no one with whom to share my thoughts and sentiments except the kindred spirits on the CB radio I will use to keep myself company, rolling through the darkness of the long interstate nights. The faceless voices.

I will live among them.

They will call me "driver."

# AFTERWORD

IT HAS BEEN SOME TIME NOW SINCE I PENNED THE NOTES OUT there that would become this manuscript. A lot has happened in my life, and I wanted to talk a little about some of those things. First, the important stuff:

All my daily-use fishing gear was stolen. Right off the back porch of my little house by the bay. I didn't even notice at first the next morning, as I sat on my patio looking at the big expanse of bare wall where rods and reels had been for so many years. I stopped in mid-coffee-sip when I realized what I was not seeing. I felt sick for a moment, and then realized I wouldn't let them, the thieves, do that to me as well. So, I collected myself and called the police for the first time in my life regarding a theft. That is a bad feeling, the sudden realization something important has been stolen, and difficult to describe.

I filed a claim against my house insurance, and they paid off, minus the deductible. The adjuster had a hard time accepting the dollar figure associated with the caliber and quantity of the gear, and that I didn't keep it put away, both of which would have made sense to him had he been a serious fisherman, but I came away from the experience with a lot of new stuff and the sad realization that my life there, in that locale, was different

371

as the result of having had that happen. I reasoned I would never feel like I could leave my home again without worry I didn't have before, and I don't like feeling like that. We all had watched out for one another when there were only a few of us out there at the settlement by the bay, as if there were something to watch out for, but the neighborhood has grown now, and new people are moving in, bringing problems we didn't have before, so I moved out. I didn't want to feel the way I did about the new folks I had for neighbors. I know that is shortsighted, that thieves are everywhere and in all income brackets, but it is just the way I viewed it at the time. More than fishing gear was taken from me, like my freedom to leave my stuff where I could get to it, and I decided to give a new location a chance at leaving me alone. But, that didn't work either; I have to lock everything up now, living in a small city but still near the bay, and I have come to despise locks. And the people that cause me to have to use them.

I got back to New York City recently, and one of the things I wanted to do was to go out to the Statue of Liberty and see that plaque attached to the base of it. I told you about my intention to do that and see if that plaque is there and if it says what I was once told it says. But, there was a problem.

Since September 11, 2001, there has been a security alert on Liberty Island, where the Statue stands, and so it was on the day I wanted to go. If the terrorists set out to change the way we live, I guess they did that. They took the Statue away from us, and because of them and some authoritative security group, the world's symbol of freedom has to be locked away, and that bothers me deeply in my Americanness somehow. I wonder what the hundreds of thousands that traded their lives to secure our freedoms would say about all that. Our freedom isn't free, you know. It never has been. Though freedom was a birthright for most of us, someone had to pay for it. Those who paid the bill have never, in any of our wars, been more than boys; they suffered and died alone, frightened, and brave a long way from home.

Our freedom also has responsibility attached. It comes with the responsibility to maintain that freedom, purchased at such a cost, to exercise it, cultivate it, and not let it be eroded away a little at a time, even by our own, until it is just as gone as if we'd lost it in a war.

I will get back to Liberty Island one day, and do what I said I would do.

I still drink coffee. That didn't change. About a potful a day at home, and my usual two mugs on the road. When I can get out there.

I decided to return to driving on occasion, after a hiatus to fish and generally mess around. I like the life, and the travel, and I have bills, like everyone else, and over-the-road driving is the only thing that will allow me to come and go as I please and still retain employment. So, since I don't require a lot of money, I am just a part-time driver. I don't do winter trucksports at all now though; I take the winters off. One winter out there should have been enough for me, but it wasn't. My truck slid on ice on three separate occasions in two winters. I stayed on the road each incident, but my willingness to deal with winter road conditions went completely away, so I just don't drive winters anymore. The fine line between shutdown for road conditions and get the load there on time is difficult to define with the best of information, and nearly impossible to define with guesswork and lousy information. So I simply will not put myself into the position of having to make that call. I once saw forty-eight off-road accidents in 60 miles after a snowstorm in Iowa. Almost one a mile, and there were about as many bigtrucks involved as four-wheelers. Those folks weren't very good at defining that line either.

Real jobs require a certain commitment, kinda like a marriage, and luckily for me, forty-eight-state trucking companies are so desperate for good drivers I can get away with just about any amount of hometime and still have them welcome me back when I get that travelin' Jones . . . as long as I don't tear up their trucks or trailers, keep my license clean, and pick up and deliver on time.

There may be other crafts out there that will allow that same latitude for job security versus time away, but I can't think of one right now, and I think about a lot of things as I drive my bigtruck along the interstates, when I am able to be out there, while I look for the road and street signs that I hope are still in place. It seems like what signs the pranksters didn't take, the cities do, in their street improvement programs. I have to believe the first casualty of any construction project is the street signs, unfortunately for us, because they are a huge part of a successful pickup or delivery.

One of the things I think about out there is how much I have enjoyed this time on the road and the things I've learned from it. I don't know that they do, but those experiences should equal many semester-hours of many subjects in some university of adversity, or diversity, and it might be a good course for lots of cardrivers to take, if someone comes up with a place and a way to teach it.

That time Trainer and I spent together seemed like no time at all, as I look back on those days and nights from this desk, here and now, back among the general population and four-wheeler operators, and I wonder if I really did it at all, as though it may have happened to someone else. Maybe everyone feels like that about some things that have happened in the past—wondering whether it was real or not. Like maybe the memories are someone else's, or part of a dream, or some wishful thinking of some kind, which causes me to wonder whether or not even my thoughts are my own. I think I'll just quit thinking one day and see what happens. But not today.

I continue to find several things right with driving for a living, and several things wrong with it. The things wrong outweigh the things right, at least for me, and I will soon enough make space for someone who wants the job worse than I do. That list is long, and there will be no shortage of candidates to fill what little void I leave, in that the dollars are attractive to someone who can put up with the problems, and the employee turnover is so high they won't miss me anyway. I didn't think it was a long-term proposition for me, nor did I enter into it with that thought. I knew going in it would be nothing more than a career change, that I, or someone close to me, might not like it, and I might move on to something else after a while.

I think on how it feels to shift the gears and turn the steering wheel, rolling out in the mornings, the vibration and sound of the engine and how the trailer feels behind the truck when it is loaded and balanced properly. Feeling the tractor drift down, or grind up a hill. How the cab tilts in a turn, and watching the tandems in the mirrors to make certain they clear the esplanades and curbs. And cars. And utility poles.

I think on how I know I will miss those things and feelings, not so much in terms of longing for them, but that I will have had them once, and I will not have them always. Life on the road has a powerful allure for me, and a day will come when I say goodbye to the road and hello to the life of a workaday person who comes home every night and lives happily ever after. I won't complain. I won't wish my life would be like it was when I was driving. That part of my existence will be behind me and I will just remember what I can, stay out of blind spots and give that driver a little extra room in the five o'clock jam, because I'll know he needs it. And I'll hope the run he is on will get him home, if that is where he wants to be.

Still, it is difficult for me to imagine, after this time of driving, that I may never hold another Kenworth steering wheel or Eaton ten-speed shifter in my hand, floating the gears in sync with the turbo as I settle into the rhythm of the interstate, knowing the ride will be long and pleasant on the cement arteries that carry the commercial lifeblood through the mesmerizing swirl of people and places and things the rest of the world knows as America. There are feelings and sensations and emotions that ride evokes like few other things do, and I tried to convey a little of that in the pages before this note, helpless as my effort may be in describing it all. Our language is one of sciences and practicality, and just doesn't have some of the words I needed.

Well, my handy-dandy pocket chart says the tide is coming in soon, and I believe it will bring a speckled trout or two along, so my plan is to be in the backbay flats when that happens. I tied a couple of new salt-water flies and I want to test-drive them, so I am headed out to do that shortly. But, before I go, I'd like to leave you with a couple of thoughts.

Firstly, when you are in traffic, at speed or creeping, leave that empty space in front of those bigtrucks empty. Don't zip in there, trying to gain a couple of car lengths. That space contains precious time the driver, and it might be me, must have to stop those forty tons, and riding with us like you did, you should know that.

Secondly, don't worry about losing your job. Look what happened to me when I lost mine.